Joining up in the Second World War

Manchester University Press

Cultural History of Modern War

Series editors

Ana Carden-Coyne, Max Jones and Bertrand Taithe

To buy or to find out more about the books currently available in this series, please go to: https://manchesteruniversitypress.co.uk/series/cultural-history-of-modern-war/

https://alc.manchester.ac.uk/history/research/centres/cultural-history-of-war//

Joining up in the Second World War

Enlistment, masculinity and the memory of the Great War

Joel Morley

MANCHESTER UNIVERSITY PRESS

Copyright © Joel Morley 2025

The right of Joel Morley to be identified as the author of this work has been asserted in accordance with the Copyright, Designs and Patents Act 1988.

An electronic version of this book has been made freely available under a Creative Commons (CC BY-NC-ND) licence, thanks to the support of OpenUP, which permits non-commercial use, distribution and reproduction provided the author(s) and Manchester University Press are fully cited and no modifications or adaptations are made. Details of the licence can be viewed at https://creativecommons.org/licenses/by-nc-nd/4.0.

Published by Manchester University Press
Oxford Road, Manchester, M13 9PL

www.manchesteruniversitypress.co.uk

British Library Cataloguing-in-Publication Data
A catalogue record for this book is available from the British Library

ISBN 978 1 5261 5723 2 hardback

First published 2025

The publisher has no responsibility for the persistence or accuracy of URLs for any external or third-party internet websites referred to in this book, and does not guarantee that any content on such websites is, or will remain, accurate or appropriate.

EU authorised representative for GPSR:
Easy Access System Europe, Mustamäe tee 50, 10621
Tallinn, Estonia, gpsr.requests@easproject.com

Typeset by Newgen Publishing UK

Contents

List of figures and tables	*page* vi
Acknowledgements	vii
Introduction	1
1 Encounters with the Great War in popular culture	39
2 Encountering Great War veterans	91
3 *You and the Call-Up*: Conscription, attitudes and agency	128
4 Attitudes to service and the Great War in the Second World War	171
5 Masculinity in the Second World War	220
Conclusion	268
Bibliography	275
Index	295

Figures and tables

Figure

3.1 Percentage of registration groups provisionally
registered as COs *page* 151

Tables

3.1 Intake of men into the Armed Forces, 1939–45 144
4.1 Success of conscripts preferring Navy or RAF 189
4.2 Registrants' relative preferences for RAF or Navy,
1939–45 191

Acknowledgements

This book has been a long time in the making, and I have many people to thank for supporting its creation. Corinna Peniston-Bird sparked my interest in war and gender, and in oral history, and has been supportive of my research ever since, including providing comments on early drafts of this work. Dan Todman has also supported my research for many years, giving encouragement, constructive criticism, time he did not have and wise counsel about academia. You would not be reading this now without their efforts.

I have been very fortunate to have found willing readers and encouragement and support from people at my various institutions, including James Ellison and Miri Rubin at Queen Mary University of London; Peter Gurney and Matthew Grant at the University of Essex; and Grace Huxford and Richard Sheldon at the University of Bristol. I also owe thanks to Sonya Rose and John Tosh for conversations about masculinity; Dorothy Sheridan for discussion about the Mass Observation Archive and representativeness; Alan Allport for an exchange about race and the British forces; Mike Roper for discussions about the familial legacy of the Great War; and Richard Grayson for comments on an earlier version of this text. Lucy Noakes has also helped to refine my ideas about gender and war, and Mass Observation, and offered encouragement along the way. Of course, any errors are my responsibility. I would also like to thank the series editors and three anonymous reviewers for their helpful comments, and my exceptionally patient commissioning editor, Meredith Carroll, and the MUP production team.

While many academic books are communal endeavours, there are hundreds of people without whom this book could not exist

viii   *Acknowledgements*

because their testimony is its foundation. I am very grateful to the men who took part in interviews with me, who generously offered their time and their narratives. And without another hundred or so men doing the same for other interviewers I could not have consulted their testimonies in the Imperial War Museum's Sound Archive, either. In addition, I am grateful to the hundreds of people who recorded their attitudes and opinions via Mass Observation, even if their role in this book would surprise them. I would like to thank the trustees of the Mass Observation Archive, University of Sussex and the Imperial War Museum for permission to quote material from their collections. I also gratefully acknowledge that the research for this book was supported by funding from the Arts and Humanities Research Council (Grant Number AH/G014655/1) and an Institute of Historical Research Scouloudi Historical Award, and that I was able to test my ideas at international conferences thanks to funding from the Royal Historical Society and QMUL's Stretton Fund.

My friends and family have heard more about this book, and for much longer, than any of them would have wished. My parents, Linda and Chris, have been ever-willing readers, occasional financiers, and have provided so much more besides. I will always be very thankful. My wife, Jade Shepherd, has lived with this project for fifteen years. As well as reading many drafts and sharing her expertise on masculinity, she has been unfailingly encouraging, and accepting of the time sacrificed to it. I am sincerely grateful for that, but even more so for everything else – the friendship, the fun and a life created together. That has included welcoming our daughter into the family. She, too, is due thanks, for bringing perspective, profound joy and laughter, and much welcome distraction – Penelope, may you never find a door you cannot open. My family have made this book possible, and I dedicate it to them.

Introduction

On 11 November 1937 newly formed social research organisation Mass Observation (MO) watched Britons observe Armistice Day. When asked for his thoughts, one man, aged about 30, told a Mass Observer that his first thought during the two-minute silence had been to remember September 1918 'when word came by first post that two cousins of mine had been killed' and he 'offered a short prayer in their memory'.[1] His cousins were among the 722,000 Britons who had died in military service during the Great War.[2] He had observed the silence at one of the many memorials that had proliferated across the nation during the inter-war years, and at which, on Armistice Day, Britons were urged to remember the sacrifice of those who had died and those who had been bereaved.[3] Having said his prayer his thoughts turned to the future and how those around him understood the Great War; he wondered 'if all these people had had all the real horror of war brought home to them and whether they come to the square as a matter of form or not. And whether they believed or not war would come again.'[4]

There was good reason to wonder whether he and his compatriots understood the war in the same way. Formal remembrance was only one of many sites of Great War memory in inter-war Britain. Britons could read, see, listen to and watch a wide variety of depictions of the Great War in elite and popular culture, many of which were not focused on 'the real horror of war'. Many people had their own memories, too. Some had experienced separation, anxiety and bereavement from the Home Front, following the fighting through newspapers and soldiers' letters.[5] More significant in relation to the memory of the Great War were 7,800,000 British Great War veterans who returned home after the war's conclusion. This included

2   *Joining up in the Second World War*

641,000 ex-servicemen in receipt of a war disability pension, many of whom were forced to adapt to a much-changed civilian life and remained visual reminders of the Great War as they did so.[6] Many more veterans ostensibly resumed their pre-war lives. They, too, carried memories and mementoes of their Great War experiences that were sometimes encountered by those they lived alongside. Ordinary Britons themselves thus sat alongside war memorials, literature and films as vectors of the Great War's wider cultural legacy. Like these cultural scripts, veterans did not offer a singular reading of what the Great War had been like, nor what it meant.

Two decades after the Great War's conclusion, conscription for the Second World War began. In those years between, a generation of young men had grown up steeped in representations of the Great War, including its evocation as 'the war to end all wars', and yet they found themselves called to join up to participate in another global conflict. Contemporaries were acutely aware of this irony.[7] Some scholars have suggested or implied that Britons' imaginings of and responses to the Second World War were shaped by their understandings of the Great War, which were informed by its cultural representations, particularly the canonical war literature.[8] Similarly, and based in part on the depictions of war experience in Great War literature, it has been suggested that the Great War weakened the significance of military service in constructions of wartime masculinity.[9] Yet, as Martin Francis has highlighted, historians have been slow to examine 'the legacy of the First World War on the subjective worlds of participants in the Second',[10] and Stephen Heathorn is right to insist that understanding whether and how the cultural representations of the Great War shaped the thinking of ordinary people requires looking 'beyond the intentions of artists and intellectuals to look at how the conflict's representation has been received and understood by the population at large'.[11] To understand the significance of the Great War's cultural legacy in relation to Second World War enlistment we need to understand which depictions of the Great War young men – particularly young working-class men – actually encountered and how they interpreted what they did encounter, not just in literature but amongst the multitude of Great War representations circulating in inter-war Britain. We also need a better understanding of how the men who had

Introduction

grown up in inter-war Britain responded to the prospect of joining up for military service in the Second World War.

Entering these young men's 'subjective worlds' and locating the Great War within them requires a novel approach. Rather than taking the cultural representations as my starting point, I have instead focused upon the experiences of young men themselves. Personal testimony is therefore at the heart of this book. It utilises fifty-five unique oral histories conducted for this research, archival oral histories and MO material. This source base is significant for two key reasons. First, it enables a new approach to investigating the legacy of the Great War. Oral history interviews offer an unparalleled opportunity to examine how 'ordinary' young men encountered and engaged with the Great War in inter-war Britain. The opportunity to ask questions and encourage reflection on specific topics enables us to establish whether or not individuals had particular experiences and whether or not particular things were considered influential. For instance, no other source offers the same opportunities to uncover what these men heard about the Great War from their fathers, mothers, brothers or uncles, or to probe how they responded. The ability to examine the presence *and the absence* of references to the Great War in men's narratives is useful; while the absence of a topic in a memoir is ambiguous, oral histories can confirm that a young man had opportunity to read *Goodbye to All That* but was more interested in boys' story papers, or that he did not mention *All Quiet on the Western Front* when narrating his enlistment because although he read it he treated it as entertainment rather than an illustration of what could await him, or that Armistice Day had simultaneously communicated the horror and cost of war and a belief in dutiful sacrifice. Such an examination enables a more complete understanding of the Great War's cultural legacy, with greater awareness of its limits, than can be achieved by finding references to the Great War as influential in memoirs. The second reason these sources of personal testimony are significant is that, in comparison to memoirs and diaries, they better illuminate the experiences of young men from across the class spectrum and enable analysis that is more sensitive to class. This is important because class likely shaped both exposure to representations of the Great War and attitudes to Second World War enlistment.

4 *Joining up in the Second World War*

Using oral history to examine the Second World War and gender is a well-established approach, precisely because personal testimonies are so well suited to this task.[12] Here, the personal testimony enables insight into Second World War veterans' subjective approaches and attitudes to military enlistment, including their conceptions of the relationship between military service and masculinity, and the significance they ascribe to their understandings of the Great War in that context. While some (often middle-class) individuals' attitudes towards Second World War enlistment can be accessed through memoirs and diaries, Francis observed that 'flyer memoirs are often formulaic and tend to emphasise narrative at the expense of meaning'.[13] Oral history interviewees, however, can be reflective about their memories and through questioning the historian can broaden their narratives, revealing the complex and private negotiations behind individuals' decisions and attitudes.

MO material can also shed light on how men from this generation felt about Second World War service at the time and whether and how they connected the two world wars. Furthermore, if the contemporary MO material revealed a substantially different picture to that drawn from the oral histories it may signal that narratives have shifted with time. This is important because the popular memory of the Great War –particularly its representation as an event that removed the nation's naivety about and enthusiasm for war – has become increasingly powerful since the Second World War, and particularly since the 1960s.[14]

Together, these two bodies of material provide a window onto men's subjective attitudes and experiences that enables detailed interrogation of their interaction with the legacy of the Great War, their attitudes to the Second World War and the relationship between the two. This book demonstrates that young men engaged with a much wider range of representations of the Great War than those focused upon in existing scholarship, and it emphasises the significance of representations of the Great War from its veterans and within the home, as well as in popular culture. Importantly, it shows that 'disillusioned' literature had limited influence, and that what young men took away from any representation of the Great War was unpredictable. This understanding complicates and challenges previous assumptions about the influence of cultural representations and public discourses in relation to both the memory of

Introduction

the Great War and masculinity. Representations of the Great War in inter-war Britain provided a variety of depictions of the relationship between war and masculinity, but crucially those that young men most commonly encountered presented this relationship in traditional terms, or even within a masculine 'pleasure culture' of war.

When it came to joining up, young men did not universally draw upon their understandings of the Great War, but many did and these understandings informed their attitudes to, and choices about, enlistment. While the fact that the vast majority complied with conscription gives the appearance that it was widely accepted, this appearance was kept up, at least in part, by State manpower controls that gave individuals some agency to negotiate the nature of their service while still conforming to the State's expectation that they would participate in the People's War. Men's private attitudes to joining up were, in fact, diverse. Some were enthusiastic about the prospect of military service, perceiving it as a route to adventure or heroism. Others could not be described as truly willing, but accepted they could not find a legitimate way out. More common, though, was a reluctant willingness to serve if duty demanded it. Given the choice, and informed by understandings of the Great War, most men would have rather joined the RAF, and certainly preferred to avoid service in the infantry.

During the Second World War the dominant masculinity in public discourse was 'temperate' – stoic, brave and good-natured, but lacking in bravado, aggression and heroism.[15] Here it is shown that young men understood that temperate masculinity was the public expectation, and that to be seen as performing wartime masculinity they should be seen in uniform, but young men's subjective conceptions of masculinity often diverged from the temperate template. Many were privately less accepting of the duty of military service than was expected, even if they ultimately conformed. For others temperate masculinity and even the soldier hero (or its Second World War equivalent, the pilot hero) were expected or desirable subjective identities, despite, and even because of, the legacy of the Great War. For some this was because representations of the 'pleasure culture' of war had provided a frame through which to imagine past and future service. For others, the understanding that a previous generation had fought in the Great War, often including their father or uncles, confirmed that they too had to join up. Ultimately,

6   *Joining up in the Second World War*

this book demonstrates that, rather than severing the association between military participation and wartime masculinity, the most influential components of the Great War's cultural legacy reinforced Edwardian conceptions of wartime masculinity in the subjectivities of those who had grown up in the Great War's shadow.

The Great War in inter-war memory

The cultural legacy of the Great War has been the subject of a great deal of research, yet this can only tell us so much about the attitudes of the wider population. In particular, scholars have examined how the Great War was depicted and the meanings ascribed to it within literary texts. An initial focus upon elite literature – including the war books boom at the end of the 1920s – led to the suggestion that British society became disillusioned with warfare after 1918.[16] Historians have since highlighted that the 'disillusioned' authors were, in fact, ambivalent about their wartime experiences and that disillusioned narratives were contested at the time.[17] In addition, as historians have examined a wider range of texts they have found greater variation in the meanings ascribed to the Great War. Significantly, media that was widely consumed in inter-war Britain such as juvenile fiction, middlebrow novels and film more commonly presented the Great War in traditional terms: redemptive sacrifice, heroic soldiering and even within a pleasure culture of war as masculine adventure.[18] Similarly, commemorative ceremonies emphasised death and loss as a result of war, but framing this as sacrifice imbued those deaths with significance and value.[19] In inter-war Britain, as Daniel Todman has argued, 'Britons want[ed] to remember very different versions of the war. Although none completely obscured the horror and the suffering inflicted by the war, the meanings derived from those experiences varied widely.'[20] While scholars have shown how the Great War was represented in many cultural texts and what literary and film critics interpreted these works to be saying about what the Great War meant or was like, we know far less about *audiences'* reactions. Vincent Trott has considered how inter-war audiences reacted to Great War literature, but to understand the effects of the Great War's wider cultural legacy, more sustained and in-depth examination is needed.[21] It is

Introduction

necessary to establish what young men encountered, and how they interpreted what they did encounter, from the extensive catalogue of available Great War representations in varied media in inter-war Britain.

Chapter 1 uses oral histories and MO material to examine young men's exposure to, engagement with and responses to representations of the Great War in inter-war Britain. It explores young men's subjective engagement with representations of the Great War in literature and film, and in juvenile literature, radio, Armistice commemorations and schools. The chapter shows that, despite the attention paid to it by scholars, the canon of Great War literature was only occasionally encountered and comprised a relatively small proportion of young men's exposure to representations of the Great War. The significant exception is *All Quiet on the Western Front*, but under-researched texts such as illustrated histories of the Great War were amongst the most influential. What individuals took from representations of the Great War was even more varied than the plethora of representations they encountered, highlighting the difficulty of inferring the messages such texts communicated about the Great War.

Focusing upon the lived experience of young men in inter-war Britain reveals how extensive and pervasive the Great War's cultural legacy was. It was not only wider than the literary works of canonical war poets and memoirists but also spread beyond popular culture. Great War veterans took the war home. Jessica Meyer suggested that the soldier identity was difficult to accommodate in post-war domesticity, but in Great War veterans' letters, diaries and memoirs 'the war retains its place as an arena in which men were defined as martial heroes and domestic protectors', and that the positive effects of even negative wartime experiences 'were as persistent in shaping men's post-war identities as more negative responses of disillusionment and fatalism, making them equally important in defining British First World War servicemen's memories and identities'.[22] Scholars have, however, paid little focused attention to whether and how Great War veterans transmitted representations of the Great War to young men in their day-to-day lives in inter-war Britain.[23] Chapter 2 demonstrates the significance of representations of the Great War in the domestic space and from Great War veterans. The oral histories show how young men

8 *Joining up in the Second World War*

encountered Great War veterans, how they learned that they were veterans, what these veterans told them and how they interpreted these narratives and impressions. Although many veterans were reticent about their experiences, most young men learned about veterans' service, some heard detailed narratives of experience and many young men considered these interactions significant within their understanding of the conflict. The chapter therefore demonstrates that veterans' narratives should be considered an important component of the body of inter-war representations of the Great War. Like representations in popular culture, veterans' narratives were understandably heterogeneous: they might include horrific and traumatic aspects or camaraderie and humour, or both. The content and tone of what veterans opted to share with young men meant these narratives more often presented a traditional impression of stoic or heroic service as duty or adventure than a story of 'disillusionment'. As such, they did little to break, and may well have reinforced, the connection between wartime military service and masculinity in the subjective understandings of the young men who heard them.

Joining up

From 1937, with the Second World War approaching, politicians began debating the introduction of conscription. The Government, drawing lessons from the Great War, was alert to the benefits of control over military enlistment.[24] Measures to direct volunteers to appropriate services and a Schedule of Reserved Occupations were published nearly a year before war began, though throughout the war the State fought to balance the demand for men (and women) in overalls with the need for men to don khaki or RAF blue.[25] Limited conscription measures were introduced by the May 1939 Military Training Act, and on the outbreak of war in September 1939 the National Service (Armed Forces) Act made all men aged 18–41 liable for conscription. Perhaps because the Great War had set a precedent, Britons ostensibly met conscription with far more compliance than resistance.[26] This acquiescence may explain historians' focus on the political debates about conscription, on Britain's broader manpower problems and on the mechanisms by which recruits

Introduction 9

were distributed to the services and transformed from civilians into soldiers, seamen and airmen.[27] While conscientious objectors have attracted scholarly attention,[28] few scholars have examined how the much larger group of men who did enlist thought and felt about it.[29] Alan Allport well illustrates that young men held a variety of attitudes towards enlistment in the Army, but he does so as part of a wider study that was never intended to explore men's attitudes to enlistment in the depth that I do here, or to include those who joined the RAF or the Navy.[30] Similarly, as part of a broader study, Frances Houghton has explored enlistment using the memoirs of Second World War veterans who had been 'at the sharp end' across all three services, and found that most claimed to have been enthusiastic recruits.[31] A wider and deeper consideration of young men's attitudes and decisions about enlistment – including those who did not covet or hold combat (or even military) roles, and considering what men said at the time as well as afterwards – reveals a more nuanced and detailed picture of conscription in Second World War than is available in the existing historiography. Beneath the overarching picture of compliance, individual young men held very varied attitudes and took varied decisions around enlistment in an effort to negotiate the nature of their Second World War service.

Chapter 3 uses MO survey material and opinion polls to explain how the British public, and particularly young men, reacted to the implementation of conscription. War Office documents and published advice guides are used to map the shifting boundaries of wartime conscription and how these affected the level of control young men could exercise over the nature of their own wartime participation. This provides the most detailed discussion to date of men's State-imposed wartime responsibilities. Unlike much existing discussion, this discussion is presented from the perspective of young men rather than the State, and personal testimony is used to examine the extent to which individuals might negotiate the State's demands and how well young men understood this at the time. The negotiation of manpower controls is explored further in Chapter 4. Oral histories and MO material are used to examine young men's attitudes to conscription and volunteering and illustrate the diversity of attitudes. It shows that, as Houghton suggests of some combat veterans, younger recruits in particular were able to conceive of wartime service in heroic, adventurous or patriotic terms, as some

10   *Joining up in the Second World War*

of their counterparts had done decades before.[32] More commonly, though, men reluctantly consented to service that they felt was an unwelcome interruption to their working and domestic lives. This variety of opinions was obfuscated by what outwardly appeared overwhelming compliance with State direction. This compliance was, however, due, at least in part, to the potential for individuals to negotiate the manpower system to obtain wartime service that suited their desires, particularly by volunteering; negotiation was often a method of ensuring entry into the forces – and especially the service a man desired – not simply an attempt to stay out of uniform. Together, Chapters 3 and 4 enhance our understandings of men's attitudes to conscription and military service during the Second World War by revealing the varied levels of willingness hidden beneath the veneer of consent for conscription.

Significantly, Chapter 4 also uses personal testimony to examine how the Great War shaped men's attitudes during the Second World War. Gary Sheffield has suggested that the continued existence of representations that presented the Great War in traditional terms explains why 'so many young men proved resistant to the trend among the intellectual elite of revulsion against the First World War'.[33] Houghton's examination of Second World War veterans' memoirs highlights that the 'pleasure culture' depictions of the Great War could spur interest in military service, and less positive understandings were included as justifications for preferring RAF service over the Army.[34] These suggestions are reasonable, but the influence of the Great War on joining up in the Second World War has not previously been the focus of a substantial study. Moreover, given that Chapters 1 and 2 show that young men's engagement with representations of the Great War was more complex than has previously been suggested, it is worthwhile exploring this topic in greater depth, and using an approach that is potentially more illuminating. As well as examining a broader range of personal testimonies, including more young men who grew up in working-class households,[35] the original oral histories provide the opportunity to probe the significance interviewees placed on the Great War, and to view their narratives of joining up in tandem with their recollections of their engagement with representations of the Great War. Chapter 4 considers the attitudes of the young men themselves, and their parents' feelings and advice. It reveals the complexity of the

Great War's influence. The attitudes and decisions of many young men, but not all, were shaped by their understandings of the Great War, but the effects were not straightforward, particularly when young men's understandings were informed by both representations encountered in popular culture and from veterans. Understandings of the Great War did not commonly cause men to withdraw their consent to serve, but did influence how men sought to spend their wartime service, most commonly discouraging service in the Army.

Masculinity

The soldier hero ideal that had been the hegemonic masculinity in 1914 was challenged by the experience of the Great War.[36] For instance, Michael Roper suggests the Great War demonstrated that character could not prevent fear and, instead, the ability to endure and to continue despite fear became the hallmark of courage.[37] Some scholars have contended that masculinity was more fundamentally reshaped during the inter-war years as the Great War had challenged the place of military participation in conceptions of masculinity.[38] George Mosse and Alison Light suggest that inter-war British masculinity became softer, more domestic, pacifistic and anti-heroic.[39] The success of the 1935 'Peace Ballot' and the popularity of the Peace Pledge Union suggested that wider society, aware of how many lives the Great War had cost, were increasingly pacifistic, too.[40] Those averse to militarism and those who feared the production of an effeminate generation clashed over teaching in schools, particularly about physical education,[41] and students at Oxford and Cambridge colleges were increasingly embracing masculine identities that did not include military service.[42] Yet Jessica Meyer has demonstrated that Great War veterans typically thought of their own service in traditional masculine terms,[43] and we know that the Great War also continued to be represented as an adventure and the realm of heroic manliness throughout the inter-war period.[44] Chapters 1 and 2 show representations containing such depictions were the ones that young men most commonly encountered, and this may have ensured the survival of Edwardian masculine ideals. Sonya O. Rose draws on Light's argument about inter-war masculinity when she suggests that the hegemonic masculinity in

12   *Joining up in the Second World War*

public discourse during the Second World War was 'temperate'.[45] Nonetheless, Rose is clear that military participation was fundamental to the successful enactment of the hegemonic temperate masculinity. Contemporaries fiercely defended combat as a masculine arena,[46] and men with military roles were more highly regarded by women.[47] This does not suggest that a substantial or durable shift in conceptions of wartime masculinity took place between the wars. Yet, whether the hegemonic construction of masculinity that Rose identified in public discourse had the same dominance in the conceptions of masculinity held by the young men who were to serve in the Second World War has not been fully explored.

Scholars have paid much attention to the subjective masculinities of those *outside* the full-time forces, including men in the Home Guard, men in reserved occupations and conscientious objectors.[48] Those *inside* the forces have not been ignored: how the body and sexuality related to masculinity in the Army has been explored.[49] Martin Francis and Frances Houghton have explored the subjective identities of those who served in the RAF; and Houghton has examined the memoirs of men who held 'sharp-end' combat roles in all three services.[50] Yet, although the distinction between serviceman and civilian was crucial in the successful performance of temperate masculinity, historians have paid limited attention to the point when this transition occurred: enlistment. Examining the significance that young men placed upon joining up reveals much about full-time servicemen's subjective understandings of the relationship between military service and masculinity, including how they related to temperate masculinity and the earlier image of the 'soldier hero'.

Chapter 5 shows that young men who entered all three services generally understood hegemonic wartime masculinity as bound up with the status of combatant, particularly in the air. This understanding shaped their attitudes towards enlistment even though not all men aspired to perform the hegemonic masculinity. Indeed, men's subjective conceptions of masculinity were often divergent from Rose's 'temperate' template. Some desired military involvement, perceived elements of service as glamorous and anticipated an exciting adventure. Such ideas were too militaristic and enthusiastic for temperate masculinity and were more closely aligned to an older perception of service as a masculine rite of passage or even the

Introduction 13

soldier hero. This finding confirms Frances Houghton's observation that veteran memoirists of all three services presented the war as a coming-of-age story; the hyper-masculine tropes discernible in their enlistment narratives were replaced over the course of the war by a temperate masculinity.[51] As Houghton cautions, however, these memoirists are 'a self-selecting group', all of whom saw war at the 'sharp end'.[52] There are other reasons that these sources are predisposed towards a hyper-masculine framing of enlistment, too.[53] Looking at a more diverse group reveals that a larger proportion of men reluctantly accepted military participation as a duty, often framed as defence of home and family. Their reluctance could be accommodated within temperate masculinity so long as they were ostensibly willing to serve. Yet willingness to serve also remained the minimum requirement in the minds of many of those brought up in inter-war Britain. Moreover, even those who did not hold this conception often conformed rather than publicly reject temperate masculinity. They could try to balance their personal preferences with their public obligations by negotiating the constraints of the manpower system. A key difference in the construction of wartime masculinity between the First and Second World Wars was not the absence of hyper-masculine expectations of military experience or the widespread wholesale rejection of military service, but rather the acceptability of publicly expressing a willingness to fight mixed with a preference for not having to do so. Significantly, the imprecision and ambiguity of the most important marker of temperate masculinity – being in uniform – camouflaged the subjective masculinities of both those who were, relative to the temperate ideal, overly reluctant or overly keen to join up.

Personal testimony

Examining subjective experience – individuals' experiences, attitudes and understandings – is central to the approach taken in this book. Oral history and MO provide two crucial sources of personal testimony. The original oral histories in particular provide an unparalleled opportunity to examine how 'ordinary' young men encountered and engaged with the Great War in inter-war Britain, and to explore their attitudes and responses to Second World War

14   *Joining up in the Second World War*

enlistment, because through questioning the historian can broaden their narratives, revealing the complex and private negotiations behind individuals' decisions and attitudes. Archival oral histories and material from the Mass Observation Archive also have a central place in this study. Both are used to shed light on how men felt about Second World War service and whether and how they connected the two world wars.

The oral histories

A common concern about oral sources is that the passage of time results in forgetting, yet a number of researchers examining veterans' oral narratives have commented on the remarkable consistency and accuracy of their recollections.[54] Indeed, most forgetting occurs very shortly after an event, after which point the passing of time has little impact on what we remember.[55] Things that seem significant to us at the time appear to be well recalled, and we record the meaning, sense and emotion of events.[56] While short-term memory wanes with age, long-term memory is significantly less affected.[57] Moreover, and beneficially for studies like this, adolescence and young adulthood are the years elderly people remember best.[58]

More significant than our capacity to recall events and feelings from the past is the understanding, based on neurobiological research, that memories are better envisaged as a jigsaw to be reconstructed than as a file archived for retrieval. The context in which we are remembering, and the possible influences of hindsight and the dominant narratives in popular culture, can shape how we reassemble them. Had there been substantial disagreement between the oral histories and the contemporary MO material it might have indicated how memories had changed over time, but that is not evident here. The Popular Memory framework developed by the Popular Memory Group can also help us to identify and understand these influences.[59] An important component is Graham Dawson's concept of composure: a narrator seeks to tell stories that make sense, enable positive self-perception and elicit a positive reaction from the audience – providing composure.[60] Recognising that narratives may be shaped by a (subconscious) need for stories that fit with an event's

Introduction 15

later significance and/or enable positive self-perception can help us to interpret 'mis-rememberings'. For example, Les Temple emphasised the importance of his brother's imprisonment as a POW in his own enlistment motivations, though this narrative does not fit with the chronology.[61] This reconstruction, however, shows us why his service *became* important to him, as well as the importance he places upon his bond with his brother. The desire to elicit a positive reaction from the audience can also have important consequences. Audiences' reactions (and narrators' expectations of audiences' reactions) are commonly informed by the popular memory, so a narrative that adheres to the popular memory is the most likely to elicit a positive reaction.[62] Consequently, the popular memory can suppress alternative narratives. For instance, Alistair Thomson illustrated that Fred Farrall felt unable to discuss his Great War experiences because they were opposed to the hegemonic narratives of Australian soldiers.[63] It was not until the Vietnam War, and increasing representations of the soldier as a victim, that Farrall was provided with a framework and popular recognition of his viewpoint, which enabled him to 'talk more easily about his experience of "the war as hell" and his own feelings of inadequacy as a soldier'.[64] Similarly, Penny Summerfield and Corinna Peniston-Bird found women who served in the Home Guard were often silenced by their absence from cultural representations of the service.[65] Popular memory does not necessarily determine individual narratives, though. Peniston-Bird has shown that an empathetic interviewing style could help male Home Guard veterans acknowledge, negotiate and contest the understanding – popularised by *Dad's Army* – of the force as aged and inept.[66] One said:

> I think [*Dad's Army* is] very funny. I don't think it was as funny as they depict but there was funny things in the Home Guard without a doubt really. I mean, there's got to be, hasn't there? But not so bad to that extent you know. Actually it was serious stuff really in the Home Guard.[67]

Peniston-Bird notes that having met a non-judgemental response, later in interviews some Home Guards 'became less likely to present their memories in the light of previous audience responses, less likely to reproduce the dominant cultural construction of the force, and more confident about asserting their own authority in interpreting the significance of the force'.[68]

I conducted two sets of oral histories. These enabled me to ask questions to examine young men's exposure to and responses to representations of the Great War from its veterans and in popular culture, as well as their experiences relating to the Second World War. The first set of thirty-five interviews with veterans of the Second World War Armed Forces was conducted in 2010 and 2011 for the doctoral research that was the origin of this book. I first met most of these men at commemorative events in Whitehall in 2009, a veterans' event at the RAF Museum, Hendon or a Russian Convoys event at the Imperial War Museum, and I invited them to participate in interviews about their early lives and their attitudes to Second World War enlistment and service. I was introduced to a small number of my interviewees by other interviewees. I also made a specific appeal for RAF ground crew in the RAF Association's South-East branch newsletter, as my initial efforts did not yield anyone who had held this position. The second set of oral histories has a more opportunistic relationship to this research. Between 2015 and 2016 I interviewed twenty-five Second World War Bevin Boys – men conscripted into mining rather than the Armed Forces.[69] Aided by the Bevin Boys Association, I invited these men to be interviewed about their early lives and their attitudes to Second World War enlistment and service as Bevin Boys. These men had also grown up in inter-war Britain and, had it not been for the Bevin Boys ballot, would typically have become veterans of the Armed Forces. I therefore took the opportunity to ask questions about their youth and exposure to representations of the Great War.

By 2010 the passing of time had largely removed the opportunity to interview those born before and during the Great War, meaning most of my interviewees were born during the 1920s and served as young men. Older men are, however, found amongst the ninety-four oral history interviews with veterans of the Second World War Armed Forces that I examined in the archives held by the Imperial War Museum and the National Museum of the Royal Navy, Portsmouth. The archival interviews increase both the weight and the diversity of the source base. While some were selected because the interview summary referred to the Great War, others were selected to help redress particular imbalances, including age, or because they had served in the Army or Navy, which helped counterbalance the number of my own interviewees who

Introduction 17

had served in the RAF. With both my own and archival interviews, I could establish interviewees' ages and where they served. Some interviewees were Jewish, a fact mentioned because it affected their enlistment motivations, but otherwise race did not feature prominently in the interviews. Everyone who responded to my calls for interviewees was white, and given the demography of British society at the time most of the archival interviewees probably were, too. Many of my interviewees were residing in South-East England when interviewed, though some had grown up elsewhere, and others had lived in and were interviewed in Lancashire, Derbyshire, Nottinghamshire and Northamptonshire. The archival interviews broaden the geographic spread further, especially a useful series with members of the Durham Light Infantry.[70]

Oral history interviewees are self-selecting. Certainly, veterans who found it difficult to compose their own narratives of the Second World War might have been less likely to agree to be interviewed, but it is difficult to ascertain which veterans were most likely to experience this difficulty. The apparent reticence of RAF ground crew veterans may have been caused by their relative absence in the cultural memory of the Second World War, overshadowed by the prominence of flyers in public narratives.[71] Conversely, Arthur Howard was particularly keen to be interviewed precisely because he felt the involvement of British forces in Burma is too commonly forgotten – the interview gave him the opportunity to add t/his history to the record. Others clearly expected they would be unable to achieve composure: one RAMC veteran declined my invitation by explaining that he found talking about what he had seen during the war upsetting. My assurances that recounting his experiences after enlistment was unnecessary did not override his awareness that his memories were not safely composed.[72] Individual interviewees also had their own motivations for being interviewed. Some were keen that their story be recorded for their families, or because they felt their service had been forgotten.[73] Conversely, three or four others had been interviewed before and one or two were well practised in the role of 'veteran'. More generally, interviewees were evidently excited about the prospect of an interested audience; most remarked that they had enjoyed the process and remembered things they had completely forgotten.[74] Most indicated some pleasure at the idea of their interview being archived, and emphasised the importance

18   *Joining up in the Second World War*

of remembering the war. The most common and often most pressing motivation, however, was frequently highlighted as I left, when interviewees were concerned to establish that they had helped me and talked about relevant topics, and often extended invitations for me to return with more questions.

Whether, or how, the broad characteristics outlined above would shape the findings of this research is, however, far less clear. There is no apparent connection between such characteristics and an individual's inter-war engagement with representations of the Great War. A greater relationship might exist between men's pre-war attitudes to enlistment and the connection between military service and masculinity and their post-war attitudes, but here too it is difficult to speculate about how this would shape the findings. While my interviewees were mainly born in the 1920s, we might hypothesise that interviewing more men born in the 1900s or 1910s might have surfaced more recollections of canonical Great War literature. Nevertheless, such references were uncommon within the responses of Mass Observers of that age.

Crucially, one thing all these men have in common is that they were invited to be interviewed about, and because of, their Second World War service. There is no reason to expect that this collection of oral histories overemphasises the significance of young men's engagement with the Great War. The resulting body of interview material thus enables detailed investigation of the legacy of the Great War within the inter-war generation, and its impact in relation to Second World War service. Importantly, however, while my own interviews were designed to explore this question, the archival interviews were not. Harry Moses demonstrated interest in his interviewees' social backgrounds, their decisions and the context in which these were taken. As a result, he sometimes asked fortuitously relevant and well-phrased questions, such as 'In your young life, looking back over those years in the late '20s and '30s, had the experiences of the First World War, were they still within the communities?' Conrad Wood put a more leading variant to Peter Taylor: 'So you weren't thinking about the terrible suffering of those in the trenches in the First World War?'[75] Generally, though, one is left to await chance mentions of the Great War. These were not uncommon in the interviews examined; interviewees often stated that an individual within their narrative was a Great War veteran,

Introduction

19

irrespective of its relevance to what followed, or mentioned the Great War in relation to their own enlistment. For instance, James Donovan remarked:

> I suppose like a lot of youngsters you'd heard tales of the First World War, and er, well I thought to myself well I'll be disappointed if I don't find out what it's like, as strange as it may seem now, but at the time I thought to myself is it going to last long enough for me to get into the Army.[76]

Who told those tales and how much he heard about his father's service was left unspoken, though. These chance inclusions are valuable evidence but because the interviewers were not seeking to explore, or confirm the upper limit of, young men's exposure to representations of the Great War it is possible that the archival interviews under-represent how much young men had learned about the Great War from popular culture or its veterans.[77]

My interviews were normally conducted at veterans' homes,[78] and were normally one-to-one.[79] Interviewees' wives were sometimes quiet presences, either to provide reassurance, out of interest or because the logistics of interviewing in homes left them few other options. Interviews were normally completed on a single day, though some were over up to three separate occasions, and ranged from an hour to five hours in length; most were between two and half to three hours long. Some interviewees, particularly those who I met more than once, incorporated social elements into our interactions – often a pause for tea and cake, sometimes lunch, and once lunch at the local pub. The interviews were semi-structured, and although they were not life histories they utilised the familiar structure of a life story: questions about family and upbringing; schooling and juvenile leisure; and teenage hopes and plans in working life were all things I wanted to hear about to understand the men's lives and see their enlistment narratives in context, but these typically 'safe' topics (at least relative to some war narratives) provided time for interviewees to develop confidence and us to develop rapport before we moved onto topics where they were perhaps less likely to have composed narratives: awareness of approaching war, enlistment and service preferences, and war service itself. A notable absence in this description of the interview structure is the Great War. Invitations to be interviewed stressed my interest in Second

World War enlistment and understanding what had influenced men's attitudes and decisions. I could not explain my interest in understanding the significance of the Great War as doing so would almost certainly have encouraged men to foreground the Great War within their narratives of joining up, and it might have discouraged potential interviewees who felt the Great War was not relevant to them. Instead, the interview structure gave interviewees the chance to explain their enlistment in their own terms, and then I asked more direct questions about enlistment, attitudes and masculinity, and followed up any organic references to the Great War before asking further questions about their contact with, and the influence of, Great War veterans and engagement with representations of the Great War in popular culture. My interviews with Bevin Boys in 2016 were conducted in a very similar way, with the same approach to structure, albeit tailored to ensure less focus on enlistment specifically and greater focus on their time as Bevin Boys.

Like Peniston-Bird, I used an empathetic interviewing style and worked to build rapport with interviewees. Oral historians are accustomed to reflecting on how their own personal markers, such as age, sex, class and education, affect the interviewee's perception of the interviewer and their relative positions in society (and vice versa), and shape the interview dynamic, and thus content, sometimes negatively.[80] I did not experience intersubjectivity as disruptive, but I shared Peniston-Bird's experience of the identity 'historian' causing an interviewee's preoccupation with the provision of dates and chronologies; some had notes or RAF log-books to hand to enable precision.[81] I suspect, too, that some interviewees would have narrated their wartime encounters with young women differently, or not at all, to a young woman interviewer. Yet gender is not the only, or necessarily the most influential, component of intersubjective dynamics. Juliette Pattinson highlights the importance of generational difference,[82] and Valerie Yow suggests that interviewees may place an interviewer into the established role of a person with similar characteristics.[83] I was similar in age to many of my interviewee's grandchildren, who were also frequently the family members with university experience, and passing comparisons were made over coffee or lunch. Dan Todman has suggested that Great War veterans found it easiest to talk to their grandchildren about their war experiences, and being placed in the position of

Introduction 21

grandchild may explain why interviewees were so willing to help and certainly seems to have helped foster a productive interview dynamic.[84] In my assessment, my approach, paired with the duration of the interviews, typically successfully built rapport, encouraged candid and reflective dialogue and gave interviewees the space and confidence to present narratives that diverged from the dominant discourse if they wished. Certainly, some worked through a process of negotiation and contestation, similar to that which Peniston-Bird describes in relation to the Home Guard, when they were discussing their enlistment motivations. They initially ascribed their enlistment to patriotism, almost as an answer which might make the question go away, but later in the interview expanded or changed their explanations. Similarly, the trope that Great War veterans did not talk about the war was one that many interviewees were able to negotiate. It must, however, be borne in mind that dominant narratives *could* have had a silencing effect, particularly on archival interviewees which were not all conducted with the empathetic style that facilitates contestation, and mentions of familial service usually occurred early in interviews before a rapport had developed.[85]

Once oral histories have been produced, it is the task of the oral historian to interpret and contextualise individual interviews and draw more general conclusions from the collection. Without assigning the historian any kind of omniscience, the distance a historian has from an individual's life narrative can enable the observation of things the interviewee has not acknowledged, or would find uncomfortable to acknowledge.[86] Moreover, analysing a collection of narratives can demonstrate themes and influences that are not perceived or even considered by an individual, particularly (normally) subconscious influences like constructions of gender. Yet, as Katherine Borland cautions, 'Our scholarly representations ... if not sensitively presented, may constitute an attack on our collaborator's carefully constructed sense of self.'[87] Most of my interviewees preferred to be named rather than anonymised and were more interested in contributing their experiences than my interpretation of them. I sincerely hope that none of my interpretations will be perceived as disparaging; it should be remembered that the attitudes these men expressed are unlikely to be unique, and the evidence presented here is illustrative of many young men rather than

22   *Joining up in the Second World War*

just the individual concerned. Presenting what interviewees said and the emotional register in which they said it requires compromises between verbatim transcription and readability. When it is illuminating, incorrect grammar and wordings have been faithfully reproduced, and false starts, pauses, changes of course, repetition, stutters, tears or laughter are included, regardless of the obstacles this poses to silent reading.[88]

Mass Observation

In 1937 left-leaning intellectuals Charles Madge and Tom Harrisson founded MO, a social research organisation that aimed to enable 'the masses to speak for themselves, to make their voices heard above the din created by the press and politicians speaking in their name'.[89] Despite the conscription of some of its staff, including Harrisson, MO continued to produce, gather and publish a wealth of material about people's opinions throughout the Second World War. Some of MO's publications and internal File Reports are used within this book, but the raw material MO gathered, much of which they never analysed, is even more valuable.

MO employed Observers who surreptitiously recorded Briton's behaviour and conversations in pubs and cafés, on public transport and on the streets.[90] Such material, especially from the Worktown study of Bolton, is drawn upon throughout. MO also conducted street surveys and, during April 1939, canvassed Londoners' reactions to the announcement that limited peacetime conscription was to be introduced.[91] An analysis of the four hundred verbatim replies is used in Chapter 3 to provide a more nuanced understanding of individuals' responses to peacetime conscription. As MO recognised, however, their researchers encountered an inevitable barrier between an individual's public and private opinions.[92] Sometimes this barrier was impenetrable; an Observer conducting the April 1939 street survey recorded the response: 'You go and Fuck Off!'[93] Conversely, some Britons voluntarily joined MO's 'National Panel', which provided the mass of MO's material. Panellists received monthly 'Directives' by post, which solicited reflective answers to open-ended questions. MO were confident that panellists were 'prepared to give us the most detailed, candid, personal reactions' because they were answering by

Introduction 23

correspondence, in their own time, and with the understanding that MO 'respect their confidence and anonymity'.[94] Directive Replies could certainly be frank: for example, an 18-year-old student asked his opinion on the Blackout wrote: 'Personally, I like the Blackout; to walk in the dark exercises the mind, star-gazing is easier, and sex more sexy.'[95] The verbatim responses to two Directive questions are used extensively here. In January 1940, male panellists were asked, 'If you think you are going to be called up this year, what are your reactions to this and how has it affected your personal plans for the future?'[96] The 164 responses are discussed in relation to wartime conscription in Chapter 4. In February 1940, male and female panellists were asked, 'How much do you think childhood impressions and incidents colour your opinions in the present war? And if you do think childhood does affect your present opinion, in what way do you feel these effects work?'[97] The 239 respondents often made reference to the Great War, or representations of it, enabling a glimpse of which representations had shaped their understandings.[98] Analysis of their responses informs Chapters 1, 2 and 4.

MO did enable Britons 'to speak for themselves, to make their voices heard', but MO's different methods amplified the voices of different groups. The street surveys asked questions of unsuspecting members of the public and were sometimes dominated by working-class voices, while the self-selecting National Panel contained a disproportionate number of lower-middle- and middle-class Britons, particularly clerks and teachers.[99] As fewer than 2,500 Britons volunteered for the Panel by the end of the war, those who did were exceptional by default.[100] More importantly, perhaps, James Hinton suggests they perceived themselves as such: 'a group of self-consciously enlightened individuals located across the class spectrum'.[101] MO characterised them as exceptional, too: the 'thinking minority'.[102] The Panel inevitably attracted those interested in ideas like MO; many had volunteered after or hearing discussion of MO on the radio or reading an MO publication, and *Britain* by Mass Observation was published in 1939 in the Penguin Paperbacks range, marketed for 'young intelligentsia'.[103] The MO Diarists, who might be characterised as some of the most engaged members of the Panel, had commonly received more education than a typical Briton; few had a degree, but they commonly held a grammar-school scholarship, and they read widely.[104] The *News Chronicle* and *New Statesman* were preferred journals,[105] and panellists were typically politically left-leaning or centrist.[106] Murray Goot has suggested they might be conceptualised as those who 'wrote letters to the editor',[107] and certainly they were keen to express their opinions, perhaps, as Lucy Noakes suggests, because they felt they were unrepresented in British society.[108] The Panel was demographically unrepresentative of the British population, too: young people, especially men, and people from South-East England, were disproportionately inclined to join.[109] Nevertheless, MO consistently stressed that the Panel were not intended to be representative. Instead, they provided qualitative material to access the 'why' of public opinion.[110]

Although the Panel was not representative, as Calder remarked of the Directive on Race, 'if one knows how the Panel was composed, then the results in part seem highly significant'.[111] As I have argued elsewhere, because most wartime panellists wrote fewer than four times and around a quarter wrote only once, it is more important to understand the composition of the respondents to the Directive in question than that of the Panel as a collective.[112] In the case of the January and February 1940 Directives, no less than 80 per cent of the male respondents were under the age of 35, and 65 per cent of the women who answered the February Directive question were younger than 35. Clearly, they do not reflect the age distribution of the British population; however, the skew towards those who had come of age during the 1920s and 1930s, and the preponderance of young men, is obviously advantageous for a study focused upon the experiences and attitudes of young men.[113] If these experiences and attitudes varied across the United Kingdom's nations, this is unlikely to be apparent in these responses. Few people wrote from Scotland or Wales. Moreover, as many as half the respondents were writing from London or the South-East of England, and respondents from the South-West, North-East, North-West and Midlands made up roughly equal proportions of the remainder. In terms of class, the January and February 1940 respondents reflect the broader picture of the panel as a whole. Some held blue-collar jobs, including a sheet-metal worker, a farm labourer and an apprentice wallpaper manufacturer. Most of those who responded, however, held white-collar jobs – they were clerks or journalists, assistant librarians or insurance salesmen. This composition need not limit the analysis, however.

Introduction 25

Indeed, as will be argued, the relative lack of exposure to depictions of the Great War in 'high' literature amongst a group of respondents weighted towards to the educated lower-middle class is even more telling than if the respondents had been representative of the national population. It is possible that the above-average education levels of panellists meant that they had a better than average understanding of the processes of conscription, and thus how to negotiate it. Yet, as the discussion in Chapter 3 demonstrates, the highly educated could misunderstand, and those who received fewer years of formal education could both transmit information about the processes and exercise agency in relation to them. Similarly, it is possible that lower-middle class young men might have more keenly felt military service as an interruption to their burgeoning careers, yet the working-class men whose opinions were captured in the April 1939 street survey expressed similar concerns about interrupted apprenticeships. There is, then, little to suggest that the self-selecting nature of these sources casts doubt upon the findings presented.

While neither the street surveys nor Directive Replies provide neat cross-sections of the British public's opinion, and the voices of different groups predominate in different kinds of MO material, the Mass Observation Archive 'provides a unique opportunity to interrogate the ideas and feelings of large numbers of ordinary men and women'.[114] The Directive responses and verbatim survey answers enable historians to re-examine individuals' subjective expressions of their opinions themselves, rather than accepting MO's analyses.[115] As Claire Langhamer states, such MO sources provide 'glimpses of "private", emotional lives, and responses to public events, unavailable from more traditional, quantitative, sources'.[116] The material proves particularly valuable here because MO asked questions so relevant to this study, broadening its scope by enabling the reflections and attitudes of hundreds of Britons to be examined in far more depth than opinion polls. The oral histories, meanwhile, provide even deeper insight and the ability to explore and interrogate particular themes within the context of a broader narrative. That the two bodies of material – one contemporary and one far more recent – are consistent with one another suggests that interviewees have been able to successfully recollect and reflect how they thought and felt at the time.

* * * *

This book is divided into two parts, shaped by the aim of bridging the gap between the two world wars. The first two chapters locate the cultural legacy of First World War in the subjectivities of men who participated in the Second World War. Examining young men's lived experience of and engagement with representations of the Great War in inter-war Britain enables a re-evaluation of the Great War's cultural legacy. It challenges the significance of 'elite' literature and instead highlights the influence of both the 'pleasure culture' of war and a broader and potentially more impactful range of representations of the Great War in domestic and day-to-day life. Having established how boys growing up in the 1920s and 1930s encountered representations of the Great War and what they took from them, the third, fourth and fifth chapters focus on joining up in the Second World War, including consideration of whether and how understandings of the Great War shaped men's attitudes. They examine how young men felt about enlistment, the preferences they expressed and the choices they made. Their attitudes were highly varied, from those who fought to join up to those sought to escape the call-up, and those who accepted it with varied levels of enthusiasm or fatalism. Young men did not universally draw upon their understandings of the Great War when facing the Second World War, but many did and these understandings informed their attitudes to, and choices about, enlistment. Men's attitudes and preferences also reveal much about their subjective conceptions of wartime masculinity. Having considered how wartime masculinity was depicted in representations of the Great War in Chapters 1 and 2, Chapter 5 examines how these young men conceptualised it in relation to their own service. It shows that their conceptions were often divergent from the temperate masculinity that occupied a hegemonic position in public discourse, but when looking at men's actions in relation to enlistment traditional constructions of masculinity appeared resilient. This appearance was kept up, at least in part, by State manpower controls that gave individuals some agency to negotiate the nature of their service while still ostensibly conforming to public expectations of masculine service in the People's War. Yet, traditional constructions of wartime masculinity did not only appear resilient; for some young men temperate masculinity and even the soldier hero remained expected or even desirable subjective identities, in spite of, and even because of, the

Introduction 27

legacy of the Great War. This book contributes to and connects the history of the legacy of the Great War and the history of gender and military service in the Second World by demonstrating that the most influential components of the Great War's cultural legacy reinforced Edwardian conceptions of wartime masculinity in the subjectivities of those who had grown up in inter-war Britain.

Notes

1 Mass Observation Archive (hereafter MOA), TC Worktown, 27/A Armistice Day 1937: LT Observations on street.
2 Ian F. W. Becket, *The Great War 1914–1918* (Harlow: Routledge, 2007) p. 440.
3 Adrian Gregory, *The Silence of Memory: Armistice Day 1919– 1946* (Oxford: Berg, 1994); Lucy Noakes, 'A Broken Silence? Mass Observation, Armistice Day and "everyday life" in Britain 1937– 1941', *Journal of European Studies*, 45 (2015) pp. 331–46.
4 MOA, TC Worktown, 27/A Armistice Day 1937: LT Observations on street.
5 Michael Roper, *The Secret Battle. Emotional Survival in the Great War* (Manchester: Manchester University Press, 2009); Helen McCartney, *Citizen Soldiers: The Liverpool Territorials in the First World War* (Cambridge: Cambridge University Press, 2005). The dissemination of civilians' memories is not the focus of this book, but occasionally such individuals, particularly Great War veterans' wives or mothers, feature.
6 Figure for 1937–8, Joanna Bourke, *Dismembering the Male. Men's Bodies, Britain and the Great War* (London: Reaktion, 1996) p. 33. See also Deborah Cohen, *The War Come Home: Disabled Veterans in Britain and Germany, 1914–1939* (Berkeley: University of California Press, 2001).
7 'The Present Salutes the Past', *Cambridge Daily News*, 21 October 1939, p. 3.
8 Paul Fussell, *The Great War and Modern Memory* (Oxford: Oxford University Press, 1975); Samuel Hynes, *A War Imagined: The First World War and English Culture* (London: Hodley Head, 1992). Michael Paris to some extent accepts Hynes's premise, which elides representation and influence, and challenges it with the *existence* of the pleasure culture of war in other *cultural* representations; Paris, *Warrior Nation: Images of War in British Popular Culture, 1850– 2000* (London: Reaktion, 2000) p. 148. Gregory, *Silence*, pp. 176–7;

28 *Joining up in the Second World War*

Jay Winter, *Sites of Memory, Sites of Mourning: The Great War in European Cultural History* (Cambridge: Cambridge University Press, 1995) p. 8. Robert Mackay suggests the canonical war books gave impetus to the peace movements, in *Half the Battle: Civilian Morale in Britain during the Second World War* (Manchester: Manchester University Press, 2002) p. 23. Dan Todman points to a wider body of popular representations as contributing to later attitudes, in *The Great War. Myth and Memory* (London: Hambledon and London, 2005) pp. 94–5. Vincent Trott uses audience reception to demonstrate that Vera Brittain's *Testament of Youth* (1933) 'fostered' the developing pacifism of some young readers, though with the caveat that they were not necessarily typical of their generation; Trott, *Publishers, Readers and the Great War. Literature and Memory since 1918* (London: Bloomsbury, 2017) pp. 115–17.

9 Alison Light, *Forever England: Femininity, Literature and Conservatism Between the Wars* (London: Routledge, 1991); Eric Leed, *No Man's Land. Combat and identity in World War 1* (Cambridge: Cambridge University Press, 1981).

10 Martin Francis, 'Attending to Ghosts: Some Reflections on the Disavowals of British Great War Historiography', *Twentieth Century British History*, 25 (2014) pp. 347–67 (pp. 360–1).

11 Stephen Heathorn, 'The Mnemonic Turn in the Cultural Historiography of Britain's Great War', *The Historical Journal*, 48 (2005) pp. 1103–24 (pp. 1111, 1122).

12 Penny Summerfield, *Reconstructing Women's Wartime Lives: Discourse and Subjectivity in Oral Histories of the Second World War* (Manchester: Manchester University Press, 1998); Penny Summerfield and Corinna Peniston-Bird, *Contesting Home Defence: Men, Women and the Home Guard in the Second World War* (Manchester: Manchester University Press, 2007); Juliette Pattinson, *Behind Enemy Lines: Gender, Passing and the Special Operations Executive in the Second World War* (Manchester: Manchester University Press, 2007); Alison Chand, *Masculinities on Clydeside: Men in Reserved Occupations 1939–1945* (Edinburgh: Edinburgh University Press, 2016); Juliette Pattinson, Arthur McIvor and Linsey Robb, *Men in Reserve: British Civilian Masculinities in the Second World War* (Manchester: Manchester University Press, 2017.

13 Martin Francis, *The Flyer: British Culture and the Royal Air Force, 1939–1945* (Oxford: Oxford University Press, 2008) p. 9.

14 Todman, *Myth and Memory*; Gary Sheffield, *Forgotten Victory: The First World War: Myths and Realities* (London: Review, 2001).

Introduction   29

15 Sonya O. Rose, 'Temperate Heroes: Concepts of Masculinity in the Second World War Britain', in *Masculinities in Politics and War: Gendering Modern History*, ed. by Stefan Dudink, Karen Hagemann and John Tosh (Manchester: Manchester University Press, 2004) pp. 177–98 (p. 177). See also Sonya O. Rose, *Which People's War? National Identity and Citizenship in Wartime Britain 1939–1945* (Oxford: Oxford University Press, 2003).

16 Fussell, *Great War and Modern Memory*; Hynes, *A War Imagined*.

17 On ambivalence: Brian Bond, 'British Anti-war Writers and Their Critics', in *Facing Armageddon. The First World War Experienced*, ed. by H. Cecil and P. Liddle (London: Leo Cooper, 1996) pp. 810–30; Brian Bond, *The Unquiet Western Front: Britain's Role in Literature and History* (Cambridge: Cambridge University Press, 2002) p. 33. On contestation: Janet Watson, *Fighting Different Wars: Experience, Memory and the First World War in Britain* (Cambridge: Cambridge University Press, 2004) ch. 5; Trott, *Publishers, readers and the Great War*, pp. 67–84; Ian Andrew Isherwood, *Remembering the Great War. Writing and Publishing the Experiences of World War I* (London: Bloomsbury, 2020).

18 Cecil, 'British War Novelists', in *Facing*, ed. by Cecil and Liddle, pp. 801–16; Paris, *Warrior Nation*; Paris, *Over the Top: the Great War and Juvenile Literature in Britain* (Westport, Conn: Praeger, 2004); Todman, *Myth and Memory*, pp. 132–3; Watson, *Fighting Different Wars*; Kelly Boyd, *Manliness and the Boys' Story Paper in Britain: A Cultural History, 1855–1940* (Basingstoke: Palgrave Macmillan, 2003); Bond, *Unquiet Western Front*; Graham Dawson, *Soldier Heroes: British Adventure, Empire and the Imagining of Masculinities* (London: Routledge, 1994); Gary Sheffield, 'The Shadow of the Somme: The Influence of the First World War on British Soldiers' Perceptions and Behaviour in the Second World War', in *A Time to Kill: The Soldier's Experience of the War in the West, 1939–1945*, ed. by Paul Addison and Angus Calder (London: Pimlico, 1997) pp. 29–39; Rosa Maria Bracco, *Merchants of hope: British Middlebrow Writers and the First World War, 1919–1939* (Oxford: Berg, 1992).

19 Gregory, *Silence*; Winter, *Sites of Memory*.

20 Todman, *Myth and Memory*, p. 17.

21 Trott, *Publishers, Readers and the Great War*. Paris attempted to consider the influence of the cultural artefacts examined in *Warrior Nation* with reference to 'the memories of those who grew to manhood under its spell', p. 10. Seeking the reflections of individuals who cite texts is preferable to assuming impact, but provides little sense of

30 *Joining up in the Second World War*

how widespread such responses were, or how commonly representations were encountered.

22 Jessica Meyer, *Men of War: Masculinity and the First World War in Britain* (Basingstoke: Palgrave, 2009) pp. 164–5.

23 See Joel Morley, 'Dad "never said much" but … Young Men and Great War Veterans in Day-to-Day-Life in Interwar Britain', *Twentieth Century British History*, 29.2 (2018) pp. 199–224; Sheffield, 'Shadow of the Somme'. Michael Roper considers the multi-generational familial legacy of the Great War, examining a range of different traces, in *Afterlives of War. A Descendant's History* (Manchester: Manchester University Press, 2023).

24 Angus Calder, *The People's War. Britain 1939–1945* (London: Pimlico, 1996) p. 51.

25 Calder, *The People's War*, pp. 72–4, 234–7, 267–70, 321–3; Daniel Todman, *Britain's War: A New World, 1942–1947* (London: Allen Lane, 2020) pp. 258–60; Jonathan Fennell, *Fighting the People's War. The British and Commonwealth Armies and the Second World War* (Cambridge: Cambridge University Press, 2019) pp. 63–6; Harold Smith, 'The Womanpower Problem in Britain during the Second World War', *The Historical Journal*, 27.4 (1984) pp. 925–45; Geoffrey G. Field, *Blood, Sweat and Toil. Remaking the British Working Class, 1939–1945* (Oxford: Oxford University Press, 2011) ch. 3.

26 Henry M. D. Parker, *Manpower. A Study of War-Time Policy and Administration* (London: United Kingdom Civil Series, 1957); Fennell, *Fighting the People's War*, pp. 64–6.

27 Parker, *Manpower*; Roger Broad, *Conscription in Britain, 1939–1963: The Militarization of a Generation* (London: Routledge 2006); Jerry H. Brookshire, ' "Speak for England", Act for England: Labour's Leadership and British National Security Under the Threat of War in the Late 1930s', *European History Quarterly*, 29.2 (1999) pp. 251–87; Nick Crowson, 'The Conservative Party and the Call for National Service, 1937–1939: Compulsion Versus Voluntarism', *Contemporary Record*, 9.3 (1995) pp. 507–28; Peter Dennis, *Decision by Default: Peacetime Conscription and British Defence, 1919–1939* (London: Routledge and Kegan Paul, 1972); Daniel Hucker, 'Franco-British Relations and the Question of Conscription in Britain, 1938–1939', *Contemporary European History*, 17.4 (2008) pp. 437–56; Daniel Hucker, *Public Opinion and the End of Appeasement in Britain and France* (Farnham: Ashgate, 2011); P. J. Wainwright, 'The National Service Debate: Government Conscription and the Peace Movement in Britain, 1936–1942' (PhD, Stamford, 1993); Daniel Todman,

Britain's War, Into Battle, 1937–1941 (London: Allen Lane, 2016) pp. 263–8; Jeremy Crang, *The British Army and the People's War* (Manchester: Manchester University Press, 2000); David French, *Raising Churchill's Army: The British Army and the War Against Germany, 1919–1945* (Oxford: Oxford University Press, 2000); Emma Newlands, *Civilians into Soldiers. War, the Body and British Army Recruits, 1939–45* (Manchester: Manchester University Press, 2014); Corinna Peniston-Bird, 'Classifying the Body in the Second World War: British Men in and Out of Uniform', *Body and Society*, 9 (2003) pp. 31–48.

28 Denis Hayes, *Challenge of Conscience: The Story of the Conscientious Objectors of 1939–1945* (London: Allen and Unwin, 1949); Rachel Barker, *Conscience, Government and War: Conscientious Objection in Great Britain, 1939–1945* (London: Routledge & Kegan Paul, 1982); Linsey Robb, 'The "Conchie Corps": Conflict, Compromise and Conscientious Objection in the British Army, 1940–1945', *Twentieth Century British History*, 29.3 (2018) pp. 411–34.

29 For instance, Broad's *Conscription in Britain* places much greater emphasis on politics and processes than on men's attitudes to conscription. Jonathan Fennell reflects on attempts to evade or defer service in *Fighting the People's War*, pp. 63–6, and Todman reflects on this and rates of conscientious objection in *Britain's War, A New World*, pp. 411–13.

30 Alan Allport, *Browned Off and Bloody-Minded. The British Soldier Goes to War, 1939–1945* (Yale: Yale University Press, 2015) pp. 60–75.

31 Frances Houghton, *The Veterans' Tale. British Military Memoirs of the Second World War* (Cambridge: Cambridge University Press, 2019) pp. 208–9, 211–13.

32 Houghton, *Veterans' Tale,* p. 211.

33 Sheffield, 'Shadow of the Somme', p. 31. See also Hew Strachan, 'The Soldier's Experience in Two World Wars: Some Historiographical Comparisons', in *A Time To Kill: The Soldier's Experience of the War in the West, 1939–1945*, ed. by Paul Addison and Angus Calder (London: Pimlico, 1997) pp. 369–78.

34 Houghton, *Veterans' Tale*, pp. 210, 214–15.

35 Houghton's memoirists were predominantly middle and lower-middle class; *Veterans' Tale*, p. 25.

36 Graham Dawson, *Soldier Heroes*. Paris's analysis of juvenile literature supports this idea – see Paris, *Over the Top*, and Paris, *Warrior Nation*.

32   *Joining up in the Second World War*

37 Michael Roper, 'Between Manliness and Masculinity: The "War Generation" and the Psychology of Fear in Britain, 1914–1950', *The Journal of British Studies*, 44.2 (2005) pp. 343–62 (p. 353).

38 The following say masculinity was challenged by the First World War: Elaine Showalter, 'Rivers and Sassoon: The Inscriptions of Male Gender Anxieties', in *Behind the Lines: Gender and the Two World Wars*, ed. by Margaret Higonnet, Sonya Michel, Jane Jenson and Margaret Collins Weitz (London: Yale University Press, 1987) pp. 61–9; Ted Bogacz, 'War Neurosis and Cultural Change in England, 1914–22: The Work of the War Office Committee of Enquiry into "Shell-Shock"', *Journal of Contemporary History*, 24.2 (1989) pp. 227–56; John Benyon, *Masculinities and Culture* (London: Open University Press, 2002); Kelly Boyd, 'Knowing Your Place; The Tensions of Masculinity in Boys' Story Papers 1918–1939', in *Manful Assertions: Masculinities in Britain since 1800*, ed. by Michael Roper and John Tosh (London: Routledge, 1991) pp. 145–67; David Glover and Cara Caplan, *Genders* (London: Routledge, 2000); Fussell, *Great War and Modern Memory*; Hynes, *War Imagined*.

39 Pattinson, *Behind Enemy Lines*, p. 13.

40 Sheffield, *Forgotten Victory*; Watson, *Fighting Different Wars*. Bond cites the impact of casualty figures in *Unquiet Western Front*.

41 Bourke, *Dismembering the Male*, ch. 4.

42 Sonja Levsen, 'Constructing Elite Identities: University Students, Military Masculinity and the Consequences of the Great War in Britain and Germany', *Past and Present*, 198 (2008) pp. 143–83 (p. 167).

43 Meyer, *Men of War*.

44 Paris, *Over the Top*, p. 161. See also Bond, *Unquiet Western Front*; Isherwood, *Remembering the Great War*; Paris, *Warrior Nation*; Sheffield, *Forgotten Victory*; Strachan, 'The Soldier's Experience in Two World Wars'; Watson, *Fighting Different Wars*.

45 Rose, 'Temperate Heroes'. See also Rose, *Which People's War?*

46 Gerard De Groot, 'Whose Finger on the Trigger? Mixed Anti-aircraft Batteries and the Female Combat Taboo', *War in History*, 4.4 (1997) pp. 434– 53, and Penny Summerfield, ' "She Wants a Gun not a Dishcloth!" Gender, Service and Citizenship in Britain in the Second World War', in *A Soldier and a Woman*, ed. by G. J. DeGroot and C. M. Peniston-Bird (Harlow: Pearson, 2000) pp. 119–34.

47 On the significance of military roles to women's subjective attitudes to men, see, for example, Summerfield, *Reconstructing Women's Wartime Lives*, pp. 120–1.

Introduction   33

48 Pattinson, McIvor and Robb, *Men in Reserve*; Chand, *Masculinities on Clydeside*; Linsey Robb, *Men at Work: The Working Man in British Culture, 1939–1945* (Basingstoke: Palgrave Macmillan, 2015); Summerfield and Peniston-Bird, *Contesting Home Defence*; Robb, 'The "Conchie Corps"'.

49 Newlands, *Civilians into Soldiers*; Peniston-Bird, 'Classifying the Body'; Emma Vickers, *Queen and Country: Same-Sex Desire in the British Armed Forces, 1939–45* (Manchester: Manchester University Press, 2013).

50 Francis, *The Flyer*; Frances Houghton, 'Becoming "a Man" During the Battle of Britain: Combat, Masculinity and Rites of Passage in the Memoirs of "the Few"', in *Men, Masculinities and Male Culture in the Second World War*, ed. by Lindsey Robb and Juliette Pattinson (Basingstoke: Palgrave, 2018); Houghton, *Veterans' Tale*.

51 Houghton, *Veterans' Tale*, p. 219.

52 *Ibid.*, p. 243.

53 For further discussion, see Chapter 5.

54 Hoffman cited in Corinna Peniston-Bird, 'Oral History: The Sound of Memory', in *History Beyond the Text: A Student's Guide to Approaching Alternative Sources*, ed. by Sarah Barber and Corinna Peniston-Bird (London: Routledge, 2009) pp.105–21 (p. 108); Earl Walton Rodney, 'Memories from the Edge of the Abyss: Evaluating the Oral Accounts of World War II Veterans', *The Oral History Review*, 37.1 (2010) pp. 18–34; Peter H. Liddle and Matthew J. Richardson, 'Voices from the Past: An Evaluation of Oral History as a Source for Research into the Western Front Experience of the British Soldier, 1914–18', *Journal of Contemporary History*, 31.4 (1996) pp. 651–74.

55 Alistair Thomson, 'Memory and Remembering in Oral History', in *The Oxford Handbook of Oral History*, ed. by Donald Ritchie (Oxford: Oxford University Press, 2007) pp. 77–95 (p. 83). See also Paul Thompson, *The Voice of the Past* (Oxford: Oxford University Press, 2000) pp. 129–30.

56 Lynn Abrams, *Oral History Theory* (London: Routledge, 2010) ch. 5.

57 *Ibid.*, p. 86.

58 Douwe Draaisma, *Why Life Speeds Up As You Get Older: How Memory Shapes Our Past* (Cambridge: Cambridge University Press, 2001) pp. 172–4 (pp. 193–200). See also Thompson, *Voice of the Past*, p. 137.

59 Popular Memory Group, 'Popular Memory: Theory, Politics, Method', in *The Oral History Reader*, ed. by Robert Perks and Alistair Thomson

(London: Routledge, 2006) pp. 43–54; The Popular Memory Group, 'Popular Memory: Theory, Politics, Method', in *Making Histories: Studies in History*, ed. by R. Johnson, G. McLennan, B. Schwartz, and D. Sutton (London, 1982) pp. 205–52.

60 Dawson, *Soldier Hero*, pp. 22–5.

61 Lesley Temple (Author, 2010).

62 Dawson, *Soldier Hero*, pp. 22–5.

63 Alistair Thomson, 'Anzac Memories: Putting Popular Memory Theory into Practice in Australia', *Oral History*, 18.1 (1990) pp. 25–31. See also Vincent Trott, 'Remembering War, Resisting Myth: Veteran Autobiographies and the Great War in the Twenty-first Century', *Journal of War & Culture Studies*, 6.4 (2013) pp. 328–42.

64 Thomson, 'Anzac Memories', p. 31. See also Thomson's discussion of the problems Percy Bird had in composing a narrative, in Alistair Thomson, ' "Unreliable Memories?" ' The Use and Abuse of Oral History', in *Historical Controversies and Historians*, ed. by William Lamont (London: UCL Press, 1998) pp. 23–34. For an illustration of how veterans can construct their narratives against the idea that their war has been forgotten, see Grace Huxford, 'The Korean War Never Happened: Forgetting a Conflict in British Culture and Society', *Twentieth Century British History*, 27.2 (2016) pp. 195–219.

65 Summerfield and Peniston-Bird, *Contesting Home Defence*. For popular memory's silencing effect, see also Summerfield, 'Culture and Composure: Creating Narratives of the Gendered Self in Oral History Interviews', *Cultural and Social History*, 1 (2004) pp. 65–93.

66 Corinna Peniston-Bird, ' "I Wondered Who'd Be the First to Spot That." Dad's Army at War in the Media and in Memory', *Media History* 13.2–3 (2007) pp. 183–202. See also Kathleen Ryan, ' "I Didn't Do Anything Important": A Pragmatist Analysis of the Oral History Interview', *Oral History Review*, 36.1 (2009) pp. 25–44; Dorothy Sheridan, 'Ambivalent Memories: Women and the 1939–45 War in Britain', *Oral History*, 18.1 (1990) pp. 32–40; Morley, 'Dad Never Said Much'. Michael Roper suggests examining individuals' psychic motivations for narration, which can be more influential than popular memory; 'Re-Remembering the Soldier Hero: The Psychic and Social Construction of Memory in Personal Narratives of the Great War', *History Workshop Journal*, 50 (2000) pp. 181–204.

67 Interview with John Shuttleworth, 21 March 2000, cited in Peniston-Bird, 'I Wondered Who'd Be the First to Spot That', p. 194.

68 Peniston-Bird, 'Sound of Memory', p. 107.

Introduction 35

69 Amongst my twenty-five interviewees there are a small number of 'optants', who chose to enter mining in preference to the Armed Forces.

70 While the essentially random geographic spread of the body of interviews used here is positive overall, it does not lend itself to examining the effects of regional variations in either the impact of the Great War or attitudes to service in the Second World War. Comparing these findings with interviews conducted with members of chapel communities in Wales, with members of communities like Bury where a particular Great War event dominated local experiences (Geoffrey Moorhouse, *Hell's Foundations: A Town, Its Myths and Gallipoli* (London: Hodder & Stoughton, 1992)) or with servicemen from areas where a large proportion of the community were in reserved occupations during the Second World War (Chand, *Masculinities on Clydeside*) may prove illuminating.

71 Four ground crew responded; two worried they had nothing of interest to tell me.

72 Alistair Thomson provides the similar example of Percy Bird, who avoided public representations which triggered memories of his Great War experiences of witnessing death that he had not assimilated into a composed narrative. Thomson, *Anzac Memories*, p. 206.

73 Frank Webster, a member of RAF ground crew, was particularly clear about this, as were a number of Bevin Boys.

74 I do not know that any interviewees *did not* enjoy the process, but not all were asked.

75 Russel King, IWM-SA-18512, 1998; Peter Douglas Taylor, IWM-SA-10484, 1988.

76 James Donovan, IWM-SA-20316, 2000.

77 On the utility of using archival oral histories, particularly those conducted with a life history method, to explore themes other than the interview's primary interest, see April Gallwey, 'The Rewards of Using Archived Oral Histories in Research: The Case of the Millennium Memory Bank', *Oral History*, 41.1 (2013) pp. 37–50. See also Joanna Bornat, 'A Second Take: Revisiting Interviews with a Different Purpose', *Oral History*, 31.1 (2003) pp. 47–53; Libby Bishop, 'A Reflexive Account of Reusing Qualitative Data: Beyond Primary/Secondary Dualism', *Sociological Research Online*, 12.3 (2007).

78 The first interview with Gordon Mellor, and first two with Jack Abbott, took place at QMUL. Abbott and Reg Elson were also interviewed, separately, at the Victory Services Club.

79 At their request two pairs and one trio were interviewed.

80 Valerie Yow, 'Do I Like Them Too Much? Effects of the Oral History Interview on the Interviewer and Vice Versa', in *The Oral History Reader*, ed. by Robert Perks and Alistair Thomson, pp. 54–72 (p. 62); Peniston-Bird, 'Sound of Memory', p. 111.

81 Peniston-Bird, 'Sound of Memory', p. 115.

82 Juliette Pattinson, ' "The thing that made me hesitate ...': Re-examining Gendered Intersubjectivities in Interviews with British Secret War Veterans', *Women's History Review*, 20.2 (2011) pp. 245–63.

83 Yow, 'Do I Like Them Too Much?' p. 65.

84 Todman, *Myth and Memory*, pp. 195–6.

85 See Corinna Peniston-Bird, ' "All in it together and backs to the wall": Relating Patriotism and the People's War in the 21st Century', *Oral History*, 40.2 (2012) pp. 69–80 (p. 78).

86 Katherine Borland, ' "That's not what I said" Interpretive Conflict in Oral Narrative Research', in *The Oral History Reader*, ed. by Robert Perks and Alistair Thomson (London: Routledge, 2006) pp. 310–21. For further discussion of who controls the interpretation, see Tracy E. K'Meyer and A. Glenn Crothers, ' "If I See Some of This in Writing, I'm Going to Shoot You" ': Reluctant Narrators, Taboo Topics, and the Ethical Dilemmas of the Oral Historian', *Oral History Review*, 34.1 (2007) pp. 71–93.

87 Borland, 'That's not what I said', p. 317.

88 Alessandro Portelli, 'The Peculiarities of Oral History', *History Workshop Journal*, 12.1 (1981) pp. 96–107 (p. 98).

89 James Hinton, *The Mass Observers. A History, 1937–1949* (Oxford: Oxford University Press, 2013) p. 3. Coincidentally, both Harrisson and Madge had Great War veteran fathers. Madge's father was killed in France in 1916; Hinton, *Mass Observers*, pp. 4–6.

90 On their training for conducting fieldwork, see Hinton, *Mass Observers*, pp. 261–3.

91 Mass Observation, TC Forces (Men) 1939–56, 29/142/1/C. [Verbatim responses to Military Training Bill Street Surveys, 26 and 27 April 1939.]

92 Neil Mercer, 'Mass Observation 1937–1940: The Range of Research Methods', Working Papers in Applied Social Research Number 16 (University of Manchester, 1989).

93 MO, TC29/142/1/C [Verbatims]. Investigator MER, 27 April 1939.

94 Mass Observation, *War Begins at Home* (London: Chatto & Windus, 1940) p. 20; Wilcock, 'Mass-Observation', p. 456.

95 MO, DR1141, January 1940 Directive.

96 MO January 1940 Directive Replies, Question 7 [Attitudes to conscription].

Introduction   37

97 MO, February 1940 Directive Replies, Question 8 [Influence of childhood impressions].

98 155 men and 84 women provided legible answers that can be sensibly interpreted in relation to the question. Tony Kushner has demonstrated MO Directive Replies can be used to test the assumed impact of cultural representations, *We Europeans:Mass-observation, 'Race' and British Identity in the Twentieth Century* (Aldershot: Ashgate, 2004).

99 Nick Stanley, 'The Extra Dimension: A Study and Assessment of the Methods Employed by Mass-Observation in its First Period, 1937–1940' (Unpublished PhD thesis, Birmingham Polytechnic, 1981).. Hinton puts it at 52% – *Mass Observers*, p. 271. James Hinton, 'The "Class" Complex': Mass-Observation and Cultural Distinction in Pre-War Britain', *Past & Present*, 199:1 (2008) pp. 207–36 (pp. 210–11).

100 Hinton, *Mass Observers*, p. 267.

101 *Ibid.*, p. 276.

102 Murray Goot, 'Mass Observation and Modern public Opinion Research', in *The SAGE Handbook of Public Opinion Research*, ed. by Wolfgang Donsbach and Michael W. Traugott (London: SAGE, 2008) pp. 93–103 (p. 97).

103 Fiona Courage, ' "The National Panel" Responds: Mass Observation Directives 1939–1945.' Mass Observation Online, Essays.

104 Tom Jeffery, 'Mass Observation: A Short History', MOA Occasional Paper No. 10, Mass Observation Online, Essays. For the comparative engagement of panellists and diarists, see Hinton, *Mass Observers*, pp. 267–8.

105 *News Chronicle* published BIPO polls, and MO's inaugurating letter was published in *New Statesman* in 1937 – Joe Moran, 'Mass-Observation, Market Research, and the Birth of the Focus Group, 1937–1997', *Journal of British Studies*, 47.4 (2008) pp. 827–51 (p. 831).

106 Jeffery, 'A Short History'; Hinton, *Mass Observers*, p. 277.

107 Murray Goot, Mass Observation Anniversaries Conference, July 2012.

108 Lucy Noakes, *War and the British: Gender, Memory and National Identity, 1939–1991* (London: I. B. Tauris, 1998) pp. 76–7.

109 Stanley, 'Extra Dimension', table 3, pp. 159, 163–4.

110 MO, *War Begins at Home*, p. 20; Madge and Harrisson, eds. *First Year's Work 1937–38 by Mass Observation* (London: Drummond, 1938) p. 66; Tom Harrisson, 'Preface', in Mass-Observation, *The Pub and the People: A Worktown Study* (London: Gollancz, 1987)

p. xv; Bob Wilcock, MO, Draft for Handout, 30.01.1947. In Polls Apart, Unpublished Manuscript, MOA, University of Sussex, cited by Goot, 'Mass Observation', p. 99. Wilcock also defends the qualitative in 'Mass Observation', *American Journal of Sociology*, 48.4 (1943) pp. 445–56.

111 Angus Calder, 'Mass Observation 1937–1949', in *Essays on the History of British Sociological Research*, ed. by Martin Bulmer (Cambridge: Cambridge University Press, 1985) pp. 121–36.

112 Joel Morley, 'The Memory of the Great War and Morale During Britain's Phoney War', *The Historical Journal*, 63.2 (2020) pp. 437–67. For figures about inconsistent participation, see Stanley, 'Extra Dimension', p. 155, and table 1. And Hinton, *Mass Observers*, pp. 267–8.

113 National Panel and General Population figures from Stanley, 'Extra Dimension' 159, based on 'The National Register Statistics of Population on 29 September 1939', HMSO, 1944.

114 Claire Langhamer, 'The Live Dynamic Whole of Feeling and Behaviour: Capital Punishment and the Politics of Emotion, 1945–1957', *Journal of British Studies*, 51.2 (2012) pp. 416–41 (p. 419).

115 This was not MO's motivation; qualitative collection increased the explanatory power of 'Don't Know' answers: Goot, 'Mass Observation', p. 100. Moran, 'Mass-Observation', pp. 835–6. Penny Summerfield highlights MO and War Time Social Survey established that a significant minority of women were unwilling to do war work, but MO's qualitative answers could explain *why*; 'Mass-Observation: Social Research or Social Movement?', *Journal of Contemporary History*, 20.3 (1985) pp. 439–52 (pp. 449–50).

116 Langhamer, 'The Live Dynamic Whole of Feeling and Behaviour', p. 419.

1

Encounters with the Great War in popular culture

Introduction and sources

The oral histories of the young men who grew up in the 1920s and 1930s highlight the existence of multitudinous and disparate representations of the Great War in this period. George Stagg was intrigued by a painting depicting John Cornwall winning the Victoria Cross at the Battle of Jutland that hung in his school's assembly hall.[1] John Malling saw huge battle re-enactments with fireworks at Belle Vue Gardens amusement park in Manchester. He recalled, 'we would hear that was what the First World War was like' and he and his brother 'would go home and have battles ...'.[2] Military reference points and a pleasure culture of war remained components of popular culture. Interviewees recalled playing with toy soldiers – though Jim Stephens re-enacted 'Waterloo usually ... [it had] to be one that we won [laughter]'[3] – and when Edward Kirby was awarded a school scholarship his veteran father rewarded him by taking him to a military tattoo at Wembley stadium, which was 'wonderful, exciting entertainment for a young boy, there was no horror of war, it was all the colour, the marching, the music'.[4]

Throughout the inter-war years, new representations of the Great War, in various cultural forms and varied tones, joined those created during the war but which endured after its end.[5] Some of these cultural artefacts have subsequently been the subject of considerable academic attention. An initial focus upon elite literature and the post-war peace movements led to the suggestion that British society promptly became disillusioned with warfare after 1918.[6] As historians acknowledged that representations of the Great War were far more ubiquitous than this, however, a more nuanced

40   *Joining up in the Second World War*

picture emerged, of a plurality of competing narratives of the Great War within popular culture. This period was, as Dan Todman has argued, one in which 'Britons want[ed] to remember very different versions of the war. Although none completely obscured the horror and the suffering inflicted by the war, the meanings derived from those experiences varied widely.'[7] Although the Great War was represented as a cause for disillusionment as the inter-war years went on, this was always a contested narrative.[8] The war could also be presented in more traditional forms: in terms of redemptive sacrifice; heroic soldiering; and even within a pleasure culture of war as masculine adventure.[9]

The focus of this chapter is young men's engagement with the Great War in popular culture between 1918 and 1939. Representations of the war were widely available, not only in juvenile literature, novels and poetry, but also encyclopaediae, school textbooks and (illustrated) children's histories of the Great War. The Great War was re-enacted on the nation's cinema screens and in theatre and radio plays, and young men themselves featured as actors or spectators in rituals of commemoration in both schools and local communities in the 1920s and 1930s. Existing studies have tended to focus upon the production and popularity of representations of the Great War, and have aimed to infer societal attitudes.[10] The reception and influence of these texts, however, tend to have been assumed rather than established through examination of the subjective experiences and attitudes of those who consumed them. This chapter uses personal testimony to explore how young men accessed and responded to representations of the Great War. It highlights the breadth of places where young men encountered representations of the Great War and thus confirms that scholars' shift to consider a wider range of cultural artefacts was necessary, and affirms that the scope merits still further expansion. The chapter makes clear that young men encountered some of these artefacts more commonly than others, which was partly affected by social class, but young men's own interests and preferences also had considerable influence. Those that were encountered most often tended to offer a depiction of Great War experience that was either compatible with traditional ideas of war as heroic, masculine adventure or at least had redeeming features. Yet, young men responded in varied and unpredictable ways to the representations they did encounter, whether they were

The Great War in popular culture 41

positive, negative or ambiguous about war. It is therefore difficult to generalise about the effects of a particular representation, and young men's responses could be framed by understandings from other sources. How individuals' memories of the Great War might be transmitted to others within everyday life and the domestic sphere is analysed in detail in Chapter 2.[11]

Three bodies of personal testimony are the foundation of this chapter. The first two are my own interviews with veterans and the archival oral histories. Although the sources were discussed in the introduction, it is important to emphasise the different values they have for the subject under discussion here. In the former, I was able to ask interviewees which representations of the Great War they had and had not encountered, and explore their reactions to them. In the latter, references to representations of the Great War are chance inclusions. This does not diminish their usefulness. When analysing my own interviews I have been alert to whether references were organic elements of the narrative or were narrated in response to questioning. But these archival interviews do offer a 'Rumsfeldian' problem of 'unknown unknowns' – they do not provide the same opportunities to examine which representations were not encountered, or were encountered but were not mentioned because they were not asked about.

The third body of material is contemporary survey material. This includes, but is not limited to, the responses provided by those who had grown up in inter-war Britain to a MO Directive question asked in February 1940: 'How much do you think childhood impressions and incidents colour your opinions in the present war? And if you do think childhood does affect your present opinion, in what way do you feel these effects work?'[12] A detailed examination of these previously unused responses in relation to attitudes towards Second World War service also informs Chapters 2 and 4. Here, however, the responses of young men, and occasionally young women, which often contained references to the Great War, supplement the oral histories and surveys as a means to explore how young men in inter-war Britain were learning about the Great War.[13] The respondents were, like most MO panellists, employed in lower-middle and middle-class positions,[14] and there is nothing to suggest that they did not share the broader characteristics of others interested in MO, as discussed in the Introduction. They were,

42 *Joining up in the Second World War*

then, probably better educated and read more widely than average Britons, meaning they were more likely than most, and definitely no less likely, to have encountered representations of the Great War in high culture.[15] They were also more likely to be of left-leaning politics and to have some interest in pacifism.[16] It must be recognised, therefore, that this was a group that was probably more sensitised than most to the influence, if any, of anti-war literature.[17]

Reading the Great War

Reading was a very popular form of entertainment for young people between the wars.[18] It was in close competition with sport as the most popular pastime amongst Merseyside schoolboys in a 1934 survey.[19] Likewise, a survey of boys in St Pancras, London in the early 1930s found only carpentry was a more popular hobby, and half of these children read three or more 'books', normally story papers, each week.[20] When Annette Kuhn interviewed members of the same generation in the 1990s about their cinema-going in the 1930s she found reading and listening to the wireless were the most popular alternatives,[21] and most of my interviewees had also liked to read as children.[22] A 1932 survey of the preferred reading categories of 853 boys in the Central Junior Library in East Ham sheds light on *what* boys liked to read and highlights the popularity of books about the war. The five most popular topics were Adventure, School Life, War, Sea and Ships, and History. The Great War, or warfare in imagined forms, may have featured in adventure literature and the librarian noted that the ' "distressingly high" preference for "War" stories ... referred to tales of the Great War; anything earlier was rejected as "ancient history" '.[23]

Juvenile literature

Traditionally, juvenile literature had proffered the adventurous imperial warrior as a masculine role model, and sought to inculcate in young readers the belief that wartime military service was a man's duty.[24] Michael Paris argues that depictions of the soldier hero continued during the Great War, as writers such as Brereton,

Westerman and Strang depicted it as an epic adventure: a crusade to liberate peoples occupied by a barbarous nation which threatened the Empire, death in such a cause was a noble and worthwhile sacrifice, and victory had brought an end to war itself.[25] Although such fiction recognised significant casualties and the destructive power of new weaponry, 'in the final analysis their fictions and visual images reveal an essentially romantic and chivalric war fought for high moral purpose' and an adventure that 'was the crowning experience of [men's] lives'.[26]

Post-1918, war remained a staple setting of adventure tales in juvenile literature.[27] Publishers made veteran authors a selling point, and titles such as the *Aldine War Stories* series (1930–1), inexpensive sixty-four-page novelettes, offered a 'continuation of the fiction of the war period', similar to Henty and Westerman.[28] Inter-war stories still communicated British heroism, but moved away from trench warfare to the war of movement, which was 'more palatable and more exciting to young readers'.[29] Budgen observes that 'Flying and spying hardly reflected the experience of the majority during the Great War, but they became more prominent themes in children's fiction.'[30] Meanwhile, the works of Brereton, Westerman and Strang were reissued, sold well and remained popular with education authorities, Sunday schools and parents as prizes or gifts.[31] As Paris highlights, those choosing these texts were often veterans, but 'they consciously made the decision to pass on to the next generation a heroic and justified representation of the war, rather than stories ... that portrayed it as degrading and futile'.[32] These texts were popular with boys themselves, too. In 1926, when 750 boys in Croydon's public libraries were asked to name their favourite author, Westerman, Strang and Henty shared 84 per cent of the votes.[33] Westerman received around a third of the vote when *The Times* asked young readers in Stepney the same year.[34]

Most interviewees did not, however, recall having read novels about the Great War.[35] Jack Abbott felt he was not 'terribly interested in the First World War anyway, apart from the fact that I knew my father had been in it in some way I don't think it really was something that concerned me much'.[36] Reg Day preferred to read 'about cowboys and Indians'[37] and Don Browne regularly borrowed Bulldog Drummond and Sexton Blake detective novels and PC Wren novels about the Foreign Legion from his local library.[38]

44 *Joining up in the Second World War*

Stories about the war in the air, especially *Biggles* stories, published from 1932, were, however, read by some interviewees who were otherwise uninterested in the Great War in fiction.[39] According to Paris, while Biggles stories demonstrated the cruelty of modern war, they did not suggest it was futile or unjust, and the stories could not fail to feature the excitement of flying and aerial combat.[40] Five years after the 1932 East Ham survey, a schoolchild in Middlesbrough told MO, 'Books which I prefer most are books of air stories by "Johns" usually thrilling episodes of Biggles and Co.'[41] Another commented: 'Flying stories often tell of the difficulties of … the difficulties in the war when at first machine guns could not fire through the air-screw … War stories are sometimes very far-fetched but most of them show the grim horrors of war and many dangers which have to be endured.'[42]

Working-class children often only acquired books 'second-hand or as gifts (notably the ubiquitous Sunday school prizes), borrowed, inherited, or scavenged'.[43] Biggles, however, had initially featured in the boys' story papers, and it was these to which the working and lower-middle class children of St Pancras were referring when they reported reading three books a week. The boys' story papers had huge readerships. In the 1920s the weekly circulation of the Amalgamated Press's ten boys' titles was greater than 1,000,000 copies, and the Religious Tract Society published the middle-class, and more expensive and less popular, *Boy's Own Paper*.[44] Yet surveys usually showed that boys preferred D. C. Thomson's 'Big Five' – *Adventure*, *The Rover*, *The Wizard*, *Skipper* and *The Hotspur* – to Amalgamated Press's biggest sellers – *Magnet* and *Gem*.[45] *The Wizard* alone sold over 800,000 copies a week throughout the 1930s.[46]

Like many other of my interviewees, Jack Pragnell recalled he would 'have *The Hotspur* every week and then you'd swap it with somebody [who] had *The Wizard* and then swap with somebody who had *The Rover* …'.[47] Don Browne read a series of magazines about the Great War which 'somebody would buy and then they'd sell it to somebody else for a bit cheaper and that's how it got passed along'.[48] By such methods, boys read more papers than they could otherwise have afforded. The industry assumed each copy reached at least three boys, thus McAleer suggests that 'each Thomson paper was read by between 600,000 and 1,500,000 boys (and girls) *per week* between the wars'.[49] Undoubtedly, most young people in Britain were regularly reading a story paper.

The Great War in popular culture   45

Boys' story papers were enthusiastically recalled by the majority of my interviewees, who commonly remembered having enjoyed the public school stories like Billy Bunter, but most did not remember encountering Great War stories in the story papers.[50] Reg Day remembered 'gung-ho stories' about the Empire, and indeed a frequently recalled character was the Wolf of Kabul, who controlled Afghan tribesmen with the assistance of a servant brandishing a 'clicky bar' – a cricket bat adorned with barbed wire.[51] Fred Pond felt that warfare was 'never glorified' in the story papers, but conversely Stagg thought its portrayal in the comics was in 'jovial ways ... never depicted as gory or anything like that, ... the Germans were the bad boys, the English were the good boys, you know'. Stagg felt that, as an adolescent, 'to a certain extent it gave you [the] impression it was thrilling, the gory side of it never entered it, it was an adventure ...'.[52] Derrick Thurgood said the story papers had given him an 'impression of the first war, of the dreaded Hun, Boche, attacking the brave British soldiers in their trenches and our brave chaps fighting them back, giving them a touch of the old cold steel'.[53]

These impressions were similar to traditional representations of warfare as adventure. Paris suggests that in order that such representations could be continued, the Great War increasingly made way for battles policing the empire, futuristic wars in space or historic wars more distant than 1914. Publications could thus present historic or imagined battles in glamorous and adventurous tones, whilst also solemnly considering the costs of the Great War.[54] For instance, an issue of *Boy's Own* once both glamorised a historic war and emphasised the importance of Armistice Day in educating young men about the realities of war.[55] Thus Paris suggests that depictions of war in the boys' story papers were a 'vital and exciting element of the pleasure culture'.[56]

Another response to the horrors of the Western Front, and the challenge to the notion that individual skill brought success or even survival, was the emergence of characters who had mastered mechanised warfare: highly trained assault troops or pilots. At this time the RAF promoted military aviation as the future of warfare.[57] Some took this on board; Peter Woodard expected the Second World War to be different from the First because of airpower, which Biggles, the 'superstar in the Flying Corps', had shown him

46   *Joining up in the Second World War*

had been involved at the end of the Great War.[58] Frank Webster read fictional stories about the Royal Flying Corps in *The Ranger* and also recalled *Baldy's Angels*.[59] Jack Thomas, born 1924, had read all 'the Biggles books of course, Biggles was a great hero, yes [laughs]' and recalled that aged 9 or 10 he read the '*Boy's Own* paper ... very good authors like W. B. Johns and people, and I used to read a series of stories about a chap who was a pilot on an air craft carrier, and I thought when I grow up I'm gonna be a pilot on an aircraft carrier ...'. He recalled that 'as kids [war] was an adventure more than anything else'.[60] Readers of non-fiction did not, however, necessarily receive a different impression/think of war as less of an adventure.

Non-fiction

There was undoubtedly significant public interest in the Great War. Winston Churchill's *The World Crisis* (1923–31) was the most successful non-fiction work of the inter-war period.[61] Similarly, David Lloyd-George's war memoirs, published in the 1930s, were also widely purchased; an inexpensive two-volume edition released in 1938 quickly sold more than 100,000 copies.[62] His highly critical stance on Douglas Haig, who he depicted as incompetent, inflexible, unintelligent and uncontrollable, fuelled interest.[63] Heathorn states this 'helped solidify amongst the general public an increasingly negative opinion of the army leadership during the Great War'.[64] Such texts may well have informed popular understandings of the competency of Great War generals, who were 'figures of mockery' for some by the end of the 1930s,[65] but the texts themselves did not feature in the oral history interviews, probably because those who read them were typically older than the interviewees. Nevertheless, the interviews reveal other kinds of non-fiction through which young men in inter-war Britain encountered representations of the Great War and these representations shaped their understandings of the conflict.

Thurgood had 'read a lot about [the Great War]', and had twenty-four volumes of *The Children's Story of the Great War*, published during or at the end of the Great War, which had 'pictures of the Boche bayoneting babies and things like that, because all the myths

The Great War in popular culture

if myths they were, of the behaviour of the Germans, the Hun of the First World War, were perpetuated in these books'.[66] Periodicals and part-works were regularly recalled, even if exact titles were not forthcoming. Don Browne read a series of magazines called '*The Great War something*',[67] and Jim Stephens described a periodical written by 'Brig. Hammerstein or something like that' – probably Hammerton's *War Illustrated*.[68] Similarly, Derrick Davies, born in 1923, read the twenty-two-volume *The Illustrated News History of the 1914–1918 War*.[69] Peter Woodard got a four-volume set of *War Illustrated* when he was apprenticed aged 15, and may have also had a set of books called *The First Pictorial Knowledge of the [Great]War* before the Second World War.[70]

In 1933 the *Daily Express* opined that their own publication of that year – *The First World War: A Photographic History* – was 'the most dreadful book of bloodshed ever printed' and argued that 'there is no glamour left in war after turning those pages'.[71] Yet looking at texts like these from a modern perspective it is hard to classify them as 'anti-war' – they frequently mentioned British heroism and clearly celebrated victory – and some of them, particularly those produced as the spectre of another conflict loomed during the 1930s, were undoubtedly sensationalist. *War Illustrated* included photographs of Victoria Cross winners,[72] and illustrated reports of heroic acts.[73] Even when the illustrations depicted challenging combat the tone of accompanying text suggested courage and sometimes martial adventure.[74] Given that death and injury were not absent (though British causalities appeared less frequently than German) it is important to note that although often accompanied by text heralding bravery,[75] what readers took away – particularly from the images involved – could be very different from the content of the text.

The images of the Great War encountered in illustrated histories were a particularly common source of young men's conceptions of the Great War.[76] Allan Florence found, and occasionally looked through, a 'whole pile of books on the Great War' his parents 'had gathered somehow or other'. They were difficult reading for Florence, aged between 5 and 8, but the photographs of the Army in France enabled an understanding; he saw the 'terrible states some of the men were in, er, parts of bodies blown off and all that, lying around ....'[77] Pearson, a keen reader, remembered

48   *Joining up in the Second World War*

he had been interested in a book about the Great War owned by his brother George. '[O]ccasionally when George brought it out' Pearson would look at the pictures 'of the trenches' and he remembered he was impressed by photographs of the Highland regiments who frightened the Germans, and also saw images of men going into action.[78] Illustrated histories of the Great War were also one of the representations of the Great War in popular culture more commonly referenced by MO respondents. A civil servant, born in 1920, had, when he was 'very small', been given a war book – presumably an illustrated book given his age – which had prompted nightmares, and said this was behind his 'intense horror and dislike of war'.[79] Another, born in 1919, felt 'war is outrageously barbaric. The seeds of this opinion were, I believe, sown by reading the serial magazine *War Illustrated* issued during the last war. I did this in my childhood and some of the pictures still remain in my memory.'[80] A music student the same age, though, implied he had taken a similar impression from 'the pictorial history of 1914–18' as from 'the usual "glorious" war stories in books and magazines'.[81]

A few of my interviewees had read avidly about the war even as children. Given the choice, Bob Woodhams would have opted for a book about the Great War ahead of other topics, and had read about the Army's experiences on the Somme. He recalled that the books he had read had included illustrations of

> people going over the top and what it was like in the trenches, you know, used to explain it all, about the mud and when they used to lay down all these duckboards and that, and actually digging 'em and where they actually dug under the German lines, to dynamite 'em, to blow 'em up, I remember reading that part, so there was different things that stuck in your mind about that.[82]

Brian Spragg said he had known 'quite a bit, I used to read about it'. While he thought much had gone over his head, he remembered reading about the internment of prisoners during the Great War. Interestingly, he noted that 'pretty well all' of his friends' fathers were veterans, so he and his friends would talk about the war. From around the age of 8, Ken Hay was borrowing war books from the adult section of the library because he 'found them quite exciting'. He said:

The Great War in popular culture

> I think I read every book in the library concerned with air warfare, ...
> I can recall some from the Navy, the Battle of Jutland and things
> like that, I think I was very interested in the war but as an event, not
> something that was coming, a something that was in the past and
> even when the war did come I can't recall ever associating the two
> things, one was history almost happening you know and I didn't see
> that as history ....[83]

Hay's enthusiasm was unusual amongst the interviewees, but his interest in air warfare was not. More interviewees had read about the air aces than any other aspect of the Great War.[84] Bob Lowe, aged between 10 and 12, had 'avidly' read his brother's books 'all about the flying aces of the First World War', 'about all these blokes in these little bi-planes going up and shooting Germans down and all the rest of it and getting shot down themselves ... so I had a fair idea of what happened there'.[85] Maurice Marriot read about Great War pilots and aircraft and subscribed to *Aeroplane* magazine, which was about 'all the latest aircraft'.[86] Often an interest in the Great War flyers related to a more general fascination with aviation, and reading about air races and the feats of flyers like Amy Johnson. Visits from Alan Cobham's Flying Circus were particularly well remembered,[87] while a few had attended military air displays, like the Hendon Air Pageant, which the League of Nations and the Fellowship for Reconciliation and Peace sought to ban, believing it encouraged militarism.[88] The Air Ministry agreed, and therefore supported displays like Hendon, and the later Empire Air Day, which saw hundreds of thousands attend aerodromes across the country, to participate in a form of popular militarism especially attractive to British youth.[89]

Representations of the war in the air inevitably put innovative technology and individual military heroes centre stage. This topic had particular appeal to young men in inter-war Britain, but the personal testimonies also highlight that illustrated histories of the Great War were a commonly encountered and easily accessible representation that could also leave a lasting impression. While such texts demonstrated the human costs of the Great War in potentially graphic ways, they could also provide narratives of heroic action compatible with traditional scripts of military service as adventure and a test of masculine character. Moreover, readers' responses were varied; some were horrified, but others were impressed.

50   *Joining up in the Second World War*

War literature

Around four hundred works of fiction representing the Great War were published in Britain between the wars.[90] Erich Maria Remarque's *All Quiet on the Western Front*, published in English in March 1929, was probably the most widely read.[91] By July 1929 133,000 copies had been sold.[92] It occupied the best seller list from April to October, 'an astonishing achievement for any book, in any genre, in this period'.[93] More significantly, it was serialised in the *Sunday Express* in autumn 1929, a decision that was perceived to have increased the paper's circulation.[94] Hugh Cecil argues, however, that the success of *All Quiet* and R. C. Sherriff's play, *Journey's End* (also serialised in the *Evening Standard* in October 1929),[95] obscures the fact that 'book for book, the British Public, over a thirty year period, seem to have preferred the patriotic to the disenchanted type of war book'.[96] Trott has highlighted that texts that celebrated Tommys' achievements and offered a consoling vision of the Great War, like *Peter Jackson, Cigar Merchant*, sold well,[97] and Ernest Raymond's *Tell England*, published in 1922, had sold 300,000 copies by 1939.[98] In the 1920s and 1930s, it was middlebrow novels that occupied the bookshelves of libraries and middle-class homes.[99] Middlebrow novels typically connected the Great War with traditional military ideals to alleviate the shock of the Great War, and to maintain middle-class values.[100] Daniel Todman has noted that it was possible for texts like *Tell England*, which depicted the Great War 'in terms of Christian redemptive sacrifice and made use of traditional visions of heroism', to portray the war as horrifying whilst also investing it with essentially positive meanings.[101] It sold out eleven imprints.[102] Even texts that were labelled 'anti-war', like *Journey's End* and Robert Graves's *Goodbye to All That* (1929) contained ambiguity; authors might demonstrate that war was destructive and deadly but remain far more equivocal about the war as a whole and stress positive wartime experiences.[103] Indeed, Robert Graves and Sherriff resented the moniker 'anti-war'.[104]

Trott suggests that publishers attempted to cater to an inter-war book-buying public that was divided about how to interpret the war; both romanticised and disillusioned depictions found a market.[105] Janet Watson's exploration of the war books controversy

The Great War in popular culture

illustrates this division. While some heralded the 'disillusioned' war books as telling the 'truth' about the war, others argued that while the war had been horrible, 'To dwell on that only ... and to argue that coping with its horrors was beyond the capacities of British soldiers, was to malign the past (including the dead), to criticise the present, and even to jeopardise the future of the nation.'[106] Charles Carrington's *A Subaltern's War*, published in July 1929, was intended to counter the disenchanted war books. Carrington 'contend[ed] that he and his fellow volunteers had known from the outset that they faced a terrible ordeal but were determined to see it through'.[107] Veterans had letters published in the conservative press declaring that the disenchanted books did not mirror their experience,[108] though it is noteworthy that their high rank suggests they were professional soldiers who may therefore have approached the conflict with a different perspective to their amateur or conscripted counterparts. Still, veterans' organisations, which preferred to celebrate more positive aspects of war experience, tended to disapprove of the disenchanted war books.[109] Veteran Sidney Rodgerson, in *Twelve Days* (1933), praised the courage, resolution and cheerfulness of ordinary soldiers, and expressed his irritation that 'the soldier looks in vain for the scenes he knew' in war books which portrayed an experience manipulated 'by the ... agents of peace for all time......this post-war propaganda, piling corpse on corpse, heaping terror on futility'.[110] Conversely, a critic praising the realism of Blunden's *Undertones of War* wrote that 'all should have been recreated, so that a youth reading might experience exactly what Second Lieutenant Blunden experienced at the time'.[111]

The hope or fear that disillusioned literature might diminish the next generation's martial spirit and patriotic sentiment or cultivate a commitment to peace was also visible in newspaper opinion pages and in the comments of civic figureheads.[112] It is the fact that it was a *youth* doing the reading that Watson sees as fundamental to the interest in these texts. There was little new about the depiction of war they offered; the unpleasantness of trench life was illustrated in traditional literature in the early 1920s, and disillusioned representations of the war had appeared regularly without attracting critical or public attention.[113] What was different was the readership; a younger generation of readers encountered this literature, and subsequently saw the war 'not for what it had achieved, but for what it

52 *Joining up in the Second World War*

had cost'.[114] Moreover, Watson has observed that *All Quiet* appears to have had particular resonance with 'those who came of age just after the war and who wanted to understand the experiences that had been so formative for their older brothers. *All Quiet* seems to offer them a window into that shadowy time. They could, they felt, know what *really* happened.'[115]

Some of the archival interviewees belonged to the age group Watson is referring to, but none made reference to *All Quiet*. References to 'disillusioned' war literature were even uncommon amongst the MO respondents, but they did occur and support Watson's suggestion that the war books provided a sense of understanding for those who had been excluded from the war experience. These respondents had lived through the war as young children – girls, in fact, though their responses suggest little reason some boys would not have responded in the same way. A young woman, born in 1914, who gave her occupation as 'reader', had indistinct memories of wounded soldiers and unhappiness in those around her, but these memories were bolstered by the 'war novels of the late 1920s and early 1930s' which she read 'almost like advice', 'I suppose because I had to fill in the facts about the war of which I had such vivid though such vague childhood impressions. I remember the bitterness and disillusion of those war books and I shared it.'[116] A housewife, born in 1910, wrote that she had 'read a terrific amount of books on [the war]' and that her 'horror of war' is 'based on my reading of the suffering and futility of the Great War ...'.[117]

Although they were generally younger than either the MO respondents who mentioned the war books, or those who 'came of age' just after the war, a small number of those interviewed for this research had read *All Quiet* between the wars. In contrast, as will be seen below, it was the film of *All Quiet* which would have probably the greatest impact of any cultural product of the inter-war years on interviewees' remembered attitudes to war. Their responses provide insight into how they had approached the war books.[118] Ken Hay, who also read lots of non-fiction about the Great War, read *All Quiet* and *Goodbye to All That* and treated them as historical, although he understood they were novels.[119] Derrick Thurgood had read *All Quiet* at least twice, aged 10 or 11 in 1936/7, and later saw the film. He was attracted to the story because:

The Great War in popular culture   53

> I was very interested in the First World War, erm, I, I found it difficult
> to believe that men could go over the top into a hail of machine gun
> fire knowing that their friends were all falling down and they were
> the next ones ..., erm, er, there didn't seem to be anything heroic
> about it on the one hand, on the other hand it was a sort of subject
> that you couldn't, I couldn't, leave alone ....[120]

At a similar time Thurgood read Howard Spring's *Oh Absolon,
(my son my son)*, which he found stunning because it showed an
officer could be on the battlefront in the morning 'and get on a
train and that evening be back in Victoria taking a girl to dinner ...
having only just left the ghastliness of the First World War trenches,
and I found that riveting'.[121] Stagg felt that he had learned about
the experience of fighting the Great War through fiction from the
library, although he was uncertain which titles. He thought that
some used fiction to 'build up the momentum they were fiction but
er the basic principles of 'em were true'. His response to the books
demonstrates a similar ambivalence to that displayed by Thurgood;
they were 'thrilling to a certain extent but at the same time you
thought there was really horrendous you know'.[122]

In March 1940 MO asked fifty young men attending sixth form
colleges, and mostly born in 1922 or 1923, to complete a questionnaire about literature.[123] Their responses suggest they were, on
the whole, keen readers. Thirty-five read book reviews, typically
those in the *Observer* or *Sunday Times*, and a couple even read
the *Times Literary Supplement*. Even so, nearly four times as many
said their book purchases were 'spur of the moment', influenced
by the author or the type of book, rather than in response to book
reviews; this is noteworthy when considering the influence of literary critics. Charles Dickens topped the list of the young men's
favourite authors overall, while P. G. Wodehouse was by far their
favourite humorous author. Thirty-five of the fifty had liked a book
so much that they had read it more than once. Among the revisited titles were *The Pickwick Papers* (4 respondents), *The Wind
in the Willows* (3 respondents), *Winnie the Pooh* (2 respondents)
and *Alice's Adventures in Wonderland* (2 respondents). Great War
novels – whether canonical or middlebrow – were, however, absent
from lists of their favourite novels and novels they had revisited, and
while titles about Gladstone, Disraeli and monasteries featured in
their favourite historical books titles about the Great War did not.

54   *Joining up in the Second World War*

Some certainly had read Great War books, though. Hemingway's *Farewell to Arms* and Sassoon's *Memoirs of a Fox Hunting Man* were each named once among the eighty-four titles that had given readers 'the greatest satisfaction', and one respondent mentioned *All Quiet on the Western Front* when asked if they read foreign books in translation. As well as asking about their favourites, the questionnaire solicited readers' feelings about particular authors. If their familiarity to readers is indicated by the number of responses then Edmund Blunden (3 responses) was relatively unknown compared with Charles Dickens (18), William Thackery (11) and Aldous Huxley (10). Nevertheless, those who had something to say about Blunden were positive, considering him 'the best novelist of the war, beating Mottram by a short head', and recalling *Undertones of War* as 'the best war novel I have read' and 'a very enthralling and movingly realistic picture of the war'.[124]

Taken together, the personal testimonies and surveys show that young audiences clearly did read war books and could find them affecting, but the responses to MO's 1940 questionnaire summarised above also reiterate that we should see such texts as only a component of the reading matter individuals in inter-war Britain consumed and as something that *some* but not all young men engaged with, rather than conceiving them as texts that impressed their representation of war experience upon a generation.

Poetry

Poetry, like literature, provided varied depictions of the Great War. An 'incoherent' canon developed.[125] Wilfred Owen and Siegfried Sassoon achieved critical recognition and featured in collections of poetry that sold well,[126] but 300,000 copies of Rupert Brooke's *Collected Poems* had been sold by 1930.[127] Both Brooke and Owen's work featured in the BBC's Armistice Day radio programme in 1930.[128] Clearly, disillusioned poetry certainly did not sit wholly outside mainstream culture, but it appears that works that celebrated traditional values remained popular and better known during the inter-war period.

The works of Sassoon and Owen were, at least before 1945, largely unfamiliar to my interviewees. Moreover, they rarely recalled having read any poetry about the Great War. Pond commented that 'most of the poetry I knew were filthy'; the one poem he could recall related to the Great War was about 'diddling in [a German's] eye' and suggested that people should feel no sympathy towards the Germans.[129] The small minority of interviewees who had encountered war poetry, often at school, most commonly remembered reading Brooke's *The Soldier* and McCrae's *In Flanders' Fields*.[130] Thurgood doubted they made any impact, and Lowe said the same of Owen and Sassoon, whose work he thought he 'probably didn't understand because they all seem to be a metaphor really [laughter]'.[131] Jack Pragnell read the 'very thoughtful' 'peaceful poems' of Sassoon and Graves at school, but also read Brooke, Kipling and Tennyson; it was the latter's *The Charge of the Light Brigade* which was his favourite.[132]

The responses of those who reflected on the influence of childhood impressions for MO confirm that war poetry did have the potential to shape understandings and attitudes, though. A writer and businessman, born in 1901, wrote:

> ... fellows who had been at school with me were killed in their teens. This I believe affected my later attitude. I think my later war reading affected me much more than childhood. The romanticism of war as seen by a child has been obliterated by intellectual approaches, the poetry of Sassoon and Owen etc.[133]

Notably, though, this respondent identified his profession as a writer, suggesting he may have had greater interest in literature than most. Of those whose testimonies have been examined here, only a minority had encountered 'disillusioned' war poetry and those who had did not typically deem it influential.

Watching and listening to the Great War

Literary texts were by no means the only, or even the most significant, means of cultural production that represented the Great War to inter-war audiences. Films, plays and radio programmes were produced, and literary and stage representations were adapted for radio and cinema. Indeed, the cinematic adaptations of *Journey's End* and *All Quiet on the Western Front* were two of the most

56 *Joining up in the Second World War*

successful inter-war war films.[134] It was undoubtedly the case that most of those who encountered these stories did so via these means of dissemination.

Film

The Battle of the Somme was probably the most widely seen cinematic representation of the Great War.[135] In the months following its release in 1916 the majority of Britons watched battlefront recordings and, unbeknown to audiences, re-enactments that vividly depicted the action that had taken place in France two months previously.[136] The next film in the series, *Advance of the Tanks*, shown in June 1917, proved a box office failure. With audiences wanting to escape the war, few subsequent feature films were made about it until the Armistice.[137] When the Great War returned to the screen, Paris argues, it was generally portrayed in a positive light; sacrifice had occurred, but it was worthwhile. Therefore, Paris suggests, cinema 'helped to disseminate heroic images of violence and war'.[138]

Traditional and patriotic portrayals of war outnumbered those that 'raised even some ambiguously phrased doubts about whether such sacrifice could ever be justified' even when anti-war sentiment became more widespread.[139] In any case, those films that were more ambiguous about the war's meaning, like *Reveille* (1924), enabled audience members with conflicting views to see what they wanted. Paris suggests that British Instructional Films *The Battle of Jutland* (1921), *Mons* (1922, remade 1926) and *Ypres* (1925) were widely seen by children as they were perceived as educational,[140] and were popular with audiences.[141] These films provided a similar version of the war to that expressed in inter-war popular fiction: 'sanitised, heroic images, testaments to courage, patriotism and the nobility of sacrifice'.[142] They were not recalled by my interviewees, who were largely too young to see them upon release, but nor did they feature, by name at least, in the archival interviews examined here.

Throughout the 1930s there were between eighteen million and nineteen million cinema attendances a week, a number that leads Ross McKibbin to suggest that 'no other cultural activity of the period' was as popular, and it was adolescents who went most.[143]

The Great War in popular culture

57

A quarter of the school-age boys asked in Merseyside in 1934 went to the cinema weekly.[144] In the 1990s Annette Kuhn surveyed nearly two hundred 1930s cinema-goers, 'probably reasonably representative of "ordinary" picture goers of their generation', about their film tastes.[145] Almost half had been educated past 14, most were first employed in positions typical of the lower-middle class, and their median year of birth – 1923 – was similar to that of my interviewees.[146] Nearly all went to the cinema at least once a week, which Kuhn suggests 'does not exaggerate the cinema-going habit in the 1930s'.[147] Nearly a third went regardless of the picture playing, and stars were a more important attraction than plots. They had favourite films and genres, though; films adapted from books or plays were most popular – about three times more popular than war films – and were also the type of film most often cited as having made an impression.[148]

Two of the most successful inter-war war films, though, were both adapted from books or plays *and* were war films: *Journey's End* and *All Quiet on the Western Front*.[149] The film adaptation of *All Quiet* had greater reach than the original novel. Released in 1930, it 'played to packed theatres in Britain'[150] where it apparently 'fared better ... than anywhere else in the world'.[151] A clerk, born in 1922, wrote to MO in 1940 that:

> One of my habits when young was seeing all the war films that I could – and this possibly made me dread war. I can vividly remember *All Quiet on the Western Front* when I was about 10. I remember I was petrified with horror and disgust as I was later when I read the novel.[152]

All Quiet was the favourite film of 11 per cent of the men Annette Kuhn surveyed about their 1930s cinema-going.[153] How typical this was may, however, be open to question. Sue Harper has analysed one of the few remaining attendance ledgers of the period, from the Regent Cinema, Portsmouth. The cinema's immediate catchment was 'clearly lower-middle-class' and 'young-ish', an audience who liked to see films that confirmed their essentially conservative attitudes.[154] *All Quiet* was shown in the week beginning 4 April 1931; admissions were the third lowest of that year, some 4,000 below the average.[155] Harper suggests that audiences avoided *All Quiet* because 'it was too depressing'.[156] In comparison, *Gunga*

58   *Joining up in the Second World War*

Din and *Cavalcade*, both of which had a more traditional military aspect, were hits at the Regent.[157] The war films of the 1930s were not generally disillusioned, but often simple depictions of war as adventure.[158] Duty and sacrifice were the key themes of *Tell England* (1931) and *Journey's End* (1930), and the latter focused more upon 'the enduring heroism of the soldiers than ... anti-war rhetoric'.[159] *Forever England* (1935) – which drew big audiences at the Regent in Portsmouth[160] – emphasised individual heroism, and while war was unpleasant, it remained a man's duty to endure it.[161] That *Forever England* was a naval tale may have been significant in its success. The last British film set in a trench was *Suspense* (1930).[162] Paris suggests that with another war on the horizon films about the Great War became more positive in their attitude, and filmmakers turned to earlier wars that 'could still be portrayed as high adventure and were well received by the public'. This, he concludes, shows 'that the nation's pacifism was not perhaps as deeply held as we have been led to believe, or at least did not extend to entertainment'.[163]

When asked about the cinema, interviewees often recalled Saturday morning matinees, often Westerns, in the 'Fleapit' or 'tuppenny rush'.[164] Far from all who went to the cinema regularly recalled having seen films about the Great War as they grew up, but a number of films about war were recalled by individuals, including the *Four Horsemen of the Apocalypse*[165] and *Lives of a Bengal Lancer*.[166] Jim Hayes had seen 'a good many films' about the Great War, including some staring Victor McLagan.[167] Frank Webster recalled that he had found one Great War film 'rather callous'; it depicted an American soldier who 'fired the shot and he said to his mate "Went up like a so-and-so and down like a so-and-so, stiff as a board", it was almost glorifying the fact that he killed a bloke'.[168] The popularity of the cinema notwithstanding, however, not everyone went. Thomas Leask, born in Newcastle in 1923, spent much of his leisure time at the swimming baths, which was 'very popular because it was so cheap, we couldn't afford to go to cinemas and things like that'.[169]

Significantly, the film *All Quiet* was re-released in 1939, at which point the men interviewed for this research were closer to the coming-of-age Watson describes.[170] *All Quiet* was the war film that most often appeared naturally in interviewees' narratives.[171]

The Great War in popular culture   59

Those who remembered it tended to agree with Brian Spragg's overall assessment: 'I was very sad when somebody was shot [laughter]', and it was 'rather a sad film as much as anything'.[172] There was much greater variation, however, in what men took from the film. Jim Stephens remembered that the 'slaughter they depicted there was absolutely horrible'.[173] Frank Webster remembered that *All Quiet* 'frightened [him]' and always remembered the final scene, but thought he was 'too young to understand that much' in relation to its message.[174] Similarly, Tom Knowlton, who had either read or seen *All Quiet*, felt its impression was limited: 'it didn't sink in because I wasn't clever enough to understand it, put it that way'.[175] Conversely, Don Browne had understood the film to be about the 'futility of war', but he had gone to see it 'as entertainment' and while 'it was a very sad film', he felt that it had little long term effect on his views about war.[176]

George Stagg, who like many others recalled the final scene,[177] suggested that the film had 'showed you an insight that the German people ... was on the same principles what we were, working-class people all with their sons and sending 'em off to kill and be killed'. Whether Stagg had understood this at the time or whether this is how he understood it on reflection is unclear, however, as he also said that 'at that time, being that age, it don't sink in properly, it was still to a certain extent sort of storytelling'.[178] Reg Day remembered it was about 'trenches and fighting and killing, it was about the Western Front I guess'. It was, however, 'just a film to us, we weren't old enough to be serious about things like that, our life was too young and sweet wasn't it, we didn't think about what had gone ...'.[179] Reg Elson, on the other hand, was 'very much impressed' and felt that he took *All Quiet* and the film adaptation of *Journey's End* as accurate depictions of war experience: 'Oh I think we thought it was real, I think we thought it was realism, truly I never thought of it as fiction ....'[180]

For Fred Pond *All Quiet* provided a window onto an experience he was otherwise unable to access, as Watson suggests. The Great War 'wasn't part of history' at school, so 'all we got was what Tom, Dick or Harry would say to you, you know, my dad was this' or knowledge from veterans they knew. Still, 'we heard very little of trench warfare but we knew of it because I think they made a film of it, *All Quiet on the Western Front* the film was called, ... that's

60 *Joining up in the Second World War*

the only way we got what happened in the trenches'. Pond was sure that other war films existed, but *All Quiet* which he saw aged 12 or 13 'was the main one, er, and that was, that was impersonating the trenches, completely in trenches, but they were German trenches and about German people, the story was about how they got on up against the enemy which was us'.[181]

Pond's responses about *All Quiet*'s impact were complex and conflicting. He repeated that *All Quiet* had been the only thing that had given him an idea of what the Great War had been like, but had earlier said that it had not left any impression because films were 'all stories'. When we returned to the topic, he said he had known nothing about the Great War 'except that we got out of films, stories and plays, American ones, you know where you'd see a dogfight or they were being bombed but you saw them and you thought "all that's what happened" ...'. I pressed Pond further and mentioned that he had said that *All Quiet* 'told [him] a bit about the trenches and I think you suggested that what you knew about trenches put you off the Army, is that something that you think is true?'. Pond replied that it could have put him off, but 'it wouldn't have stopped me from going in the Army had I wanted to go in the Army, no that wouldn't have stopped me because it was a film, it may have been reality but we never treated it as reality or even dangerous'.[182]

The other key trend that came through from my interviews was the distinct effect cinematic representations of aerial warfare had on the boys who grew up in the 1920s and 1930s. Although men did not suggest they were films that had influenced their attitudes about war itself, how they were spoken about suggests they contributed to enthusiasm about aerial warfare. Tom Knowlton recalled *Hell's Angels*, which featured Alan Cobham, was about 'the First World War air battles, it was a wonderful film that was', and Derrick Thurgood remembered *Dawn Patrol* had 'some really spectacular biplane dogfights'.[183] *Dawn Patrol* was one of the few cultural artefacts referred to within archival enlistment narratives. Charles Patterson, born in 1920 and taught about the horrors of the Great War by his mother, was interested in flying and took from *Dawn Patrol* an image of aerial warfare as adventurous and exciting. He said he was:

> very much influenced in what I wanted to do if there was a war by the film *Dawn Patrol* .... It may sound a bit odd and unlikely but

The Great War in popular culture 61

[it] really did have a tremendous influence on me. Because it struck me that although the casualties were very heavy it was much the most exciting and wonderful way to go to war. ... I could never – I thought at the time and certainly know now – have stood up to the rigours of fighting on land in the dust and heat and dirt and so on. That simply would have been quite beyond me. Also flying seemed to offer an outlet for personal initiative and individual initiative.[184]

While *All Quiet* had given some, though significantly not all, the impression that the infantryman's Great War had been horrific, cinematic representations of war in the air had none of the same connotations.

Stage and radio plays

Journey's End could be seen on cinema screens from 1930, but had started life on stage. War plays were not popular during the 1920s; R. C. Sherriff's was a notable exception, and sold a record-breaking 175,000 copies when published.[185] Sherriff did not consider the play to be anti-war but it was ambiguous about the war, with Stanhope's heroism demonstrated in his selfless endurance rather than courageous acts of valour; many reviewers perceived it to be both exceptionally realistic and a 'brilliant indictment of the futility of war'.[186] *Journey's End* was also broadcast on the radio on Remembrance Day in 1929.[187] The *Radio Times* devoted two pages to publicising the broadcast, including a full-page article: 'Mr Sherriff's Play and What It Stands For'.[188] Charles Morgan opined that while it might 'by a side wind, have the effect of making men more reluctant to enter into war, to consider it from that point of view is to misinterpret it'.[189] Instead it was significant because it provided listeners access to a scene that is,

and always was, remote from the visual experience of all English women and of the greater number of Englishmen. Those who served in the trenches were a minority even in the years of war; as time advances, that minority shrinks. The period is not far distant when, except to a few old men, the struggle of 1914–1918 will be no more than a tale that is told.[190]

62   *Joining up in the Second World War*

The play would bridge the experiential and generational gap: listeners 'almost believe themselves to be listening to the conversation of men they themselves have known and loved'. Morgan rejected the suggestion that *Journey's End* maligned soldiers by playing too much emphasis upon cowardice and drunkenness:

> It is true that fear and the use of drink to make endurance possible do appear in the play. Why not? They appeared in the trenches. They were part of the suffering of those days; they are ... evidence of heroism. ... The fight against personal deterioration was greater than the fight against the enemy.[191]

In this assessment, listeners to *Journey's End* could learn something of the experience of the Great War, and understand that it was a battle to retain or achieve masculine character as much as anything else. It appears that broadcast of *Journey's End* was generally well received; in 1931 the *Radio Times* wrote that it had drawn 'more letters than any single broadcast of the last two years; only one of these hundreds of letters protested against its inclusion.[192] Bracco reveals that commentators at the time wondered about the effect of war literature on young people. In 1929, the BBC rejected a realistic war play written by Henry Williamson in part because 'one had to be careful about the influence of the "Glory of War" on listening children'.[193] Sherriff subsequently assessed the impact of *Journey's End* on three juvenile boys, and concluded the experience prepared them for wartime service.[194] In 1931 journalist Kathleen Conyngham Greene wrote that a young man who saw the play would subsequently ' "in his inmost heart ... rather like an opportunity of trying" the military experience'.[195] Emily Curtis Walters observes that some young men wrote to their local newspapers in response to seeing the play; published letters suggest that the War Secretary Sir Laming Worthington-Evans was correct that the play would show them 'the terrible things that their fathers came through in the Great War'.[196] Nevertheless, some asserted that they would go to war if it were needed.[197] Reg Elson, who saw *Journey's End* as a film, presumably aged 8 in 1930, was impressed by it, and said he had 'thought it was realism, truly I never thought of it as fiction, way back then ...'. Even so, Elson desired to join the Army as a child.[198] Only one other interviewee recalled encountering *Journey's End* in any medium, and recalled it as a play 'about

The Great War in popular culture 63

the follies of war', but he did not show that it shaped his attitudes towards service in the Second World War.[199]

Journey's End was not the only depiction of the Great War to feature on BBC radio in the inter-war years. A German radio play, *Brigade Exchange*, was broadcast four times between the wars, first in March 1930 to the London regional audience and again on 10 November 1930 to a national audience, and then on television in August 1938 before a national radio broadcast a few weeks later.[200] *Brigade Exchange* provided realistic and graphic depictions of British attacks on German lines from the perspective of German troops at a telephone exchange.[201] The *Radio Times* listings in 1930 sought to draw attention with a dedicated centre-column illustration and a header at the top of the page – 'A German radio war play' – and noted that it had proved popular in Germany. Gregory suggests that the use of *Brigade Exchange* in the context of Armistice Day in 1930 is 'an indication, perhaps, of how far *All Quiet* changed attitudes in the space of a year'.[202] Nevertheless, plays centred around the Great War were uncommon on the inter-war BBC, though it seems this changed to an extent in 1938, when *Brigade Exchange* was just one of five Great War plays aired.[203] Radio plays were popular with the listening public as a whole, but perhaps had more appeal to older adults than young men; interviewees did not regularly recall Great War plays on radio.[204]

The Great War on the air

When *Journey's End* and *Brigade Exchange* were first broadcast on the BBC, perhaps a quarter of households had a radio; a decade later the BBC estimated this had grown to four-fifths, though the proportion of lower-working-class homes with a licence was less than three-fifths.[205] Interviewees from working-class homes generally recalled their family radio as a relatively recent acquisition in the late 1930s. Different households, and different members of households, consumed radio content in different ways. Ross McKibbin suggests that 'there was a tendency in working-class households to turn the set on and leave it on. Middle-class households were more discriminating: the set was turned on for particular programmes and turned off when they ended.' McKibbin observes the radio 'was

64   *Joining up in the Second World War*

like a piece of furniture ... especially if it was on all the time. It was simply there; an accompaniment rather than an alternative to something else.'[206] As a result, young people often consumed other people's programme choices passively and incidentally, as well as choosing content themselves.

Radio was an important mode of mass media, but only one of the people writing to MO in February 1940 referred to representations of the Great War on the air; a woman born in 1921 recalled her mother 'hated to talk of the war or listen to any radio programmes about it'.[207] Interviewees rarely recalled representations of the Great War on the radio either, but Peter Woodard was quite right to recall that 'they did quite a few radio programmes at one time' about the Great War.[208]

While uncommon, the appearance of such recollections in personal testimony suggests that the presence and tone of representations of the Great War on radio deserves more scholarly consideration, particularly given radio's reach. Great War radio plays were far from a regular feature, but special programmes for Armistice Day were an annual event, and just as Eleanor O'Keefe has observed in relation to local press, the Great War 'seeped into the calendar of civic life well beyond Armistice season'.[209] In addition to extensive Armistice Day programmes, the BBC broadcast no fewer than eight commemorative ceremonies between 1923 and 1939,[210] and as late as 1936 military bands were BBC listeners' third-most popular programme type.[211] While memorials and ceremonies were important elements of remembrance, programmes intended to illicit reminiscences of the Great War, typically through music, were more frequent on the BBC. According to the *Radio Times* the 1925 'Radio Pageant of the Great War' would 'renew ... memories of the pathos, wit and music of the times, as well as the spirit of self-sacrifice shown by all people',[212] and 'Army Reminiscences' (June 1929) which featured songs of the route march and songs of the trenches, would 'revive old army memories'.[213] Songs such as 'Tipperary' and 'Oh, We Don't Want to Lose You' featured in 'War in Song', broadcast October 1928, and 'Marching Songs of the Great War' (which included mouth organ illustrations) was broadcast nationwide in August 1926. The descriptions of these programmes suggest that they were intended to appeal to veterans, and a desire to remember positive aspects of war experience including the camaraderie.

The same desire appears to have underpinned the apparent popularity (probably particularly amongst veterans) of 'Concert Party' radio programmes. During the war Concert Parties featuring bawdy songs and jokes had 'brought all ranks together in a spirit of community' and 'helped dispel any tensions within a unit, often by making light of recent events or by parodying less favourable aspects of military life'.[214] The Roosters' Concert Party performed one particularly popular example. The amateur troupe was formed from servicemen overseas in 1917 and subsequently reformed, with some new members, in 1923.[215] They then performed humorous songs and sketches regularly on BBC Radio, as well as at seaside resorts and British Legion events.[216] Their 'Evening of Army Reminiscences' Concert Party was broadcast on BBC London in June 1924,[217] and 'in response to many requests' they repeated it in October of the same year, and the programme was broadcast nationally on Armistice Day.[218] They performed again for Armistice Day in 1925 and 1926. As late as May 1938 the Roosters delivered a Remembrance Concert to an audience of veterans, broadcast on the BBC.[219] Their Army sketches and songs, backed by a raucous ensemble, sought to evoke the atmosphere and humour of the wartime Army. In November 1926 the *Radio Times* wrote:

> This party must be almost the last of the original Army troupes extant, and wherever they perform this feature of their entertainment the scenes and humours of army life in war time is continually asked for. [...] On Armistice night this year the 'Roosters' will once again give one of the Army scenes – a typical Y.M.C.A. concert of the 1914–1918 period complete with Padre, piano (with a past), good-hearted but amateur performers and a generally ribald audience.[220]

By the late 1920s veterans were becoming marginalised in Armistice Day commemoration,[221] but nostalgic recollection and camaraderie were given greater prominence in the national commemorative radio coverage when the *Daily Express* orchestrated a change in the tone of the Armistice Day Festival of Remembrance. It had been held at the Royal Albert Hall since 1923, and centred around a performance of Fould's World Requiem, conceived as a universal appeal to peace. This music was, however, considered too elitist for the masses and too boring by the musical elite.[222] In 1927 the *Daily Express* effectively co-opted the event and championed a much more populist

66 *Joining up in the Second World War*

programme of wartime songs, expressing a less pacifist, patriotic remembrance that made space for military solidarity.[223] Fifty thousand veterans applied for the ten thousand free tickets to attend the event at the Royal Albert Hall, keen to take the opportunity to gather as comrades and sing marching songs, and the forty thousand who missed out could still participate by listening to the BBC radio broadcast.[224] The programme included hymns and humorous songs, but also cynical and unheroic songs, such as 'I Want to Go Home'.[225] In a period of conflict about the most appropriate modes of commemorating the Great War, it seems many veterans considered this format to strike a balance between the pleasant and the reverent; it facilitated reunion and comradeship, nostalgia and remembrance. H. V. Morton attended the Royal Albert Hall Festival of Remembrance, and wrote of the effect of the songs:

> We were young once more as we can never be again and we went deeper into our memories [...] We looked into an abyss of memories where long columns passed and repassed over the dusty roads of France, where grotesque, unthinkable things happened day and night – the brief joys, the sharp sorrows of those days, the insane injustices of fate, and above it all the memory of the men we knew so well ... It seemed to be that we had caught the only decent thing in the war – the spirit of comradeship.[226]

I have contended that the existence of representations must not be conflated with evidence of their reception or influence, and I have not found evidence of how young men received these specific representations. Nevertheless, this examination sheds greater light on what was possible and plausible. Veterans' requests for and responses to renditions of wartime songs and concert parties on BBC Radio do suggest that such representations befitted the ways they sought to remember the Great War.[227] This resonates with the evidence elsewhere that comradeship, moments of enjoyment and comic fatalism were frames through which veterans sought to remember. When paired with what we know about how radio was consumed and the nature of inter-war housing, it is highly likely that some young men consumed these representations directly and certainly indirectly.[228] Moreover, much as a mother's feelings about the Great War could be read from her insistence that radio programmes about it were switched off, a veteran listening to (and

The Great War in popular culture

67

potentially insisting the rest of the family listened to) such programmes implied that they endorsed this representation of how Great War experience might be understood.

Some interviewees did recall other Great War representations on radio. Bob Woodhams felt that the little he knew about the Great War as a young man had come from 'what we read, and flashbacks on the radio then'. Woodhams, having initially questioned the accuracy of his recollection, described a programme involving interviews with veterans, with the Somme as the main topic.[229] Based on digitised searches of the inter-war *Radio Times*, occasions when Great War veterans discussed their experiences on radio appear to have been limited. Such items were certainly a feature of Armistice Day programmes, though the radio listings provide insufficient information to establish the content or tone of these narratives. Beyond Armistice Day, I have identified fewer than ten episodes or programmes broadcast on the inter-war BBC that, based on the *Radio Times* descriptions, focused on veterans' stories. They typically aired in the latter half of the 1930s and typically focused on the 'remarkable' experience and on heroic action. For instance, in 1938, listeners to 'Up Against It – Escape from Capture' heard Lieutenant-General Sir Tom Bridges describe 'an exciting episode in ... the early days of the Great War – August, 1914 – he was involved in the skirmishing between the British Expeditionary Force and the advance sections of the German Army. In one day he twice escaped from capture and then only by the skin of his teeth, after a succession of hairbreadth adventures.'[230] The same year listeners of 'Hunted by Kurds' heard that Commander Oliver Locker-Lampson 'took a British armoured car unit across Russia from the White Sea to the Caucasus to take part in the fighting in the north of Turkey'. While crossing 'twenty miles of plain "with only one abominable track" in an open touring car accompanied only by driver, orderly, and interpreter ... they were ambushed by Kurds – enemies so cruel that Locker-Lampson was advised to poison himself rather than fall into their hands alive – ... how they got away will be told in this exciting talk'.[231] Great War veterans featured more than once in a 1932 series called *Hazard* in which men recounted experiences of 'adventure' and 'thrills' that had resulted in narrow escapes in war or exploration. The third programme, 'Zeppelin Raid on London', featured the Commander of a German Zeppelin unit during the

68   *Joining up in the Second World War*

Great War, who was on board an airship 'forced down in the North Sea'. The *Radio Times* remarked that 'The hazards of war are common to men on both sides, and the telling of them can only serve the cause of union.'[232] Whether this message would have stood out to a youthful audience when within a programme that stressed hyper-masculine adventuring spirit and the thrill inherent to taking risks and beating the odds, is less than certain, however.

When considered as a whole, representations of the Great War on radio emphasised the Great War as adventure and/or as an occasion of masculine camaraderie – either of which were compatible with traditional images of military service and with a wider pleasure culture of war – or as the subject of commemoration, where the war's meaning was necessarily ambiguous and from which, as we will see, young people did not necessarily glean in-depth understanding.

Being taught the Great War

In addition to coming to 'know' about the Great War through cultural representations, young people in inter-war Britain might be more consciously educated about the Great War at school, by what might be broadly termed peace organisations, and through Armistice Day commemoration. A civil servant, born in 1917, was most likely thinking of the latter two factors when she remarked to MO that 'all people of my age [have been] educated to peace', and that she had always 'heard of the Great War as a terrible thing which had happened in the past, to make a new world possible. It was a bad mistake which would never be made again.'[233]

Few of my interviewees remembered having been taught about the Great War in the classroom. History lessons focused upon the 'Kings and Queens going back to William the Conqueror',[234] or 'the Battle of Hastings, Trafalgar, Nelson absolutely, anything to do with the empire as well'.[235] A minority of interviewees, seemingly where an individual teacher felt it was important or interesting, were taught about aspects of the Great War. A veteran teacher lectured Fred Pond's class, not about the fighting but 'normally ... true stories that happened to him, and there was nothing really spiteful, it was a bit of humour, it was good entertainment yeah ... just what happened to him, with the Indians, he liked the

The Great War in popular culture 69

Indians ...'.[236] Elson was taught that concealed international affairs had caused the Great War, and Stagg and his peers also received lectures about why the Great War happened and the battles, but recalled 'we wasn't given the gruesome parts of it', 'we wasn't given numbers of dead and so forth, things like that, we was only taught the fundamental parts of it'.[237] Aged 10 or 11, Les Temple was taught about various battles and 'the dreadful conditions of trench warfare and so on, ... that's really all we were concerned with with the First World War'.[238]

Of course, there could be no guarantee that pupils would be particularly struck by such lessons or treat it any differently to other school topics; an MO respondent, born in 1921, wrote that when he heard about the war in school it 'was just history'.[239] Nevertheless, the personal testimony above reflects what we know about the content of school textbooks. Chapters about the war were included in new editions of existing textbooks and dedicated textbooks were produced. These typically presented the war in military and political terms, stressed that Germany had caused the conflict and portrayed Britain's involvement as legitimate and worthwhile.[240] Reference was made to the horrors of war, but limited emphasis was placed on the number of dead or the experience of battle.[241] In 1925 the Incorporated Association of Assistant Masters in Secondary Schools reflected that boys' interest in the details of battle did not make it a more important topic than 'the causes and consequences of wars', and covering it risked encouraging militarism.[242] As in other media, descriptions of the experience of warfare could have the effect of emphasising the heroism, stoicism and sacrifice of those who experienced it.

More balanced and critical discussions of the Great War appeared later in the inter-war period.[243] Although apparently not widely (or immediately) adopted, a school textbook written by two veteran teachers in 1929 honestly reflected the ambiguous attitudes veterans could have towards the war.[244] They made 'frequent reference to British courage, portray[ed] the High Command positively' and saw death as noble sacrifice, though most performed no heroic deeds. War had 'redeeming features': the estaminet, the cheerful billet and comradeship. They were thankful, though, that 'memory lets slip the unpleasant and leaves the pleasant uppermost', for it had been tiring, terrifying, gruesome and often monotonous, and

70   *Joining up in the Second World War*

ultimately 'not one of those who felt the scorch of war would willingly live through his or her experiences again'.[245] The youngest of those landing on D-Day *might* have seen a schoolbook written in 1936 for children aged 11 which explained that 'in all countries men who fought did not want to kill each other; they were caught up in something bigger than their private wishes [....] In all countries men long that peace may not again be broken.'[246] A similar sentiment was described by some of the younger respondents to MO; they had been taught to think of the Germans as just as unfortunate to suffer the war as Britons, but this lesson was most commonly imparted outside the classroom.[247]

Great War commemoration

On 11 November, the Great War and its dead were deliberately and publicly remembered by and for the nation. Commemorative ceremonies had a distinctly local focus, clustered around town and village war memorials on Armistice Day itself and on the Remembrance Sunday that followed. From 1928, radio provided a popular way for people to join Armistice commemorations as the BBC broadcast the ceremony from the Cenotaph,[248] and components of the wider programme, such as the Roosters' evening Concert Party, were also broadcast nationally.

The majority of interviewees remembered the strict observation of the silence as Ken Hay described: 'at 11 o'clock on November 11 there was a big maroon ... that boomed right across the town, and everything stopped, buses, traffic and you wherever you were stopped, and in my case said a prayer for the deceased ... and then [the maroon] went again and you carried on'.[249] In rural Derbyshire, Arthur Howard and an acquaintance halted their walk home from their allotments to observe the silence.[250] The ritual of the silence was entrenched, but its enactment alone might communicate little about the Great War. To Reg Day it 'was just Armistice Day, it was the day the war ended and that was it, didn't know anything about it'. The maroon 'would be heard all over the town and [people stopped] because there were still a lot of veterans about from the First World War ... they knew what they were remembering'.[251] Jack Abbott, born in 1925, said Armistice Day and British

The Great War in popular culture 71

Legion poppies served as the 'two reminders that there had been a world war ... the war to end all wars as they called it'. But he also described 'a generation of grown-ups, older people, who were more aware of what had happened and they wanted to remember more ....'[252] These latter narrations suggest the gap that could exist between those who had experienced the war and a younger generation who might observe the silence out of obligation. This interpretation fits with Adrian Gregory's discussion, drawing on MO's work on Armistice Day, about the way in which its meanings changed during the 1930s,[253] and with Lucy Noakes's finding that throughout the 1930s Armistice Day remained significant and potentially traumatic for those who had direct experience of the Great War, or who had been bereaved by it, but that 'rituals of remembrance' had little affective resonance for many, especially those too young to have a personal connection to the war.[254] That young men had understanding of the ritual and the obligation to participate, and that doing so often had limited resonance, is clear in men's recollections.

Armistice Day and Empire Day were marked by schools 'come hell or high water', Don Browne remarked, but with the exception of observing the silence schools' commemoration was varied.[255] Browne did not recall being told anything about the war, but they sang 'Oh God, Our Help in Ages Past' and a prayer was read. Pond, who observed the silence in his school hall, felt that he and his peers had understood from a young age and without explanation that 'everybody in the nation had to stand still for two minutes', and that the silence was 'to remember the dead, if you knew any'.[256] George Cash's school held an assembly that coincided with the silence:

> we would go in and sing a hymn that was relevant to Armistice Day and then of course we would say a prayer and then [the headmaster] would say that today we're not celebrating but we're thinking about all the men who were killed during the war and explain[ed why people were] wearing poppies and things like that ... so that we would think to ourselves if we saw a lady with a poppy 'oh yes she's remembering somebody', but it wouldn't sink in tremendously ....[257]

Brian Spragg's school would sometimes mark Armistice Day with a visit to a local cenotaph, and the significance of the Armistice,

72 *Joining up in the Second World War*

particularly the casualties, was impressed upon them.[258] Casualties were the most commonly recalled focus; at Les Temple's school the emphasis was upon 'paying our respects to the people that died fighting for us', and they were also shown slides about the war.[259] Pearson felt he and his peers were unaware of the extent of the casualties, though his teachers stressed that the dead should be remembered, poppies – which were obtained by financial donation – were widely worn at his school in a very poor area of Manchester, and 'we all had to stand to attention no matter what' for the silence.[260]

Only a minority of those interviewed for this research attended commemorative events outside school.[261] Shrines were visible in the streets surrounding George Cash's home. On his street, a shrine listed the names of those who had 'gone from that street' and every November

> they held a little service ... but even that didn't really bring it home to us, all it was was that we used to go and stand and watch and listen and then some of the older people would talk amongst themselves, do you remember old so and so ... his boy's name is on there and that sort of thing it didn't really strike home exactly what it all meant.[262]

Lowe and Woodhams both sometimes watched the parades for the spectacle. Woodhams lived close to the local war memorial, and his mother would say, ' "There's a band down" ... so we used to go down there and just watch the band more or less, that was the big attraction'. Woodhams found the silence and the Last Post very impressive, though he gave the impression he understood little more about the Armistice than that it marked when the war had finished. It was with his own service that it had gained emotional resonance; he understood 'more now than what I did ... when I was a nipper'.[263]

Even involvement in the ceremonies might not ensure 'lessons' were learned.[264] Tom King had been part of the Armistice parade as a member of the Church Lads Brigade, but commented, 'it didn't have any meaning excepting that we were getting dressed up for the day and marching to the war memorial'.[265] Stagg's scout troop had its own service, and marched in a service at the local memorial. Stagg's mother, who had lost her first husband in the Great War, would attend, and also took Stagg annually to the Field of Remembrance at Westminster Abbey 'because we always used to

The Great War in popular culture

put a cross in his section ... I used to go there as a boy, and do it ....'[266] As a result of his attendance at these various ceremonies, he had been told 'that it was the war to end wars and all the rest of it, but to grasp it all, you can't, because you're too young', though he thought it had an effect to 'a certain extent'.[267]

Others attended commemorative activities because of familial involvement in the Great War. On one occasion Jim Hayes's father told him he was going to participate in a local march, and Hayes volunteered to polish his medals, and 'I saw him on the march and that and he was proud to be marching'.[268] Reg Elson's veteran father took him to a local service every year, though Elson's primary interest was not the content of the service but soldiers stood on each corner of the memorial who performed a rifle drill at the end of which they 'turned the rifle completely, slowly, upside down and lowered it onto the instep of the boot ... then the Sgt Major would say "Down", so there would be four soldiers in First World War ... uniforms and they would stay like that throughout the whole ceremony, called the sleeping sentry', and the padre would preach his service from a horse trough and those gathered would sing 'Abide with Me'.[269]

Todman has suggested that Armistice ceremonies were a

> significant means by which a younger generation were educated in what war had meant. The commonly expressed idea that young Britons owed a debt of loyalty to the men who had sacrificed their lives for the liberty of future generations, bound them together in a concept of duty and responsibility.[270]

But assessing children's response to Armistice Day is difficult. The absence of emotional reactions evident in the oral histories is mirrored in observations from and closer to the time. Gregory quotes someone who observed children listening to an explanation of Armistice Day: 'No emotion, I should say, in children, but interest in something that is spoken on so much in their hearing.'[271] When those writing to MO in 1940 reflected on their attitudes towards warfare some cited Armistice ceremonies as being influential but, regardless of the intended message, the reported effect was mixed. An electrical inspector, born in 1921, felt the 'solemn and impressive' ceremonies conducted at his school had contributed to his 'general dislike of war', but a medical officer at a sanatorium, born

74 *Joining up in the Second World War*

in 1916, felt his sense of duty and patriotism was developed 'in my childhood by literature, armistice services, patriotic songs, and historical tradition etc.'.[272] In retrospect, however, few of my interviewees felt they were learning anything of significance about the war other than that they should remember those who had died.

Yet, even if Armistice commemorations did not teach young people a great deal about the events or experience of the war, the responses to MO's February 1940 Directive do emphasise that communal remembrance of the Great War continued to have a significant didactic and rhetorical function because it communicated the idea that the Great War was the war to end all wars.[273] This message was reinforced by organisations such as the Peace Pledge Union (PPU) and the League of Nations Union (LNU), which mobilised the Great War to educate young Britons to peace.[274] These were not insignificant organisations; the strictly pacifist PPU reached 120,000 members, while the 'pacificist' LNU, which would countenance war only if all other measures failed, could state that one million Britons had been members between 1920 and 1933.[275] The LNU provided schools with guest speakers and teaching resources, and established junior branches and study circles.[276] An education on peace clearly continued to resonate with some of those who had come of age after the Great War, like a male clothing manufacturer's assistant from Ipswich, born in 1922, who said: 'Childhood told me war was always unnecessary and also taught me to hate it. I still hate, I still think it unnecessary.'[277] Similarly, a 25-year-old teacher from Chesterfield felt the waste of lives and resources made the Second World War 'sheer stupidity' because she had been 'brought up to believe that the Great War was a war to end wars' and for a long time 'could not realise how statesmen could be such fools as to allow wars to develop'.[278] While this pair did not describe the origins of their attitudes, their views mirror the proselytising of the PPU and LNU, and others directly recall their influence. A 23-year-old civil servant from Harrow expressed her 'present scepticism about the war. Also from earliest times I had heard of the Great War as a terrible thing which had happened in the past, to make a new world possible. It was a bad mistake which would never be made again. I did not dream that it could happen again.' She was, along with all her school peers, a member of the LNU; like 'all people of my age ... we were educated to peace. It is

The Great War in popular culture   75

hard now to change one's attitude to war'.[279] A male solicitor from London, aged 24, had a similar experience and expressed a similar attitude. He 'felt that after our peaceful upbringing we should not be much use if called upon to fight after all; it also made me wonder if it could be right to ask us to make such a complete switch round in our attitude'.[280] Notably, these Directive respondents were relatively young and held lower-middle- and middle-class occupations. This could be simply be symptomatic of the demographic composition of MO's panel, a collective who were probably more likely than the average Briton to be exposed to and receptive to the PPU and LNU. At a local level the LNU was predominantly middle class,[281] and working-class oral history interviewees did not commonly recall knowing about or interacting with peace organisations. Nevertheless, it appears that their messages were in step with popular feeling in the mid-1930s; the responses of eleven million Britons to the 1935 'Peace Ballot' suggest widespread support for a 'prudent middle way between isolationism and militarism'.[282]

Conclusion

This exploration of how young men might encounter the Great War in inter-war Britain has emphasised the vast variety of representations of the conflict circulating in multiple different media within popular culture between 1918 and 1939. Some of these, such as those in boys' story papers, films and illustrated histories, were encountered very frequently. Others, such as poetry or plays, were less commonly seen. Broadly speaking, representations that intended a positive depiction of the Great War appear to have been more widely encountered than those that intended negative depictions. These were understandings of the Great War that fitted neatly into, or at least resonated with, traditional depictions of war as a venue for adventure and a test of masculine character. The relative absence of references to 'disillusioned' representations, even within Directive Replies to MO, should inform our expectations of their relative impact. Moreover, examining the representations that informed young men's subjective impressions of the Great War allows us to gain a more nuanced sense of which texts were influential and encourages us to explore an even wider range of cultural media. They were often, for example, shaped by illustrated histories of the Great War, some of them directly aimed at children: notably, this is a field of representations which remains under-researched.

Looking at how young men (rather than critics) responded to a variety of cultural artefacts shows that the responses of audiences were even more numerous than the number of representations. This in turn illustrates the difficulties of generalising about how a particular representation shaped the thoughts of individuals. Even those representations that resonated with individuals might shape them in unpredictable directions. For example, many young men might have seen *All Quiet* but their responses show that how much of its intended message they understood varied widely. So too did their feelings about how they should react, which depended largely on whether they considered themselves to be watching something that was more fact than fiction, or vice versa. Moreover, even such a negative portrayal of the war was received in concert with all manner of conflicting representations of war as heroic adventure.

Crucially, however, popular cultural texts were not the only sources available to young men to learn about the war. Nor were they even necessarily the most influential. In fact, the interviews conducted for this research, the archival interviews and the MO responses, all suggest the importance of representations in familial and social settings. These versions of the war are the focus of Chapter 2.

Notes

1 George Stagg (Morley, 2010). In fact, a copy of this picture was displayed in every London County Council school. Paris, *Warrior Nation*, p. 136.
2 John Malling (Morley (& Cash & Dann), 2010). See also Samuel Pearson (Morley, 2011). For more, see Robert Nicholls, *The Belle Vue Story* (Manchester: Neil Richardson, 1992) pp. 39–43.
3 Jim Stephens (Morley, 2010). See also Pearson (Morley, 2011). MO DR1264, journalist, born 1916, and DR1310, February 1940 Directive. Roper notes that tens of millions of toy soldiers and First World War toys, including replica tanks, were sold in Britain after 1914. *Afterlives of War*, pp. 176–7.

The Great War in popular culture 77

4 Edward Kirby, IWM-SA-16084, 1995. Frank Webster (Morley, 2010) similarly enjoyed the marching bands at the Aldershot Tattoo.

5 Historians have examined how popular understandings of the war have shifted over the twentieth century; see particularly Sheffield, *Forgotten Victory* and Todman, *Myth and Memory.*

6 Fussell, *The Great War and Modern Memory*; Hynes, *A War Imagined.*

7 Todman, *Myth and Memory*, p. 17.

8 Watson, *Fighting Different Wars*; Isherwood, *Remembering the Great War.*

9 Paris, *Warrior Nation*; Todman, *Myth and Memory*; Watson, *Fighting Different Wars*; Boyd, *Manliness and the Boys' Story Paper*; Bond, *Unquiet Western Front*; Dawson, *Soldier Heroes*; Sheffield, 'Shadow of the Somme'.

10 Paris has attempted to consider the influence of the cultural artefacts he examines in *Warrior Nation* with reference to 'the memories of those who grew to manhood under its spell' (p. 10). Paris's approach – seeking the reflections of individuals who cite particular texts – is certainly preferable to assuming the impact of a representation, but unlike the approach employed here – examining which texts people cite, and what they say about them – it provides no sense of how widespread such responses were, or even how commonly representations were encountered, nor is he as sensitive to the class of those who reflect on the representations as one might like.

11 I have not overlooked the fact that there were Great War veterans who also fought in the Second World War, but their experiences, decisions and attitudes are beyond the scope of this book. Of greater relevance are the many veterans who served in organisations like the Home Guard, where they came into contact with young men yet to enlist in the full-time services. This is discussed in Chapter 2.

12 MO February 1940 Directive Replies, Question 8 [Influence of childhood impressions]. Subsequent references to Directive Replies [DR] in this chapter are to this directive, unless otherwise stated. It appears likely that MO asked this question as part of an investigation into how 'ordinary people form their opinions on current events', which Harrisson told Mary Adams about on 16 January 1940. See Hinton, *The Mass Observers*, p. 143.

13 Panel membership was particularly attractive to young men, and this panel was no exception. Here, men under the maximum conscription age of forty-one have been examined.

14 More than half of the panellists in June 1939 would probably have been perceived as middle-class by their contemporaries. Hinton, 'The "Class" Complex', pp. 210–11.

78   *Joining up in the Second World War*

15 Jeffery, 'Mass Observation: A Short History'. As is common to MO Directive Replies, the respondents' geographic distribution better reflects the population of England than it does Scotland and Wales, who are significantly under-represented.

16 Analysis of the MO January 1940 Directive Replies (Question 7 [Attitudes to conscription]), suggests conscientious objectors were over-represented amongst those particular respondents.

17 Murray Goot has suggested that treating the respondents as a most likely case to test a hypothesis is a good use of MO directives. Mass Observation Anniversaries Conference, University of Sussex, 4–6 July 2012.

18 Joseph McAleer, *Popular Reading and Publishing in Britain, 1914–1950* (Oxford: Clarendon, 1992) p. 244.

19 D. Caradog Jones (ed.), *The Social Survey of Merseyside* III (London, 1934) cited in McAleer, *Popular Reading*, table 5.1, pp. 219–20.

20 J. H. Engeldow and W. C. Farr, 'The Reading and Other Interests of School Children in St Pancras', Passmore Edwards Research Series, no. 2 (London, 1933) cited in McAleer, *Popular Reading*, p. 139.

21 Annette Kuhn, 'Cinema-going in Britain in the 1930s: Report of a Questionnaire Survey', *Historical Journal of Film Radio and Television*, 19.4 (1999) pp. 531–43 (p. 535).

22 Four would actively avoid it, however, and one found reading exceedingly difficult. Wally Harris (Morley, 2010); Jim Hayes (Morley, 2010); Arthur Howard (Morley, 2011); Edward (Ted) Roberts (Morley, 2010); Alf Wyke (Morley, 2010).

23 See table 5.3 based on 'What Children Read', *The Publishers' Circular*, 12 November 1932, p. 561 cited in McAleer, *Popular Reading*, pp. 143–4.

24 Michael Paris, *Over the Top*, pp. xxi, xv.

25 *Ibid.*, p. 155.

26 *Ibid.*, p. 145.

27 Paris, *Warrior Nation*, p. 181; David Budgen, *British Children's Literature and the First World War. Representations since 1914* (London: Bloomsbury, 2020) p. 78.

28 *Ibid.*, pp. 81–2.

29 *Ibid.*, p. 83.

30 *Ibid.*, p. 83.

31 Paris, *Warrior Nation*, p. 150. See also Paris, *Over the Top*, pp. xv and 156.

32 Paris, *Over the Top*, p. 158.

33 'An Analysis of Child Reading', *The Publishers' Circular*, 20 November 1926, p. 759 cited in McAleer, *Popular Reading*, p. 141.

The Great War in popular culture 79

34 'What East End Children Read', *The Times*, 23 September 1926, p. 14 cited in McAleer, *Popular Reading*, p. 141. MO found that working-class adults were less adventurous than middle-class readers, more often choosing familiar authors. If working-class parents assisted their children with their reading choices it may have resulted in conservative reading tastes. MO File Report 2018, p. 100 cited in Jonathan Rose, *The Intellectual Life of the British Working Classes* (New Haven: Yale University Press, 2002) p. 140.

35 Jack Abbott (Morley, 2010); Reg Day (Morley, 2011); Ron Meades (Morley, 2010); Pearson (Morley, 2011); Stephens (Morley, 2010); Percy Walder (Morley, 2010); Robert (Bob) Woodhams (Morley, 2010); Webster (Morley, 2010).

36 Abbott (Morley, 2010).

37 Day (Morley, 2011).

38 Don Browne (Morley, 2010). Fred Pond tried to read Drummond but lost patience with novels; Fred Pond (Morley, 2011).

39 Thomas Knowlton (Morley, 2010); Bob Lowe (Morley, 2010); Jack Pragnell (Morley (& Marriot), 2010); Lesley Temple (Morley, 2010); Peter Woodard (Morley, 2011).

40 Paris, *Warrior Nation*, pp. 162–3. See also Budgen, *British Children's Literature*, pp. 84–7.

41 MO TC 'Reading' 1/B (9 September 1937) cited in McAleer, *Popular Reading*, p. 147. Francis has asserted that Biggles was 'an object of unqualified hero-worship' for schoolboys in the 1930s. Francis, *The Flyer*, p. 16.

42 McAleer, *Popular Reading*, p. 147.

43 Rose, *Intellectual*, p. 121; Steve Chibnall, 'Pulp Versus Penguins: Paperbacks Go to War', in *War Culture: Social Change and Changing Experience in World War Two Britain*, ed. by Pat Kirkham and David Toms (London: Lawrence & Wishart, 1995) pp. 131–49, notes that even by the Second World War reading 'remained organised around divisions of class' (p. 134) and cites MO research suggesting that most working-class adults considered books other than pulp-fiction 'outside their economic scheme' (MO File Report 1332 [Books and the Public, 1942], p. 12 cited on p. 133).

44 McAleer, *Popular Reading*, pp. 3, 134.

45 *Ibid.*, p. 140. See figure 6.1, p. 172 for sales figures of the first issue of each paper.

46 Paris, *Warrior Nation*, p. 163 citing figures from Kevin Carpenter, *Penny Dreadfuls and Comics* (London, 1983) p. 65.

47 Pragnell (Morley (& Marriot), 2010). See also Roberts (Morley, 2010); Woodhams (Morley, 2010); Reg Elson (Morley, 2010);

80 *Joining up in the Second World War*

Stephens (Morley, 2010); Stagg (Morley, 2010); Derrick Thurgood (Morley, 2010). Woodard (Morley, 2011) and Ken Hay (Morley, 2010) both noted that without getting papers as they were passed around they would have been unable to afford to read them.

48 Browne (Morley, 2010).

49 McAleer, *Popular Reading*, p. 140.

50 For public school stories, see Abbott (Morley, 2010). Elson (Morley, 2010); Pond (Morley, 2011); Woodard (Morley, 2011). No recollection of BSP war stories: Abbott (Morley, 2010); Charles (Wag) Jeffries (Morley, 2010); Meades (Morley, 2010); Stephens (Morley, 2010) and Woodhams (Morley, 2010).

51 The Wolf of Kabul, and accompanying 'clicky bar', were well recalled – Day (Morley, 2011); Thurgood (Morley, 2010); Meades (Morley, 2010); George Cash (Morley (& Dann & Malling), 2010). It was Spragg's favourite; Spragg (Morley, 2010).

52 Pond (Morley, 2011); Stagg (Morley, 2010).

53 Thurgood (Morley, 2010).

54 Paris, *Over the Top*, p. 160. See also Budgen, *British Children's Literature*, p. 78.

55 See Paris, *Warrior Nation*, pp. 155–6.

56 *Ibid.*, p. 157.

57 Francis, *The Flyer*, p. 16.

58 Woodard (Morley, 2011).

59 Frank was 'sure' that these had an impression on him, though he did not say what impression. Webster (Morley).

60 Jack Thomas, IWM-SA-27342, 2005.

61 Todman, *Myth and Memory*, p. 88.

62 Stephen Heathorn, *Haig and Kitchener in Twentieth-Century Britain* (Farnham: Ashgate, 2013) p. 164, citing George W. Egerton, 'The Lloyd George *War Memoirs*: A Study in the Politics of Memory', *Journal of Modern History*, 60.1 (1988) pp. 55–94.

63 Heathorn, *Haig and Kitchener*, pp. 158–64.

64 *Ibid.*, p. 159.

65 Todman, *Myth and Memory*, p. 94.

66 Thurgood (Morley, 2010).

67 Browne (Morley, 2010).

68 Stephens (Morley, 2010).

69 Derrick Davies cited by Rose, *Intellectual*, p. 377.

70 Woodard (Morley, 2011).

71 *Daily Express*, 21 October 1933 in Adrian Bingham, 'Writing the First World War after 1918. Journalism, History and Commemoration', *Journalism Studies*, 17.4 (2016) pp. 392–7 (p. 393).

The Great War in popular culture 81

72 For example, J. A. Hammerton (ed.), *The War Illustrated: A Pictorial Record of the Conflict of the Nations*, 5.110 (London: Amalgamated Press Ltd), 23 September 1916, 'For Valour: More Heroes of the Victoria Cross', p. 144.

73 For example, Hammerton (ed.), *The War Illustrated*, 5.113, 14 October 1916, 'One British Soldier Routs Twenty Germans', p. 205.

74 Hammerton (ed.), *The War Illustrated*, 5.108, 9 September 1916, 'The Campbells are Coming!', p. 88.

75 Hammerton (ed.), *The War Illustrated*, 5.112, 7 October 1916, 'The Two Extremes of Courage on the Field', p. 181.

76 Photographs of the Great War were found outside specifically war-related publications. Lowe (Morley, 2010) and Ralph Harris (Morley, 2010) saw photographs in newspapers, and thus they understood, as Harris said, 'that the trenches were filthy, we knew that they were dying in their hundreds'. Allan Florence ((Morley, 2010) saw photographs in inserts that came with his story paper. Lowe (Morley, 2010) and Pragnell (Morley (& Marriot), 2010) encountered images of the Great War in encyclopaediae – Pragnell recalled 'about half of one of the volumes was on the [Great War], showed this bloke going up and down blowing the bagpipes, that sort of historical event and it showed the trenches and the trees all broken down and what have you'. Harold Harper (IWM-SA-10923, 1990) made reference to unspecified images of the Great War within popular culture, and Ian Carmichael (IWM-SA-10297, 1988) also referred to 'horrifying pictures of trenches and mud and bayonets and all this sort of thing which anyone with a vivid imagination could see'. Arthur Flint (IWM-SA-899, 1977) and Charles Patterson (IWM-SA-8901, 1985) also drew on unpleasant images of Great War infantry service.

77 Florence (Morley, 2010).

78 Pearson (Morley, 2011).

79 MO DR2419.

80 MO DR2363.

81 MO DR1310.

82 Woodhams (Morley, 2010).

83 Hay (Morley, 2010).

84 Day (Morley, 2011); Hay (Morley, 2010); Knowlton (Morley, 2010); Lowe (Morley, 2011); Marriot (Morley (& Pragnell), 2010); Pragnell (Morley (& Marriot), 2010); Spragg (Morley, 2010).

85 Lowe (Morley, 2011).

86 Marriot (Morley (& Pragnell), 2010).

87 Tom Knowlton was one of many who, unable to afford a ticket, had 'stood on the outside of the canvas awning watching', Knowlton

(Morley, 2010). Lowe (Morley, 2011); Meades (Morley, 2010); Spragg (Morley, 2010). Stanley Brand got around the cost of the ticket by crawling in through a hedge (Stanley Brand, IWM-SA-27347, 2005). Some were fortunate enough to have their first flights at such events (Thomas, IWM-SA-27342, Richard Griffiths, IWM-SA-29574, 2007).

88 Elson (Morley, 2010) watched Croydon from outside. Hendon-Webster (Morley, 2010); Rupert Parkhouse, IWM-SA-15476, 1995; Gregory, *Silence of Memory*, p. 125.

89 Rowan G. E. Thompson, ' "Millions of eyes were turned skywards": The Air League of the British Empire, Empire Air Day, and the Promotion of Air-Mindedness, 1934–1939', *Twentieth Century British History*, 2 (2021) pp. 285–307. See also Brett Holman, *The Next War in the Air: Britain's Fear of the Bomber, 1909–1941* (Ashgate: Surrey, 2014).

90 Hugh Cecil, 'British War Novelists', in *Facing Armageddon*, ed. by Cecil and Liddle, pp. 801–16 (p. 801).

91 Cecil, 'British War Novelists', p. 801. It sold 25,000 copies in the first fortnight. *Daily Mail*, 30 April 1929 cited in Bracco, *Merchants of Hope*, p. 145. Modris Ekstiens has discussed *All Quiet* as a publishing success, but has not examined its reception amongst everyday audiences. Modris Ekstiens, 'All Quiet on the Western Front and the Fate of a War', *Journal of Contemporary History*, 15.2 (1980) pp. 345–66.

92 Trott, *Publishers, Readers and the Great War*, p. 31.

93 Isherwood, *Remembering the Great War*, p. 45.

94 Bingham, 'Writing the First World War after 1918', p. 393. Trott also observes that library lending data shows huge demand for *All Quiet*, and that some local councils refused to buy the book because of its message. *Ibid.*, pp. 67–8.

95 Trott, *Publishers, Readers and the Great War*, p. 68.

96 Cecil, 'British War Novelists', p. 803.

97 Trott, *Publishers, Readers and the Great War*, pp. 22, 25.

98 Bracco, *Merchants of Hope*, pp. 15. 29.

99 *Ibid.*, p. 11.

100 *Ibid.*, p. 2.

101 Todman, *Myth and Memory*, pp. 132–3.

102 Isherwood, *Remembering The Great War*, p. 42.

103 Bond, 'British Anti-War Writers and Their Critics'.

104 Bond, *Unquiet Western Front*, p. 33.

105 Trott, *Publishers, Readers and the Great War*, chapter 1.

106 Watson, *Fighting Different Wars*, p. 213.

The Great War in popular culture   83

107 Bond, 'Anti-War Writers', p. 824; Cecil, 'British War Novelists', p. 804.
108 Trott, *Publishers, Readers and the Great War*, pp. 70–2.
109 *Ibid.*, pp. 70–2.
110 Sidney Rodgerson, *Twelve Days* (1933) in Graham Greenwell, *An Infant in Arms* (1972) p. xiii cited in Bond, 'Anti-War Writers', p. 826.
111 Henry Williamson, 'Reality in War Literature', *London Mercury*, 19.111 (January 1929), cited in Watson, *Fighting Different Wars*, p. 199.
112 Trott, *Publishers, Readers and the Great War*, pp. 73–4.
113 Watson, *Fighting Different Wars*, p. 188.
114 *Ibid.*, p. 195.
115 *Ibid.*, pp. 203–4.
116 MO DR2052.
117 MO DR2176.
118 Florence (Morley, 2010); Hay (Morley, 2010); Thurgood (Morley, 2010). Marriot thought he had Marriot (Morley (& Pragnell), 2010).
119 It is noteworthy that what most stuck in Hay's mind from reading Graves's book was the protagonist's involvement in a *ménage à trois* rather than a military incident; Hay (Morley, 2010). Allan Florence's response to *All Quiet* suggests he too saw it as factual; Florence (Morley, 2010).
120 Thurgood (Morley, 2010).
121 Thurgood (Morley, 2010).
122 Stagg (Morley, 2010).
123 MO FR 62, Literary Questionnaire, March 1940.
124 *Ibid.*
125 Trott, *Publishers, Readers and the Great War*, pp. 57–9; Todman, *Myth and Memory*, pp. 162–3.
126 Trott, p. 59.
127 Corelli Barnett, *The Collapse of British Power* (1972) pp. 428–9 cited in Bond, 'Anti-War Writers', p. 822.
128 *Radio Times*, 7 November 1930, p. 396, broadcast 11 November 1930.
129 Pond (Morley, 2011).
130 Brooke: Thurgood (Morley, 2010); Marriot (Morley (& Pragnell), 2010); Pragnell (Morley (& Marriot), 2010). McCrae: Marriot (Morley (& Pragnell), 2010); Pragnell (Morley (& Marriot), 2010); Woodhams (Morley, 2010). These poems were often not remembered by name, but can be identified from the lines that could be remembered. See Jon Silkin (ed.), *The Penguin Book of First World War*

84 *Joining up in the Second World War*

Poetry (Harmondsworth: Penguin, 1979); Brooke, p. 77; McCrae, p. 80.

131 Thurgood (Morley, 2010); Lowe (Morley, 2011); Browne (Morley, 2010); also thought he read them. Ken Hay was interested in poetry, though not war poetry specifically, and may have read Sassoon at school; Hay (Morley, 2010).

132 Pragnell (Morley (& Marriot), 2010).

133 MO DR1460.

134 Trott, *Publishers, Readers and the Great War*, p. 84.

135 N. Reeves, 'Through the Eye of the Camera', in *Facing Armageddon*, ed. by Cecil and Liddle, pp. 780–800 (pp. 782–4).

136 Reeves, 'Through the Eye of the Camera', p. 784, citing Nicholas Hilley, 'The Battle of the Somme and the British News Media', *Centre de Recherche de l'Historial de la Grande Guerre*, Peronne, 21 July 1992.

137 Michael Paris, 'Enduring Heroes: British Feature Films and the First World War, 1919–1997', in *The First World War and Popular Cinema. 1914 to the Present*, ed. by Michael Paris (Edinburgh: Edinburgh University Press, 1999) pp. 51–73 (p. 52).

138 Paris, *Warrior Nation*, p. 152. John Whiteclay Chambers II states that few notable Great War films were made in the 1920s, the exceptions being *What Price Glory*, *The Four Horsemen of the Apocalypse* and *Wings*. ' "All Quiet on the Western Front" (1930): The Anti-War Film and the Image of the First World War', *Historical Journal of Film, Radio and Television*, 14.4 (1994) pp. 377–411 (p. 380).

139 Paris, 'Enduring', p. 60.

140 Paris, *Warrior Nation*, p. 153.

141 Paris, 'Enduring', p. 57.

142 *Ibid.*, pp. 55–6. The 1926 version of *Mons* showed individual heroics and bayonet charges.

143 Ross McKibbin, *Classes and Cultures, England 1918–1951* (Oxford: Oxford University Press, 1998) p. 419.

144 D. Caradog Jones (ed.) *The Social Survey of Merseyside* III (London, 1934) in McAleer, *Popular Reading*, pp. 219–20.

145 Kuhn, 'Cinema-going', p. 540.

146 Kuhn found that people remembered the act of going to the cinema more easily than specific films and why they had made an impression. *Ibid.*, pp. 538–9. Similarly, my interviewees often found it difficult to recall what had made a film impressive.

147 *Ibid.*, p. 535.

148 *Ibid.*, pp. 535–7.

149 Trott, *Publishers, Readers and the Great War*, p. 84.

The Great War in popular culture 85

150 Chambers, 'All Quiet', p. 394.
151 Andrew Kelly, 'All Quiet on the Western Front: "brutal cutting, stupid censors and bigoted politicos" (1930–1984)', *Historical Journal of Film, Radio and Television*, 9.2 (1989) pp. 135–50 (p. 138).
152 MO DR2201.
153 Kuhn, 'Cinema-going', table 15, p. 538.
154 Sue Harper, 'A Lower Middle-class Taste-Community in the 1930s: Admissions Figures at the Regent Cinema, Portsmouth, UK', *Historical Journal of Film, Radio and Television*, 24.4 (2004) pp. 565–87 (pp. 567–8, 577).
155 *Ibid.*, pp. 578–9.
156 *Ibid.*, p. 576.
157 *Ibid.*, table 4, p. 570.
158 Paris, 'Enduring', p. 61.
159 Paris, *Warrior Nation*, p. 153.
160 Harper, 'Regent', p. 572.
161 Paris, *Warrior Nation*, p. 153.
162 Paris suggests it was perhaps becoming too painful, but is mute about why it would become so at this point, and this did not deter audiences from viewing *All Quiet*, which is absent from his discussion.
163 Paris, 'Enduring', p. 65.
164 Abbott (Morley, 2010); Lowe (Morley, 2010); Pearson (Morley, 2011); Roberts (Morley, 2010); Webster (Morley, 2010); Woodhams (Morley, 2010).
165 Stagg (Morley, 2010).
166 Webster (Morley, 2010).
167 Hayes (Morley, 2010).
168 This could have been *Wings* (1927). Webster (Morley, 2010).
169 Thomas Leask, IWM-SA-21602, 2001.
170 Kelly states details about the re-releases are hard to find. The 1939 edition, apparently only briefly available, was notably shorter than the original, and contained an anti-Nazi commentary as well as a documentary preface including newsreel of the First World War and the rise of the Nazis. Kelly, 'All Quiet', pp. 141–2.
171 Browne (Morley, 2010); Day (Morley, 2011); Elson (Morley, 2010); Howard (Morley, 2011); Jeffries (Morley, 2010); Knowlton (Morley, 2010); Pearson (Morley, 2011); Pond (Morley, 2011); Ted Roberts (Morley, 2010); Spragg (Morley, 2010); Stagg (Morley, 2010); Stephens (Morley, 2010); Temple (Morley, 2010); Thurgood (Morley, 2010); Webster (Morley, 2010). Pragnell and Lowe thought they had probably seen it – Pragnell (Morley (& Marriot), 2010); Lowe (Morley, 2011). Despite its success, some interviewees did not

86   *Joining up in the Second World War*

recall seeing it, however – Abbott (Morley, 2010); Florence (Morley, 2010); Ralph Harris (Morley, 2010); Wally Harris (Morley, 2010); Hayes (Morley, 2010); Marriot (Morley (& Pragnell), 2010); Meades (Morley, 2010); Walder (Morley, 2010); Woodhams (Morley, 2010); Wyke (Morley, 2010).

172 Spragg (Morley, 2010) had been particularly interested in scenes involving aeroplanes and observation balloons.

173 Stephens (Morley, 2010).

174 Webster (Morley, 2010).

175 Browne (Morley, 2010).

176 Browne (Morley, 2010).

177 Stagg, however, narrated a composite of endings of the 1930/9 and 1979 versions of the film. That *All Quiet* has been remade and replayed so often may be one reason it is well remembered now. Stagg (Morley, 2010).

178 Stagg (Morley, 2010).

179 Day (Morley, 2011). Charles Jeffries (Morley, 2010) similarly thought he did not treat it seriously.

180 Elson (Morley, 2010). Pearson also recalled he had thought it 'true to life'; Pearson (Morley, 2011).

181 Pond (Morley, 2011).

182 Pond (Morley, 2011).

183 Browne (Morley, 2010); Thurgood (Morley, 2010). Pond (Morley, 2011) thought *Dawn Patrol* was 'a lot of rubbish'. Temple (Morley, 2010)remembered *Hell's Angels* and *Dawn Patrol* when prompted, but did not feel any films made any impression.

184 Patterson, IWM-SA-8901.

185 Bracco, *Merchants of Hope*, pp. 145–7 (p. 151).

186 *Ibid.*, pp. 152–68.

187 *Ibid.*, pp. 149–51. The film adaptation was shown on television on Armistice Day in 1937, and repeated 15 November 1937 (see *Radio Times*, 736, 5 November 1937, p. 20).

188 See also *Radio Times*, 319, 8 November 1929, p. 406–7.

189 Charles Morgan, 'Mr Sherriff's Play and What It Stands For', *Radio Times,* 319, 11 November 1929, p. 407.

190 *Ibid.*, p. 407.

191 *Ibid.*, p. 407.

192 'A History of Broadcasting on Armistice Day', *Radio Times*, 6 November 1931, p. 453, cited in Gregory, *Silence*, p. 138.

193 *Daily Mail*, 12 June 1929, cited in Bracco, *Merchants of Hope*, p. 176.

194 Bracco, *Merchants of Hope*, p. 176, citing the *New York Herald Tribune*, 27 April 1930.

The Great War in popular culture   87

195 *Ibid.*, p. 176; Kathleen Conyngham Greene, 'The War-Wise Generation', *Daily Mail* (Bombay, India), 17 April 1931.

196 'The War Secretary at "*Journey's End*"', *Manchester Guardian*, 7 February 1929, cited in Emily Curtis Walters, 'Between Entertainment and Elegy: The Unexpected Success of R. C. Sherriff's *Journey's End* (1928), *Journal of British Studies*, 55 (2016) pp. 344–73 (p. 372).

197 See *ibid.*, p. 372.

198 Elson (Morley, 2010).

199 Browne (Morley, 2010).

200 *Radio Times*, 338, 21 March 1930, p. 33, broadcast 25 March 1930; *Radio Times*, 371, 7 November 1930, p. 29, broadcast 10 November 1930; *Radio Times*, 778, 26 August 1938, p. 19, broadcast 30 August 1938; *Radio Times*, 779, 2 September 1938, p. 46, broadcast 7 August 1938.

201 Todman, *Myth and Memory*, p. 17; Ernst Johannsen, *Brigade Exchange, A Telephone Story of the Great War* (New York; Los Angeles: Samuel French, 1932).

202 Gregory, *Silence*, p. 139.

203 'C'est La Guerre' (1939); 'The White Chateau' (TV, 1938); 'A Source of Irritation' (1938); 'The Thin Red Line' (1938); 'The Old Lady Shows Her Medals' (1938).

204 "What Listeners Like, May 1939", table 1, BBC R9/9/3/LR/71, cited in Rose, *Intellectual*, p. 205.

205 'Listeners' Listening Habits, Autumn 1939', 22 December 1939; BBC R9/9/3/LR/86 cited in Rose, *Intellectual*, p. 204. McKibbin offers 71% of households in 1939; *Classes and Cultures*, p. 457.

206 McKibbin, *Classes and Cultures*, p. 458.

207 MO DR2038.

208 Woodard (Morley, 2011). Woodhams (Morley, 2010) also recalled radio programmes.

209 Eleanor K. O'Keefe, 'The Great War and "Military Memory". War and Remembrance in the Civic Public Sphere, 1919–1939', *Journalism Studies*, 17.4 (2016) pp. 432–47 (p. 434).

210 Search of BBC Genome database, extracted from *Radio Times*: https://genome.ch.bbc.co.uk/genome

211 McKibbin, *Classes and Cultures*, p. 466.

212 *Radio Times*, 112, 13 November 1925, p. 354, broadcast 19 November 1925.

213 *Radio Times*, 297, 7 June 1929, p. 517, broadcast 11 June 1929.

214 Emma Hanna, *Sounds of War: Music in the British Armed Forces during the Great War* (Cambridge: Cambridge University Press, 2020) pp. 207–8.

88 *Joining up in the Second World War*

215 BBC Radio, 'Desert Island Discs' with Percy Merriman, 17 August 1964.
216 Desert Island Discs with Percy Merriman, 1964.
217 *Radio Times*, 38, 13 June 1924, p. 492.
218 *Radio Times*, 54, 3 October 1924, p. 64; *Radio Times*, 59, 7 November 1924, p. 296.
219 *Radio Times*, 27 May 1938, p. 36, broadcast 31 May 1938.
220 *Radio Times*, 162, 7 November 1926, 'The Roosters' Concert Party', p. 346.
221 Gregory, *Silence*, p. 84.
222 James G. Mansell, 'Musical Modernity and Contested Commemoration at the Festival of Remembrance, 1923–1927', *The Historical Journal*, 52.2 (2009) pp. 433–54 (p. 446).
223 *Ibid.*, p. 452.
224 Gregory, *Silence*, p. 78.
225 *Ibid.*, p. 82.
226 H. V. Morton, *Daily Express*, 12 November 1927, p. 2, quoted in *ibid.*, p. 82. See also Hanna, *Sounds of War*, p. 239.
227 Hanna notes that wartime songs were heard on inter-war football terraces (Hanna, *Sounds of War*, p. 240) and communal singing of wartime songs became a more prominent feature of Armistice Day events.
228 Hanna suggests that the 'melodies of 1914–18 would also be preferred by the next generation' as they fought the Second World War (*ibid.*, p. 231) and various accounts cite Great War songs being sung during the second conflict. Younger men must, then, have become familiar with the songs somehow; such broadcasts may have been one route.
229 Woodhams (Morley, 2010).
230 *Radio Times*, 19 August 1938, p. 54, broadcast 26 August 1938.
231 *Ibid.*, p. 46, broadcast 25 August 1938.
232 *Radio Times*, 452, 29 May 1932, p. 578.
233 MO DR2248. See also DR2239, DR1284, DR2285, DR2435.
234 Abbott (Morley, 2010).
235 Stephens (Morley, 2010).
236 Pond (Morley, 2011).
237 Elson (Morley, 2010); Stagg (Morley, 2010).
238 Temple (Morley, 2010).
239 MO DR1310.
240 Budgen, *British Children's Literature*, pp. 97–100, 107.
241 *Ibid.*, pp. 103–5.
242 *Memorandum on the Teaching of History* (1925) p. 17, cited in *ibid.*, p. 103.

The Great War in popular culture 89

243 Budgen, *British Children's Literature*, p. 109.

244 Todman, *Myth and Memory*, p. 5. In France, Winter and Prost suggest, representations in schoolbooks had a wide audience and tended to be patriotic in tone, until 1930 when a veteran named Jules Isaac wrote a balanced account which was influential. They note, though, that he felt it impossible to explain the infantryman's experience and turned to soldier's accounts as the best representation, and the final image in the book showed a military cemetery. Jay Winter and Antoine Prost *The Great War in History. Debates and Controversies, 1914 to the Present* (Cambridge: Cambridge University Press, 2005) pp. 176–7.

245 Todman, *Myth and Memory*, pp. 5–6 citing G. Craig and H. Scott, *An Outline History of the Great War for Use in Schools* (Cambridge, 1929) pp. 260–2.

246 C. B. Firth, *From James I to George V* (London, 1936) pp. 95–6 cited in Todman, *Myth and Memory*, p. 134.

247 MO DR2248. See also DR2239, DR1284, DR2285, DR2435.

248 Gregory, *Silence*, p. 135. MO material suggests that it was a popular way to join the commemorations, p. 168.

249 Hay (Morley, 2010). See also Meades (Morley, 2010); Florence (Morley, 2010); Marriot (Morley (& Pragnell), 2010); Pragnell (Morley (& Marriot), 2010); Day (Morley, 2011).

250 Howard (Morley, 2011).

251 Day (Morley, 2011).

252 Abbott (Morley, 2010).

253 Gregory, *Silence*, pp. 166–7. See also Mass Observation, *Britain* (Harmondsworth: Penguin, 1939) chapter 7: Two Minute Story.

254 Noakes, 'A Broken Silence?', pp. 332, 335–6, 339.

255 Browne (Morley, 2010). Empire Day was commonly remembered in tandem with Armistice Day as special days at school. For brief discussion of Empire Day and lyrics to the song 'What Is the Meaning of Empire Day?' recalled by some interviewees, see Hugh Cunningham, *The Invention of Childhood* (London: BBC Books, 2006) pp. 180–2.

256 Pond (Morley, 2011).

257 Cash (Morley (& Dann & Malling), 2010).

258 Spragg (Morley, 2010).

259 Temple (Morley, 2010); Florence (Morley, 2010).

260 Pearson (Morley, 2011).

261 Thurgood (Morley, 2010). Eight of 28 interviewees who were asked directly.

262 Cash (Morley (& Dann & Malling), 2010).

90 *Joining up in the Second World War*

263 Woodhams (Morley, 2010); Lowe (Morley, 2010). Elson (Morley, 2010) also remembered Armistice parades with the Territorial band as the only military parade he would see.
264 As a choirboy and scout Tom Knowlton was involved in the parade. He recalled watching 'all the old veterans from the First World War with all their medals on coming into church and our organist was a First World War veteran as well, and I remember we always had to have Psalm 46, God is our refuge and strength and ... various British Legion members reading the lesson'. There was no sense that this involvement had shaped Knowlton's attitudes, however. Knowlton (Morley, 2010).
265 Tom King, IWM-SA-9571, 1986.
266 Stagg (Morley, 2010).
267 Stagg (Morley, 2010).
268 Hayes (Morley, 2010).
269 Elson (Morley, 2010).
270 Todman, *Myth and Memory*, p. 132.
271 MO S43, 11 November 1937, cited in Gregory, *Silence*, p. 171.
272 MO DR2438, DR2276.
273 Including in schools – see DR2038.
274 Noakes, 'A Broken Silence?', p. 337. See Gregory, *Silence*, pp. 150–63.
275 PPU: Martin Ceadel, *Semi-Detached Idealists: The British Peace Movement and International Relations, 1854–1945* (Oxford: Oxford University Press, 2000) p. 334; LNU: Helen McCarthy, *The British People and the League of Nations. Democracy, Citizenship and Internationalism, c1918–45* (Manchester: Manchester University Press, 2011) pp. 3–4.
276 Helen McCarthy, 'Democratizing British Foreign Policy: Rethinking the Peace Ballot, 1934–1935', *Journal of British Studies*, 49 (2010) pp. 358–87 (p. 365).
277 MO DR2265. See also DR1190, DR2285, DR2239, DR1284.
278 MO DR2047. See also DR2239.
279 MO DR2248.
280 MO DR2362.
281 McCarthy, 'Democratizing British Foreign Policy', p. 372.
282 Martin Ceadel, 'The First British Referendum: The Peace Ballot, 1934–5', *The English Historical Review*, 95 (1980) pp. 810–39 (p. 838). See also Martin Ceadel, *Pacifism in Britain 1914–1945: The Defining of a Faith* (Oxford: Clarendon Press, 1980).

2

Encountering Great War veterans

Ron Holloway recalled that his uncle Fred '… wouldn't talk about the 1914–18 war and I was told strictly never, never to mention it to him …'. Nevertheless, Holloway 'spotted a framed citation on the wall and I read it and I couldn't believe it': Fred was shot by a sniper, but travelled a mile to warn others at headquarters. This explained Fred's incapacitated right arm. Fred was one of 'perhaps half a dozen' Great War veterans Holloway was acquainted with as he grew up in inter-war Britain. It 'seemed to be the general rule that any chaps of my father's age with any wartime experience didn't talk about it, they bottled it, … I got the impression that you didn't ask them anything at all.' Yet:

> occasionally they would say something, like I made a remark to one chap, I said 'Cor dear, I do feel hungry' and he looked at me and said 'Tha's never been hungry' and described how he got into a truck … when he was being relieved from the trenches, coming back, they picked up all the odd bits and pieces that the troops coming in had thrown on the floor and they ate them …, and he said 'That's when you're hungry, when you'll eat what somebody else has thrown away.'[1]

This chapter explores whether, how and what young men heard about the Great War from its veterans. It shows that Holloway's experience typifies those of young men in inter-war Britain: they knew that veterans were present in their day-to-day lives; they found veterans were generally reticent about their wartime experiences; and, nevertheless, they were typically exposed to occasional representations of Great War experience by these veterans, or learned something about their wartime service through other means. Veterans are popularly imagined as either expressive poets or silent (traumatised) warriors.[2] In reality, most were neither of these archetypes. The moments when they spoke of the war are elusive after the fact: often fleeting, private and not always recognised at the time. Yet oral history interviews and MO material reveal that veterans in inter-war Britain divulged elements of their experiences and attitudes to the young men around them more commonly than has previously been acknowledged. Learning that men were veterans or hearing them discuss their service, tell war stories or express attitudes to conflict all provided young men with impressions of wartime service and understandings of the Great War.

Although young men's interactions with veterans, and the narratives they heard from them, were a significant and influential way by which young men came to 'know' about the Great War, they are largely overlooked in the extensive body of scholarship about representations of the Great War in the 1920s and 1930s. Very little research considers veterans' non-literary accounts, and the transmission of narratives of the Great War within the family has remained largely unexplored. The notable exception to this is a published conference paper by Gary Sheffield, which examined how Second World War servicemen drew upon the Great War. Sheffield suggested that some had heard about the Great War from their fathers and that this affected their service preferences. He argued that whilst the 'First World War was a terrible experience ... it was also for many survivors the most important and rewarding period of their lives, and this perspective was passed on to youngsters.'[3] Sheffield's suggestion was, understandably given its origins in a conference paper, based upon a small evidence base. This chapter uses a significantly larger body of personal testimonies, including fifty-five purpose-designed oral histories and fifty-four archival interviews that include a reference to Great War veterans, to examine the topic more thoroughly.[4] These sources also enable insight into the experiences of a more socially varied group of men than those Sheffield examined. This breadth matters because class shaped father-son relationships in inter-war Britain, and therefore what veterans shared, and because class shaped how the Great War was experienced, and therefore what there was to tell. The sources used here enable a wider investigation, and a more nuanced understanding, of what young men heard from veterans.

Encountering Great War veterans 93

This chapter begins by examining the extent to which veterans were present in young men's day-to-day lives in the inter-war period, before exploring the potential explanations for veterans' reticence about their Great War experiences. The second section examines how young men established that men they knew were veterans and how they learned more information about their wartime service; day-to-day conversation and artefacts within the home, including veterans' bodies, could reveal wartime service and transmit at least an impression of their experience. The third section considers the occasions – sometimes prompted by day-to-day occurrences, objects or wounds – when young men heard more expansive and deliberate narratives from veterans themselves. The content and tone of these narratives varied; veterans ascribed heterogeneous meanings to the war. What they chose to pass on, and what they preferred not to talk about, meant that young men more often heard broadly positive messages about the experience of the Great War than explicitly negative ones. The Great War was not typically presented to, or understood by, young men as an experience entirely lacking positive or redeeming features, such as pride in having served or comradeship, and it remained possible to position these narratives as representations of adventure, rewarding endeavour or redemptive sacrifice, each of which could place military service within established conceptions of masculinity. Positive framing could even be used when young men heard from others about family members who had been killed during the Great War. The final section shows that during the Second World War the Home Guard became a site where young men encountered, and often respected, veterans prior to their own full-time military service, but, even in a setting where discussing military experience had cachet, young men typically found veterans talked amongst themselves rather than sharing their experiences with the next generation.

Encountering veterans and silences in inter-war Britain

Great War veterans were common in inter-war Britain; more than seven million Britons had served and returned home. Young men found them conspicuous, nevertheless. Perhaps the most conspicuous were the more than one million disabled veterans, most

94   *Joining up in the Second World War*

of whom 'lived with their disabilities not in institutions ... but at home, in domestic spaces and local communities'.[5] Young men certainly noticed and remembered disabled veterans on the streets, 'selling matches or selling razor blades, whatever they could sell to live off'.[6] Harry Parkes remembered a 'victim of the First World War' who begged at Nottingham Cathedral and 'travelled home by swinging on his hands', and Jack Pragnell recalled a 'shell-shocked' man who would do a 'jerky march' past his house.[7] They also watched veterans in Armistice parades, and irrespective of outward markers of 'veteran' status, they considered it noteworthy when they learned a man they knew was a veteran. These were often men with significant roles in their lives; thirty-four of my fifty-five interviewees knew their fathers were veterans, and the vast majority counted ex-servicemen amongst their uncles or elder brothers, or amongst men they regularly interacted with as part of their day-to-day lives: friends' relatives, neighbours, teachers, colleagues or fathers-in-law. All of these figures were potential narrators of Great War experiences; indeed, all were cited as such. Only two interviewees had not knowingly encountered a Great War veteran before joining up in the Second World War.[8]

The presence of, and the knowledge of, veterans in young men's lives did not necessarily ensure that they heard detailed or extensive narratives about the war, though. Ten of my thirty-four interviewees with veteran fathers heard nothing from them during the inter-war period about their Great War service, and some others heard imprecise or abridged information. Gwyn Grogan knew that his father had been a decorated Brigadier General, but he 'did not really talk about it very much'. Instead, Gwyn learned about his achievements by reading the official histories.[9] Joseph Drake apparently knew only basic details about his brother's service and wounds, Brian Folkes had two veteran uncles who did not discuss it and George Elliot knew his uncle had been decorated by the Belgians in the Great War, but said 'no member of the family knew what he had received it for, that I can guarantee'.[10] Even when fitting opportunities for story-telling presented themselves, they might not be taken: John Riggs's Officer Training Corps master had won a Military Cross on the Western Front but 'never mentioned it much'.[11] Most young men established at least basic details about the service of veterans they knew, and some found

Encountering Great War veterans 95

that veterans would occasionally narrate select fragments of their war experiences, but few were regularly regaled with stories by the veterans they interacted with. The trope of the 'silent veteran' certainly makes too little allowance for occasional oration, but it is not without foundation.[12]

It might seem unnecessary, even impudent, to ask why veterans might not have discussed their – potentially traumatic – wartime experiences in the earshot of young men. Yet, the oral histories demonstrate the importance of acknowledging the variety of possible, and not mutually exclusive, explanations. A desire to move on should not be dismissed; it was explicit in Len Pettet's experience. Pettet's father 'didn't say much, anything about it at all', but his mother revealed that his father had served in a rifle corps in France before becoming a prisoner of war (POW). Pettet asked his father about it 'on one or two occasions but I was given rather negative answers, "That's all gone by now boy, we've got to live for the future and that's gone", he didn't really want to know'.[13] Pettet (later) postulated that this reticence was probably because his father's experiences had been horrific. Trauma undeniably underpinned some veterans' silence, but this need not be our default assumption.[14] Veterans may also have struggled to compose a coherent narrative of combat, or have been discouraged by the belief that those who had not been there would not understand.[15] They might have held back out of concern that their stories would upset their audience; the desire to avoid causing distress had shaped soldiers' letters home during the war itself.[16] Silence could also result from a veteran's perception – arrived at either by comparison with representations in popular culture or by objective assessment – that their service was uninteresting; as Dan Todman has reasoned: 'If Daddy had spent his war shifting packing cases in Le Havre, he might not want to talk about it not because it was horrific but because it seemed humdrum.'[17] Another possibility, and one perhaps most applicable to those in 'humdrum' roles, is that men who enlisted 'for the duration' and who had not fully identified as soldiers during the war did not embrace the identity of veteran at its conclusion. Oliver Wilkinson suggests that while a minority joined veterans' associations most 'easily jettisoned [military identity] in favour of civilian identities and affiliations that predated the war and/or prevailed in its aftermath'.[18]

Far more prosaic reasons, unrelated to war experience, were also important. Fred Pond had little opportunity for conversation with his father, who worked nights as a baker; while Pond knew his father had served he was uncertain about what he had done.[19] Some veteran fathers died when their children were young.[20] Others' fathers seemingly had the opportunity but opted not to discuss their war service.[21] Conversational conventions could be important. Todman has pointed to the working-class tradition that work stayed at work,[22] and some young men felt that their parents' pasts simply were not topics of discussion. Dennis Hagger knew his father had become a machine gunner after the horses he worked with in the Royal Horse Guards were killed. When asked if his father had talked about his wartime service Hagger replied, 'No, I don't think he talked about anything to me of his past, I mean he never said much about his time in Australia [where he had emigrated briefly as a young man].'[23]

Another prosaic but nonetheless significant factor worthy of recognition is that veterans were not necessarily silent in the face of persistent questioning. Gordon Waterhouse noted that his father 'wouldn't talk about it unless you approached him and asked these things',[24] but my interviewees' recollections suggest that children did not commonly do so.[25] Some simply were not sufficiently curious about the war. Although Fred Pond had rarely had the opportunity to ask questions of his father, he explained that he would not have been inclined to in any case: 'I don't think I was interested in the war, no, just because we'd never been taught about it so it wasn't a subject to us.'[26] Derrick Thurgood, on the other hand, was interested in the Great War and conscious of his father's service, yet had not thought to question his father.[27] Fathers were increasingly involved, and friendly, with their children in inter-war Britain,[28] but some did not expect to be questioned or pestered by their children after a day's work.[29] In other families it was fathers, rather than children, who directed the topics of conversation. Ken Hay and his brother listened 'if my Dad chose to tell us something' and 'could ask him anything', but

> on things like the war we just relied on him to tell us and if he didn't tell us I don't think we rationally thought well he doesn't want tell us because it's horrible, we didn't think to ask I don't think, or I didn't,

Encountering Great War veterans

I don't think my brother did either because my brother would have told me, 'here, did you know dad said so-and-so'.[30]

The freedom to ask about anything did not extend to all households. Some youngsters were dissuaded from asking about the Great War by other family members, who either understood or presumed that a veteran relative did not want to discuss it. Ron Holloway 'was told strictly never, never to mention it' to his veteran uncle, and an estimator, born in 1918, told MO in 1940 that he had grown up with three uncles who 'had gone through the war and two had been wounded, but they would never tell of their experiences. I was discouraged from ever asking them, and in fact so far as that household was concerned, the last war might never have been fought at all.'[31] Alternatively, mothers and older siblings could assume the role of gatekeeper: Reg Elson's father had answered his questions about elements of his experiences, yet other family members would not. When Elson was aged about 12 his father suffered rheumatism as a result of his wartime service. Elson was told 'it's because "Dad was wet in the trenches", things like that, "Dad has rheumatism from the war", but no more detailed than that and indeed come to think of it if one kept asking one would be told "be quiet, it's none of your business".'[32] Whether it was any of their business or not, and despite the varied reasons that veterans might not have been voluble about their wartime experiences, most young men did, however, establish basic details about the service of veterans who they knew.

Learning about veterans

Young men learned about the wartime service of family members and other veterans in a number of different ways. Some were directly told a limited amount about their service. Percy Walder's father had told him 'just the facts': he was in the Army, although Walder was unsure of his role, and he was gassed at Ypres.[33] Jack Abbott felt his father wanted to move on from the war and so 'didn't talk much about it'. Still, without asking questions, Abbott 'picked up different pieces about how he was in Italy and ... Turkey and ... Egypt', knew he was involved with vehicles and saw some photographs of his father in uniform.[34] Importantly, the deliberate reminiscence envisaged in the 'Daddy, what did YOU do in the Great War?' recruitment poster was far from the only way that children established that men they knew were Great War veterans, or gained an understanding of their experience.[35]

Because wartime service had intruded upon men's lives, references to it could emerge from more familiar conversational scripts about careers, family life and travel. For instance, William Coster knew that his father had started his business 'after he came out of the First World War in 1919'.[36] Stanley Brand was told the familial tale of his parents' first meeting, when his grandmother invited soldiers from the local Army depot to her home in an attempt to marry off her daughters.[37] While the Great War's destructive capacities enshrined it within many family histories, its end served as a reference point for the resumption or beginning of family life in many more. Children were designated as memorials to both death and love in connection with the Great War: Harry Gould understood that he was named after an uncle killed at Passchendaele, while Denys Owen's name was chosen because it was popular in northern France, where his father had served during the Great War and where his parents subsequently spent their honeymoon.[38] Wartime service was also referred to because of its contemporary relevance. Arthur Howard was not the only interviewee to learn of his father's service through his mother's complaints about an unawarded war pension; in Howard's case this was attributed to his father having absconded from hospital while being treated for exposure to gas.[39] Conversely, Ken Hay recalled that what his father had learned in the RAMC qualified him as the household expert when they had minor ailments.[40] Family gatherings provided another situation when young men might encounter representations of the Great War. Frank Webster recalled his father and his father's brother-in-law enjoying playing Great War marching songs on the piano and a banjo on Sundays, and at other family occasions young men (over) heard about family members service.[41] Gordon Mellor recalled that when his extended family gathered his uncles would discuss their war experiences over dinner while his aunts swapped tales of their time in domestic service.[42] Brian Spragg's uncle told him his father had been 'brave' and his grandmother gave him an insight into trench conditions when she told him that 'when [his father]

Encountering Great War veterans 99

came home on leave, he'd come virtually out of the trenches and be in a filthy condition and she virtually had to burn his uniform [laughter] full of lice and dirt and mud'.[43] On other occasions, children overheard conversations that they were not intended to; Ruth Armstrong recalled her veteran father 'told me nice stories'. He reserved the 'nasty stories' for her mother; 'I was outside the door one day and I overheard him telling her about the things that he saw, and what the Germans had done. They had no idea I was listening.'[44]

As children explored, and simply lived in, the domestic space they might encounter wartime objects and artefacts that indicated the presence of a veteran in the family. This chapter opened with Ron Holloway's recollections of learning about his uncle's wartime service through a citation on the wall of his home, and Abbott's testimony above indicated that photographs reinforced his under-standing of his father's service overseas. Photographs, particularly photographs of family members in uniform, were the objects that young men most consistently recalled as having provided them with any information about familial Great War service.[45] How informa-tive they were depended on whether they could be connected to other knowledge, as in Abbott's case, or if they were accompanied by a narration. Samuel Pearson, whose father died when he was aged nine, knew that his father had been a regular in the Royal Navy and had heard about the battle to obtain his war service pen-sion, but it was family members who showed Pearson photographs of the ships he had served on and told him mainly adventurous and humorous tales about his time in the Navy.[46] Similarly, Maurice Marriot, who was 8 years old when his father died, later saw a pho-tograph of his father in uniform and was told basic details about his service by family members.[47] Viewed in isolation, however, photographs offered limited depth. Frank Webster learned of his uncle's service from a photograph, but without further information his knowledge was incomplete: 'I know he had another brother, me father had another brother who was in the Cameroons I believe it was, but I only know that because I saw a picture, but I don't know any details.'[48] Still, this could be informative if one had previously known nothing; Alf Wyke claimed he only knew of his father's ser-vice because he saw a photograph of him in uniform.[49] In some homes photographs were ever present because they performed a

100 *Joining up in the Second World War*

commemorative function: George Stagg remembered a photograph of mother's first husband in uniform that was hung in memoriam.[50] Other families preserved photographs in albums. In his family's photograph album, Ron Meades found posh silk postcards from the frontline, which told him a little about the Great War.[51] Such cards were expensive, and some soldiers requested that the recipient keep them as souvenirs.[52] This was as close as any interviewee came to referring to wartime letters and/or a diary. The wealth of letters now within British archives proves that families did retain letters, but the fact that interviewees do not remember encountering them suggests that in the inter-war years they were typically stored – treasured or forgotten – rather than regularly examined.[53]

The family home could also house wartime mementoes. Like photographs, these were more informative if accompanied by a narrative, but they could reinforce knowledge of a family member's service or prompt questions. Stanley Brand was given his uncle's Royal Navy Air Service helmet, ensuring he knew that his uncle had served and creating a tradition of service in Brand's mind.[54] Souvenir collecting was a popular habit amongst British soldiers,[55] and Derrick Thurgood's father had brought home a Poilu's helmet and a shell head, which Thurgood felt had ensured he had always been conscious of the Great War. Little scholarly work has sought to excavate the meaning that veterans themselves attached to their souvenirs, but Paul Cornish suggests that they 'resonate with memories of life and death situations, suffering or glory'.[56] Nicholas J. Saunders suggests that for those who had lost loved ones, artefacts and trench art were reminders of the dead,[57] and triggered feelings of grief, guilt or relief.[58] Yet, these objects did not necessarily carry the same meaning to those who encountered them on the mantelpiece rather than the battlefield, particularly if their owner had come home with them at the end of the war. Thurgood's consciousness of the Great War did not prevent him and his brother from enjoying playing with the shell head; their understanding that their mother feared it would detonate increased their enjoyment.[59] Other boys utilised such objects within the pleasure culture of war, too. Wilf Curtis recalled a friend's father had a decommissioned hand grenade from the Great War, 'and my friend one day pulled the pin out and we were waiting for it to explode, but of course it never exploded. Boys being boys ...'.[60]

Encountering Great War veterans

101

Medals were more intrinsically informative than photographs, indicating not only that people had served, but also where, and whether they had served with particular distinction. Ted Roberts, whose father never spoke about his war service, learned about his father's service by covertly retrieving his medals from a drawer. As Roberts stated that his father never spoke about his war service it is possible the medals were the only way he learned his father had served in the Boer and Great Wars.[61] Conversely, objects had the potential to provoke questions. Phil Robinson knew that his father had served 'because of his medals' and when he was school age his interest was piqued because his father 'had a German helmet with a spike on, and erm, what was it, [mimics excited voice] "How many Germans did you kill, Dad?", he'd never tell you, never tell you'.[62] Other fathers were more forthcoming, or found themselves in situations where either the questions or the answers were deemed more appropriate. When Jim Hayes was shown his father's medals prior to an Armistice parade he was made aware of his father's pride in his service, and remembered when 'I was only a kid, [Dad] brought a German pistol out, Luger, and he was taking it to pieces and showing me and cleaning it and he said he took it off a German that got killed ...'.[63] Any answer Robinson's father had provided would have lacked such ambiguity about *who* killed the German.

Veterans' bodies could also provide a lasting record of some of their war experiences.[64] Jessica Meyer has noted that the close confines and 'wider physical intimacy' of working-class family life in inter-war Britain made hiding wounds difficult,[65] and Oliver Wilkinson uses the case of Arthur Hoyland – a Great War veteran and POW – to illustrate that fact that 'war disability could be starkly visible at home': ' "the deformed thumbs, the whip marks that stood out on his back, and the gaping hole in his arm" were all visible to family members when Hoyland stripped in front of the fire for his bath [and] carried with them the testimony of his captivity experiences to family members'.[66] Other veterans were even less able to conceal the damage the war had wrought upon their bodies from their children. Stuart Underdown's father 'would never talk about it. Erm he was badly knocked up, lost an arm, his left arm, shrapnel in his head, and back, which was there 'til his dying day'.[67] Similarly, Cyril Price recalled being very conscious of his father's disability, which resulted from his Great War service:

> Father was twice wounded, once in the leg and secondly he had a bullet through the front of his helmet that ploughed a rift in the front of his head and came out of the back and er he suffered from the effects of that for the rest of his life ....[68]

Even when wounds were no longer obvious, though, sustaining wounds seems to have been a common detail for even reticent veterans to narrate.[69] When asked if his father spoke fondly of the services, Des Radwell replied, 'Dad was wounded twice badly in the First World War, through the leg and through the mouth ... I believe he had a pretty hard war, but he never used to say too much about it at all.'[70] As Meyer suggests, 'the ex-serviceman's damaged body formed a persistent reminder of the loss of war'.[71] Unless wounds had been sustained in particularly heroic fashion they were unlikely to be perceived as a positive representation of war experience, or to be interpreted within a 'pleasure culture' framework, but they did demonstrate service and sacrifice.[72] Like objects, veterans' wounds might illustrate service and its effects, but the extent to which they provided information about an individual's experience was determined by what was said about them. Indeed, wounds could prompt more expansive narratives about the incident in which they were sustained.

Hearing from veterans

When he thought his son was old enough to understand, Frank Webster's father explained the circumstances that resulted in his missing arm. In explaining how he was wounded, he provided an insight into his experiences. Webster's father had been at Passchendaele:

> [T]hey were being shelled, me father thought 'Oh dear, there's some poor devil's legs sticking out of the ground,' and he was near that, and said that the stench wasn't very pleasant so he crawled away to get somewhere else, and then he laid on his left side, and then another shell came over and apparently a little distance away of course, the legs disappeared but of course they caught him on the right arm and the right hip, and erm, he er, he was attended to and the [Medical Officer], whoever, said that I doubt whether this chap will reach the casualty clearing station alive, because he's lost so much blood ....

Encountering Great War veterans 103

A blood transfusion 'kept him going ... and apparently his arm turned gangrenous and he was happy enough for it to be removed'.[73] Wounds might also prompt children to ask questions. Elson recalled that his father 'didn't go on about the First World War' but he 'had been shot in the arm, we used to look as children and say "Dad, what's that?", where the bone had been taken out there was kind of a big circle ...'. This prompted a detailed explanation.

> He told us he was detailed to gather in wounded and was with some stretcher bearers when he bent down and the next thing he knew his arm was slung around here and he was terrified because he thought his arm had gone and he couldn't feel anything, what happened was the bullet had entered his arm just above his left elbow and swung his arm over and it had caught on ... his braces so he's going around thinking he's lost an arm.

That the incident was ultimately presented not as horrific but as humorous, with the emphasis on his arm catching on his braces, is notable; it made the narrative more acceptable for a young audience, it increased the chances of a positive response and it could serve as a coping strategy. Elson commented that his father more often told them funny anecdotes.[74] Gordon Waterhouse's father had been a sergeant in the 'Kings Liverpool', and was wounded twice – Gordon 'could actually put [his] fist in the side of [his father's] back where he got wounded with shrapnel'.[75] Gordon heard about his service on the Western Front:

> I can remember him telling us [Gordon and a friend] stories about when they were in the trenches in France and the battle of Ypres and all that, and they'd have their fixed bayonets and they'd put, for pastime I suppose, bully beef on the end, and put it on the parapet and the rats would come and take it ... and he said he stood for weeks and weeks in water, with the puttees round their legs, and then he told us about when they got this thing to go over the top, when they went over, and he got wounded, I think it was in Delville wood, I remember him saying, and he was in hospital, but one of the chaps that carried him back, pulled him back out of the thing, he actually lived ... quite near where my father lived, and I can always remember ... when my father had a few shillings or anything, he'd give it to him and he always used to say 'Thank you very much Albert' and it was only because he had saved his life actually ....

104 *Joining up in the Second World War*

Gordon Waterhouse characterised his father as reluctant to talk about the war, yet he appears to have been a willing narrator when given an interested audience and would answer questions, even those asked by one of Gordon's friends, who 'used to love talking about the war'. His service in Ireland appears to have been his preferred topic: 'he told us stories about all that, what happened when he was there'. He discussed the IRA threat and going in civilian clothes to hear Michael Collins speak, and stumbling upon an armed bank robbery when in uniform: 'all of a sudden there's two hands touch them on their shoulders and they said "If you move you are next", he said, and they just froze and when they got up afterwards there was nobody there, so he always told us that tale. "If you move, you're next."'

Regularly hearing extended narratives about the Great War from one of its veterans was unusual. The oral histories make clear, however, that, even without wounds or wartime objects as prompts, many young men did occasionally hear fragments of wartime narratives from usually reticent veterans. These were varied in terms of content and emotional effect. Thirteen of my thirty-four interviewees with veteran fathers heard deliberate, but normally singular or irregular, reflections about their fathers' experiences. Some heard tales from more than one veteran. George Stagg heard tales from two uncles, his neighbours and a colleague.[76] Wilf Curtis, who also heard from multiple veterans as he was growing up, said, 'The only thing that I knew about [the Great War] was stories that people who had served in the war had told us about it.' Curtis's father had 'quite a soft job', driving 'the Colonel around ... he was very, very lucky, so he never went to France, so he told me about his trips in the staff cars and things like that, but he didn't speak *a lot* about the war'. Aged around 11, Wilf heard from a friend's father about France: 'he never told us much about the actual fighting, talking more about how they had to struggle to live ... in trenches'. Wilf 'just listened to the tales he was telling us, I was too young to ask any sensible questions'.[77] Others also received an insight into trench living conditions. As a child, Stagg's veteran neighbours spoke about 'what they had to go through, their rations and things, and how they used to eat with the cats and shaving in the morning if they were lucky, and things like that, in the trench and when it rained'.[78] Jack Pragnell, camping on the village green as a child, received a

Encountering Great War veterans   105

similar brief insight into trench life when he saw a stranger drinking from a water tank: 'there was a slug in the water, and we said "Ergh, look at that!" and he said "Ah, that's nothing compared to what we drank in the trenches"'.[79] That such details were shared with youngsters suggests that they were perceived as appropriate narratives for children to hear: devoid of the violence of war, they were perceived as unlikely to upset children (or their parents), perhaps because trench conditions were frequently depicted in popular culture.[80] Nevertheless, such tales, and the response to Holloway's complaints of hunger, could fulfil a didactic function. Veterans illustrated a model of stoic masculinity by emphasising to young men how much harder life could be and how much softer they were than the previous generation, while legitimising their veteran status by highlighting their trench experience.

Others heard more detailed narratives of events on the frontline. Frank Webster heard a 'frightening' story from a neighbour-cum-family friend about an instance when 'a colleague got shot in the head or something and I think he went to bandage him and all his brains came out somehow'.[81] Brian Spragg heard 'bits and pieces' about his father's service, including

> how terrible it was at Passchendaele ... he said whole wagons, some horses would disappear in the mud and flood ... and he did tell me that he was stuck for two days in a shell hole in no man's land wounded before he was brought out, but he never went on to sort of explain things to me a great deal probably until after the Second World War.[82]

Tom Knowlton heard a similar story as his veteran colleagues discussed their service. Although they rarely talked about combat, one spoke about being 'in the fighting area somewhere ... looked for a hole to get into and saw a crater, jumped in, and there were two dead Germans there you see, I remember him telling me that'.[83] George Cash's father 'never really spoke much at all' about the Great War, but 'occasionally my dad would reminisce'. He once told Cash and his brother about being a courier, and having 'to find his way in the dark and so on and so forth', and about guiding an officer:

> [A]s they went along the route Dad said that some of the landmarks had been blown away with shells and so on and he came to a point

106   *Joining up in the Second World War*

> where he just didn't know where to go and this young officer lost his temper with him and brandished his revolver and said 'If you don't take me, I will shoot you', you know, well fortunately my dad managed to find a reasonable landmark which he made for and then he got this man where he wanted to go but he used to make a joke of it and say that was the nearest he came to anything happening to him sort of thing but none of my uncles sat down and talked about the war as such and my dad never did, it was just, with my brother and I, just an occasional thing and we didn't pump him [because we were not that interested or knowledgeable].[84]

Hay heard mention of similar issues in 'some horrific tales' about his future father-in-law's time as a runner in the Post Office Rifles, and learned he had been wounded twice, once being shot through both arms. These 'horrific' tales were, however, mixed with some more positive tales about his time in Syria in charge of some horses and Indian drivers.[85]

It seems that more graphic recollections of front-line experience were more often heard by young adults, while children heard about trench conditions. Graphic representations may have simply been considered inappropriate for children, but age also influenced the intergenerational dynamic. While childhood was associated with innocence and play, as sons approached working age their fathers commonly sought to prepare them for the wider world and teach them about manliness,[86] and treated them more like 'pals'.[87] Either of these shifts may have enabled or prompted more revealing narrations. What both groups of narratives communicated about the experience of war or masculinity was, however, potentially equivocal. From such descriptions, trench conditions could be imagined as unbearable, or a test of stoicism and grit. Stories of life or death runs through featureless trench networks, or taking cover from artillery fire in shell craters could sit comfortably within juvenile adventure fiction, but would not be out of place in *All Quiet on the Western Front*.[88]

Some narratives were more clearly disillusioned. Thomas Leask's father served in the Dardanelles, where his battalion took heavy casualties. He spoke little of his experiences but when he did he angrily expressed his disdain for senior commanders and the

> dreadful waste of life, I remember him telling me quite clearly when they first got to Gallipoli they could actually walk ashore and they

Encountering Great War veterans

could have taken the whole peninsula, but ... they had to wait until the powers that be were ready to invade and by that time of course the Turks backed by the Germans were ready for them, and so it was a disaster ....[89]

Peter Woodard also received a striking negative impression of service at Gallipoli, and its after-effects, from his father, who had been a radio operator in a Signals unit. He 'didn't talk about it, never did talk about it', but traumatic memories meant he provided an involuntary narrative; he would 'have a bender now and again and he used to live Gallipoli all over again'. One evening Peter and his brother were trying to get their father home from a club 'and he was bobbing up and down behind hedges and swearing like hell about the Turks [...] He was reliving it all again, but he couldn't tell us what he was reliving or anything like that, he was just there.'[90] Edward Kirby's father came close to the stereotypical disillusioned veteran. He suffered from neurasthenia, 'wanted to get back into normal civilian life' and was 'rather scornful' of Edward's veteran uncle who wore his medals and attended veterans' events. Kirby said he 'never never spoke about the war, I only remember one thing he told me':

> [S]o the trenches they were in, they were in them for a long time, and the dead were left there for a long time, and he remembered, this is the one thing that he spoke about to do with the horror, he never spoke about the horrors of the war, but there was a corpse, a man, with his head [hanging] over the parapet with his mouth open, and he watched this corpse turn into a skeleton, they were long enough for this body to decompose but nobody moved it and he had to walk past it every day and er he came back, that couldn't have been the only corpse he saw, but it was the awful position, the mouth open and the teeth showing, er ....[91]

Kirby was not alone in understanding his father had not enjoyed his wartime service. Pragnell's father had been a regular in the Royal Engineers and, while he passed on the Morse code and French he had learned, Pragnell understood that he 'detested war, he'd see the bad side of it'. He 'didn't tell us a lot about the trenches or about the war but he'd tell us more when we got him talking now and again, more about the Boer War and when he was in India in the cavalry which was a much nicer thing'.[92]

108   *Joining up in the Second World War*

While some veterans clearly did express disillusion, it seems to have been more common to avoid some topics or to opt to talk about the 'much nicer thing'. Pragnell, and Phil Robinson – whose father 'would never tell' how many Germans he killed – were not alone in their awareness of silences and selectivity in what veterans would recount. Silences could themselves cause interest;[93] Thomas Chilton's father passed on tales about Thomas's uncle's time in the Navy, but 'the tales he would *not* tell me about was when he was in the trenches, he would not speak about it, he used to say "It was tough son" but ... across the bridge of his nose he had ... a piece of shrapnel [that] he carried ... until he died'.[94] Although his response, 'It was tough son', served to refuse an extended narrative, in combination with the shrapnel, Chilton took away the impression that his father's trench experience had been unpleasant. Chilton's questions were repeatedly rebuffed, but with war looming in 1938 Chilton 'could finally get him to talk sometimes, not about what he went through, but about what happened in the First World War, why they went to war and all this sort of business'. Chilton's father was happiest to talk about the Great War indirectly. George Stagg experienced a different kind of selectivity. When he was 18 years old Stagg worked on a delivery lorry with Bill Palmer. Stagg learned Palmer was a 'First World War hero' who won the Military Medal while driving for the Army Service Corps, and Stagg heard a detailed narrative about this incident and other elements of his service, but Palmer refused to discuss more unpleasant memories. Stagg recalled:

> he used to tell me about the runs he used to make, from different regiments, 'cause he was driving a solid wheel truck, what used to carry ammo and food and everything, ... and he was going from one place to another and [came] under heavy machine gun fire, very heavy, in fact Bill had a finger and he could waggle it about, [the bone was detached] and what had happened was that he had to go to this other area or this headquarters and he said he went through this lane down there and he came under heavy machine gun fire and a bullet hit the column of the steering wheel, and bounced and hit his hand and it was pouring with blood and he still ... drove on and he won the MM for that, he showed me that medal ....

Encountering Great War veterans

JM And did you ever ask Bill questions about the First World War to try and find out more, were you interested in knowing more?

GS Well yeah, whenever he was, but I sorta considered his feelings at times just in case he didn't want to talk about it.

JM Right. So were there times when you wanted to ask something more?

GS Well I asked him and you know he'd say oh you don't want to know nothing about that.

JM Do you remember what kind of things he'd say that to?

GS Well, different times I asked him about if he'd carried any wounded fellas about like, and he says well you don't wanna know nothing about that, 'cause I think he used to not only carry ammo and stuff like that, he used to use it as ambulance as well if it was required ...

Establishing why veterans avoided discussing unpleasant aspects of service is difficult; self-protection from traumatic memories, maintaining a stoic appearance or a sense that such narrations were unsuitable for adolescent audiences, could all have played a part. It is also plausible that, perhaps in an attempt to achieve composure, men's difficult experiences were related with the emphasis placed upon the 'silver lining'; George Cash heard that his father-in-law had been gassed, but 'he used to climb over the [hospital] wall and go and meet Emily who he eventually married [so] even that was something romantic that had happened'.[95] Ironically, however, this selectivity may have reinforced the cultural tendency that continued to construct military service in positive terms. Certainly, what Palmer was happy to share with Stagg could be told in heroic, exciting, adventurous tones, particularly given the award of the Military Medal, and would not have been out of place in a *Boy's Own* story.

As Gary Sheffield suggested, positive or rewarding aspects of military service appear to have been shared more commonly than negative ones. Some young men heard about the novelty of veterans' experiences. James Mann's father mainly spoke about France as a country, promising to take him to visit, Richard Griffiths heard about his father's experiences learning to fly, and John

110   *Joining up in the Second World War*

Riggs's uncle recounted the famous artists he served with in the Artists' Rifles.[96] A number of young men heard tales that they took to communicate their fathers' pride; notably, this was not limited to men who had served in combatant roles. Mr Sweetland's father 'used to tell us he was one of the Royal Engineers who probably laid the French railway lines as they were more or less up to the present day'.[97] William Coster heard a detailed account of the places his father had served and how he had received 'a smashed finger', and knew he 'was always very proud of being a sergeant in the RASC [Royal Army Service Corps]'.[98] Richard Todd heard a detailed narrative of his father's service in a medical role; he had 'a fairly active and good, if you can use the word good, erm, certainly active First World War, got a good Military Cross ... because of him I think my thinking as a boy was pretty militaristic'.[99] Others heard apparently exciting tales. As a child William Jalland's father 'used to tell me about being at Shoeburyness [in the Royal Artillery] and the shooting down of a Zeppelin at Potter's Bar and er, I suppose that was the reason that I started getting interested'.[100] Jack Thomas had heard a heroic version of his father's experiences, which certainly were unusual. Thomas understood his father to be one of only two private soldiers to escape from a prisoner-of-war camp in Germany. He was subsequently posted to the Intelligence Corps, where he won a medal for his involvement in the arrest of two German spies. Perhaps unsurprisingly, Thomas recalled that as children he and his friends perceived war as 'adventure more than anything else'.[101] Watson has argued that the adventurous soldier was a valid identity at the time,[102] and, as was discussed in Chapter 1, depictions of war as adventure persisted in inter-war popular culture. That young men interpreted veterans' narratives as such is clear in a number of the descriptions of narrative transmission above. Jim Hayes's veteran father was unusual in that he was known to like talking about the war.[103] When Jim asked about the war his sister would object – ' "Don't start him off again!" ' – but Hayes was 'all ears ... give me the worst ...'. He heard 'a lot about the trenches', about his father's hatred of trench rats and about 'snipers getting a couple of his pals and dropping down in the trenches, they had to think what to do for them and all that'. Hayes's father also told him about an occasion when his unit had to retreat hastily:

Encountering Great War veterans

[F]or four days and four nights they galloped and galloped and galloped, stopped for a drop of water and all that but the Germans was 20 minutes behind them all the time and I thought what a nerve test and that was, and I didn't like that much but other than that I was all for going in the war if there was a war, you know, it wasn't frightening to me.[104]

Hayes's tone suggests that he placed his father's narratives within a 'war as adventure' framework as a youth, and despite his unease and recognition that war could be a test of nerve, he was not deterred from envisaging his own service. Pride and enjoyment appear to have dominated in the understandings of others who heard more ambivalent narratives of veteran's service. George Iceton's father was a driver for the engineers,

he used to have to get the stuff up to the back trenches and they were manhandled through the trenches to the front line, and so I had had a fairly vivid account of the war from my father, and also from a lot of his comrades because erm, with having a farm my mother and father seldom took holidays together so I went with my father ... to visit his old war comrades, so yes I had heard this discussed, and again, for all they did mention some bad times of the war, most of their memories were happy, erm joyful, erm, I don't think I was let into all of their secrets but er, as a young boy, big ears, I heard quite a lot.[105]

Mr Parkhouse knew his father had become an officer in the RASC, before volunteering for the Royal Flying Corps. Although Parkhouse knew that he had been 'badly shot up on three occasions' and ultimately returned to the infantry diagnosed temperamentally unfit to fly, Parkhouse understood his father was proud of having flown artillery observation sorties during 1918, and 'very proud of the fact he was a member of Kitchener's Army'.[106] Similarly, Elson, whose father had narrated his being wounded with black humour, would 'occasionally talk about a buddy lost', but Elson understood his father was 'very proud of his old regiment', and he had more commonly told his children humorous anecdotes. Ultimately, Elson felt that the Great War 'was romanticized in young men's minds ...'.[107]

Pride, although not romance, could even be taken from objectively horrific narratives. Ron Womack's father became a POW in France after German forces overran his trench. He did not volunteer information about this experience, but when Ron was aged about 10 he asked his father, who provided frightening accounts

112 *Joining up in the Second World War*

of the abuse and starvation he had suffered at the hands of the 'Prussians' while being used as forced labour in railway marshalling yards, and about a friendship he developed with an 'Anglo-Saxon German' who had worked in England prior to the war, who would sneak him food. Ron understood that his father's experiences were frightening and horrific – they were difficult to interpret another way – and he later discouraged Ron from joining military youth organisations. When asked whether hearing about this had given 'any particular impression or feeling about the First World War as a youngster', Ron responded, 'I think like most children of my age we were proud of our fathers having fought in the war, fought against the Germans ....'[108]

As these examples illustrate, despite the selectivity that some veterans exercised, many young men heard representations that revealed that military participation could be dangerous, challenging, unpleasant, even horrific, but this did not invalidate expressions of duty and pride in service. If anything, the understanding that veterans had endured it in spite of this amplified the pride they felt. Narratives could be presented within the frame of adventure or rewarding endeavour, and young men could also interpret them as such, but challenge and sacrifice could be accommodated within, and even bolster, conceptions of military service as a test of masculinity or adventure. Veterans' narratives were not necessarily understood in cultural isolation, and the presence of representations of war as adventure, rewarding endeavour or redemptive sacrifice might well have encouraged such interpretations.

Hearing about veterans

In August 1918, as he lay mortally wounded on a battlefield in France, a British serviceman wrote to his wife:

> With my last strength God bless you and the kiddies. I am glad to give my life for my country. Don't grieve over me – be proud of this fact. Goodbye and God bless you. Fred.
>
> When the kiddies get older, tell them how I died.[109]

Fred was just one of the 145,000 British men who left a widow, and his children were just some of the 360,000 who lost fathers.[110]

Encountering Great War veterans 113

Fred's wife never received his instructions about how to remember his death, and we cannot know what she told the children. For those who had lost loved ones, the meanings attached to the Great War could be conflicting; a worthwhile heroic sacrifice for King and country – the dominant construction in wartime rhetoric and commemoration – contrasted with the wasteful, destructive event of an individual death, which often also caused long-term financial hardship for families. Scholarship about British war widows has typically focused upon how they coped post-war, particularly their battles for (albeit inadequate) pensions or their decisions to remarry.[111] Less is known about how widowed mothers presented the Great War and their husbands' wartime deaths.[112] Richard van Emden's interviews with children who lost fathers confirm that children experienced both the positions described above.[113] Violet Baker remembered her mother was, and remained, 'so angry' about Violet's father's death; she was 'disgusted' by the Death Penny, insulted that the State would give '[t]hat for a husband', and called the pension she received 'blood money'.[114] Violet's mother tried to avoid being reminded of her husband, and Violet never saw his medals.[115] Conversely, Donald Overall's mother told her children about their father's character and hobbies, and took them to the Cenotaph on 11 November 1920. Donald, then aged 8, felt 'dumbfounded' during the service and felt most for his crying mother.[116] His mother continued to demonstrate her pride in his father's service by adorning her dresses with buttons from his regiment,[117] and she told Donald details about his service that emphasised his loyalty and duty:

> She told me about the snipers and how they went over the top and how scared they were and how, when his mates were killed, he had to carry on. That's why he wouldn't take Corporal's stripes on his arm because he didn't want to be separated from his mates, what were left of them. I was really proud of my dad and I always wished I could be like him.[118]

My own interviewees were mostly born too late to have lost their fathers during the Great War, but the testimonies of George Dann and George Stagg provide insight into how information about a deceased father's service might be passed on. Dann was born in 1921, but his father died in 1922 as a result of being gassed during the war. When Dann was about 5 years old his mother took him to the local Armistice ceremony, showed him his father's name on

114   *Joining up in the Second World War*

the war memorial and explained what had happened. They continued to go the ceremonies, where Dann recalled he saw veterans marching with their medals and 'used to think, cor, you were in the war and nothing happened to you ...'. He thought that as a youngster he had respect for them because they had helped to win the war. George had seen a photograph of his father in uniform, and a small, flat soldier's tobacco tin that had belonged to him, and in his late teens, Dann received his father's Military Medal from his mother. Perhaps surprisingly, she did not tell him the circumstances in which he won it, but she told him 'more or less what they had to put up with and we obviously won [the war] but I only really knew that he was in the trenches and that's how they did things, apart from what you read in other things ...'.[119] George Stagg's mother lost her first husband in the Great War. Although George was not his son, George's mother involved Stagg in his commemoration, as we heard in Chapter 1. In addition, a photograph of him in uniform was displayed in their home and Stagg saw 'the medallion for the wounded and all his medals'. As Stagg grew up, his mother told him about his death and showed him a letter a Canadian nurse at a clearing station had written, which detailed his wound and death. Stagg's mother did not discuss her own views of the war with him, but he was conscious that the loss of her first husband contributed to her anxiety when it was clear her three sons might serve in the Second World War. Sadly, her worry was not misplaced. During the Second World War she lost her second husband, a railwayman, in the bombing of Bishopsgate, and her eldest son was killed in the Navy. Four of the archival interviewees' fathers were killed in the Great War. Their testimonies reveal little about what they had learned about their fathers' service, but they do show sons were not necessarily deterred from the military; two enlisted between the wars in the same service arm as their fathers.[120] They perhaps, like Donald Overall, 'wished [they] could be like him'.[121]

Hearing from veterans in the Home Guard

As is evident in a number of the instances described above, veterans' narratives could result from a number of prompts: objects, wounds, or particular contexts such as Armistice Day or the approach of the Second World War. The Civil Defence organisations that were formed as a result of the Second World War provided another context in which young and old were brought together to participate in the defence of Britain. '[M]illions of greying veterans ... offered themselves for service ... in bodies such as the Home Guard and the Air Raid Precautions.'[122] Similarly, many young men joined the Home Guard, whose local branches routinely ignored the theoretical minimum age threshold,[123] before enlisting for full-time military service. All those interviewees who had joined the Home Guard remembered it as a site where they encountered Great War veterans.[124] Ken Hay joined the Home Guard aged just 15 in 1940. He remembered 'it was all the old sweats ... when you went on parade there were blokes who limped by from war wounds of the First World War' as well as one or two younger men in reserved occupations.[125] The 'ex-serviceman' identity could bring recognition within the Home Guard, and the leaders of units were often veterans.[126] The veterans in Norman Bowdler's Home Guard battalion 'were considered senior figures 'cause they'd done a bit'.[127] Likewise, the NCOs in James Donovan's unit were mostly veterans. Donovan recalled that 'they would try and pass on a bit of their expertise as best they could' and 'some of them were really good' because 'they'd been through it so they knew what it was all about'.[128] Such respect was typical,[129] but it was not guaranteed; Charles Seibert recalled that when a rifle was accidentally fired 'most of the older men seemed to be trying to clamber up the walls of the hut in the corners [laughs]'.[130] As well as being an environment in which young men and veterans interacted, Todman has suggested that the Home Guard also encouraged ex-servicemen to reminisce.[131] George Nicholson, who had joined the Home Guard aged 17 in 1941, once found his father and other Home Guard members, most of whom were ex-servicemen, in the pub singing First World War songs.[132] Reminiscence also occurred in Civil Defence units; Jessica Hammett reports that one air raid warden reflected that the words ' "In the last war" ... have begun countless reminiscences with which Civil Defence workers have wiled away the watches of the night'.[133] Yet, interviewees rarely recalled being deliberately involved in or overhearing veterans' reminiscences in the Home Guard.

In some cases limited interaction between members of different ages curtailed the opportunities for the dissemination of narratives.

116   *Joining up in the Second World War*

Fred Pond found that members tended to talk with those of their own age, explaining that the difference in age was significant enough that the others were 'old to us',[134] and spatial separation cemented this division: the veteran members of the unit ensured they got some sleep by delegating their guard duties to the enthusiastic young members who were – although technically messenger boys – only too happy to relieve them of the rifle and head out into the night. In Reg Day's experience it was the veterans who undertook duties while he was confined to headquarters. He too felt distant from them because 'they were old men to me', though he admired them because 'they'd been and done it'.[135]

Even some of those who spent time around the veteran members of their companies did not hear anything about the Great War.[136] Derrick Thurgood, who joined in 1942, also aged 15, knew that many of the members of his Home Guard were veterans, but they did not discuss the Great War in front of him. It was only 'by accident' that he had heard that one of his superiors had won an MC in the Great War.[137] Bob Woodhams remembered that all of those in charge in his company were veterans, and they would talk amongst themselves about 'their experiences'; 'they used to have a chat now and again, of how they was lucky to come through like different battles they'd been in', and sometimes Woodhams 'might get the tail end of the conversation but you wouldn't know what they was talking about' and he would not be included in such conversations.[138] His experience supports Todman's suggestion that the Home Guard encouraged reminiscence primarily between veterans, rather than across generations. None of the interviewees recalled veterans volunteering narratives while conducting Home Guard duties, nor had they asked veterans questions about their service. That veterans appear to have traded stories with other veterans or drawn upon common memories, rather than discussing experiences with younger men, in some ways mirrors the dynamic of Old Comrades Associations.[139] While veterans might have perceived their Great War role as sufficiently different to that in the Home Guard that they did not see the relevance of sharing their experiences, it is nevertheless surprising that narratives of the Great War were not volunteered or requested in such a fitting setting, and where veteran status was valued. While it seems that young men typically respected veterans and perceived their Great War

Encountering Great War veterans   117

experience as having some relevance to and utility in the context of Second World War Civil Defence, this finding also supports the broader argument that veterans were typically reticent about telling war stories to the younger generation, and highlights the importance of representations within the family.

Conclusion

When discussing what they had heard from veterans, interviewees' often characterised them as reticent and began discussion with phrases like 'he never said much'. This phrase, however, belied a striking variety of experiences; discussion often revealed that the interviewee actually had heard about wartime experience, and sometimes extensive or significant narratives. Phillip Foster's case is an illustrative example. Foster knew his father had been responsible for clearing up RAMC field operating theatres, but felt 'I never really got very much, he'd tell the odd story but he never said very much.'[140] Despite this assertion, 'one of his stories' – phrasing which implies that his father told, and retold, stories – detailed clearing up after an amputation:

> ... this fella had supposedly died and had been taken into the mortuary and my father came across this leg, he said, and thought 'Well I'd better put that with this chap' so he tucked this leg under his arm and went down to the mortuary tent and ... suddenly the fella sat up and said 'Can I have a drink of water' [...] He says 'I shot out of that tent and then I came to my senses and went back in and organized him being taken out of there, so I don't really know what happened to him but if ever a bloke deserved to survive then he did', but only very small, he didn't talk about it much, but he must have had a hundred of equivalent sort of experiences.

Foster's insistence that his father 'never said very much' is perhaps partly explained by the fact that his father, like many other veterans, exhibited reticence and only spoke about the war occasionally, but it hints at something else, too: Foster believed there were stories that his father left untold. Nevertheless, as this chapter has shown, young men in inter-war Britain learned about Great War experiences from veterans in their day-to-day lives more frequently than has been previously acknowledged. This was not always transmitted directly or deliberately: objects in the home, innocuous passing comments and veterans' bodies could all provide clues to veteran status and experience. Although most veterans appear to have been reticent, a significant proportion of young men heard occasional, detailed recollections of aspects of their service. Most were not regularly regaled with war stories; more often their knowledge was gleaned from singular or irregular insights. What triggered these narratives is not always clear but was certainly varied: sometimes they were solicited by young men's questions; sometimes something war-related, such as wounds or wartime objects, triggered narratives (or young men's questions); and sometimes triggers were indirect, such as discussion of parents' work, travel or relationships, or young men's complaints about comparatively trivial matters.

Like representations of the Great War in inter-war popular culture, veterans' narratives were heterogeneous. Veterans expressed not only a wide variety of attitudes, but also of *experiences*. Trenches, shell holes and being wounded – culturally available images of the Great War – were components of many narratives, but some spoke about more banal activities absent from representations in popular culture. Moreover, and contrary to Todman's suggestion based on a desire to provoke thought rather than on primary research, some men who had served as drivers, engineers, in medical facilities or in Britain were not silenced by their own inability to tell 'war stories' that related to combat or the increasing dominance of the trench soldier in popular understandings of the war. If anything, it seems that activities away from front-line trenches were more commonly discussed. The fact that no one version of the conflict dominated between the wars may have made young men more receptive to varied stories: they too were not necessarily bound by a single version of what wartime experience should mean. This open-mindedness may have enabled non-combatant veterans to be more communicative, and narrating experiences that diverged from more popular understandings might have been easier within a family environment.[141] As Meyer observed in relation to wartime letters and post-war memoirs, though, families were not an appropriate audience for narratives of killing or committing violence.[142] While the scarcity of such narratives no doubt partially reflects the fact that many veterans did not have direct engagement with enemy troops, this silence perhaps speaks to the incommunicability

Encountering Great War veterans 119

of violence and the difficulty of comfortably accommodating tales of such violence within the domestic sphere. Although horrific or traumatic incidents were certainly recounted, it seems young men more often heard about camaraderie or humorous incidents, or narratives that illustrated stoicism or heroism. The selectivity veterans exercised tended to deny young men access to more negative narratives, and equivocal narratives outnumbered the clearly disillusioned. When exposed to such representations, young men seem to have taken away affirmative rather than disillusioned elements, such as pride in service, as has been suggested in relation to ambivalent Great War literature. These findings sit comfortably alongside Todman's suggestion that when veterans were together they were keen to recollect positive elements of their war experience,[143] with Isherwood's observation that veterans' memoirs presented the war as meaningful and emphasised comradeship,[144] and with Paris's suggestion that veterans selecting literature for children chose 'a heroic and justified representation of the war'.[145] They also add substantial support and depth to Sheffield's suggestion that it was the rewarding elements of Great War service that were passed on to young men.[146]

What young men heard from veterans encouraged an understanding of war as a duty to accept, a challenge to overcome or even an adventure to be had, more often than as a futile endeavour to denounce. Those who heard about challenging aspects of the war, such as being wounded or falling into shell holes, or about veterans who had died, may have better understood the potential for war to be horrific, but that understanding served to amplify rather than lessen the stoicism and bravery of the veterans they had heard from or about. Veterans' narratives were also uniquely positioned to shape young men's understandings of war and masculinity, coming from older men, and often those who younger men respected, sought to emulate and from whom they might expect to learn about manliness. While this may not have been intended by the narrator or perceived by the audience, veterans' narratives of the Great War affirmed particular masculine traits. Stoicism, even in the face of fear or injury, and pride in service, duty and camaraderie were all common themes, and sacrifice and gallant heroism were present too. Veterans' narratives typically offered little that would decouple war and masculinity. Instead, war remained a theatre in which young

120 *Joining up in the Second World War*

men could perform masculinity, as the previous generation had. In this respect what young men most commonly heard from veterans was similar in tone to the representations in popular culture through which young men might otherwise 'know' about the Great War. Reg Day even remarked that what he had heard from his veteran grandfather about his service in Mesopotamia 'was all unbelievable, it was the things you read in *Hotspur*'.[147] Yet, the unmediated, and often familial, nature of veterans' narratives may have given them greater significance. They were fleeting and ephemeral representations but were nonetheless significant. Although previously subjected to limited examination, they are an important component of the cultural memory of the Great War because, as we shall see, they sometimes shaped the attitudes and decisions of young men when they faced the prospect of service in the Second World War.

Notes

1 Ron Holloway (Morley, 2016).
2 Todman, *Myth and Memory*, p. 8.
3 Sheffield, 'Shadow of the Somme', p. 31.
4 47 of these 54 made reference to their fathers being veterans, and many knew other veterans as well. Only 7 of those who referenced veterans did not state that their father was a veteran.
5 Jessica Meyer, 'Wounded in a Mentionable Place: The (In)visibility of the Disabled Ex-serviceman in Inter-war Britain', in *Veterans of the First World War: Ex-Servicemen and Ex-Servicewomen in Post-War Britain and Ireland*, ed. by Oliver Wilkinson and David Swift (Abingdon: Routledge, 2019) Ebook. For discussion of efforts to rehabilitate wounded veterans, see Julie Anderson, *War, Disability and Rehabilitation in Britain. Soul of a Nation* (Manchester: Manchester University Press, 2011), chapter 2, 'Attitude: Disabled Ex-servicemen after the First World War'.
6 Stagg (Morley, 2010). See also Charles Seibert, IWM-SA-18485, 1998. On the challenges faced by disabled veterans in Britain, see Cohen, *War Come Home*.
7 Pragnell (Morley, 2010); Bevin Boy Harry Parkes (Morley, 2016).
8 Florence (Morley, 2010); Frank Rose (Morley, 2016).
9 Gwyn Grogan, IWM-SA-2236, 2002.
10 George Elliot, IWM-SA-10602, 1993; Joseph Drake, IWM-SA-20791, 2000; Brian Folkes (Morley, 2016).

Encountering Great War veterans   121

11 John Riggs, IWM-SA-22346, 2001.
12 Roper also found that silence about the Great War stood out to many interviewees; Roper, *Afterlives of War*, pp. 65–70, 142.
13 Len Pettet (Morley, 2016). Oliver Wilkinson argues that 'a desire to forget was clear amongst some veterans, including ex-POWs'; Oliver Wilkinson, 'Ex-Prisoners of War, 1914–1918. Veteran Association, Assimilation and Disassociation after the First World War', in *Veterans of the First World War*, ed. by Wilkinson and Swift.
14 On trauma and silence, see Jay Winter, 'Shell Shock, Gallipoli and the Generation of Silence', in *Beyond Memory: Silence and the Aesthetics of Remembrance*, ed. by Alexandre Dessingue and Jay Winter (Abingdon: Routledge, 2016) pp. 195–208.
15 Todman, *Myth and Memory*, pp. 9–10.
16 Michael Roper, 'Maternal Relations: Moral Manliness and Emotional Survival in Letters Home During the First World War', in *Masculinities in Politics and War: Gendering Modern History*, ed. by S. Dudink, K. Hagemann and J. Tosh (Manchester: Manchester University Press, 2004) pp. 295–316; and Roper, *Afterlives of War*, p. 142.
17 Todman, *Myth and Memory*, p. 10. See also Penny Summerfield, 'The Generation of Memory. Gender and the Popular Memory of the Second World War in Britain', in *British Cultural Memory and the Second World War*, ed. by Lucy Noakes and Juliette Pattinson (London: Bloomsbury, 2014) pp. 25–45 (p. 31).
18 Wilkinson, 'Ex-Prisoners of War'.
19 Pond (Morley, 2011).
20 Maurice Marriot (Morley, 2010); Samuel Pearson (Morley, 2010).
21 Howard (Morley, 2011); Roberts (Morley, 2010); Thurgood (Morley, 2010); Wyke (Morley, 2010).
22 Dan Todman, ' "Sans Peur et Sans Reproche": The Retirement, Death and Mourning of Sir Douglas Haig, 1918–1928', *The Journal of Military History*, 68.4 (2003) pp. 1083–1106 (p. 1105).
23 Dennis Hagger (Morley, 2015).
24 Gordon Waterhouse (Morley, 2016). See also Ronald Womack (Morley, 2016).
25 One exception was Thomas Chilton, who appears to have pestered his father for information: Chilton, IWM-SA-27345, 2005.
26 Pond (2011).
27 Hay (Morley, 2010); Thurgood (Morley, 2010).
28 Roper, *The Secret Battle*, pp. 293–4. Tim Fisher shows serving soldiers were interested in their children's day-to-day lives during the First World War; 'Fatherhood and the Experience of Working-Class Fathers in Britain, 1900–1939' (Unpublished PhD Thesis, Edinburgh

122   *Joining up in the Second World War*

University, 2004) p. 166. On friendly fathers, Laura King, *Family Men: Fatherhood and Masculinity in Britain 1914–1960* (Oxford: Oxford University Press, 2015) pp. 116–18.

29 Fisher, *Fatherhood*, pp. 194, 215–16; King, *Family*, pp. 103–4, 125.

30 Hay (Morley, 2010).

31 MO DR2349, February 1940 Directive.

32 Elson (Morley, 2010).

33 Walder (Morley, 2010).

34 Abbott (Morley, 2010).

35 'Daddy, What Did YOU Do in the Great War?', Saville Lumley for the Parliamentary Recruiting Committee, 1915. IWM PST0311.

36 William Coster, IWM-SA-28723, 2006.

37 Brand, IWM-SA-27347.

38 Harry Gould (Morley, 2016); Denys Owen (Morley, 2016). Neither had learned more about their relatives' service. That Great War-related baby names were a wider phenomenon is illustrated by Jessamy Carlson: 'Battle Babies', 18 February 2016, https://blog.natio nalarchives.gov.uk/battle-babies/

39 Howard (Morley, 2011); see also Pearson (Morley, 2010).

40 Hay (Morley, 2010).

41 Webster (Morley, 2010).

42 Gordon Mellor (Morley, 2010). Bob Atkinson mentions hearing his father talk to different folk about it; IWM-SA-18738, 1999.

43 Brian Spragg (Morley, 2010).

44 Ruth Armstrong, in Richard van Emden and Stephen Humphreys, *All Quiet on the Home Front: An Oral History of Life in Britain during the First World War* (Chatham: Headline Book Publishing, 2004) p. 305.

45 Hayes's home had a photograph of his father in uniform on display. Hayes (Morley, 2010). Roberts recalled seeing a small number of photographs of his father in uniform, and Stagg recalled a photograph of his mother's first husband in uniform hung in their home. Roberts (Morley, 2010); Stagg (Morley, 2010).

46 Samuel Pearson (Morley, 2011).

47 Marriot (Morley, 2010).

48 Webster (Morley, 2010).

49 Wyke (Morley, 2010).

50 Stagg (Morley, 2010).

51 Meades (Morley, 2010).

52 Alex Mayhew, ' "A War Imagined": Postcards and the Maintenance of Long-Distance Relationships during the Great War', *War in History*, 28.2 (2019) pp. 1–31 (p. 18). See also P. Tomczyszyn, 'A Material Link between War and Peace: First World War Silk Postcards', in

Matters of Conflict: Material Culture, Memory and the First World War, ed. by N. J. Saunders (Abingdon: Routledge, 2004).

53 This practice mirrors that of bereaved families in inter-war Australia identified by Tanja Luckins in her research about the National Memorial in Canberra's appeal in the 1930s for letters of Australian War Dead, and recollections noted by Michael Roper: Tanja Luckins, 'Collecting Women's Memories: The Australian War Memorial, the Next of Kin and Great War Soldiers Diaries and Letters as Objects of Memory in the 1920s and 1930s', *Women's History Review*, 19.1 (2010) pp. 21–37; Roper, *Afterlives of War*, pp. 78–82. On families donating Great War objects, including letters and diaries, to museums, see Ann-Marie Foster, ' "We Decided the Museum Would Be the Best Place for Them": Veterans, Families and Mementos of the First World War', *History and Memory*, 31.1 (2019) pp. 87–117.

54 Brand, IWM-SA-27347.

55 Paul Cornish, ' "Just a boyish habit" British and Commonwealth War Trophies in the First World War', in *Contested Objects. Material Memories of the Great War*, ed. by Nicholas J. Saunders and Paul Cornish (Abingdon: Routledge, 2009) pp. 16–25.

56 Paul Cornish, ' "Just a boyish habit" ', p. 24; Nicholas J. Saunders, *Trench Art. Materialities and Memories of War* (Oxford: Berg, 2003) pp. 153–4.

57 Nicholas J. Saunders, *Killing Time. Archaeology and the First World War* (Stroud: The History Press, 2010) pp. 61–2.

58 Nicholas J. Saunders, 'Apprehending Memory: Material Culture and War, 1919–1939', in *The Great World War, 1914–1945*, ed. by John Bourne, Peter Liddle and Ian Whitehead, vol. 2 (London: Harper Collins, 2001) pp. 476–88 (p. 480).

59 Thurgood (2010).

60 Wilf Curtis (Morley, 2010).

61 Roberts (2010). Stagg saw a medallion for the wounded; Stagg (2010).

62 Philip Robinson (Morley, 2016).

63 Hayes (2010). On objects as triggers to narratives within oral histories, see Donald Ritchie, *Doing Oral History: A Practical Guide* (Oxford: Oxford University Press, 2003) p. 99, and Elizabeth Tonkin, *Narrating Our Pasts: The Social Constructive of Oral History* (Cambridge: Cambridge University Press, 1995) pp. 94–5.

64 Michael Roper has explored the effects of being the child of a disabled veteran, but does not discuss whether children heard about how wounds were sustained, in 'Subjectivities in the Aftermath: Children of Disabled Soldiers in Britain after the Great War', in *Psychological Trauma and the Legacies of the First World War*, ed.

124 *Joining up in the Second World War*

by Jason Crouthamel and Peter Leese (Basingstoke: Palgrave, 2016) pp. 165–92.

65 Meyer, 'Wounded in a Mentionable Place'.

66 Richard van Emden, *Prisoners of the Kaiser: The Last POWs of the Great War* (Barnsley: Pen and Sword, 2009) p. 183 cited in Wilkinson, 'Ex-Prisoners of War'.

67 Stuart Underdown, IWM-SA-31699, 2008.

68 Cyril Price, IWM-SA-28775, 2006.

69 For example, Alfred Cox, IWM-SA-22167, 2001; George Forster, IWM-SA-2824, n.d.

70 Des Radwell, IWM-SA-28531, 2005. See also Folkes (Morley, 2016).

71 Meyer, 'Wounded in a Mentionable Place'.

72 Veterans' wounds disturbed some children: Roper, 'Subjectivities', p. 173.

73 Webster (2011).

74 Elson (2010).

75 Waterhouse (2016).

76 Stagg (2010).

77 Curtis (2010).

78 Stagg (2010). See also Browne (Morley, 2010).

79 Pragnell (2010).

80 By 1921 book reviewers considered tales of trench conditions all too familiar: Watson, *Fighting Different Wars*, p. 189.

81 Webster (2011).

82 Spragg (2010). Spragg received fuller explanations when the pair could trade wartime experiences.

83 Tom Knowlton (Morley, 2010).

84 Cash (Morley, 2010).

85 Hay (2010).

86 Fisher, *Fatherhood*, pp. 228–9.

87 King, *Family*, pp. 116–18.

88 E. Remarque, *All Quiet on the Western Front* (1929), and the 1930 film adaptation directed by Lewis Millstone.

89 Leask, IWM-SA-21602.

90 Woodard (Morley, 2011).

91 Kirby, IWM-SA-16084.

92 Pragnell (2010).

93 See MO DR2349, February 1940; For Ted Hughes's fascination due to his father's silence, see Winter, 'Shell Shock', pp. 204–7.

94 Chilton, IWM-SA-27345.

95 Cash (2010).

Encountering Great War veterans

96 James Mann, IWM-SA-18513, 1998; Griffiths, IWM-SA-29574; Riggs, IWM-SA-22346.

97 Mr Sweetland, IWM-SA-10452, 1988.

98 Coster, IWM-SA-28723.

99 Richard Todd, IWM-SA-29069, 2006.

100 William Jalland, IWM-SA-11944, 1991. Curtis (2010) also heard colleagues telling a story in the adventure frame.

101 Thomas, IWM-SA-27342.

102 Watson, *Fighting Different Wars*, pp. 50–1.

103 See also Harold Sell, IWM-SA-10403, n.d.; John Wilson, IWM-SA-17985, 1998.

104 Hayes (2010).

105 George Iceton, IWM-SA-11938, 1989.

106 Parkhouse, IWM-SA-15476.

107 Elson (Morley, 2010).

108 Womack (2016).

109 Richard van Emden, *The Quick and the Dead: Fallen Soldiers and Their Families in the Great War* (London: Bloomsbury, 2011) p. 89.

110 *Ibid.*, p. 303.

111 Janis Lomas, 'Soldiering On: War Widows in First World War Britain', in *The Home Front In Britain*, ed. by Maggie Andrews and Janis Lomas (Basingstoke: Palgrave Macmillan, 2014); Andrea Hetherington, *British Widows the First World War: The Forgotten Legion* (Barnsley: Pen and Sword, 2018); and Joy Damousi, *The Labour of Loss. Mourning Memory and Wartime Bereavement in Australia* (Cambridge: Cambridge University Press, 2010). On war widows' place in commemoration, Susan R. Grayzel, *Women's Identities at War. Gender, Motherhood and Politics in Britain and France during the First World War* (Chapel Hill, North Carolina: The University of North Carolina Press, 1999) chapter 7, 'Public Spaces and Private Grief: Assessing the Legacy of War', pp. 226–43.

112 Van Emden's interviews also suggest that death was not explained to some children or ascribed meaning; instead, they were expected to accept it and look after their mother. This was certainly the case with the death of a brother; see van Emden and Humphreys, *All Quiet on the Home Front*, pp. 104–16.

113 Van Emden's *Quick and the Dead* reveals more about children's perceptions of others' trauma and how families coped with the loss than about what was communicated to children themselves. Some children were told nothing more than that their father would not be coming back; p. 318.

126 *Joining up in the Second World War*

114 The state issued around 1,000,000 Next of Kin Memorial Plaques, or 'Death Pennys'; see Ann-Marie Foster, 'The Next of Kin Memorial Plaque and the Family Connection', https://blogs.kent.ac.uk/muniti ons-of-the-mind/2019/07/08/the-next-of-kin-memorial-plaque-and-the-family-connection/ and Imperial War Museum, 'Next of Kin Memorial Plaque, Scroll and King's Message' https://iwm.org.uk/hist ory/first-world-war-next-of-kin-plaque
115 Van Emden, *Quick and the Dead*, p. 316.
116 *Ibid.*, pp. 262–3.
117 *Ibid.*, pp. 313–14.
118 *Ibid.*, p. 319.
119 Stagg (2010).
120 Francis Frederick Hill, NMRN; Fredrick William Hann, IWM-SA-3962, 1978. All were aged four or younger when the Great War broke out, and two had no memory of their fathers, which perhaps lessoned the emotional impact of their death.
121 Van Emden, *Quick and the Dead*, p. 319.
122 Sheffield, *Forgotten Victory*, p. 10.
123 Summerfield and Peniston-Bird, *Contesting Home Defence*, p. 233.
124 Hay (2010); Webster (2011); Wyke (2010); Pond (2011); Thurgood (2010); Bob Woodhams (Morley, 2010); Norman Bowdler, IWM-SA-27347, 2005.
125 Hay (2010).
126 Hay (2010); Webster (2011); Wyke (2010); Thurgood (2010); Leask, IWM-SA-21602; Seibert, IWM-SA-18485; Bowdler, IWM-SA-27347; Donovan, IWM-SA-20316. Jessica Hammett found veterans often used their experience to claim authority in Civil Defence; ' "It's in the Blood, isn't it?" The Contested Status of First World War Veterans in Second World War Civil Defence', *Cultural and Social History*, 14.3 (2017) pp. 343–61 (p. 343).
127 Bowdler, IWM-SA-27347.
128 Donovan, IWM-SA-20316.
129 Summerfield and Peniston-Bird, *Contesting Home Defence*, p. 220.
130 Seibert, IWM-SA-18485.
131 Todman, *Myth and Memory*, pp. 189–90. Hammett has suggested the same of Civil Defence, 'It's in the Blood', p. 345.
132 George Nicholson, Correspondence, 15 December 1999, cited in Summerfield and Peniston-Bird, *Contesting Home Defence*, p. 224.
133 *Queen's Review: ARP in the Queen's District of Willesden*, 12 (August 1941) p. 8 cited in Hammett, 'It's in the Blood', p. 357.
134 Pond (2011).
135 Day (Morley, 2011). They also seemed old to Seibert, IWM-SA-18485.

Encountering Great War veterans 127

136 Webster (2011); Hay (2010); Wyke (2010); Seibert, IWM-SA-18485.
137 Thurgood (2010).
138 Woodhams (2010).
139 Todman, *Myth and Memory*, pp. 189–90.
140 Philip Foster (Morley, 2016).
141 Thomas McKay, 'A Multi-Generational Oral History Study Considering English Collective Memory of the Second World War and Holocaust' (Unpublished PhD Thesis, University of Leicester, 2012) pp. 75–6, 139–40.
142 Meyer, *Men of War*, p. 141.
143 Todman, 'Sans peur', p. 1105; *Myth and Memory*, pp. 188–9.
144 Isherwood, *Remembering the Great War*, pp. 21–31, 163.
145 Paris, *Over the Top*, p. 158.
146 Sheffield, 'Shadow', p. 31.
147 Day (2011).

3

You and the Call-Up: Conscription, attitudes and agency

Introduction

From 1938 to 1945 the relationship between the British State and the British people changed considerably, as the State gained and exercised substantial power to direct Britons into work and the Armed Forces. The limits of the State's power shifted regularly and significantly over the course of the war, and so too did Britons' individual agency. For some this had limited and quotidian consequences, but for others it fundamentally changed the nature of day-to-day life for the duration of the war and had profound effects upon people's life courses, as careers were upended, people were relocated, doors opened or closed on relationships or lives were cut tragically short. Chapters 1 and 2 established the variety of ways young men encountered the Great War as they were growing up. Chapter 4 explores how understandings of the last war affected perspectives on service in a new conflict. To set the context within which men were applying these understandings (or not) in relation to their own potential service, this chapter examines the introduction of State structures to control manpower and what these meant for an individual's agency, as well as analysing Britons' attitudes towards conscription and military service in 1939.

First, the chapter outlines the coming of conscription in 1939. It describes the debates about the introduction of conscription in peacetime, which were partly influenced by memories of the Great War. It then uses opinion polling data and previously unexamined responses to an MO street survey to examine how the British public reacted to the introduction of conscription, particularly those young men who were to be affected by it.

You and the Call-Up 129

With the outbreak of war in September 1939, the State's control over men with regard to military service drastically increased. It extended still further over the course of the war. The third and fourth sections of this chapter examine who was liable to be made to do what, when. War Office documents, contemporary advice guides, MO material and personal testimony are used to map the shifting boundaries of wartime conscription and to detail how these affected the individual registering under the National Services Acts over the course of the war, how individuals might negotiate the demands of the State, how well young men understood the options open to them at the time and the ways men were able to exercise agency, legitimately and illegitimately. This chapter provides a foundation for Chapter 4, a detailed examination of the ways in which men's attitudes and enlistment decisions were shaped by their understandings of the Great War. While detailing changes to manpower controls, and how the public reacted, the chapter highlights the influence of Great War memories and the relationship between wartime masculinity and military service that the State was enforcing through legislation. The chapter provides the most detailed discussion of men's State-imposed wartime responsibilities to date, and – in conjunction with Chapter 4 – enhances our understanding of men's attitudes to conscription and military service during the Second World War. It shows that varied levels of willingness hid beneath the veneer of consent displayed towards conscription.

The coming of conscription

In 1937 Chamberlain stated, 'We shall never again send to the Continent an army on the scale of that which we put into the field in the last war.'[1] Before the Second World War, there was considerable debate about the nature of British military involvement in any future conflict and the extent of the compulsory military service that would be required. The attitudes of Britons – those with power and those without – reflected the continued influence of memories of the Great War. While it ultimately became widely accepted that military and perhaps also industrial conscription would be required in the event of the outbreak of major hostilities, these forms of compulsion remained politically and culturally unattractive so long

130   *Joining up in the Second World War*

as peace survived. Nor was it a foregone conclusion in the mid-1930s that Britain's participation in a second world war would take the form that it ultimately did. With Britain's leaders trying to limit the costs of the Army and in any case reluctant to recruit another great army for another attritional war, Britain adopted a position of limited liability to continental security. As Todman explains, 'No British politician of any stripe wanted to precipitate another world war, and Labour and Liberal defence policies shared the Government's strategic logic: a large air force and navy, a reliance on economic power, and no great army to be sucked into the trenches of another western front.'[2] The British public had not generally become pacifist over the inter-war years, but there is evidence of greater scepticism and reluctance to accept war as a method of resolving international tension. The Peace Pledge Union had over 100,000 members in the late 1930s and the 'pacifistic' League of Nations Union, which would countenance war only if all other measures failed, could state that one million Britons had been members between 1920 and 1933,[3] and the responses of eleven million Britons to the 1935 'Peace Ballot' suggest widespread support for a 'prudent middle way between isolationism and militarism'.[4] The British public appear to have been of a similar mind about military commitments as their political leaders. In January 1937, according to a British Institute of Public Opinion (BIPO) poll, three-quarters of Britons were against compulsory military training.[5] Nor were Britons necessarily eager to serve on a voluntary basis: in November 1937 only 38 per cent of men asked by BIPO replied that they would volunteer in the event of a future war, and only 22 per cent of women expected they would pressure their husband to do so.[6] The latter years of the Great War arguably set both the expectation that this would be how armies would be raised if they were needed and the expectation that conscription was the lot of the young man in wartime. In March 1938 MO asked Britons whether individuals could do anything about the international situation. MO suggested that the responses indicated a high degree of fatalism. Certainly, a number of responses indicate cynical resignation, but they are not without resolve: 'Worker, 40: "Have to fight I suppose. We'll probably get conscription". Worker, 25: "Go out and get shot". Worker, 30: "We've got to fight if we've got to fight".'[7] What is also clear in these responses is that many Britons expected conscription

You and the Call-Up 131

if war broke out. Six months later, in the midst of the Sudeten Crisis of September 1938, some had accepted their lack of control over events in the international arena and much closer to home: when MO asked a 20-year-old Londoner about the crisis he replied, '[I] [d]on't take any notice mate. What's the good? If they want yer they'll take yer. They don't ask your permission like.'[8] In the process of normalising conscription, the Great War had, for some at least, disrupted the expectation of voluntarism.

Shortly after the Sudeten Crisis in September 1938, MO canvassed working-class residents in West Fulham. Clearly, it was not only political leaders whose perspective on current events was filtered through memories of the previous conflict. A 55-year-old woman told them, 'it scared my wits out, thinking of the last war. They said it was going to be this week, and I heard the milkman say this morning that we can say the worst has passed now.'[9] Time, and Hitler, would make fools of both the milkman and Chamberlain. After the Munich Agreement, there was growing public disillusion with appeasement.[10] A woman aged 30 told MO:

> If there's one thing we want, it's no more war. But I can't see what we are going to do when he keeps on wanting things that he says, like that Czechoslovakia. I know what I'd do if I had him. My husband says, and I agree, that we will have a bigger war now sooner or later for this.[11]

Her mention of 'no more war' echoes the 'war to end wars' rhetoric of Great War commemoration, and the Great War was explicit in other's reactions. A man aged 34 told MO, 'For once in my life I'm damned well ashamed to be an Englishman. I think the worst possible thing has happened to them Czechs now. It puts me in mind of a song they used to sing during the last war: "You can send who you like, but for God's sake don't send me." '[12]

Britons shared their leaders' disinclination to participate in another large-scale war. Yet as international tensions increased the French government made clear that they did not 'intend England to fight her battles with French soldiers',[13] British politicians recognised that limited liability had to be abandoned, and the British people came to accept that conscription was coming. Following the apparent deferring of conflict at Munich, demands for conscription in order to strengthen Britain's defences became increasingly forceful. By October 1938

132   *Joining up in the Second World War*

public opinion remained evenly divided on conscription,[14] but three-quarters of those polled by BIPO favoured a National Register, suggesting a desire to be prepared.[15] Nonetheless, conscription remained a difficult political issue. It was popular with some Conservative MPs,[16] but Chamberlain remained concerned about both the diplomatic message that would be sent by the introduction of compulsory service and the political consequences of the bargaining that it would require with the trade unions. From the very different perspective of the Labour party, allowing the national government to control manpower – and hence perhaps to conscript unionised workers – was also problematic.[17] As late as November 1938, Chamberlain argued to the House of Commons that conscription might yet be proved unnecessary: 'It must be remembered that we are not today in the same position as we were in 1914, in this respect: that we are not contemplating the equipment of an army on a continental scale.'[18]

Some Britons did not need to be conscripted, of course. In March, September and November 1938, hundreds of thousands of men responded to the heightened international tensions of the Anschluss, Sudeten Crisis and Kristallnacht by volunteering for the Territorial Army, Air Raid Precautions and Auxiliary Police.[19] It was Britons' voluntarism, quite aside from any strategic need to increase enlistment for the forces, that created pressure to implement a system of registration and direction in order to avert industrial disruption. As the Ministry of Labour would later explain, there was a strong awareness that the Great War 'had shown the folly of indiscriminate recruiting'.[20] A voluntary National Register was announced on 1 December 1938 and on 25 January 1939 the Voluntary National Service Campaign was launched to encourage enrolment.[21] Promoting the campaign on the radio, Chamberlain told listeners: 'Compulsion is not in accordance with the democratic system under which we live, or consistent with the tradition of freedom we have always striven to maintain. We are confident that we shall get all the volunteers that we need without recourse to compulsion.'[22] Two hundred and seventy-five National Service Committees were established to promote recruitment and advise individuals how they could serve, particularly those covered by the newly published Schedule of Reserved Occupations (SRO). Every household received a copy of *National Service: A Guide to the Ways in which the People of this Country May Give Service*, which was

You and the Call-Up

intended to 'give the public a concise description of the various forms of national service open to them'.[23] The guide included an application form and explained the commitment and qualifications that each role required, as well as cautioning that people should not volunteer for positions they would be prevented from fulfilling in wartime. While most people supported the idea of the Register, in practice volunteerism was more attractive when other people were the ones doing it. In December 1938, when the voluntary National Register was announced, only a third of those polled who had not yet volunteered for some form of National Service intended to do so under the 'national register system'.[24] Interest in the Voluntary National Service campaign diminished as early as February, particularly after press reports of willing volunteers being turned away.[25] By the end of the campaign in August 1939, 1.5 million had enrolled, but three-quarters had enrolled for Civil Defence, 'an indication of the defensive mood of the country'.[26] As Todman has highlighted, 'Left to themselves, most people were not getting ready for war.'[27]

Conversely, by the start of 1939 the State's preparations for war were difficult to miss. Numerous RAF airfields and Army training camps were created, along with their associated stores, and munitions and aircraft factories were built at great State expense.[28] Gas masks had already been issued and in some regions local authorities hastened their construction of public air raid shelters and started distributing Anderson shelters for installation in Britons' gardens; in others they began enquiring who would be willing to open their doors to evacuees.[29] Hundreds of thousands of Britons, motivated by a sense of duty, volunteered for largely part-time roles in Air Raid Precautions.[30] Attitudes to conscription in 1939 have to be seen in the changed international context: 'By the start of 1939, Munich was clearly seen as a postponement rather than a deliverance.'[31] Britons had been relieved not to go to war in 1938, but as Hitler and the Nazis repeatedly took advantage of Chamberlain's policy of appeasement and escalated tensions towards war, and persecuted European Jews in acts such as Kristallnacht, a majority of Britons believed that peace could not be maintained honourably, and resolved that there was little to be gained through delay.[32] An increasing number of Britons now agreed with the sentiments a man aged 20 had expressed to MO after the Munich Agreement: 'I'd give Hitler hell for this lot. He's going to get it too before long, you bet he will.'[33]

134 *Joining up in the Second World War*

Chamberlain was slow to see that Britons' mood had shifted.[34] In February 1939, Britain restated its commitment to defending French territory – a point demonstrated in March by a doubling of the Territorial Army.[35] According to BIPO polls in April, a narrow majority of the public favoured filling these nearly 200,000 spaces by voluntarism, and the public remained evenly divided on the question of compulsory National Service.[36] In the event, volunteers were not hard to find, with 88,000 new recruits in April, aided by the removal of 630,000 men from the SRO.[37] After Germany's invasion of the rest of Czechoslovakia in March, Britain committed itself to the defence of Polish independence. In April 1939, Chamberlain accepted that peacetime conscription was a necessary symbol of British commitment to European security. On 26 April the Secretary of State for War, Leslie Hore-Belisha, announced the Military Training Bill: men turning 20 who were not in reserved occupations would be required to complete six months' full-time training, followed by three and a half years in the reserves.[38] Unless war broke out, men could not be sent overseas, employment was to be reinstated after service and provision was made for conscientious objectors and students. Men were primarily to be trained for air defence at home rather than continental war. That Chamberlain was moved more by the symbolism of this act than the utility of an expanded force or a shortage of volunteers is well illustrated by the fact the Army had not been consulted; Allport writes that 'When the deputy chief of the Imperial General Staff ... heard the news, he gave a look of "almost incredulous bewilderment".'[39] The sudden shift from voluntarism to compulsion left Labour in a difficult position, too: some of its MPs were angered by what they saw as Government trickery, but the party was unwilling to be seen as simultaneously opposing the bill and demanding a strong stance against Hitler.[40] On 26 May 1939 the Military Training Act was passed, introducing conscription in peacetime for the first time in British history.

Responses to peacetime conscription

In the days immediately following the announcement of the Military Training Bill, MO's investigators went door-to-door in London, particularly the East End, to assess reactions.[41] The 405 responses

You and the Call-Up

provide a much richer understanding of the immediate public reaction to peacetime conscription.[42]

Conscription was favoured by 44 per cent of those MO asked, while 33 per cent opposed it; the remainder were uncertain, uninterested or unwilling to answer.[43] By Tom Harrisson's reckoning, more support was to be found amongst middle-class households, but still a small majority of working-class households favoured conscription. In both cases, Harrisson suggested, the responses of 'families where some member is directly concerned in conscription are LESS favourable to it than the rest', but this had less impact on the middle-classes, for whom job security was less of a concern, and OTC training in secondary school increased the chances of a commission.[44]

The verbatim replies reveal individuals' reasoning.[45] Most of those unaffected by conscription thought it positive because it was necessary given the circumstances or it was important to enhance national preparedness. At a point when voluntarism was being emphasised, some noted that 'young fellows of that age are joining the Territorials. It doesn't seem right to me that some should join, and others who are not public spirited enough should be able to keep out of the Army.'[46] Conscription would ensure the burden was evenly spread. Another common favourable reaction disassociated military training from its military purpose and endowed it with that of social regeneration: it would 'help the fellows off the street corners, and give them something useful to do, instead of chasing after girls all night', or solve the problem of having 'too many mothers' boys in the country. Conscription would make a man out of them'.[47] Such ideas reflected a wider, long-standing contemporary discourse about masculinity and military service, and inter-war concern about soft boys.[48] Around a quarter of those unaffected by conscription expressed definite opposition to it, most commonly owing to a belief that the voluntary principle should be maintained, that conscription wrongly removed British freedom, or sometimes as a result of a more general desire to avoid war altogether.

For the parents of young men conscription contained an obvious tension between personal impact and assessments of ideology and necessity. As the father of one 20-year-old said, 'From a father's point of view it is not a good thing, from a patriot's point of view, there ought to be some form of national service.'[49]

136 *Joining up in the Second World War*

Fathers expressed greater recognition of the necessity of conscription than mothers, and were more often convinced that military training would benefit their sons. Most mothers expressed their objection: some were concerned about employment and comments such as 'We want the jobs guaranteed after conscription or a war. Half the men were caught that way in the last war' were not uncommon; some disagreed on that basis that Britain was a 'free country'. The majority of mothers, though, expressed an unwillingness to subjugate parental duty to patriotic duty: 'A mother's opinion is: not conscription, much as she would like to see everything all right.'[50] Another simply said, 'Nobody wants to give their sons away. Certainly not me.'[51] Even though war would not be declared for another five months, some parents were evidently imagining their sons doing more than training. Memories of the Great War, which informed the demand for job guarantees above, more explicitly underpinned some parents' objections. One father replied, 'I fought in the last war, and I can tell you that my lad is not going to be conscripted by this government nor any other. I did my part, and it's left me no reward ....'[52] And mothers, too, might look to the personal costs of the previous conflict: one replied, 'No I am opposed to conscription [...] My husband was killed at Vimy Ridge, and he left me two sons, and I pray to God that he won't take them like he did my old man.'[53] These responses show that individuals' recollections of the Great War informed their attitudes to conscription, but we can also read these responses as responding to, or at least aligned with, commemorative scripts of the Great War. Sacrifice, and sacrifice represented as primarily borne by mothers,[54] was at the heart of commemorative practice, and rhetorical efforts to imbue that sacrifice with purpose had promised the reward of a brighter future, including the promise of peace. Yet for most Britons the 1930s had proved distinctly overcast even before the clouds grew darker and more ominous in 1938. These responses reflect not only gendered codes of expression, but also a gendered framing of Great War memory: fathers reflected on how service would benefit their sons, weighing the merits of the contract of masculine citizenship, sometimes based on their own experience. Mothers, on the other hand, anticipated what it would cost *them*, and determined they were unwilling to pay that price.

Around two-thirds of the potential conscripts themselves (and most of their girlfriends) were opposed to conscription. A minority thought conscription a good idea, commonly because it would benefit men to be prepared if or when war arose. Some felt that others their age required social improvement – it would provide their peers with employment, 'stop them hanging around street corners, keep them fit', and 'wake one or two of the boys' ideas up'.[55] Most of conscription age, however, expressed their opposition to conscription, and more vehemently than those unaffected, in conjunction with resignation that they would be unable to avoid service.

Expressions of self-interest, in the form of not wanting to lose their job or simply not wanting to participate, were as common as expressions of ideological opposition. Respondents expressed their feeling that conscription signalled the erosion of liberty, or described conscription as the first encroachment of totalitarianism; one feared that soon 'We shan't be able to speak without being spied upon, like they are in Germany.'[56] A small number of respondents alluded to soldiering as a task that fell upon the working classes as a consequence of the actions of the ruling classes. And of course, for some all these complaints coalesced to form the following sentiment: 'No I am not in favour of conscription. I shall try to get exempt, I have just finished my time [apprenticeship] and now I earn a fairly good wage, and I'll be fucked if I'm going to lose it already because of the bleeding capitalists. It's a bloody grand state of affairs when all our liberty is taken away from us.'[57]

Conscription found significantly greater favour amongst those just below conscription age, many of whom wanted to join up or had volunteered. The little opposition that existed tended to be based on the assumption that others would also volunteer. A lower-middle-class 19-year-old said, 'I'd much sooner they relied on the spirit of the young people to volunteer. I'm a Territorial.'[58] At least half of those aged 22–25 expressed approval of conscription, although again this view tended to come from those who had joined or wanted to join the services anyway.

MO also asked those just *above* conscription age 'who will be affected in the next draft' whether conscription would 'induce you to volunteer now for Territorials or some other service'.[59] In fact, it was those just *below* conscription age, who would turn 20 the following year, who would be liable for the next draft. Yet MO's

138   *Joining up in the Second World War*

question and the responses suggest that individuals expected the expansion of the act to higher age groups, an expectation which may itself have drawn on knowledge of the pattern of conscription in the Great War. A significant group expressed an apparently genuine desire to join the Territorials, like a 23-year-old lower-middle-class man who felt conscription 'a very good thing. I don't know what there is against it. I only wish I were of age to join. I shall join some sort of national service as quick as I can.'[60] Equally common, though, was a self-serving rush to the colours by those who opposed conscription, certainly if it was to affect them. Joining the Territorials or the Auxiliary Fire Service in an attempt to obtain exemption from the Act was one way for a man to retain his job, as this young man expressed:

> Well people of my age have missed it so far but they are not going to catch me. I am going to join up for something, the Auxiliary Fire Brigade if I am old enough. You see I work as a clerk with a £3 a week job, it's alright employers being public spirited and say the job will be left open, it wasn't in the last war and it won't be this time, so I'm not taking any chances on that, you can't blame me can you.[61]

We can only speculate about what had focused the attention of men in their early twenties on the fragility of guarantees to workers twenty years earlier, but one can imagine how an older man's warning – at home or at work – could seed such thinking, which then spread amongst peers. Certainly, it seems that J. B. Priestly was preaching to the choir when, two years later, he cautioned his listeners to remember the fate of those who returned from the Great War to poverty and unemployment.[62] Between 1–29 April 1939, 88,000 new members 'were enlisted or in the process of enlistment for the Territorial Army'.[63] This no doubt partly reflected both the unstable appearance of international relations at the time – TA enlistment had also surged during the Munich Crisis in 1938 and with the invasion of Czechoslovakia in March[64] – and the announcement in March that it would have double the number of divisions. Still, in the spring of 1939, a proportion of those enlisting in the Territorials were, as the young clerk's response explains, not expressing their patriotic voluntarism but participating in a pragmatic negotiation of their service. Those who had enrolled in the Territorials or auxiliary forces by 27 April would be unaffected by the Bill,[65] an exemption

You and the Call-Up 139

Territorial officers were not above using to stimulate recruitment. In East Anglia on the evening of 26 April, fifty-four recruits signed up at Saffron Walden's drill hall after two Territorial officers had driven 'around Saffron Walden, Dunmow and Stanstead in a lorry … urging young men, through a megaphone, to volunteer before they were conscripted'.[66] From early May it was decided that those subsequently enlisting in the Territorials would be diminishing the time they would spend in the reserves after their six months training.[67] Militia-age men continued to rush to enlist.[68] The potential conscript had every incentive to join. If war broke out quickly his peers would soon join him in uniform, and if not those who enlisted before 27 April would have traded the disruption of six months in the Army for part-time soldiering, and those who were slower off the mark were reducing their time in the reserves.

The responses provide a sense that such respondents would have objected less had Britain been at war, but during peacetime six months in the forces and away from one's employment was too great a sacrifice. Those who were to become militia men were largely disgruntled. A significant proportion of those a few years older looked to pre-empt the spectre of peacetime conscription through self-serving voluntarism and other methods of avoiding compulsory military service. Students could defer their conscription, and R. Douglas Brown suggests it was no coincidence that in 1939 Cambridge saw its largest intake of freshmen since 1919.[69] Those who were keen to participate in military service look to have been volunteering under the National Service Campaign, regardless of conscription, while a large proportion, if not a majority, of young men sought to delay service if at all possible. Probably thanks largely to the deteriorating international situation, the reaction to conscription in peacetime amongst the general population was favourable, though a significant minority objected. On a national level it appears that public opinion about conscription was moving in step with the Government's reactions to the shifting international situation. Although the public had preferred voluntarism in April, in May, after the announcement of the Military Training Bill, BIPO found three-fifths of those polled approved of conscription,[70] and by July, shortly after the first 34,500 were enlisted as militiamen, most were happy with conscription as it stood, and those favouring its expansion outnumbered those calling for its abolition by 2:1.[71]

140   *Joining up in the Second World War*

Analysis of the responses to MO's street survey, however, highlights the majority of the young men who were expected to prepare for war did not favour the prospect of doing so in its absence.[72] Wartime conscription would evoke reactions that were different, but not wholly dissimilar.

Wartime conscription: registration and enlistment

By 1945, 32 per cent of the male working population were in the armed or Civil Defence forces, and optimal mobilisation of the available manpower (and woman-power) inside and outside the forces was crucial to the war effort.[73] Reporting after the war, the Ministry of Labour and National Service noted the success it achieved was largely dependent on the 'willingness with which men and women accepted restrictions and hardships in order that the war might be brought to a successful conclusion'.[74] The Government's authority to regulate, restrict and direct Briton's employment dramatically increased over the course of the war, as did the number of Britons upon whom this authority to could be brought to bear. This generally limited the choices people had about the role they would play, although the range of service options available was occasionally broadened due to manpower demands. Still, individuals retained a certain amount of agency and were able to negotiate their service, in both legitimate and illegitimate ways. It is important to lay out the ways in which the boundaries of compulsion changed during the war in order to understand the circumstances in which reactions to service were formulated.

With the outbreak of war, the National Service (Armed Forces) Act 1939 was passed. It made British men aged 18–41 'liable by Royal Proclamation to be called up for service in the Armed Forces of the Crown'.[75] A compulsory National Register was completed by the end of September, and on 1 October 1939 the first proclamation made those aged 21 liable for service, along with those who had turned 20 since 3 June when those already aged 20 had been called to the militia.[76] After 'deducting medical rejects, conscientious objectors, exempted classes and men covered by the schedule of Reserved Occupations', the first proclamation was expected to provide around 200,000 men for the forces, who were to register

You and the Call-Up

on 21 October 1939 and to be called for medical examination to enable their enlistment in November.[77] The next required age groups were to be made liable for National Service by subsequent proclamations, along with those who had turned 20 in the intervening months; thus on 1 December 1939 those aged 22 were made liable along with those born between 2 October and 1 December 1919.[78]

On 15 December 1939, Ernest Brown, Minister of Labour and National Service, suggested altering this system, and instead making an annual proclamation on 1 January 'making liable the age-groups which are expected to be required for the year'.[79] The Government gave significant consideration to effects on morale when making decisions over the course of the war.[80] Manpower was no different. Brown explained an annual proclamation would not only increase administrative efficiency, ease the identification of those not registered and provide employers with greater notice of which staff they were to lose, but would be beneficial to morale and politically expedient, too;

> a Proclamation on 1st January next making liable for service all men up to 28 would have a profoundly good effect in France ... and would also have a stimulating effect in this country. It would come at a time when it can be expected that the strain of waiting may well be having some deleterious effect on morale, and action of this kind taken on New-Year's Day, demonstrating our determination and resolve, would, I suggest, provide a fitting opening for 1940.[81]

When, on 19 December 1939, the War Cabinet discussed the suggestion, the Chancellor of the Exchequer suggested the proclamation should be accompanied by speeches that 'correct the impression in France and elsewhere that we were not contributing our fair share of man power to the common struggle'.[82] And it did not go unnoticed that an annual proclamation justified the presentation of aggregate figures of the manpower to be committed to the Armed Forces that year; those age groups were expected to provide 850,000 men, 'but the number of registrations would probably exceed 1,000,000 and it might be possible to use this figure in any statement issued, so as to increase the effect on public opinion at home and abroad'.[83] The King signed the proclamation on 1 January 1940, after a 'full press conference at the Press and Censorship Bureau of the Ministry

142　　　　*Joining up in the Second World War*

of Information which was attended by representatives of the foreign as well as of the British press'.[84] The existing system of calling each age group to register as they were required was to remain unchanged, and it was stressed that those aged 19 would not be registered until they turned 20. By the end of January 1940, then, all those men born between 1916 and 1919 had been assigned a registration date or had actually registered.[85] In addition, those born between 1912 and 1915, and those born in 1920, had been made liable to be called to register and were awaiting the announcement of a registration date.[86]

In April 1940, just three months after proclaiming those who were to register in that calendar year, the Committee on Recruitment for the Armed Forces was already discussing how to obtain the next required batch of recruits with the least damage to public morale. They debated whether young men currently reserved by the SRO should be fished out before older men engaged in non-essential work were called, but decided that 'it would be wrong at this stage to withdraw trained men from industry'.[87] The decision to limit the next proclamation, on 9 May 1940, to those up to the age of 37, rather than the upper limit of 41, was shaped by concern about the potential for public discontent because they had not first implemented the alternative discussed.[88] The public's main concern, however, appears to have been less nuanced. Journalist Douglas Reed complained that the call-up seemed 'to progress with the speed of an elephant trying to compete in the Derby',[89] and the Government's Home Intelligence reports suggest that at least some of the British public were frustrated that men were not entering the Forces faster, and particularly about the delay between registration and actual call-up. The report from Birmingham on 24 May 1940 noted that 'Demand for further acceleration of calling-up and armament activity is common.'[90] In June, similar reports were made from Birmingham, Bristol, Reading, Edinburgh[91] and Nottingham, which reported 'increasing indignation at slowness of call-up: "turn playing fields into drill fields; don't wait for rifles" '.[92] A report from London stated 'Ex-servicemen disturbed by "large number of young men about streets and getting exemption" '.[93] Despite the accusatory undertone in this statement, the presence of men on the streets was a poor indicator of men's interest in serving, particularly given other reports. On 18 June, shortly after the British Expeditionary

Force had been evacuated from Dunkirk, the report from London claimed, 'Men in many districts rushed to Recruiting Offices yesterday and today. Were turned down and told to wait for registration. Much dissatisfaction the result and criticism of the present government.'[94] The same week, people in Birmingham remained frustrated at delays: ' "men lose their enthusiasm waiting" '.[95]

On 29 January 1941 the King proclaimed the remaining age groups between 18 and 41 to be liable.[96] A proclamation on 5 March 1942 raised the upper age limit to include men up to the age of 46. The National Service Act 1942, passed on 17 December 1942, enabled men to be called to register at the age of 17 years and 8 months in order that they could be called-up at 18. This power was utilised by the final proclamation, on 13 January 1943, which made men automatically liable upon turning 18. From this point registrations were less frequent as it was only necessary to register those who had reached 17 years and 8 months since the previous registration.[97]

Who was liable for military service and what they could be directed to do changed a number of times over the course of the war in an effort to meet the manpower demands of the war. On 10 April 1941 the National Service Act (NSA) 1941 gave the government authority to call-up men for Civil Defence, which included the Police War Reserve, the Auxiliary Fire Service (later renamed the National Fire Service) and the Civil Defence Reserve.[98] The NSA 1941 (No. 2), on 18 December 1941, enabled men to be called up at 18½ instead of 19, and extended liability to those up to the age of 51.[99] It also authorised the significantly greater power of 'imposing on all persons of either sex a general obligation for service in the armed forces, civil defence, industry or otherwise', including the Royal Observer Corps and Special Constabulary.[100] For the first time in Britain, women aged 20 to 30 could be conscripted to the women's military auxiliaries.[101] From January 1942 men aged 18–51 could be directed to serve in the Home Guard; 946,200 were by September 1944.[102] Finally, those who registered between 14 December 1943 and 22 April 1945 were included in the unpopular ballots for Bevin Boys, which selected 21,800 men to do their bit mining coal from beneath the green and pleasant land.[103] By the end of 1945, the NSAs had called 3.2 million men into the forces.[104]

144 *Joining up in the Second World War*

Table 3.1 Intake of men into the Armed Forces, 1939–45

	Men registered under NSA[1]	Men conscripted into Army, Navy or RAF[2]	Men volunteered for Army, Navy or RAF[3]
3 September–31 December 1939	727,000	122,200	210,800
1940	4,100,000	1,044,600	499,600
1941	2,222,000	632,700	300,300
1942	399,000	547,200	209,100
1943	465,000	347,400	197,200
1944	286,000	254,500	90,900
1945	156,000	231,300	70,700
Total	8,355,000	3,179,900	1,578,600

[1] [CMD 7225] p. 12.
[2] Parker, *Manpower*, table IV, p. 485.
[3] *Ibid.*

Held back: reserved occupations and essential work

The challenge of providing sufficient manpower to both the Armed Forces and essential industries was complicated by the fact that all men were not equal; Britain's skilled labourers were never sufficiently numerous to satisfy the demands of the Armed Forces and industry.[105] In May 1938, the Minister for the Co-ordination of Defence told the House of Commons that 'any Government dealing with the use of manpower today would be almost criminal if they did not take account of the lessons of the Great War'.[106] The State was more conscious that an army fighting for an extended period required manpower to equip and supply it as well as to serve in it,[107] and therefore as Ernest Brown, Minster for Labour, stated to the House of Commons in December 1938, 'One of the clearest lessons of the Great War of 1914–18 was the necessity for conserving the supply of skilled workmen employed in war industries.'[108] A system to exempt men from conscription and direct their labour

You and the Call-Up

145

was therefore required to keep or place millions of men in roles that optimised their contribution to the war effort. Exactly *who* was reserved changed throughout the war, and the teeth of the conscription comb became finer and finer as the State refined its methods. What remained constant, though, was that who was exempted and why was complicated, difficult for individuals (including MPs) to understand and sometimes open to question.[109]

The provisional SRO, published on 29 January 1939, was introduced to optimise the application of the available manpower. Men employed in the trades and professions listed in the SRO, and over an occupation-specific age threshold, were conferred 'immunity from conscription'.[110] The SRO listed some 2,500 roles, including those in industries directly essential to the war effort, and those that provided commodities or services that were necessities of daily life. It protected five million men working not only in working-class roles in heavy industry but also in white-collar professions.[111] From November 1939, employers could also apply for deferment for men not covered by the SRO, and 116,000 men who were either conducting work of national importance but were below the industry reservation age, or whose skills were essential to the viability of their employer's concerns, were deferred.[112]

The immunity offered by the SRO was not necessarily permanent, though, because the SRO *deferred* rather than removed an individual's liability to military service, and the SRO was never static; occupations were added or removed, age thresholds were altered and exceptions could be made if a man wanted to volunteer for a particular service role.[113] The SRO was revised in April, May and August 1939 and continued to change during the war. MO perceived repeated changes to the SRO to have created doubt about when reserved men would be called, yet some in ROs who responded to an MO's Directive about conscription in January 1940 appeared quite definite in their understanding of what would happen to them.[114] Many did express uncertainty about when they would be called, but this actually indicates that they understood that reservation was inherently uncertain. For example, a 26-year-old time-study engineer clearly expressed that he understood his position but this did not remove uncertainty: 'I might be called up: the [SRO] changes and I might not be on it at some future date. I would in many ways prefer not to be called up. But since somebody

146   *Joining up in the Second World War*

must do the job, why shouldn't I be somebody?'[115] From the State's perspective, the SRO's adaptability was one of its strengths, but this uncertainty must have been disorientating and unsettling for individuals affected. For instance, in April 1939 the removal of some occupations from the SRO meant some 630,000 men who had been reserved in January found they were not any longer. Conversely, in August 1939 changes to the reservation-age threshold in some industries meant more young men found themselves reserved.[116] Those who were too young to be reserved could enter the Armed Forces, but were theoretically only to be posted as tradesmen rather than for general service.[117] Eight thousand men who had joined the Territorial Army before the war began and who were therefore mobilised at the outbreak found themselves pulled back to work because their occupations were on the SRO and they were not working at their trade in the Army.[118] During 1940, to make more manpower available for the forces, some jobs were removed from the SRO and reservation-age thresholds were increased, and reserved men were permitted to volunteer for RAF aircrew and specific service trades.[119] A more significant 'combing out' of industry was achieved in April 1941 with the issue of a new SRO with higher reservation-age thresholds, which were raised further in June or October 1941, or sometimes both.[120]

Despite continual refinement, a more precise system than the SRO was required to enable the application of the principle that what mattered was less a man's occupation and more what his occupation produced and how essential it was that *he* be the one to do it. Thus, in December 1941 a different principle was adopted to the allocation of deferments: manpower policy transitioned from the block reservation system – which reserved people who were working in specific occupations and over a given age – to a system of individual deferments granted on the basis of a man's occupation, age and the wartime importance of his employer. This resulted in substantial changes to the management of manpower. By the end of 1941, 100,000 businesses deemed to be doing work of national importance were listed on the Register of Protected Establishments; they employed more than 600,000 men.[121] At the same time, a system of 'double ages' was applied to the SRO. An occupation in a Protected Establishment was typically assigned a lower reservation-age threshold than the same occupation outside a Protected

Establishment. Then from January 1942 the age thresholds in all occupations were increased by one year each month, until almost no occupation was automatically reserved.[122] With each monthly increase in the age threshold, a new cohort of men had their existing 'block' deferment reassessed and either replaced with an individual deferment or cancelled. As a general principle, men under the age of 25 were likely to have their deferment cancelled,[123] and men entering a reserved occupation would not be granted deferment.[124] Men who moved from a Protected Establishment to an unprotected one ceased to be reserved, but men could move in the opposite direction and remain deferred, so long as they provided notice before they were to be enlisted.[125] This process, then, was calculated make more young men available for the forces and to encourage skilled workers to relocate to employers who were doing the most essential work, while ensuring Protected Establishments (and the men they employed) were effectively shielded from the application of a finer-toothed comb to Britain's manpower.[126]

While movement *into* Protected Establishments was encouraged, movement *between* employers in essential industries created inefficiency, and was another challenge for the Ministry of Labour.[127] The solution was the Essential Work Order, issued on 5 March 1941.[128] Employees covered by the EWO could neither resign nor be sacked by their employer without authorisation from the National Service Officer.[129] It also gave the State the power to direct labour. In return, employees received guarantees about pay and conditions.[130] By the end of 1941 EWOs covered 30,000 employers and 5,750,000 employees who were deemed to be doing work of national importance.[131] By December 1944 the EWOs tied 6.1 million men to their jobs.[132]

You and the Call-Up: conscription and the individual

The SRO, EWOs and individual deferments shaped how millions of men contributed to Britain's war effort, but the default overarching constraint on individual agency was conscription. One way for the individual to take control of their military service was to volunteer, an option that was open to a majority of men throughout the war, though there were restrictions upon some in ROs. How and

148   *Joining up in the Second World War*

why they might do this is discussed in greater detail in Chapter 4. Yet despite increasing State control, even the conscript retained a certain amount of agency and a number of choices, particularly if they understood how to negotiate the complexities of the call-up system. By April 1940 War Facts Press were offering *Joining Up? A Handy Guide for Every Recruit,* which promised 'All you want to know! 6D. Registration – the call up – training – food – kit – pay – promotion – allowances – leave – postponements and exemptions. Army. Navy. Air Force'.[133] *Joining Up* assumed a decidedly positive and reassuring tone; and in his Foreword, Ernest Brown sought to mobilise a rhetorical pillar of Great War commemoration: young men's duty to their father's generation, who had already fought for them. He wrote, 'It is to you, and thousands more like you, that Britain looks to safeguard the rights and the freedom which your fathers have won for you. That you will do it, and do it with a stout heart, I know!'[134] By contrast, the front cover of *You and the Call-Up. A Guide for Men and Women,* published in 1942, emphasised legitimate routes to avoid unwanted service: 'Your liability to Compulsory Service in the Forces, Industry, the Home Guard, and Civil Defence – When you may not leave your job – The Essential Work Order – Postponement and Deferment – Conscientious Objection, etc etc – are all fully explained'.[135]

After being proclaimed liable to be called to register men were free to continue their lives as usual, and when they were needed or the system had capacity to cope with them a registration date for the group was publicly announced and circulated by the BBC and the press. Notices were posted at labour exchanges, post offices and police stations which detailed the age group required to register, the penalties for failing to do so, and who was exempt. *You and the Call-Up* informed readers that at this point:

> The person liable must make an application to be registered at such time and such local office as may be specified by the Minister of Labour [...] On registering he ... will be given a certificate of registration in the form of a postcard, and his ... name will be entered in the military service register.[136]

Registration was one of the few opportunities a man had left to exercise the little influence he had over his future for the rest of the war. It was now that 'all the particulars of [his] education, experience, trade or profession and any specialist qualifications' were recorded, and that he was asked to express a preference for the Army, Navy or RAF, or had the opportunity to state a conscientious objection.[137]

At some points during the war shortages in specific areas resulted in more options being proffered. When those aged 36 registered in January 1941 demand was such that they also had the option of 'service in the Police War Reserve or the National Fire Service as an alternative to the Armed Forces'.[138] From April 1941, some men could also express their preference for Civil Defence.[139] Mining was offered as an alternative to military service to men under 25 years of age from September 1942, and to all fit men being called up for the forces from August 1943.[140] *Joining Up* optimistically informed readers:

> It is a recognised principle that men shall go to the branch of the service they chose, whenever possible; but obviously the numbers required for the Royal Navy and the Royal Air Force are limited. Remember, whatever branch of the Service you eventually find yourself in is an honourable one and you'll find good pals there.[141]

Two years later, *You and the Call-Up* simply warned, 'These preferences will be recorded, but ... there is no guarantee that the applicant's wishes will be given effect to.'[142]

Upon registration, a man also had to provide details about his employment and employer, to establish whether he was affected by the SRO. If he was then his call-up was deferred; if his occupation was but he was below the reservation age it was noted that he should only be called into the services as a tradesman, not for general service.[143] There was a striking level of compliance with conscription. Relatively few men persistently attempted to dodge service by failing to register. Some 500,000 cases of failed registration were investigated during the war, but over 200,000 of these men were discovered to be in the services or were not liable for service. Ralph Harris recalled a friend finding the police at his door because he had not attended his registration when expected, but he had joined the Territorials in the middle of 1939 and thus was in the Army when war broke out.[144] Many others had either already registered or did so once enquiries began. Those in the latter group might have simply needed the reminder that a visit from the local

150   *Joining up in the Second World War*

constabulary provided, or they might, perhaps, have been seeking to delay their military service as long as possible by placing the onus on the State to find them and personally request their registration. Either way, only around 1,000 liable men determinedly resisted registration.[145]

Men liable for registration under the National Service Acts could request postponement or exemption from service. Deferment could be granted to those for whom call-up would cause hardship over and above that which conscription would impose on all, such as those expecting a child within three months, or needing time to arrange the running of their business in their absence.[146] Students and apprentices could apply for deferment to complete their course or to sit imminent exams, though from 1943 this was granted only to science students, who would have a useful application in war-related work upon graduation, and from early 1944 apprentices were no longer inevitably deferred.[147]

Individuals who chose to express a conscientious objection could object to all war-related service, to military service or to combatant duties. They were provisionally placed on the register of conscientious objectors pending a tribunal. Assuming he objected to serving entirely, his tribunal had four possible outcomes: he could be placed on the register of conscientious objectors unconditionally; he could be placed on the register on condition he performed specific civil work, such as forestry or agriculture; or from 1941 he could be required to perform Civil Defence;[148] he could be liable to be called to serve in the military in non-combatant duties, such in the Royal Army Medical Corps, or – from April 1940 – the Non-Combatant Corps;[149] or he could be removed from the register of conscientious objectors and be liable to call-up on the same terms as the rest of his age-group.[150]

It is difficult to suggest what proportion of men *held* a conscientious objection. Just as we might suspect that some expressed insincere objections, we can presume others held such a conviction but opted not to express it. Public disapproval towards COs surely encouraged some pragmatists to keep a sincere objection to themselves because they expected to be deemed medically unfit for military service or to be reserved due to their occupation. For instance, Bernard Smith, a committed member of the Socialist Party of Great Britain, opted to work in mining for the duration but stated that he would have objected if he had expected to be enlisted in the services.[151] Only 67,047 men *expressed* a conscientious objection upon registration, just 0.8 per cent of the 8,356,686 men who were registered.[152] COs were not only a very small group but were also increasingly invisible in registrations as the war went on. More than half of wartime conscientious objections were expressed before May 1940, and 80 per cent by the end of that year.[153] The majority therefore occurred when the younger men were registering, and when the war situation appeared less serious.[154] The perceived severity of Britain's situation at the point of Dunkirk may have made conscientious objection less attractive. As Figure 3.1 illustrates, the proportion of each registration group expressing an objection had been gradually decreasing before Dunkirk, but in June, following the evacuation order, the decrease (25 per cent) was distinctly sharper than in May.[155]

Peace Pledge Union membership also declined after Dunkirk: 6,000 people had joined between August 1939 and May 1940, but between Dunkirk and March 1941, resignations exceeded new members by more than 2,000.[156] From April 1941, not more than 0.5 per cent of a group of registrants expressed a conscientious objection.[157] Over the course of the war, the tribunals heard fewer than 60,000 cases, and 12,204 of these were unsuccessful.[158] A total of 3,577 men were registered unconditionally, 28,720 were registered conditionally and 14,691 were registered for noncombatant duties.[159] By 30 June 1945, perhaps 2,000 men had been

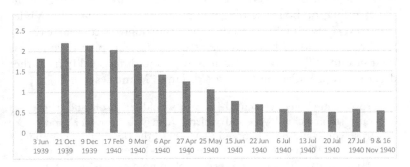

Figure 3.1 Percentage of registration groups provisionally registered as COs

152 *Joining up in the Second World War*

fined or sentenced to imprisonment for failing to comply with a condition of their registration or failing to submit to medical examination having been refused CO status.[160] Although conscientious objectors were a culturally conspicuous component of Britain's war, ultimately only a tiny proportion of men eligible for conscription refused to contribute to the war effort in some way.

Unless an individual was reserved, deferred or awaiting a tribunal to determine the validity of his objection, his registration details were passed to an Allocation Office, which would then call him to a Combined Recruiting Office for his medical and interview.[161] Men could attempt to avoid or delay service by neglecting to attend the medical examination, but by June 1945 only 4,931 men had been convicted of doing so.[162] *You and the Call-Up* provided sound motivation for attending: 'The penalty for failing to attend for medical examination when required is a fine of £5 or imprisonment in default of payment of the fine, up to one month on conviction before magistrates.'[163] *Joining Up*, of course, framed the experience more positively, remarking, 'As a civilian you would have to pay each of these doctors at least a couple of guineas for a similar examination!'[164] In practice, each of the thirty or so men in attendance passed under the scrutiny of four civilian doctors, each of whom had only a few minutes to conduct their assessment. One investigated medical history, mental condition and vision; one checked physical size, lungs, pulse, and eyes, nose, throat and teeth; one checked the heart rate, pulse and physical development; and the last tested hearing, urine, abdomen and heart.[165] They then made a collective determination as to each man's grade, with the chairman of the examination board settling any differences of opinion.[166] While some interviewees felt the medical was thorough, particularly those who were found to have problems or those who placed value on their grading,[167] veterans' accounts tended to differ starkly from the description provided by *Joining Up*. James Mann was

> surprised anybody ever failed [... you would] strip off and a man would stand behind you and whisper 'can you hear me?' and of course you could hear him and they'd hold the optics and that and the size of them you couldn't help but [see] and they tested your chest with a stethoscope and then grabbed hold of you and tell you to cough and I think that was about your medical, they asked you if

You and the Call-Up

> you had any ill health or anything like that, really it wasn't much of a medical ... it was a bit of a hit and miss thing.[168]

Some medical professionals and politicians shared this view, and concerns were raised in parliament about men who seemingly should not have been passed as fit but nevertheless had been. In 1942, Samuel Silverman MP told the House of Commons: 'People are saying that a medical board examining a recruit is interested only in getting him into the Forces by any reasonable means it can use, and therefore, if there is any doubt about a man's medical condition, the Army gets the benefit of it.'[169]

The potential recruit learned their medical grade immediately after the examination. The classification system became more complex as the war progressed and the need for manpower increased – by 1945 it had no fewer than ninety-two sub-categories[170] – but it can nevertheless be described in broad terms. Grade I (A) designated an individual as suitable for any role. Grade II (B) described those with minor health defects, but capable of considerable exertion; those with poor vision or poor feet were often in this class, and were marked, for example, II(a)(Feet). Grade III (C) restricted one to particular roles that, theoretically at least, did not require strength or exertion, and Grade IV (D) marked an individual as unfit for military service. Seventy-eight per cent of men under the age of 25 were placed in Grade I, and only 6 per cent of the same age group were deemed unfit for military service.[171] Medical grading could not be appealed, but a man could attempt to gain re-examination by presenting evidence of his fitness, or lack thereof.[172]

Corinna Peniston-Bird has highlighted that 'Medical Boards were the subject of popular classification themselves, located on a spectrum of leniency. Classification could thus be negotiated, with varying degrees of success, by careful choice of board.'[173] Moreover, Newlands has suggested that each board was 'a site of bargaining and resistance'.[174] Men might negotiate their service by attempting to present their health, through dishonesty or omission, as either better or worse than it was. That men might attempt to trick a recruiting sergeant by playing blind, deaf or dumb was understood widely enough that it could feature as the premise of a 1940 music hall skit.[175] While fictitious attempts evidently could be a laughing matter, Newlands rightly observes that failing the medical exam

154   *Joining up in the Second World War*

was 'perhaps the best option' for those who wished to 'dodge' military service, and some were determined to do so.[176] Some simply tried to feign symptoms, but in June 1940 eight Londoners were imprisoned after paying a man with heart disease to impersonate them at the examination, and several doctors were struck off for selling fake medical documents.[177] Men who were unable to pay large sums of money, or who were unwilling to break the rules so explicitly, could still attempt to bend them. An MO investigator conducting 'overheards' research in an East End café in July 1940, recorded the following exchange.[178] Fred, aged approximately 25, walked in and told his friends the medical board had graded him C-3 (fit for Home Service only).

Albert Here, come on, out with it. How d'you do it? It's my turn next- got to get used to the idea, what do you say?

Fred Nah, it wasn't nothing. They just passed me C-3.

Albert Cripes! I bet they pass me A-1. Just my luck.

Gerald That's what they done to me, A-1.

Arthur enters, to be asked by George, 'Here, Arthur, which'd you think was the healthiest? Gerald or Fred? Arthur: Fred.

Fred Well, I'm C-3 and he's A-1.

Arthur Bloomin' swindler – what d'you say to them? Told 'em you got a weak heart?

Albert Here, out with it, I want to know for when I go.

Arthur You want to get out of it, as well?

Fred Why not? Besides, we won't get out of it. They're taking fellows with one eye and one arm, so …

Albert Still, they'll keep us on the ground, if we're C-3.

Fred Sure – I'll be on the ground.

Arthur What's the secret?

Fred Well, I got one leg longer than the other, and a weak limp and flat fleet, and …

Albert A weak brain.

George I bet it's easy to get C-3 if you want it. I bet it's easy.

Fred Sure, then, you get it. Easy? Why didn't all them other geysers get it then?

George Here come's Alf. Hey Bill – he's C-3!

Bill C-3 is he? Good luck to him.

You and the Call-Up

Arthur clearly saw Fred and Albert as trying to manipulate the system in order to shirk, but his discouragement was not so vehement as to make the topic unacceptable among the group. That Fred's apparent success in beating the system was received with as much admiration as condemnation might in part be due to the attitude of Albert and Gerald, who seem to see military service as an unwelcome imposition from above.[179] More generally, their discussion illustrates the widely held view that military medical examinations were, at best, unselective.

This imprecision was, however, certainly also utilised by men who were keen to ensure that they *were* deemed fit for service. It is difficult to suggest the frequency with which this may have successfully occurred, but the press reported instances of healthy men paid to stand-in for men who knew they would fail,[180] and the oral histories provide multiple incidents of men attempting to present their health as better than it was.[181] For example, Don Browne withheld a family history of TB to enter the Navy.[182] Reg Elson was determined to join the Territorials despite his weak left eye. He attended his medical without his glasses, knowing that 'they didn't take you if you had glasses', and 'All [the medical officer] asked you to do was to place a card in front of one eye and say "can you read that" and they said "that was fine" and ... [he] put it on my right eye and I recalled the one that was on my other eye and "that's fine" he said, where I could hardly see, well I could see some but not clear enough, but that was as simple as that ....'[183]

Many men found self-worth and pride in confirmation of their physical fitness, while those who failed the medical and were therefore prevented from joining the services often recognised that they were denied access to the most culturally exalted masculine wartime identities.[184] Some young men clearly worried that they would not be seen as living up to their responsibilities because they were unfit, even if their position was entirely legitimate. At his examination Albert Parker was asked if he wanted to be passed fit and replied, 'Of course I do. All my mates have passed and I want to go with them.'[185] One young man,

> injured in the leg, reserved in essential work even if he were fit for military service, hates the thought that people may think he's dodging the call-up: 'My conscience is quite clear. But somehow I don't

156   *Joining up in the Second World War*

like to explain all this, even to myself. It always has the sound as though I was trying to cover myself up in some way. And when I'm asked the time-honoured question in years to come – "What did you do in the Great War, Daddy?" the above will sound pretty foolish.'[186]

Newlands also provides the example of a diarist who said that he had had an 'inferiority complex' and worried that he 'wouldn't be able to look a woman in the eye' if he had been passed Grade 2.[187] The discomfort and emasculation of those who failed the medical was made even more pronounced by the popular perception that the bar was low: Ken Hay recalled it was commonly said that as far as the Army was concerned, if 'your body is warm you are in [laughter]'.[188]

After the medical examination men were interviewed by a Recruiting Officer from the service they hoped to join. He would recommend where an individual should be posted, and from these recommendations names would be added to a list of men available for posting, with tradesmen separately listed.[189] The three services informed the Ministry of Labour of their manpower requirements, who then issued instructions telling an individual where, when and with which unit he was to enlist.[190] Some men were unpleasantly surprised upon receiving letters sending them to training centres for an unexpected service. *Joining Up* reassuringly represented the Recruiting Officer as 'a sort of guide, philosopher and friend to the soldier to be. Tell him what branch of the service you fancy. Let him know all your special qualifications ... [he] will guide you, although he can't give you any guarantee of any particular corps or regiment.'[191] Individuals' descriptions of their enlistment suggest that the experience of the process was not this straightforward. Some men were interviewed by Recruiting Officers from all three services as their first and second preferences had no interest. George Stagg recounted:

They examined you and then said 'A1' or whatever it might be, then they said 'What service would you like, RAF, Army or Navy' and of course I said 'the Navy please' and they said 'Oh, Sorry, we don't want anybody ... you'll have to see that chap next door', they had like three cubicles ... where they had an interviewing officer and I went into the Army one and they said 'what would you like to do in the Army, would you like to be a dispatch rider', so I said 'that's alright', 'the signals?' so I said 'yes that's fine' ... they said 'right you'll hear from us in a few weeks time'.[192]

Others claimed not to have had the opportunity to express a preference at all. When William Bell was called to interview he

> was asked what work I was doing and I mentioned the fact that I'd worked on ships in repair and one thing or another and straight away the guy who was interviewing me said 'Righto, you're going to be in the Navy' and that's as much choice as I had, mind you I'm pleased about it because I didn't particularly want to be in the Army, but it was just taken out of my hands really.[193]

These two examples indicate a lack of individual agency, but Charles Seibert's testimony demonstrates that the quick-thinking conscript could try to shape his service at the point of interview. Upon learning that Seibert had worked in foundries his interviewer asked

> 'So you know all about furnaces and boilers then?' so I thought well whatever that is I don't like the sound of it, so I said 'No, I don't know anything about those', I had visions of being put in the engineers in a hospital or something, shovelling coal into a boiler [laughter], so at that time, you know, being a youngster, enthusiastic, I said that I wanted to go in the Tank Corps ... but when I got my call up papers I was posted to ... heavy anti-aircraft [....][194]

That registration and call-up could be confusing is demonstrated by the experience of Arthur Finn. Having heard the radio announcement that Britain was at war with Germany, Arthur and his neighbours gathered in the street. He and a neighbour of the same age were talking and decided that they 'ought to volunteer. For no reason other than the fact that my father had served in the Merchant Navy in the First World War, I suggested that we should offer our services to the Royal Navy.' The pair discovered the Recruiting Office was closed, and returned the following day to be told that volunteering for the duration was not an option; it was twelve years or eighteen, which neither wanted. Finn returned to work at the Bristol Aeroplane Company, until February 1940 when he turned 20 and was required to register for National Service. He was asked to express a service preference and stated the Navy. When, in July, he attended his medical examination he was disappointed to learn

158 *Joining up in the Second World War*

the RAF were conducting it, but his protests were ignored. He asked, 'eventually what the nearest thing was to the Navy, [and] was told Coastal Command would be something similar and so I accepted this offer'. In early September 1940 he received his call-up papers:

> I had a quick look, noticed that I had to report to Exeter on 16 September, put the envelope in my pocket and hurried off to work where I informed my workmates that I would soon be off to join the RAF. One of them looked at the papers and laughingly pointed out that I was being called up into the Army. Efforts to get this changed at the various recruiting offices were fruitless and so I accepted the inevitable, enjoying the doubtful record of having volunteered for the Navy, been medically examined by the RAF and called up into the Army.[195]

How much the majority of conscripts knew about the processes in which they were involved has to be open to question. MO's research suggested that creating public understanding of wartime schemes was difficult. Although households were barraged with booklets of official instructions a minority of people reported reading them and some said they never saw them at all. MO noted that even in August 1939, with official leaflets a novelty and air raids a genuine cause of anxiety, 'in a sample of 1,000 people (near Bolton and London) nearly half had not attempted to read or look at the official leaflets distributed to every household'.[196] Campaigns to teach Londoners how to extinguish incendiary bombs educated only two-thirds of those surveyed,[197] and when MO investigated public awareness of clothes rationing they also found significant levels of misunderstanding, notwithstanding what they considered relatively good dissemination of information.[198] When asked specifically about conscription, Mass Observers themselves displayed an understanding of their own liabilities for service, but even among these respondents, who were evidently interested in the world around them and disproportionately well educated, a significant minority were demonstrably misinformed about what would happen to them and when.[199]

The understanding demonstrated by interviewees also varied significantly. Some volunteered with little knowledge of what they were volunteering for and without understanding that they could have been reserved if they had stayed put. Others, as will become clear in discussions in Chapters 4 and 5, well understood how to manipulate the system to increase their chances of serving, or not serving, where they wished. The oral histories also suggest those approaching conscription age gained some understanding from the experiences of older peers and siblings, as well as from more official channels, and the 'overheard' conversation in the café well illustrates how this could occur. Members of Air Training Corps appear to have had particularly good understandings of conscription, perhaps because one had to be particularly proactive to ensure entry into the RAF and unit leaders were able to educate young men in how to go about it. Indeed, former ATC members often said that they had joined the ATC *because* they had firm ideas about the role they wished to obtain during the war and hoped it would help. The interviews also demonstrate that while some young men discussed their enlistment aspirations with friends, and some went to the Recruiting Office with mates, young men's decisions about enlistment were often taken alone and parents were often not consulted. Interviewees who had not conferred with their parents commonly explained that they had expected their parents to be unhappy at their decision to volunteer or to attempt to dissuade them from enlisting any sooner than was necessary. As was illustrated earlier in relation to MO's street survey, some parents expressed objections to their sons' military service that were informed by their own memories of the Great War, and as will be discussed in Chapter 4, oral histories show some sons assumed that their parents' knowledge of the Great War would lead them either to worry about or object to their sons enlisting voluntarily.

Conclusion

As the Second World War loomed, both British politicians and the British public looked backwards to the Great War and hoped that conscription would not need to be introduced. One lesson from the previous conflict, though, was the importance of introducing conscription and manpower controls early. Ultimately, conscription began before the war, and over the course of the Second World War the National Service Acts and related legislation gave the State

160 *Joining up in the Second World War*

increasing control over manpower in wartime Britain. Nevertheless, the imposition of conscription and strict controls on who would work where did not generate widespread resistance. By the time Chamberlain had conceded conscription was a necessity a majority of Britons had accepted its inevitability and between 1939 and 1945 those who were directly affected by conscription remained broadly acquiescent.

In April 1939, Britons' responses to peacetime conscription were largely positive. Some of the young men of militia age felt the same way, though they were largely 'public-spirited' volunteers, and the majority of those who were to spend six months in the forces were against the idea. Most disliked that conscription would disrupt their lives and careers, some simply found the idea undesirable, some complained that it impinged upon their liberty and for some it was another class's war, or a combination of these factors. Once the war had broken out, however, few men actively opposed conscription. Few men were convicted for failure to register or attend medical examinations, and even those taking the legitimate route of conscientious objection were insignificant in number. This does not, however, mean that Britons universally accepted the effects of conscription or passively awaited instructions from the State. Indeed, the lack of opposition to manpower controls may have been because, as this chapter has shown, men who understood the system retained a surprising degree of agency. They regularly exercised this agency to negotiate the terms of their service, in ways less visible than conscientious objection and more legitimate than failing to register. By changing employers, enlisting in the Territorials or enrolling at university, or through their military medical examinations and interviews with recruiting sergeants, men attempted to influence how they would participate in Britain's War. As has been suggested here, and will be demonstrated more fully in Chapters 4 and 5, men could use the system not only to get out of but also to get *into* the forces, and to control their positioning within them. These aspects of the individual navigation of military experience – and the implications in terms of how men thought about war – have not previously been considered in scholarly works on wartime service.

The various pieces of manpower legislation during the war were attempts to solve a particular problem of resource allocation, rather than tools to communicate a particular construction of wartime masculinity, but as formal, legal statements of what was expected of specific groups of citizens they nevertheless had that effect. Moreover, by examining them we can see some of the State's assumptions about men and military service. Faced with the need to be ready for rapid expansion of the forces, the Militia Act of 1939 asserted that it was *young men* on whom the expectation of wartime service fell first and foremost. This principle continued throughout the war. The much more expansive National Service (Armed Forces) Act 1939 affected a significantly wider age range, but it too was limited to men, and while it made men up to the age of 41 liable for service, it was the youngest who were called first. Prior to making the proclamation of May 1940 the State had considered combing out young men from reserved occupations rather than forcing older men to enlist, and from January 1942 the shift from block reservation to individual reservation also prioritised removing the youngest men from ROs first. The system of reservation acknowledged that some men were more valuable as civilians than as soldiers, but the system's default assumption remained that a man was most useful in the services unless a case could be made otherwise. This was reinforced by the principle of dilution, which 'released' men for the forces. While the National Service Act 1942 enabled the conscription of women into the forces, combat remained reserved for, and the duty of, men.

Examining men's attitudes to conscription and military service helps to explain the decisions men made and did not make, and why some used the agency they retained as they did. Perhaps because conscription was established quickly, evolved slowly and caused little outward dissent, MO did not frequently or consistently investigate how men felt about conscription and military service during the war, despite their evident interest in morale.[200] The next chapter, however, makes use of MO material from January 1940 and oral history interviews to look at responses to conscription over the course of the war. Crucially, these sources also enable deeper investigation of men's motivations, the ways in which they wanted to serve, and the means by which they attempted to negotiate the system. These extensive enlistment narratives also allow a much fuller exploration of a thread that has been highlighted throughout this chapter: that when Britons – be they politicians or labourers,

162 *Joining up in the Second World War*

parents or adolescents – thought about what military service would be like in a second global conflict, they often drew on their imagined reconstructions of the last great war.

Notes

1 Cited in Hucker, 'Franco-British Relations', p. 441.
2 Todman, *Into Battle*, p. 133.
3 PPU: Ceadel, *Semi-detached Idealists*, p. 334; LNU: McCarthy, *British People and the League of Nations*, pp. 3–4.
4 Ceadel, 'First British Referendum', pp. 810–39 (p. 838), and see Ceadel, *Pacifism in Britain*.
5 George Gallup, *The Gallup International Public Opinion Polls, Great Britain, 1937–1975* (New York: Random, 1976) p. 1.
6 *Ibid.*, p. 3.
7 Mass Observation, *Britain*, p. 46.
8 *Ibid.*, pp. 30–1.
9 *Ibid.*, p. 66.
10 Hucker, *Public Opinion*, pp. 249–52.
11 MO, *Britain*, p. 76.
12 *Ibid.*, p. 76.
13 Quoted in Allport, *Browned Off and Bloody-Minded*, p. 41.
14 *Daily Mail*, 12 October 1938, cited in Hucker, 'Franco-British Relations', p. 443. *Daily Mail*, 26 October 1938, cited in Dennis, *Decision by Default*, p. 149.
15 *News Chronicle*, 19 October 1938, cited in Hucker, 'Franco-British Relations', p. 443.
16 Crowson, 'The Conservative Party and the Call for National Service'.
17 Brookshire, 'Speak for England', pp. 265, 275.
18 HC Debates Vol. 331 col. 86, 1 November 1938, cited in Broad, *Conscription in Britain, 1939–1963*, p. 34.
19 Dennis, *Decision by Default*, pp. 189–90. Dennis notes the Government were frustrated that young fit men were opting for these services rather than the TA. Peter Dennis, *The Territorial Army, 1906–1940* (Woodbridge: Boydell, 1987) pp. 234–5.
20 Ministry of Labour and National Service. Report for the years 1939–1946 [CMD 7225] House of Commons Parliamentary Papers Online, p. 3.
21 *Ibid.*, p. 7, see pp. 5–8.
22 Quoted in Dennis, *Decision by Default*, p. 163.
23 [CMD 7225] p. 6.

You and the Call-Up 163

24 Gallup, *Gallup*, p. 12.
25 Dennis, *Territorial Army*, pp. 236–7.
26 Barker, *Conscience, Government and War*, p. 10.
27 Todman, *Into Battle*, p. 182.
28 *Ibid.*, p. 179.
29 *Ibid.*, pp. 180–2.
30 *Ibid.*, pp. 181–2.
31 *Ibid.*, pp. 185.
32 *Ibid.*, pp. 184–90; Hucker, *Public Opinion*, p. 249.
33 MO, *Britain*, p. 77.
34 Hucker, *Public Opinion*, pp. 249–52.
35 Dennis, *Decision*, pp. 196–200.
36 Gallup, *Gallup*, p. 16.
37 Todman, *Into Battle*, p. 180. Nevertheless, plans were not in place to equip or train these additional recruits. Allport, *Browned Off and Bloody-Minded*, p. 46.
38 Those wishing to enter the RAF or Navy rather than the Army were able to. [CMD 7225] pp. 8–9. For draft of the Bill, see Cabinet, Military Training Bill, 30 April 1939, TNA, CAB 24/285.
39 French, *Raising Churchill's Army*, p. 82 cited in Allport, *Browned Off and Bloody-Minded*, p. 42.
40 Hucker, 'Franco-British Relations', pp. 450–1.
41 MO, TC29/142/1/C [Harrisson, letter to Darlow, 28 April 1939]. Boys' conscription age – 42, boys just above – 36, parents – 130, girlfriends and fiancées – 13, unconcerned households – 166. Harrisson noted only 15 people of upper/upper-middle class had been reached, in comparison to 94 lower-middle and 293 working.
42 MO File Report 361 [Attitudes to Military Training Bill, 1939].
43 MO, TC29/142/1/C [Verbatim responses to Military Training Bill Street Surveys, 26 and 27 April 1939]. The verbatim responses recorded on the microfiche number 204 men and 201 women; 6% were undecided, 6% uninterested and 5% unwilling to answer.
44 Harrisson, letter to Darlow.
45 MO, TC29/142/1/C [Verbatims].
46 *Ibid.*, unpaginated. The responses are anonymous and without identifying numbers.
47 *Ibid.*
48 Melanie Tebbutt, *Being Boys. Youth, Leisure and Identity in the Inter-War Years* (Manchester: Manchester University Press, 2012) p. 88.
49 MO, TC29/142/1/C [Verbatims].
50 *Ibid.*

164 *Joining up in the Second World War*

51 *Ibid.*
52 *Ibid.*
53 *Ibid.*
54 Gregory, *Silence*, p. 40.
55 MO, TC29/142/1/C [Verbatims].
56 *Ibid.*
57 *Ibid.*
58 *Ibid.*
59 *Ibid.*
60 *Ibid.*
61 *Ibid.*
62 Martin Pugh, *We Danced All night. A social history of Britain between the Wars* (London: Vintage, 2009) p. 443.
63 Hore Belisha, Parliamentary Debates, House of Commons, 5th Series, vol. 346, col. 2230, 5 May 1939.
64 Dennis, *Territorial*, pp. 234–5. See also Flint, IWM-SA-899; Taylor, IWM-SA-10484; Harper, IWM-SA-10923.
65 [CMD 7225] p. 9 and CAB 24/285.
66 R. Douglas Brown, *East Anglia 1939* (Lavenham: Terence Dalton, 1980) p. 152.
67 Sir V. Warrender, Parliamentary Debates, House of Commons, 5th series, vol. 347, col. 493 (10 May 1939).
68 Dennis, *Territorial*, p. 249.
69 Brown, *East Anglia*, p. 187.
70 Gallup, *Gallup*, p. 16.
71 *Ibid.*, p. 21.
72 MO, TC29/142/1/C [Verbatims].
73 Based on Parker, *Manpower*, table 1, p. 481.
74 [CMD 7225] p. 4.
75 War Cabinet, The Calling Up of Men for the Armed Forces, Memorandum by the Minister of Labour and National Service, 15 December 1939, TNA, CAB 67/3/40.
76 The Calling Up of Men for the Armed Forces, Memorandum by the Minister of Labour and National Service, 28 September 1939, TNA, CAB 67/1/22.
77 CAB 67/1/22.
78 CAB 67/3/40.
79 *Ibid.*
80 Mackay, *Half the Battle*, pp. 9–12.
81 CAB 67/3/40. Ultimately, the announcement had to be made on 31 December 1939 for legal reasons – see War Cabinet, Conclusions of a Meeting of the War Cabinet, 19 December 1939, TNA, CAB 65/2/53.

You and the Call-Up

165

82 CAB 65/2/53.

83 *Ibid.*

84 War Cabine, Eighth report submitted by the Minister of Labour and National Service covering the period 16–31 December 1939, TNA, CAB 68/4/12.

85 Those who turned 21, 22, 23 or 24 during 1940.

86 Those who turned 25, 26, 27 or 28 during 1940, and those who turned 20 in 1940.

87 War Cabinet, Manpower available for the Armed Forces, 30 April 1940, TNA, CAB 67/6/16.

88 *Ibid.*

89 Douglas Reed, *A Prophet at Home*, p.187 quoted in Calder, *People's War*, p. 51.

90 Paul Addison and Jeremy Crang (eds), *Listening to Britain: Home Intelligence Reports on Britain's Finest Hour, May–September 1940* (London: Vintage Digital, 2011) p. 27.

91 *Ibid.*, pp. 93, 99, 114, 128, 163.

92 *Ibid.*, p. 124.

93 *Ibid.*, p. 132.

94 *Ibid.*, p. 129.

95 *Ibid.*, p. 140. See also Nottingham, p. 221, 12 July 1940.

96 [CMD 7225] p. xix.

97 *Ibid.*, pp. 11–12. For registration dates, see appendix 1, p. 355.

98 About 5,700 men were posted under the National Service Acts to the Police War Reserve, 24,400 to the National Fire Service and 262 to the Civil Defence Reserve; *ibid.*, p. 29. Most were optants, but 'for a short time is was necessary to call up for the National Fire Service'; Parker, *Manpower*, p. 164. Postings to the PWR were suspended in December 1942, to the NFS in July 1943 and Civil Defence Reserve in October 1944. Men aged over 30, or over 25 who had been reserved, were considered for direction to Civil Defence.

99 [CMD 7225] p. 10. For draft of this bill, War Cabinet, The National Service (No. 2) Bill, TNA, CAB.67.9.12.

100 [CMD 7225] pp. 10, 29.

101 From April 1941 women aged 21, and later 18–24, had been able to be directed, with the force of compulsion, to useful war work. Summerfield, *Reconstructing Women's Wartime Lives*, p. 45.

102 This authority was granted by Order in Council (SR and O 1942, no. 91) January 1942 [CMD 7225] p. 30. For its effects upon the Home Guard, see Summerfield and Peniston-Bird, *Contesting Home Defence*, p. 48.

166   *Joining up in the Second World War*

103 [CMD 7225]. This number does not include those who opted to enter mining. For the subjective experiences of Bevin Boys, see Tom Hickman, *Called Up, Sent Down* (Stroud: Sutton, 2008).

104 Parker, *Manpower*, table IV, p. 485.

105 *Ibid.*, p. 154.

106 House of Commons Debates, 30 May 1938, vol. 336, 1765–96 quoted in Pattinson, McIvor and Robb, *Men In Reserve*, p. 61.

107 Parker, *Manpower*, p. 41.

108 House of Commons Debates, 20 December 1938, vol. 342, 2713–833, quoted in Juliette Pattinson, ' "Shirkers", "Scrimjacks" and "Scrimshanks"? British Civilian Masculinity and Reserved Occupations, 1914–1945', *Gender and History*, 28.3 (2016) pp. 709–27 (p. 712).

109 Chand, *Masculinities on Clydeside*, pp. 5–11.

110 Pattinson, McIvor and Robb, *Men in Reserve*, p. 50. See also [CMD 7225] pp. 13–14. Until May 1940 the SRO also prevented the enlistment of men who were unemployed but had worked in trades on the SRO; from May they could enlist if unemployed for two months or more. Pattinson, McIvor and Robb, *Men in Reserve*, pp. 69–70.

111 Pattinson, McIvor and Robb, *Men in Reserve*, p. 62.

112 See [CMD 7225] pp. 16–17.

113 [CMD 7225] pp. 13–14. On service role, see Pattinson, McIvor and Robb, *Men in Reserve*, p. 75.

114 MO, *US*, 3, Mass-Observation's Weekly Intelligence Service, 17 February 1940, pp. 5–8.

115 MO DR2009, January 1940 Directive.

116 Pattinson, McIvor and Robb, *Men in Reserve*, p. 68. [CMD 7225] pp. 15–17. In mining the age threshold was lowered, which potentially trapped young miners who had been intending to leave.

117 *Ibid.*, p. 69.

118 *Ibid.*

119 *Ibid.*, p. 77.

120 Parker, *Manpower*, pp. 145–6.

121 *Ibid.*

122 Pattinson, McIvor and Robb, *Men in Reserve*, pp. 84–5.

123 Parker, *Manpower*, p. 299.

124 [CMD 7225] pp. 15–16.

125 *Ibid.*, pp. 14–15. Parker, *Manpower*, p. 299.

126 Parker, *Manpower*, pp. 145–6.

127 *Ibid.*, pp. 122–3.

128 Essential Work (General Provisions) Order (SR and O 1941, no. 302). Some specified industries were exempted.

129 Parker, *Manpower*, pp. 108–9.

You and the Call-Up 167

130 *Ibid.*, pp. 137–43.
131 *Ibid.*, p. 141.
132 *Ibid.*, table XI, p. 497. Much like registration under the NSA, the Registration for Employment order, in place from April 1941, required men aged 41–50 (and women) to register and detail their employment in order that they could be directed to essential work. [CMD 7225] pp. 13–17.
133 *Joining Up. A Complete Guide to Those Joining the Army, Navy or Air Force, Etc* (London: War Facts Press, 1940).
134 *Ibid.*, Foreword by Ernest Brown.
135 Robert Pollard, *You and the Call-Up. A Guide for Men and Women* (London: Blandford Press, 1942).
136 *Ibid.*, p. 6.
137 *Joining Up*, p. 51.
138 [CMD 7225] p. 29.
139 *Ibid.*
140 *Ibid.*, p. 25. Up to the end of June 1945 about 22,300 men had become 'optants' (chosen mining).
141 *Joining Up*, pp. 7–8.
142 Pollard, *You and the Call-Up*, p. 6.
143 Parker, *Manpower*, p. 151.
144 Ralph Harris (Morley, 2010).
145 Parker, *Manpower*, p. 151.
146 Pollard, *You and the Call-Up*, p. 16.
147 Science Students – Broad, *Conscription in Britain*, p. 47. Apprentices – [CMD 7225] pp. 18–19.
148 This condition was only applied to about 800 COs, who all willingly joined the National Fire Service [CMD 7225] pp. 24–5. See Barker, *Conscience, Government and War*, pp. 56–8 for discussion of COs in Civil Defence.
149 Tribunals recommend those allowed non-combatant duties joined the RAMC, which most managed, but with the exception of the Chaplain's Corps, all other corps could be requested to take up arms. Confusion about where to place COs was eased by the creation of the Non-Combatant Corps, 'formed expressly for the purpose of receiving objectors into the Army'. Barker, *Conscience, Government and War*, p. 25. For more, see Robb, 'The "Conchie Corps"'.
150 By 1942 the RAMC only had space for those with special qualifications. COs could be asked to do anything that was not combative, including passive air defence. Pollard, *You and the Call-Up*, p. 12.
151 Bernard Smith (pseudonym (Morley, 2016)).

168   *Joining up in the Second World War*

152 Based on Parker, *Manpower*, table VI, pp. 488–90. Barker refers to 1.2% of the five million called up, but as an objection was expressed when registering, it is more sensible to see them as a proportion of those registered, or even as a proportion of those *asked to serve* and also include those who volunteered, which makes them only 0.67%. Still, Barker is correct that objection was more common than during the Great War. Barker, *Conscience, Government and War*, p. 121.

153 This was disproportionate to the number of men registered. With registration on 27 April 1940, over half of conscientious objections had occurred, though only a quarter of NSA registrations had taken place. 80% of conscientious objection occurred by the end of 1940, by which point 58% of NSA registrations had taken place. Based on Parker, *Manpower*, table VI, pp. 488–90.

154 Examining the registration groups and the proportion of COs demonstrates that the bulk of COs were born between 1912 and 1921, which suggests pacifist ideas had a particular pull for this generation. Though constraints of time and space have not permitted the development of this idea here, this suggests the potential productivity of examining PPU membership records to establish the extent to which PPU membership was drawn from a particular generational cohort.

155 In May the proportion objecting was 1.056%, and in June it was 0.775%. 25% fewer men objected in June than had objected in May. The change between April and May's registration was -15%, the same as the median month-on-month changes between February and May (range -12% to -17.5%). Based on Parker, *Manpower*, table VI, pp. 488–90.

156 It still claimed 135,000 members in February 1941. MO File Report 610 March 1941 [Attitudes to Conscientious Objectors].

157 All statistics based on data in Parker, *Manpower*, table VI, pp. 488–90.

158 [CMD 7225] p. 25.

159 Parker, *Manpower*, p. 157.

160 Failure to comply, 250 – see [CMD 7225] p. 24. Failure to submit to medical, 1,891, but figures run to 1948 without annual breakdown – see Barker, *Conscience, Government and War*, p. 26.

161 Parker, *Manpower*, p. 151.

162 [CMD 7225] p. 22.

163 Pollard, *You and the Call-Up*, p. 8.

164 *Joining Up*, p. 12.

165 Newlands, *Civilians into Soldiers*, p. 27.

166 *Ibid.*, p. 28.

167 Those examined for the RAF had a second, more stringent, medical examination.

You and the Call-Up 169

168 Mann, IWM-SA-18513. See also Donovan, IWM-SA-20316.
169 House of Commons Debates, 29 April 1942, vol. 379, col. 1044, quoted in Newlands, *Civilians into Soldiers*, p. 40.
170 Newlands, *Civilians into Soldiers*, p. 32.
171 Based on Parker, *Manpower*, table VIII, p. 495. Definition of medical grades can be found in [CMD 7225] appendix 2. See also Newlands, *Civilians into Soldiers*, pp. 30–2.
172 Parker, *Manpower*, p. 152.
173 Peniston-Bird, 'Classifying the Body', p. 36.
174 Newlands, *Civilians into Soldiers*, p. 27.
175 MO File Report 33, February 1940.
176 Newlands, *Civilians into Soldiers*, p. 42.
177 *Ibid.*, pp. 42–3.
178 MO Topic Collections 29, Microfiche Reel 142. Section 1/B [Observations in Stepney, 29.7.40].
179 MO File Report 274 [Attitude of Civilians to Military/Talk about conscription on the streets] noted that the ambition to not achieve A-1 status was also expressed by a middle-class man drunk in a night-club, who kept repeating 'They passed me A-1 Fit, can you believe it? It's just bloody', and concluded that this desire was not therefore confined to the one particular class.
180 Newlands, *Civilians into Soldiers*, p. 44.
181 Peniston-Bird comments on the scarcity of sources to establish this, but notes that the police investigated a number of cases of incorrect medical certificates being purchased. Peniston-Bird, 'Classifying the Body', p. 40.
182 Browne (Morley, 2010).
183 Elson (Morley, 2010).
184 See Peniston-Bird, 'Classifying the Body', p. 35 and Newlands, *Civilians into Soldiers*, pp. 44–5.
185 Albert Parker, IWM-SA-14788, quoted in Newlands, *Civilians into Soldiers*, p. 45.
186 FR 1402 Civilian War Work MO Bulletin (to panel), September 1942.
187 MOA Diary 5039, February 1941, pp. 7–8, quoted in Newlands, *Civilians into Soldiers*, p. 44.
188 Hay (Morley, 2010). Donovan, IWM-SA-20316, said if you could breathe you were in.
189 Men who had expressed preference for the Royal Navy but had not been accepted were, if they were willing, considered for the merchant Navy. [CMD 7225] p. 26.
190 The process differed slightly for those joining the Army after 1942, as they completed basic training at a General Service Corps, after which

170   *Joining up in the Second World War*

their abilities were assessed and they were assigned a branch. Broad, *Conscription in Britain*, p. 129. For discussion of the adoption of this process and evolving Army selection measures, see French, *Raising Churchill's Army*.

191 *Joining Up*, p. 12.

192 Stagg (Morley, 2010).

193 William Henry Bell, IWM-SA-22585, 2002.

194 Seibert, IWM-SA-18485.

195 Arthur Finn, BBC People's War website, Article ID A4119851 written 1994, contributed 2005 by his daughter. www.bbc.co.uk/history/ ww2peopleswar/stories/51/a4119851.shtml It is worth noting the distinctly anecdotal nature of this story with its tri-service punchline, but its indication of the vagaries of the process fits with details recounted by several interviewees, including being turned away by the Navy when volunteering only for the duration early on in the war.

196 *Home Propaganda, A Report Prepared by Mass Observation for the Advertising Services Guild*, Change, no. 2, Bulletin of the Advertising Service Guild, September 1941, p. 37.

197 *Ibid.*, pp. 7–8.

198 *Clothes Rationing Survey. An Interim Report prepared by Mass Observation for the Advertising Service Guild*, Change, no. 1, Bulletin of the Advertising Service Guild, August 1941.

199 MO DR1276, DR2375, DR2101, DR1532, DR2085, January 1940 Directive.

200 The introduction of the conscription of women in December 1941 did spur a small amount of research; MO FR 1009 [Manpower and Conscription, December 1941]; MOA 1.2.75.5.c.4– [Manpower conscription questionnaire results 1941].

4

Attitudes to service and the Great War in the Second World War

Introduction

On 11 November 1939, a woman in a Bolton fish shop commented that her son would soon be conscripted. A fellow customer offered reassurance – 'He'll be alright, you've nothing to worry about' – but she was not appeased: 'Yes, but I won't be alright. I had enough last war – they took my husband then, and now they want my two lads.'[1] Her response illustrates that the effects of conscription were felt beyond those who were to be called up and that the memory of the Great War continued to shape how many Britons anticipated and responded to the Second World War.[2] The sense that mothers in particular were being asked to lend their sons to the service of the State, and that they were not willing to do so, pervades discussion of familial responses to men's wartime enlistment. Men themselves were often reluctant, too. This chapter uses oral histories and MO material to explore young men's attitudes to conscription and volunteering during the Second World War and to examine how these were influenced by understandings of the Great War.

Perhaps because the Great War had set a precedent, Britons ostensibly met conscription with far more compliance than resistance.[3] This may explain why sustained examinations of what young men thought and felt about conscription and enlistment remain uncommon,[4] though attention has been paid to the relatively inconsequential proportion of British men who expressed a conscientious objection.[5] This chapter adds a wider and deeper consideration of young men's attitudes and decisions about enlistment to the historiography. Alan Allport well illustrates that young men held a variety of attitudes towards enlistment in the Army, but the RAF and Navy

172   *Joining up in the Second World War*

were beyond the scope of his book.[6] Similarly, within a study with broader aims, Frances Houghton has explored how Second World War veterans who had been 'at the sharp end' from all three services presented enlistment in their memoirs, and found that most claimed to have been enthusiastic about their enlistment.[7] This chapter includes the views of those who did not covet or hold combat (or even military) roles, and considers what men said at the time as well as afterwards. It reveals a more nuanced and detailed picture of conscription in the Second World War. A distinct lack of unanimity was camouflaged by what outwardly appeared overwhelming compliance with State direction; individual young men held diverse attitudes and took varied decisions around enlistment in an effort to negotiate the nature of their wartime service. Younger recruits in particular were able to conceive of wartime service in heroic, adventurous or patriotic terms, as some of their counterparts had done decades before, and as Houghton has suggested of some combat veterans.[8] More commonly, though, and unlike Houghton's memoirists, men reluctantly consented to service that they felt was an unwelcome interruption to their working and domestic lives. Their compliance was, however, at least in part, due to the potential for individuals to negotiate (or at least attempt to negotiate) the manpower system to obtain wartime service that suited their own desires. Chapter 3 highlighted the extent to which men retained agency despite the implementation of conscription. This chapter gives further consideration to how men used that agency to position themselves within the forces, rather than to stay out of uniform. It shows that volunteering – the most obvious expression of agency – was often a method of negotiation to ensure entry into the forces, and especially the service a man wanted. Discussion of why some men opted to wait for conscription and what motivated others to volunteer is followed by explanation of men's service preferences over the course of the war. Crucially, understandings of the Great War often shaped men's service preferences.

The second half of the chapter addresses the Great War's influence and illustrates how complex this was. As was discussed in the Introduction, the connection between attitudes to the two wars has not been the subject of extensive historical discussion. As was explored in Chapter 1, within the breadth of representations of the Great War in popular culture in inter-war Britain, the most popular

Attitudes to service 173

and commonly encountered were those that placed the conflict in a traditional framework. Sheffield has suggested that young men remained fascinated by war, and that the continued existence of representations that presented the Great War in traditional terms explains why 'so many young men proved resistant to the trend among the intellectual elite of revulsion against the First World War'.[9] Trott cites examples of men who engaged with 'disillusioned' literature as young men in the inter-war period and notes that they did not necessarily turn to pacifism as a result, and for some this even fostered curiosity about war; Christopher Isherwood felt ashamed that he had not taken part, and George Orwell felt 'less of a man' because he had missed it.[10] Houghton has observed that the Great War features in Second World War veterans' memoirs; the 'pleasure culture' depictions of the Great War could spur interest in military service, and less positive understandings were included as justifications for preferring RAF service over the Army.[11] These suggestions are plausible, but the influence of the Great War on joining up in the Second World War has not previously been the focus of a substantial study. Given that Chapters 1 and 2 demonstrate that young men's engagement with representations of the Great War was more complex than has previously been suggested, it is worthwhile exploring this topic in greater depth, and using an approach that has the potential to shed more light. As well as examining a broader range of personal testimonies, including more young men who grew up in working-class households,[12] the original oral histories provide the opportunity to probe the significance interviewees placed on the Great War, and to view their narratives of joining up in tandem with their recollections of their engagement with representations of the Great War. The chapter considers how young men's attitudes, and the feelings and advice of their parents, were affected by their understandings of the Great War. It reveals the complexity of the Great War's influence. The attitudes and decisions of many young men, but not all, were shaped by their understandings of the Great War, but the effects were not straightforward, particularly when those understandings were informed by both representations encountered in popular culture and from veterans. Understandings of the Great War did influence how men sought to spend their wartime service, most commonly discouraging service in the Army, and

174   *Joining up in the Second World War*

especially the infantry, but did not commonly cause men to withdraw their consent to serve.

Conscription in the Phoney War

In January 1940, in the midst of the 'Phoney War', the Ministry of Labour and National Service announced that all men aged 20–8 would be liable for conscription before January 1941. In response MO asked their Panel of observers: 'If you think you are going to be called up this year, what are your reactions to this and how has it affected your personal plans for the future?'[13] More than 150 men responded. Half had already been made liable for conscription or even registered and so could report their reactions to being conscripted based on experience, and many others responded even though they did not anticipate being called up in 1940.[14] Ten per cent were over conscription age, but they were largely willing to participate in the war effort.[15] One Great War veteran, far from disillusioned, complained that the government had so far 'spurned the services of ex-servicemen' and somewhat presciently remarked they 'will be glad of us before long (if bombing raids come for example)'.[16] Another, who had enlisted in the Great War aged 15 and served three years in the infantry, wrote that fighting ruined men and he 'would rather face it again than let my son go', but also wrote, 'Strangely enough there is something about the smell of dead men, high explosives and earthy smells that does link my mind with a desire to get down to it again.'[17] More importantly, though, half the respondents were aged 20–8; a fifth were older but still under 41, the maximum age for conscription; and a fifth were under 20 but old enough that they would be eligible for conscription if the war lasted a year or two. For most of the respondents the question was therefore highly relevant.

As a declaration of war was notably absent when MO first assessed attitudes to conscription in the street surveys of April 1939, the reactions men on the panel expressed in January 1940 are a useful comparison and enable a more accurate suggestion of attitudes to conscription and military service *during* wartime.[18] When MO wrote about the January 1940 replies in February 1940 they looked to the Great War and noted with surprise that young

Attitudes to service

men did not feel they were 'fighting for the mistakes of the older generation', but saw amongst the responses 'little positive enthusiasm for the war, plenty of strong support for the negative idea of "stopping Hitler"'.[19] Re-evaluating the verbatim material provides little reason to quarrel with MO's assessment about overall morale, but does provide a greater understanding of what respondents' attitudes towards conscription were, what underpinned them and how this varied according to age. Men's attitudes were, of course, diverse, ranging from those inclined to grasp any socially respectable opportunity of exemption to those who keenly anticipated wartime service. MO – characteristically pessimistic about Britons – worried that young men in 1940 exhibited 'nothing comparable to the fervour and energy shown by those who bore the brunt of the last war'.[20] They were right that only a minority of potential recruits exuded enthusiasm, but they were wrong to misremember enthusiasm as the dominant reaction to the outbreak of the Great War;[21] consequently, they missed the similarities between reactions in 1914 and 1940.

In his study of working-class volunteers in the Great War, David Silbey found escape and adventure to be motivations for enlistment.[22] He reminded his reader that 'no sombre thoughts of trenches and gas masks troubled the clerks and greengrocers ... who joined up in their thousands'.[23] Those facing conscription twenty-six years later could not say the same, and yet a minority of respondents were eager to enter the services. They tended to be younger men who saw the possibility of adventure and an escape from humdrum lives. A 21-year-old student who had applied for his conscription to be postponed to complete exams had heard nothing further at the point of writing to MO. He was:

> rather at the crossroads about it, however, as common sense tell[s] me to make every effort to get postponement and finish my course but I have a sort of feeling that there is in this thing a chance of adventure. I keep telling myself this second business is all rot and war nowadays isn't an adventure but I still hope. I might perhaps get to China, Egypt, Palestine, or even France. I wouldn't care much if I had to go.[24]

Implicit in his apparently unwanted awareness that 'war nowadays isn't an adventure' is the suggestion that the Great War should have

176   *Joining up in the Second World War*

taught him something, yet adventure remained an alluring prospect, just as representations of warfare as adventure had remained commonly encountered in popular culture. Similarly, a 24-year-old vegetable salesman was looking forward to his call-up, 'aside from a natural dislike of the possibility of being polished off in my prime', because '[i]t will make a change from the daily grind anyway. I am a bachelor, no strings, no dependants, and every possibility of my job being kept open ....'[25]

For many others, just as in 1914, domestic and economic considerations shaped attitudes to enlistment. Particularly for older men, responsibilities to family trumped responsibilities to the State, and enthusiasm was contingent on ensuring that they would have something to return to and that their domestic duties would be met. Businesses,[26] children[27] and families had to be looked after; as a pharmacist, 32, wrote, 'if I could assure my wife and family of anything like their present circumstances, I should volunteer for the RAMC at once'.[28] Volunteering at once was not the intention of the majority of the respondents in January 1940, though. A 28-year-old teacher 'hate[d] the thought of leaving my wife quite literally holding the baby',[29] and a 39-year-old clerk wrote: 'I should certainly not volunteer, but would go without grumbling when called on [....] Talk of fighting for democracy and King and Country leaves me cold, but I should do as I was told just like the rest.'[30] The clerk demonstrated his acceptance and sense of duty but recognised his enlistment ensured domestic upheaval, and his primary concern was how his wife and child would manage the loss of income.[31] After all, what was the point of defending hearth and home against Hitler if doing so meant defaulting on the mortgage?

Amongst those respondents under the age of 20, who could see conscription approaching, resignation and fatalism characterised reluctant acceptance. A clerk, 18, hoped to be deferred to complete exams, and if this was not granted he would 'undoubtedly not have the kindest possible feelings towards "King and Country". Beyond that my feelings are fatalistic – what must be must.'[32] A conceptualisation of the process of enlistment as a negotiation where both parties could compromise is inherent in this response – if the State would limit the potential disruption of his service by granting deferment, then he would accept his service as necessary. People of all ages voiced their objections to having employment disrupted, but it was most common amongst those under the age of 20. Most perceived their service as necessary, but this did not lessen its impacts on their futures. A 17-year-old engineer's assistant's response was typical: 'My opinion is that is it a dirty job that's got to be done and the sooner done the better. I feel that all my ambitions and plans for the future are shattered.'[33] Even those prepared to look for positives in enforced service shared this annoyance. One noted that 'Army life does not seem too bad [....] I am not exactly pleased at having a carefully planned career interrupted just as it was getting under way and rendering some three years' work practically fruitless.'[34]

Some were pragmatic. A 20-year-old clerk wrote, 'Whilst I see no glory in war, I accept the situation as it is and intend making the best of it.'[35] A journalist, 24, was determined to achieve fast promotion to ensure he would profit financially,[36] while another resolved to learn to be a wireless operator to improve his future employment prospects.[37] Others, particularly the older respondents, were more accepting but unenthusiastic. A boot-repairer, 33, wrote that he had 'no burning desire to respond, but neither have I any strong desire to avoid it'.[38] A teacher, 25, had 'no desire to be a bloody hero, I do feel that the "cause" is worth fighting for. I am certainly not looking forward to the war "as a picnic" (as some of my more light-hearted acquaintances are) ... but when the time comes I'll be there.'[39] This respondent's assessment of the mood of his peers lends further support to the idea that, regardless of the Great War, it remained possible to approach the Second World War in a spirit of adventure. Nevertheless, reactions like his were more typical – these men would stoically endure service when it came, but they had no intention of accelerating their enlistment; it was 'an unpleasant eventuality to be faced when it occurs'.[40]

Most respondents disliked the prospect of military service. A civil servant, 21, resented the loss of personal freedom, 'the bother and the dislike of having to regulate my life to the military machine: of having to wear clothes I don't like; of being at the beck and call of any young officer, of having to salute him and say "sir" and click my heels and all the rest of the paraphernalia'.[41] A technician, 23, expected to 'resent being quartered with lots of fools who only think about football and women. I shall hate having to be ordered about by men whom I consider my inferiors ... I should hate badly cooked food [and] ill fitting clothes ... I might like the

178 *Joining up in the Second World War*

comradeship.'[42] Annoyance with the disruption of their domestic and professional lives, or concerns about losing access to home comforts, or the freedoms, status and authority enjoyed in civilian life, were commonly expressed reasons for men's dislike of the prospect of conscription. Without doubting the sincerity or significance of these concerns, we can note that it was socially acceptable to voice such feelings. Concern that conscription could result in death was voiced less often. A 31-year-old insurance inspector had put his affairs in order so that 'when the time comes I shall be ready to go. If I survive I hope I may be of some use to the community in the establishment of the new order.'[43] More often, such concerns were an unspoken undertone in reports of frivolous spending, quitting courses of study, breaking off relationships, rushing or delaying marriage or a lack of interest in the future. One respondent wrote he was 'unlikely to think of marrying somebody before I go, as such a lot of people seem to be doing'.[44] His observation was astute. The responses indicate that the war and conscription accelerated planned nuptials,[45] and encouraged marriages that may not have otherwise occurred; a pessimistic CO felt 'inclined to get married as [I] might as well die married as single'.[46] Between 1938 and 1940 the marriage rate increased by 28 per cent, as 'thousands of people decided to marry while they still had the chance'.[47] Conscription did not encourage such spontaneity in all. Many who were not already betrothed found their relationships became wartime casualties,[48] while others set aside contemplation of matrimony, even if they 'fell in love wholeheartedly'.[49]

MO correctly highlighted that a conscript army contained 'many whose private opinion is against joining up, but who are not bold enough to hold a public opinion in opposition to the socially accepted "public opinion" of the moment'.[50] Most disliked the prospect of being conscripted and reluctant acceptance was the most common attitude, but significant minorities of men of all ages were distinctly unhappy and would have seized a respectable exemption. This was not commonly because of an ideological objection, and notably few stated that they did not feel the war was worth fighting.[51] The significant exception to this was the 17 per cent of respondents who stated that they had or would express a conscientious objection. This is a much higher proportion than that in the general population, but this is unsurprising given what is known

Attitudes to service

179

about MO panellists' common political leaning and the age of the respondents. Respondents' conscientious objections were normally based on religious belief, but two respondents added objections about imperialistic and capitalist wars, and democracy being the only justification for war respectively.[52] Respondents were perhaps more forthright and resolute when writing to MO than when communicating with the Ministry for Labour and National Service, but the intention to conscientiously object was more common amongst younger respondents, and younger men expressed stronger convictions than their older counterparts. A farm labourer, 21, awaiting his tribunal, wrote that as only 4 per cent of COs at the London tribunal had obtained unconditional exemption and 'I shall be content with nothing less [it] looks probable ... that I shall spend the duration in prison.'[53] He was far from alone in stating such determination,[54] but some were more flexible. One, who 'look[ed] forward to the Army with the utmost annoyance, fear, and horror', accepted his non-combatant duties because 'the only alternatives are suicide, prison, or stow awaying [sic] on a ship bound for some place like Peru, and none of these seem very practicable or desirable'.[55] While this response can be read as self-consciously facetious, for others the prospect of military service appears to have caused significant distress. One would-be non-combatant, who had told MO 'he would suicide' on his New Year card two months before, explained that his increasing acceptance of military service meant that he no longer felt 'so horribly gloomy about the future as he had in December'; even if his objection was dismissed, at least the process would delay his entrance into the services by a few months.[56] Some expressed a sense that once war had begun 'the best must be made of a bad job',[57] and many were happy to accept non-combatant, normally medical, roles. On the basis of the January 1940 replies, MO argued that because it was 'extremely difficult for individuals to resist conscription *publicly*',[58] 'for every CO there were one or two "latent" objectors' who held, but felt unable to express, a conscientious objection.[59] The ratios suggested are dubious, but certainly some respondents had decided against conscientious objection after genuine contemplation, like a metalworker, 24, who had decided to 'submit [to conscription] rather than the objector's court, as I said previous I am interested in motor cycles so I shall try to join a motor cycle unit'.[60]

180   *Joining up in the Second World War*

More common than conscientious objectors – 'latent' or professed – were men who held no *conscientious* objection, nor a publicly acceptable reason to refuse, but privately rejected service. They resented being forced to enlist and were unwilling to serve, but they were more prepared to comply with the requests of the State and the nation than to face the consequences of publicly refusing to serve. This attitude was particularly clearly expressed by those who actively hoped to avoid military service by obtaining reserved occupations. For example, a 21-year-old who was 'not at all keen to join up' hoped he would be granted postponement until December 1940 to finish studying. He would then 'desperately try' to obtain the building work for which he would be qualified, and get experience as close as possible to what he had intended in peacetime.[61] Another was pleased to be in an RO: '[f]rom the point of view of personal freedom I would far rather stay as I am, as I would find life far more severe in the services. I would also find it difficult to live on 2/ a day.'[62] As will be discussed in Chapter 5, men in ROs were often perceived, or even perceived themselves, to be emasculated by their non-military role. Within all the age groups were, however, discernible and sometimes significant numbers of men who either would not voluntarily relinquish a RO, or who were unhappy about service and would have gladly taken one had it presented itself.[63] Others who knew enlistment was a much more likely prospect instead hoped the war would end. A 20-year-old clerk, more concerned about the loss of home comforts in the military than the danger that service might pose, wrote, 'Nothing would please me more than to find the war over before my services are needed ....'[64] Although most respondents were willing to accept military service, reluctantly and only if necessary, only a minority would have disagreed with his sentiment.

In April 1939, the response to peacetime conscription amongst the broader population had been largely positive. Some of the young men who were militia age felt the same way, though they were largely 'public spirited' volunteers, and the majority of those who were to spend six months in the forces were against the idea. Most disliked that it would disrupt their lives and careers, some simply found the idea undesirable, some complained that it impinged upon their liberty and for some it was another class's war, or a combination of these factors. Most of those who wrote to MO in January 1940,

Attitudes to service

181

after war had been declared, were reluctant conscripts. They had diverse reasons, but significantly, practical considerations were more dominant than ideological ones. Men still expressed concerns about careers and employment, and disruption to one's life, and older men were more concerned about the impact of military wages and their potential (permanent) absence on families than those who had been potentially affected by the Militia Act. Few men actively opposed conscription once war came, but expressions of self-interested negotiation that had been evident in peacetime replies remained common amongst wartime respondents. In terms of positive motivations to accept conscription, a crucial one was, as MO noted, 'stopping Hitler'. Explicit statements of patriotism, particularly of the gung-ho kind, were noticeably absent,[65] but statements of duty were not. Neither, though, were expectations of adventure and excitement.

Writing about 1914, Catriona Pennell has argued that 'War enthusiasm' was an oversimplification: Britons were not, on the whole, jingoistic but accepted war because they were convinced it was unavoidable and necessary, and alongside enthusiasm sat significant worry about the consequences.[66] I have argued elsewhere, based on different MO material, that the picture during the Phoney War in 1939 and 1940 was similar. Britons felt deep regret that war had not been avoided, wishfully hoped that it might not be so bad, were often frustrated, and some were impatient for the war to start if really must be fought at all. The apathy identified in some accounts, including MOs, is more difficult to find.[67] The responses to the January 1940 Directive fit neatly into the same wider picture. MO were right that men demonstrated limited fire and fury, and an attitude of 'Defendism' – the motivation was the negative aim of stopping Hitler, and Britons grumbled and groused about having to do it. Yet that should not be mistaken for meaningful apathy. Instead, it suggests they had reluctantly resigned themselves to having to fight a war they had not wanted to *defend* the status quo. Many men resented the various ways that military service would affect their immediate lives and future plans, but they typically assumed that they would do it anyway. Objections were normally individual rather than ideological, and men more often hoped to manipulate *how* they would take part in the war effort, not *if*. As we will see, the oral histories reveal a similar picture, and enable a deeper examination of men's attitudes to enlistment and service preferences.

182　　　*Joining up in the Second World War*

Conscription, volunteering and service preferences

Almost a year after the outbreak of war MO reported that the call-up remained a subject of conversation on the streets. MO concluded that those young men who were 'left are none too keen. But there is a certain amount of feeling that it is better to volunteer than to "hang about".'[68] Over the course of the war, 1,578,000 successfully volunteered, while 3,179,900 men were conscripted.[69] There are distinct limits to what these numbers reveal about men's attitudes, though. Oral history interviews provide a rich understanding of not only how men felt about military service but also why some opted to volunteer and the various factors that could constrain the agency men could exercise over their wartime service.

As we saw in Chapter 3, when a man's time came the mechanisms of conscription would direct him to a role in which he would benefit the war effort. He might take action to affect this direction in some way, but the knowledge that sooner or later he would be conscripted meant that men did not *need* to give the matter any thought or take any action beyond registering when told and awaiting instructions telling him when and where to go next. 'Hanging about' was a legitimate option, and it was the one that most men took. Jim Stephens was by no means keen to enter the forces. His narrative demonstrated little sense of agency; he and his friends did not discuss their preferred roles, but simply accepted that 'you do what you're told and that's all there was to it'. Regardless, as the fifth of eight children in a working-class family in London's East End, he 'couldn't volunteer because we needed every penny we could lay hands on, but I knew that sooner or later it would be my lot because I was twenty ...'.[70]

Stephens was not alone. Men opted to wait to be conscripted rather than volunteering for the forces for a variety of reasons, often practical considerations unrelated to the war similar to those we saw in Chapter 3 and in the MO material above. Gordon Gent was prepared to accept service, but reassured his wife and children that he would 'not leave you 'til I have to' because his enlistment would reduce their household income.[71] Young men without dependants were also often contributing to their parents' household finances, and had this to consider. Tom Knowlton, a Post Office counter-clerk born in 1922, had been fascinated by aeroplanes since

Attitudes to service

183

childhood and 'wanted to volunteer ... I was desperate' to learn to fly in the RAF. Yet, as a civil servant, by the time he came of age the State would only make up any shortfall in his pay if he was conscripted; with 'my mother in desperate straits I couldn't be a volunteer straight away, I had to wait until I was called up'.[72] Similarly, George Stagg wanted to volunteer for the Navy but was unwilling to leave his widowed mother on her own.[73] Such domestic reasons for delaying military service were similar to concerns experienced in the Great War. Adrian Gregory cites the dilemma of Harold Cousins, a middle-class man who understood his enlistment would threaten the financial security of his wife and child and so fought hard to retain his civilian employment; 'his intended answer to the question "What did you do in the Great War, Daddy?" was clearly "I tried to look after you and your mother." '[74] In a reversal of Tom Knowlton's situation, Gregory notes that a large number of businesses paid at least a proportion of enlisted men's pre-war wages, or bounties for volunteering, which removed the financial barrier of enlistment.[75] Still, a son's duty to his mother had delayed enlistment during the Great War, too; as an Essex gardener expressed it, 'his mother had done much for him, whereas the King, so far as he knew, had not rendered him any service!'.[76] The oral histories and the MO material highlight that during the Second World War both young and older men waited to be conscripted because they put their responsibilities to their families ahead of their responsibilities to the State, and sometimes their own preferences. As will be discussed, they surrendered a key method of affecting their own war experience by waiting.

Others unsuccessfully attempted to volunteer between 1939 and 1945, then waited until they were conscripted. William Reid remembered that 'like many of my young chums I thought I would [do] the fashionable thing to do I suppose, join the air force', but when told 'you're too studious a chap to go flying so we won't have you thank you very much' he decided to wait until he was called, at which point he expressed a preference for the Navy.[77]

Some simply had no desire to enter the forces before they had to. Thomas Illman, born in 1923, would, like many others, have preferred not to serve. He felt 'Apprehensive. Not too enthusiastic' about his call-up in 1942, and wished that he could have 'missed the war'.[78] Jack Abbott, born in 1926, had also hoped the war

184   *Joining up in the Second World War*

would be over before he was conscripted in March 1944. He had not considered volunteering, but reluctantly accepted conscription. He said, 'I just thought it was my duty', before saying, 'well, I suppose, erm, I suppose you wouldn't wish it on yourself really, but you know, there seemed to be no option, you had to go, you went before a medical board, you're fit, go in the Army. It's the Army for you 'cause the Army needs you.'[79] The Great War had also set the expectation that conscription was the mechanism by which men entered the forces. Bob Lowe said: 'it never occurred to me to volunteer, I'm being called up anyway, I mean you registered ... when you're 18 and I think [volunteers] would have been almost up to being called up anyway'.[80] Lowe knew that his eyesight would prevent him being aircrew, so when he was called to register he expressed his wish to be an aircraft mechanic. He was told there were no vacancies and asked to state a preference for the Navy or Army. Despite having his heart set on it, Lowe had not considered that as a conscript his wish might not be granted; ultimately his ATC squadron leader successfully intervened on his behalf.[81]

Crucially, volunteering could give men more control over which service they would join and what role they would have. Throughout the war, individuals could volunteer for the service of their choice, subject to fitness, skills and demand; the RAF and Navy sometimes only accepted volunteers for certain roles. Men who would have been deferred if conscripted might also encounter restrictions on their ability to volunteer, and needed governmental approval. Thus, men could experience ROs as a safety net or a trap; Stephen Smith 'was determined to do what I could to get out [of his RO] I tried a lot ... But each time the dreaded Essential Works Order came along and stopped it.'[82] Each branch of the services could ask for restrictions to be waived in individual cases, and from the beginning of 1941 the schedule was relaxed for men volunteering for the RAF as pilots or observers.[83] Even so, the proactive youngster in a job that would see him reserved upon reaching conscription age could force his way into the services. John Malling was working at A. V. Roe making aircraft, and told his employer he wanted to join the RAF. '[T]he first thing they said was that they can stop me from going', but Malling understood that he would only be reserved upon turning 18, so 'I'd already gone and got a number, 143250 AC2 Malling' and been accepted in the RAF Volunteer Reserve.[84]

Attitudes to service

As with responses to conscription, the reasons that men decided to volunteer were many and varied. Occasionally, the war presented the opportunity rather than the motivation. Alf Wyke volunteered just before turning 18 not because of conscription or the war effort but because of his dissatisfaction with working long, hard, anti-social hours in agriculture and a desire for change following the end of a relationship with a Land Girl. The war presented the opportunity for what he expected to be enjoyable employment as a driver in the Army. His description of the process, however, shows how little information individuals could have, and just how flexible some people's service choices were. Joining something might be more important than joining something specific. Wyke went to the Recruiting Office:

> 'I've come to join the Army' so er he said 'What you wanna go in?' and all I could think of was the Royal Army Service Corps because I was always mad on driving ... so he said 'You're too young ... What else you wanna go in?' A friend of mine from the village, he was in the Queens Royal Regiment and he used to say when he used to come home on leave how good a regiment it was, I said 'I'll go in the Queens' and I hadn't got a clue what the Queens Regiment was ....[85]

For most, though, a combination of war-related factors shaped attitudes and decisions. These can be placed in one of two broad categories. Common reasons men wanted to enter the war sooner than they would do if conscripted (or at all if they were in reserved occupations) were a desire for adventure; a patriotic desire to 'do their bit'; or a desire to meet societal conceptions of duty and masculinity (the importance of which is discussed in Chapter 5). Alternatively, or additionally, men might volunteer to exercise more control over the way in which they would serve. What made a role desirable might be far more self-serving than might be implied by the notion of the 'volunteer'. Men might volunteer in order to decrease their exposure to danger or discomfort; to maximise their financial benefit; or to prepare themselves for the post-war world.

Richard Todd, born in 1919, had prepared to follow his father into the military, passing through Sandhurst before beginning a career as an actor. When war approached at the end of the 1930s, he and his friends 'decided we were going to get in as quick as possible because it probably wouldn't last very long and if we didn't get

186   *Joining up in the Second World War*

in right away we might miss it all'.[86] John Winstanley had the same attitude. He was studying to be a doctor when war broke out but was also commissioned in the Territorial Army. He opted to stay with his regiment rather than continue his studies because 'it was all going to be a short affair' and he was 'only twenty and in a way I think it was you know a chance for adventure'.[87] It is tempting to read these two accounts as limited in various ways: limited to 1939; a peculiar quirk of those already military-minded; or limited to young, middle-class men inculcated with a particular patriotism. The memoirs examined by Frances Houghton contained similar attitudes, expressed by people with similar characteristics.[88]

Yet, even as the war continued, young working-class men might consider enlisting in the wartime services an opportunity for adventure. Don Browne was 16 in 1939, and recalled he was 'enthusiastic, well I was young, I was young, yes I think as I say we were saying we hoped it won't be over before we can get in'. As an apprentice Browne could have had his service deferred, but he volunteered for the Royal Navy on his 18th birthday because 'I think at that age I looked upon it as a big adventure ....' Browne explicitly dismissed the idea that his service was 'doing his bit': 'being a war on I wanted to go in ... I don't think it was because we wanted to fight for King and country because we just wanted to get in with the services.'[89] Similarly, as a railway clerk Maurice Marriot could have been reserved, but like John Malling, he knew that an individual's reservation was not triggered until he reached conscription age; Marriot volunteered beforehand. He 'finished up with a tribunal at the labour exchange' in order to join the RAF, which he was keen to do because of 'mainly sort of the excitement and the glamour of it, it wasn't much you know sort of fighting for King and country and all that sort of thing, the things you hear about, you know, get at the enemy and all that'.[90]

The narratives of a number of middle-class men suggest a belief that with social privilege came an expectation of leadership and the responsibility to serve. Harold Sell, born in 1910, the privately educated son of a wealthy family, was also in the Territorials when the Second World War began, and commented that he 'had been all through my life taught that I had an obligation to the country to be in [some form of national service]'.[91] Charles Patterson's testimony provides an explicit illustration of such thinking. Patterson did not

Attitudes to service

187

wish join the military, and described himself as far from a natural warrior, with a deep fear, drawn directly from his understanding of Great War, that he would undoubtedly die were there a future war. Yet when the war broke out 'joining up was just automatic. It never occurred to me that I could do anything else', and he enlisted as a pilot. He conceptualised service as his duty, and said that it had been

> very firmly implanted in my mind [that] these sacrifices and these terrible conditions [of the Great War] had been endured by the ordinary Tommy, the ordinary working-class English boy [in] conjunction with a much less number of more privileged but again young and innocent subalterns and junior officers. And what I most believed – or totally believed and was taught – was that if these young, working class boys could show such courage and such self-sacrifice it made it absolutely imperative on me to not let them down. Or endeavour, at least to make an effort, to live up to what they had done should another war come.[92]

Some working-class men also expressed patriotism or the desire to feel involved in the nation's war effort. George Stagg was willing to serve and conceived of it as something he had a duty to do. George felt he 'wasn't any different to anybody else, I mean we all had to have a go, we all saw this er looming on the horizon sort of thing, we had to safeguard our own ... we had to defend it, it was our country, it was us and we were English'.[93] Similarly, Jim Hayes rejected the opportunity to evade conscription: 'I didn't want to shirk at all' because 'we wasn't only fighting for the land, England, we were fighting for our families as well so that is what got me, you know'.[94] To some extent responses such as Hayes's demonstrate a pragmatic acceptance of the reality of the conflict: there was a self-evident need for collective participation in national defence. What is also apparent within the attitudes just discussed, though, is the survival of traditional modes of thinking about military service: adventure, duty and opportunity to prove character. As we will see in Chapter 5, military service remained strongly connected to war-time masculinity in many men's subjective conceptions.

Evidently, some men were keen to enlist, but close examination of enlistment narratives reveals how difficult it is to read the act of volunteering as an indicator of men's attitudes towards military

188   *Joining up in the Second World War*

service. It *could* indicate a desire to enter the war but it could also be self-serving. Men commonly volunteered in an attempt to exercise agency over which service they would enter or which role they would have. Indeed, this was a contributing factor in the enlistment of most of the twenty-three volunteers I interviewed, and in seven cases was the only reason they did not simply await conscription. George Cash 'wanted to beat the time when … I would be due to be called up because from what I understood if I was called up I could be placed anywhere and obviously I wanted to avoid that at all costs so I went and volunteered before that time came'.[95] Similarly, Jack Pragnell and his twin brother were well aware that 'we've got to join something, we're 18 and any minute now … the old letter [conscription papers] was going to drop and once they said "You're in the Army" [then] you're in the Army, so we decided we wanted to go in the air force for the glory of it'.[96]

The Great War had associated conscription with providing the manpower for a large army, and many assumed that was their likely destination if conscripted, regardless of which service they stated as their preference upon registration. This assumption was not without justification. The RAF and the Navy could be selective because enough men listed them as their preferred service.[97] Therefore over the course of the war, only 21 per cent of those conscripts preferring the RAF and 27 per cent of those preferring the Navy enlisted with those services. The remainder entered the Army, along with those who had expressed a preference for the Army.[98]

Those who particularly wanted to join the Navy or RAF, especially as aircrew, were significantly more likely to be successful if they volunteered. Joining the Army remained entirely achievable without volunteering, but volunteering gave the individual more control over what they would do once they were in.

Of course, a determination to serve in a particular role could combine with an enthusiasm to enter the war as quickly as possible. Allan Florence volunteered as soon as he was old enough in 1941 because he had always intended to join the Navy, but the outbreak of war had made him 'more [interested] than ever'.[99] Nevertheless, although volunteering required one to enlist sooner than if one waited to be conscripted, it did not necessarily indicate a desire or even a willingness to serve.[100] Instead, an individual's desire to hold a particular role might be self-interested rather than

Attitudes to service 189

Table 4.1 Success of conscripts preferring Navy or RAF

Date	Conscripts preferring Navy who were taken by Navy (%)	Conscripts preferring RAF who were taken by RAF (%)
3 September–31 December 1939	8	1
1940	11	11
1941	28	21
1942	71	79
1943	68	35
1944	22	36
1945	6	10

Calculated from data in Parker, *Manpower*, table IV, p. 485 and table VI, pp. 488–90.

self-sacrificing. Ian Carmichael felt obligated to serve but 'hated' the prospect of army life, and attempted to avoid service overseas by volunteering for the anti-aircraft artillery, which he hoped might enable him to stay at home protecting English cities.[101] Norman Bowdler was working in aircraft production but, having repeatedly found himself out of work due to the bombing of factories, he decided to volunteer for the Army instead. He remembered, 'if you volunteered at that time you could get into the unit of your choice, or at least they would try to put you in the unit of your choice, and … I wanted desperately to be in the Armoured Corps'. He found tanks fascinating, and 'fighting the war on my feet didn't appeal to me very much, I thought I'd sooner do it on wheels thank you very much so er I volunteered'.[102] As we will see, Bowdler's decision to volunteer to have greater certainty that he would avoid fighting the war on his feet in the infantry was certainly not uncommon.

The RAF was widely perceived as the most popular force.[103] Not only did it accept more volunteers than conscripted men but its most visible members, aircrew, were universally volunteers.[104] Even those conscripted to the RAF had generally expressed it as their preference. Conscripts to the Navy had also largely joined their preferred service, and they only marginally outnumbered volunteers.[105]

190 *Joining up in the Second World War*

The Army enlisted more than three conscripts for every volunteer, many of whom would have preferred to serve elsewhere.[106] This should not overshadow the fact that the Army enlisted 650,000 volunteers, absolutely more than the RAF or the Royal Navy, but as David French notes, the vast majority of these men volunteered before or during the summer of 1940.[107] Importantly, most volunteers chose to enter Corps rather than the infantry, until that option was removed in 1942.[108]

The numbers of volunteers each service accepted, and the preferences men expressed, do not provide a complete picture of the relative popularity of the three services. Most significantly, the numbers of volunteers who entered each service differed from the number who volunteered for it. The RAF, with more stringent medical and educational requirements, rejected many more volunteers than the Army. Additionally, even the most diligently kept records of manpower cannot account for instances, detailed in oral narratives, of men who attempted to volunteer for the RAF or Navy but, upon being told it was full, volunteered elsewhere or awaited conscription.[109] Nor can records reveal how many men were strategic in their enlistment actions, and therefore did not volunteer for or express a preference for the service which they most wanted to join; enlistment narratives illustrate that many would-be flyers never applied in the belief that their education or health, especially eyesight, all but ensured disappointment. They therefore sought to serve elsewhere.[110]

Similarly, it is impossible to know how commonly conscripts did not honestly express their preference, but asked to join their second-choice service in the belief this was more likely to keep them *out* of their least preferred service. The RAF was widely remembered as the service that most young men wished to join, and neither the testimonies nor numbers suggest this is incorrect, but the comparative popularity of the RAF and Navy amongst conscripts also altered over the war. The RAF was strongly favoured in the early years of the war, when the majority of men were registered, but from 1943 this had almost reversed.

The age of the conscripts was constant from 1942 to 1945 and so does not account for this shift, and in any case the young men enlisting in early 1941 had similar preferences to the older men who enlisted in the middle of that year. The impression that

Attitudes to service

Table 4.2 Registrants' relative preferences for RAF or Navy, 1939–45

Year	Number expressing preference for Navy or RAF	% preferring RAF	% preferring Navy
1939	265,699	65	35
1940	1,652,529	66	34
1941	1,151,937	72	28
1942	246,056	51	49
1943	298,813	40	60
1944	152,633	32	68
1945	67,100	29	71

Calculated from data in Parker, *Manpower*, table VI, pp. 488–90.

it was difficult to enter the RAF may have made the expression of a naval preference appear an increasingly more likely way of avoiding Army service. Alternatively, the Navy may have become more attractive than the RAF because it appeared a safer service, or a safer way to enjoy an adventurous war; or the Navy may have appeared more likely to fit one with a useful trade for the post-war world, an important consideration for young men whose opportunities as apprentices had been disrupted by the war.

Of course, what influenced men's choices depended upon individuals' aims, be that glory in the air, safety at home or something in between. Even some who volunteered had no fixed ideas about which service or role they wanted. Arthur Howard had agreed to join the RAF with a friend, and when they told Howard he could only immediately join the Volunteer Reserve he considered both the Army and the Navy before ultimately accepting.[111] Some sought to continue with their civilian occupations in military uniform as far as possible. Gordon Gent's preference was to serve as a butcher in the Royal Army Service Corps.[112] Similarly, Frank Clements was working in the grocery trade when the Second World War began. When his employer told him that he was to join the services before Christmas he volunteered for the RASC. After being told 'We don't want you yet' because he was 24, he successfully applied for a similar role in the NAAFI.[113]

192   *Joining up in the Second World War*

The government issued *National Service: A Guide to the Ways in Which the People of This Country May Give Service* had outlined what the service roles entailed, though as it was published in January 1939 it had emphasised Civil Defence.[114] In any case, MO research suggests that most households would not have retained the pamphlet, limiting its usefulness at the point of conscription.[115] If *National Service* had gone missing, or had not provided individuals with enough information to develop a preference for a branch of service or specific role, guides such as *Joining Up* certainly did so. Without particularly careful reading, one could establish the roles most likely to involve action, or to avoid it, and which roles were financially best remunerated.

Britons commonly understood, probably as a legacy of the Great War, that Army pay was poor. Readers of *Joining Up* could establish that that remained the case: a private soldier would earn 15s 9d a week, and if he was married and allotted 7s of this to his wife the government would add another 17s a week, with additions if they had children.[116] Less detail was provided on Navy pay, but it was clear that an Ordinary Seaman earned 14s a week, and an Able Seaman £1 1s a week, and that gaining a trade or other qualifications could add significantly to this.[117] In the RAF an armourer or instrument repairer, once trained, might earn nearly £2 a week, and £3 if he had a wife and child.[118] All but the most careless reader would have noticed that RAF aircrew earned the most. Pay was similar to a private soldier during training, but once qualified a pilot earned a minimum of £4 7s 6d a week, plus various bonuses, and if he was married then his wife also received an allowance of £1 1s a week, or £1 11s 6d a week if they had a child.[119]

As we have seen, financial considerations led some to delay entering service, and they could shape the roles men wanted. Alfred Cox wanted to become a physical training instructor in the RAF because he had heard he would find the work easy and be quickly promoted, and therefore paid more.[120] Some men accepted additional or different duties once enlisted because of increased pay,[121] but it was rare for earnings to be cited as the primary reason for preferring a particular role or service. This is not to say that men did not consider the financial ramifications. George Stagg wanted to join the Navy, but also understood that uniform allowances would leave him better off than if he were in the Army. George

Attitudes to service 193

Cash wanted to fly in any case, but said 'for me it had to be air crew because they got the most money … if I was going to go into the services I wasn't going to go in and stay on two shillings a day', but to have a 'reasonable return in respect of pay' and ensure his wife would get the best possible pension if he died.[122] George Dann had known that he would not lose out financially by joining the RAF, but for him this had been a secondary motivation to the sense that he was going to do something worthwhile.[123]

Men's preferences were also affected by what a role entailed. By far the most commonly expressed example of this was men citing a desire to fly as the reason they wanted to join the RAF. As was discussed in Chapter 1, aviation and especially military aviation occupied a prominent place in boys' culture in inter-war Britain. For many it was a long-standing interest and aspiration, and the war made it a genuine possibility. Tom Knowlton was disappointed to learn his mathematics was not good enough to be a pilot, but he would be a wireless operator/air gunner instead. Knowlton had been 'fascinated by any book or comic about aeroplanes that you would see', and having 'always dreamt of flying' he 'wasn't bitterly disappointed but I was disappointed, I wanted to be a pilot'. He conceptualised service as an opportunity to undertake 'a job I wanted to do' rather than an opportunity to do his bit or an adventure, and was interested in flying rather than joining the military.[124]

Others preferred roles because of what they would allow them to avoid. In January 1940, an MO respondent wrote that he had anticipated his impending conscription by applying to a 'technical branch of the RAF … The job is technical research and comparatively bloodless, which suits me nicely.'[125] Jim Hayes made a similar observation about volunteering for mine sweeping duties.[126] In a similar vein, Thomas Illman recalled that 'everybody had aspirations to join the RAF, I think what put you off the Army was the possibility of hand-to-hand combat, but of course you didn't get in the RAF because it was pretty full'.[127] Notably in all three examples the thing men sought to avoid was either the infantry service explicitly and/or killing in the abstract, which was certainly perceived as part of the infantryman's task, and in two of the three examples the preferred solution was to join the RAF.

Frank Webster's experience of enlistment merits detailed description as it provides a clear illustration of many of the threads

194   *Joining up in the Second World War*

identified in this chapter so far: although he had no aspiration to join the forces in peacetime, he was young and keen to participate in the war; he had a clear sense that military service was expected of men in wartime; he understood the manpower system and yet was unable to enter his preferred service due to the vagaries of service requirements; his enlistment was ultimately somewhat chaotic; and his preferences were strongly influenced by his understanding of the Great War.

As detailed in Chapter 2, Webster was very aware of his father's Great War experience because he had lost an arm and had a debilitating wound. Frank, born in 1920, recalled that after the Munich Crisis and Chamberlain's 'piece of paper and all that' there was lots of activity to drive recruitment:

> [I]f you went to the pictures you'd find coming out there'd be somebody to get you to join the Territorials and things like that, but erm, this isn't sort of, what can I say, a correct reason, but bearing in mind my father had been through what he had, I, I, I didn't feel incline to wander into the Army [little chuckle].

In March 1939 Frank had committed his thoughts on 'This Question of Conscription' to paper, which he showed me during our interview. He wrote that he would support peacetime conscription

> wholeheartedly if it wasn't for the fact that I'm an apprentice and on the threshold of a good career, which takes seven years, if not more, to thoroughly grasp. If I'm conscripted (my age is just right) it means I abandon my typographical studies and to be released when my time in the Army is finished, to what? [....] I will be just an incompleted craftsman cast into the world against heavy competition.

But Frank also understood that if 'Britain is in danger unless I fight or to quote a recent ARP poster "Protect my/your heritage" my life as briefly planned above will just the same fizzle out'. Frank recognised that 'If war came, and I hope to God it doesn't, conscription would be brought in right away, when careers or individual ideas don't mean a thing', but he felt that in peacetime provision should be made for 'youngsters like myself, who are working now to fit themselves for a secure business and social future'.[128]

Attitudes to service

As his contemporary writing suggests, Frank stated in his interview that he previously had no ambition to join the forces but felt it was expected of young men once war broke out. He recalled that with the outbreak of the war there was 'a bit of a buzz' about the prospect of joining up amongst his group of apprentices. Although he was not contemplating joining the Army, Frank was not deterred from military participation in a different service.

> Coming back to what I wanted to do, I thought there's the Army, my dear old dad, there's the air force, I didn't fancy going in that – I wasn't clever enough I didn't think – [so] in '39 I went to the recruiting place in Whitehall as it was then to join the navy and they said 'All recruiting has stopped'. I said 'What? War on and recruiting stopped?' Well the recruiting officer there, he sort of melted for a moment and said 'Well look at me', he said 'I'm a qualified gunnery instructor officer and I'm stuck in this office'. Anyway I came away from there deflated, and months went on, and erm, then Dunkirk occurred, and erm, I still wasn't in the Navy obviously, and erm, I joined the Local Defence Volunteers ... in June 1940.

Meanwhile a friend had 'been plaguing me' about joining the RAF, and in July 1940, dissatisfied with 'what I'm learning with my broomstick, as an LDV',

> Eventually I said to him, 'I'll tell you what I'll do, you come with me to join the Navy for a last chance' ... and the recruiting officer ... said to me 'How old are you?' I said '19' ... he said 'Are you any one of these trades', which I wasn't, I said 'No', he said 'Well I cant take you' and he said to my pal 'How old are you?' He said '18 and a half'. He said 'I'll take you and not you'. My pal said 'I don't want to go in the Navy', so I went along with my pal and I joined the air force.

Frank had little knowledge of RAF roles, but was content when told he would be an instrument repairer, even if he did not really know what it entailed. It enabled him to enter the forces, as he had been trying to do, and it kept him out of the Army, which he wanted to avoid 'because of my father, with his one arm and his bad wound and all that'.[129] The role that young men's understandings of the Great War had within their enlistment is the topic of the next section. As we will see, one of the key ways that young men's understandings or nebulous sense of the Great War informed their enlistment decisions was in encouraging a desire to avoid the Army.

1914–18 in 1939–45

The Great War held a significant position in the subjectivities of Britons of all ages, and many viewed the Second World War through the lens of the First. In February 1940 MO asked its National Panel about influences on their attitudes to the Second World War. The responses suggest that for at least the first nine months of the war many Britons of all ages assumed that the Great War was the inevitable reference point when thinking about the Second World War.[130] Moreover, about a third of the respondents' attitudes were demonstrably shaped by the last war. Those who could remember the war but had been too young to participate were the most likely to say it had affected their opinions, but the importance of post-war impressions is suggested by the fact that even a fifth of those who had been born after the Armistice felt that the last war was affecting how they thought about the Second World War.

Some suggested that their understandings of the Great War made them more enthusiastic, but it was more commonly cited as the cause of feelings of resignation, dismay or fear. The limited war enthusiasm – which concerned MO and some contemporaries mentioned – was, at least in part, a legacy of the Great War.[131] A sense of repetition accelerated war weariness. A 49-year-old teacher from London expressed the resentment she felt towards both world wars: the last war had spoilt her career, denied her husband promotion, 'stopped all our homemaking plans' and 'indirectly it cost me my children'. 'Now after twenty five years it has again divided our home, taken my job, left me to fight depressions and bitterness.' 'Worst of all is the dreadful feeling that none of these wars need have happened if people had been kind and sympathetic and generous to one another.'[132] But memories of wartime trauma and a sense of loss were just one facet of the legacy of the Great War that informed Britons' attitudes.[133] Understandings of the origins and effects of the Great War also encouraged scepticism in some Britons about who the war was for and their position in the nation. A woman from Bolton lamented that 'It's always us working and poor people that suffer, you know', and her son suggested that 'It's the people who put the young fellows to the war that ought to go.'[134] Similarly, a student from Yorkshire born in 1907 could not 'help thinking at times, drawing remembrances from the last war,

Attitudes to service   197

that we are being led up the garden path again. I am suspicious of anything this government says or does.' He also felt the 'immense amount of anti-war propaganda to which we have been subject in the last 20 years' has 'helped to produce the lack of enthusiasm for the war which was so pronounced in the 1914 struggle'.[135]

Gary Sheffield has suggested that the Great War functioned as a touchstone of horror for Second World War veterans; their war was not as bad as that which had come immediately before.[136] Occasionally I have found evidence to support this, but in general the influence of the last conflict seems to have been more in men's minds when they considered future service – a moment when they had more chance of reflection – than during combat. At least a third of the men of service age who wrote to MO in February 1940 drew upon their understandings of the First World War when considering the Second, and oral histories demonstrate this process occurred more widely. References to the Great War were a frequent component of enlistment narratives, including references to the issue of equipment from the Great War; as shorthand to describe the provision of obsolete weaponry; and sometimes in descriptions of inadequately prepared superior officers. As we will see, it also informed men's attitudes and decision. The MO responses and the oral histories also show that Britons' understandings of the Great War were informed by different types of knowledge: personal experiences, vicarious memories and post-war representations. Post-war familial narrations and representations of war in popular culture were considered more important by younger respondents, who lacked personal recollections.

We saw in Chapter 2 that a return to martial activities in the Home Guard encouraged reminiscence amongst ex-servicemen, and MO observed that widows of the Great War were particularly affected by seeing soldiers in the streets; one commented that she could not help staring: 'I always think of my husband, got killed in the last war. Only a youngster. We'd only been married a month. It comes hard on the youngsters, don't it?'[137] Because the Second World War stimulated recollection of the First, it created instances where young men heard reference to the earlier conflict. In December 1938, Derrick Thurgood had overheard his father and veteran friends talking of ' "having to do it all over again" or something like that as ex-servicemen tended to'.[138] Discussing Second

198   *Joining up in the Second World War*

World War events also led some veterans to make comparisons with their own experiences. Bob Atkinson remembered that his father did not talk regularly about his war during the inter-war years, but elements would come out as they discussed the war news. He felt the German advance through Poland and France would have been halted by artillery in the Great War, and when British forces were retreating prior to Dunkirk he said:

> 'They could have cut 'em off!' In first war they would have let 'em through then closed the gap, but he couldn't understand like a tank bides some stopping ... but that's what they used to do, if they came through one place they let them go through and then stop 'em going back, and when they ran out ammunition they could do nothing, they could stop as long as they wanted if they'd used their ammunition [laughs] that was what he said, let 'em go through and stop second lot.[139]

Other prompts were more personal. Jim Hayes recalled seeing his cousin shortly after he had been evacuated from Dunkirk; 'Dad and I got talking about it then ... my dad says "he's all to pieces isn't he" and he said "my God it brought back memories, I saw some folks coming out of action like that", he said "it's not a nice sight".'[140]

Great War veterans' narratives, whether from before or during the Second World War, can be seen influencing men's attitudes to Second World War service and service preferences in a number of ways. James Donovan, aged 15 in 1939, was not the only man who said that tales of the Great War had made him curious about the Second World War:

JD When war was declared I thought to myself I wonder if it will last long enough for me to go, and I think that at the back of me mind I did want it to last so that I could go and join up.

I   You did?

JD Yes definitely.

I   Why?

JD I don't know, I suppose like a lot of youngsters you'd heard tales of the First World War, and er, well I thought to myself well I'll be disappointed if I don't find out what it's like, as strange as it may seem now, but at the time I thought to myself is it going to last long enough for me to get into the Army.

Attitudes to service 199

The precise origin of these tales is uncertain, but may have been his veteran father, who 'had shrapnel in his legs ... that was never taken out and as a child I can remember he'd say "Oooh its gone round back behind me knee" ... and you could actually feel the small bits of shrapnel under his skin'.[141] Nevertheless, the effect was to make Donovan keen to experience war in order to better understand his father's experience. A desire to understand 'the soldiers'' experience, prompted by veterans' narratives, is also apparent within the more ambiguous feelings an insurance agent born in 1912 expressed to MO in January 1940. He had:

> heard so much from the soldiers of 1914–18, 'What I did in the Great War', that I have a desire to experience it 'first hand'. Nevertheless I had a feeling of horror at the possibility of having to kill another human being, particularly if it be by bayonet. I have to a degree a feeling of patriotism and of fulfilling my obligations to society but overall is a feeling of despair – not from thoughts of defeat but because of the futility of war – war only causes further wars and hatred ....[142]

Similarly, the respondent mentioned in Chapter 2 who lived with his three silent veteran uncles and wrote that 'while one half of my mind is aware of the horror and waste ... of the war, the other is prey to what I can only call a sadistic curiosity' initially considered conscientious objection, but had decided against it and was looking forward to the change in life that enlistment would bring; perhaps his curiosity won out.[143]

Even basic knowledge of veterans' experiences might shape which service young men opted to join. When conscripted, Ronald Mallabar did not have particular reason to opt for one armed force over the other two, and so 'expressed a preference for the Army because my father had been in the Army in the First World War, I couldn't think of any other reason'.[144] More extensive narratives could inspire young men's determination to serve in the same unit. John Wilson was 18 when the war broke out. He was 'anxious to get into the Army to get out the office to be honest, my father was in the Black Watch in the 14–18 war and I'd heard nothing but Black Watch from him, I think he would've joined up with me [if he could]'.[145] Wilson, seeking something more adventurous than office life, subsequently doggedly attempted to join the unit. Richard Parkhouse opted to become a pilot, having taken positive impressions of his father's service from his ambivalent narratives, and heard his mother speak in 'awed tones about how Daddy got his wings'.[146]

Conversely, some of those young men who heard about their father's negative experiences were unwilling to serve in the same way. Reg Day, who had heard about his father's gassing, wanted to avoid the Army, and Edward Kirby, whose father had suffered from neurasthenia and told him graphic recollections of witnessing a corpse decompose in a trench, was reluctant to serve.[147] Jim Hayes had expressed a preference for the Navy during his enlistment, but was told it was full. He was drafted to the Royal Ordnance Corp but left the Army during training by volunteering for work on mine sweepers. He cited his understanding of the Great War as one factor in his decision. His father had spoken regularly about his war experiences, some of which Jim had seen as exciting, a 'nerve test', but he said: 'I remember my dad telling me a lot about the trenches, snipers and that, and the rats in the trenches and all this, and that did have a bearing on it I can tell you, because I didn't fancy going in the trenches at all.'[148]

Impending military service did not only stimulate young men to think about the last war. It could also encourage veteran fathers to give their sons advice. Alf Wyke, who had little knowledge of his father's service, was instructed, ' "Whatever you do, ... don't become a sniper." ' As it happened, Wyke was a very good shot, and was offered the opportunity, but he declined as his father's advice 'had stuck in my mind'.[149] Bob Atkinson, born in 1925, had not heard a great deal about his father's war service, but knew that he had been in the King's Own Royal Regiment during the Great War, and been wounded three times and gassed. Bob's call-up papers arrived in July 1943.

> **BA** [Dad] didn't say much, he just said 'Don't go in infantry, whatever you do lad', but I'd no option.
>
> **I** You didn't have a choice?
>
> **BA** No choice whatsoever. I believe after I went in they were, in our area, they were asking for Bevin Boys, but they never asked me. It was either a stoker in the Navy or in the Army.
>
> **I** So your dad's reaction was don't go into infantry.
>
> **BA** [Interrupts] Don't go into infantry, get into artillery.

Attitudes to service 201

I What was your mum's reaction?

BA Don't go at all! [Laughs] ha ha, I don't want you to go at all I should say.

...

I But of course you have to go don't you.

BA You have to go. Conscript.[150]

Atkinson's mother worried about him serving, but Bob recalled, 'I think me dad just calmed her down by saying "Oh it'll be over soon", but he knew in his, he knew it wouldn't be over soon.' Eric Johnson was apathetic about military service – 'Oh well, I shall be called up, that's it, you know.' Until then he was happy as a youth in training at the Post Office telephone exchange. Unlike Atkinson, once Johnson had registered he did receive a letter 'asking for Bevin Boy optants. My mum got hold of this and said "Oh yes, you become a Bevin Boy, don't want you to go in the Army, you become a Bevin Boy.' Johnson was happy to because it enabled him to stay connected to his day-to-day civilian life, but in his narrative his agency had been curtailed by his parents: 'My mum more or less volunteered me to be a Bevin Boy [laughter].'[151] Eric Wakeling, who had long aspired to be a regular soldier, wrote in his memoir about turning down the offer of a commission as an infantry or gunner officer early in the Second World War on the advice of his parents, who 'of course had memories of the previous war and the early deaths of Infantry subalterns and young gunner officer in the Advanced Observation Posts, who suffered the highest losses'.[152]

Second World War events might confirm the ideas expressed by Great War veterans. George Cash's father had convinced him that the Army was not the place for him: having heard about foot-slogging and trench conditions from his father and 'after Dunkirk a few of [my mates] came back with their tales, and half of them didn't come back, and well that decided me, I wasn't going to go in, I was told by my dad to steer clear of the Army so that confirmed it in my mind'. Having experienced the Blitz, Cash became determined to be a fighter pilot, and discussed volunteering with his parents as he approached conscription age. His father advised him to 'go for the RAF if that's what you want, but for God's sake don't go into the Army'.[153]

202   *Joining up in the Second World War*

Some felt their fathers' experiences caused them to worry for their sons. Henry Brewis concealed his plans to enlist from his father, fearing he would object, expecting his father had 'fears in his inner self that it was going to be a repeat of the previous do' in which Henry's uncle had died.[154] Similarly, when war broke out Jack Abbott 'sense[d] that my parents were getting very anxious my father in particular, having been through one war, he changed a lot, erm, the [Second World] war changed him, because he had the First World War experience of knowing what war was about, it was no jolly picnic, it was jolly hard, and erm, it was going to be a different war because there were more aircraft involved, and we soon knew about that because we knew that we had to prepare for bombing'. Four years later, when home on embarkation leave, Abbott concealed his imminent overseas service from his parents because he felt his father was worried as a result of his Great War experiences: '[H]e'd not been in the fighting but he knew enough about the war to know what war was all about ....'[155] Stanley Brand's father advised him to avoid military service if possible. Brand's father had been 'a wreck at the end of the [Great] war with the gassing ...'. He was 'particularly conscious' that the war was coming, 'and he had a horror of it, because he had seen erm, Flanders, he'd seen the Italian/Austrian frontier up in the Alps and er, yes he he hoped that we would fit ourselves for some job where we would be essential at home'.[156] Brand turned down a university place in September 1939 because his veteran uncles had had qualifications but were unable to find work after the Great War and he anticipated the same thing happening to him. Instead he took a job at Imperial Chemical Industries: 'it was a reserved occupation but because I was dealing with poison gases I wanted to get the hell out of it, I didn't want to be associated with anything like that, but it was a reserved occupation'. Ultimately, Brand volunteered to join the Fleet Air Arm, which he conceptualised as a fairer and more chivalrous way to participate in warfare, and he got to fly, which he had wanted to do since childhood.

More commonly, though, fathers were perceived as understanding and stoically accepting that their sons had no choice but to serve. Brian Spragg, whose father had told him about terrible conditions at Passchendaele, understood that his father was a 'true patriot' who would have encouraged him to serve.[157] Similarly,

Jack Pragnell, whose father was 'definitely anti-war', was proud of his service with the Royal Engineers, and had taught his sons Morse code. Come 1939, he hoped they would join the Engineers too.[158]

Mothers' memories of the Great War, on the other hand, were commonly perceived as the cause of their worry and upset.[159] They were often unhappy about the prospect of their sons' service, as seen in Atkinson's and Johnson's testimony. Wilfred White's mother had lost her brother, Bill, at Ypres. Before joining his unit Wilfred had grown a moustache, and his mother 'said I looked exactly like Bill so I wasn't going in ...'.[160] White did not recall his father expressing any encouragement or opposition. He had done 'most of his service helping in the cookhouse' in the RASC; 'he obviously hadn't been in the trenches, so there was no sort of blood and guts sort of get yourself out there and kill a few for me sort of thing ...'.[161] Mothers' and fathers' (outward) reactions to their sons' conscription were themselves gendered: mothers were depicted as protective but emotional, unwilling to sacrifice their child for the State; fathers were depicted as knowing and stoic, rationally attempting to protect their wives, protect their children by steering them to the safest available path and acknowledging a man's responsibility to the wartime State.

Chapter 2 demonstrated not only that young men commonly encountered narratives of Great War experience from veterans, but also that the tone of and impressions given by those narratives were hugely varied. Here, we have seen that the influence of those narratives was varied too. Some men sought to join the Army to emulate veterans they knew and to better understand their experience. Others found their service preferences and choices were shaped by the lessons they could take from veterans' experiences; most commonly this encouraged men away from Army, and specifically infantry, enlistment, rather than away from enlistment altogether.

Representations of the Great War in popular culture also shaped men's attitudes to service and their service choices, though they were cited as influences less frequently than veterans' narratives. These representations also encouraged young men away from the infantry and towards other roles, but the texts and artefacts that were influential are not necessarily those suggested by existing scholarship on the memory of the Great War. References to canonical war literature and war poetry were almost entirely absent.

204   *Joining up in the Second World War*

The significant exception, and the only canonical cultural representation that was cited with anything approaching regularity by interviewees as having influenced their attitudes and decisions, was *All Quiet on the Western Front*. Amongst my interviewees, though, it was the film, most often the 1939 re-release, rather than the novel, which was referred to. As Jim Stephens explained, he envisaged that the Second World War would be like the First, and said that 'the question of er avoiding the infantry I think was on everybody's mind because looking at some of the detail, I watched a film called *All Quiet on the Western Front* ... just before was called up [J: Right] and the slaughter they depicted there was absolutely horrible so that put me off' service in the Army, and specifically the infantry. Stephens could not avoid Army service by volunteering because his family needed his earnings: 'when I got my calling up papers ... to get going to the Army and they told me that I've got a report to Devizes on Salisbury plain to Searchlight Regiment ... which I was highly overjoyed about because the searchlight regiment isn't like an infantry regiment. Anyway about two weeks after my calling up papers I got another one from the War Office, "Dear Jim", or words to that effect, "forget about the Searchlight Regiment you've got to go to Exeter to report to an infantry regiment, the Devonshire Regiment".'[162]

Another influence commonly discussed as discouraging men from considering service in the Army, and the infantry in particular, were the photographs of battlefronts in encyclopaediae and illustrated children's histories. Bob Woodhams was particularly interested in joining the Navy, and did not appear to have genuinely considered any of the other services. What he had learned from such artefacts about the last war confirmed his choice:

> different battles, the Somme, I used to think I don't want to be a soldier ... troops being killed like that on the Somme and that trench warfare, though nah I don't want none of that, I'd sooner be at sea, yeah, so that could have a lot of me influence as well cos you know after reading that, what they went through and that, I thought no, not for me, if I can help it, yeah.[163]

Allan Florence narrated a similar experience. He had always intended to join the Navy, but the outbreak of war had made him 'more [interested] than ever' and he volunteered as soon as he

Attitudes to service 205

turned 18 in 1941. Later in the interview, when establishing what he had known about the Great War, he said that he had read books his parents owned which included photographs that showed the 'terrible states some of the men were in, er, parts of bodies blown off and all that, lying around, don't want that, no I don't want that, yeah'. Jack Pragnell's father and all of his uncles were in the Army in the Great War – 'Dad was definitely anti-war and he didn't tell us a lot about the trenches or about the war' – but Jack and his brother liked to read:

> we got a set of encyclopaedias and a bit half of one of the volumes was on the First World War, showed this bloke going up and down blowing the bagpipes, that sort of historical event and it showed the trenches and the trees all broken down and what have you ... but we didn't discuss it much at all, that was the fear, that it was going to be the same war ... gonna be trench warfare.

When combined with the manpower requirements of Britain's forces, this fear created an incentive to volunteer. Pragnell explained:

> see if we didn't join the air force, I was just 18, gonna be called up for the Army, and the idea of the Army we got in our minds was the First World War, trench war and none of us wanted that, so we, my brother and myself and another fellow man decided we'd join the Fleet Air Arm because we liked the uniform.

Ultimately Jack joined the RAF, which had a vaunted reputation in 1940, whereas the Army had recently evacuated from Dunkirk: 'we read about the pilots and the heroics of it, I don't think anybody wanted to go in the trenches did they [little chuckle] so it was no particular sort of bravado or anything like that'.[164]

Some interviewees' narratives were conflicting. Samuel Pearson had not connected the First and Second World Wars when enlisting because he expected 'that it wasn't going to be like the First World War'. Yet, he was pleased not to be in the Army, and referred to images from his brother George's book; Pearson 'always pictured the First World War, what I knew about the First World War ... the bayonets, when they were bayonet fighting and I never fancied that'. The Army would nonetheless have been his second choice, because he did not want a non-combat role in the RAF and did not think he could be a pilot.[165]

206 *Joining up in the Second World War*

Representations of war in the air were often cited indirectly as reasons that men were keen to join the RAF, their interest in flying originating in books about the Great War aviators and the adventures of Biggles. Biggles, while well remembered, was just one example of a much larger body of representations which glamorised flying in inter-war Britain; W. E. Johns alone created a number of popular pilot characters.[166] As was discussed in Chapter 1, young men found depictions of war in the air like *Hell's Angels* and *Dawn Patrol* exciting images of combat, and often subsequently wanted to join the air force.[167] Charles Patterson was 'very much influenced by *Dawn Patrol*', the 1930 Great War film about the Royal Flying Corps, which showed him that 'although the casualties were very heavy it was the most exciting and wonderful way to go to war'.[168] This description does not resonate with imaginings of infantry service: notably, Biggles once remarked, 'Thank goodness I'm not in the infantry.'[169]

Analysis of enlistment narratives demonstrates the complexity of the interactions between various representations of the Great War. Veterans' accounts did not always dominate representations in popular culture, and vice versa. Composite impressions could be formed, and of course variations in content affected any influence. Ian Carmichael used his knowledge of his father's Great War service on Anti-Aircraft guns around Hull to identify a safe service. When told that his mathematic ability was inadequate for the Royal Artillery, he accepted an offer of service in the Royal Armoured Corps, because of an understanding of the Great War informed by images in popular culture:

> the distance between the two wars was still so short and although I was born in 1920 ... there were horrifying pictures of trenches and mud and bayonets ... I thought it's better to drive into battle and have a bit of armour round you rather than going in on foot ....[170]

Peter Woodard wanted to join the RAF because he was interested in flying, but he also wanted to avoid the Army. When asked why he explained, as was described in Chapter 2, that his father had occasionally 'lived Gallipoli all over again' and had flashbacks when drunk, 'so that's one reason I thought, oh, and I had read about the First World War of course [J: Right] and the privations of the infantryman and the army in general so that's why I thought I don't want to be a soldier [little chuckle]'. In Woodard's case the representations he had encountered on a private level matched those he had encountered in wider culture.

Young men's attitudes to service were not necessarily shaped by the representations of the Great War they had encountered, though, regardless of the variety or extent. Ken Hay, who had read avidly about the Great War at his local library, conceived it as an interesting event in the past with little contemporary significance when the Second World War broke out: 'I don't think I was conscious at that time of war being a terrible thing or being anything at all, you know it was something that has happened like Barking had just missed out on the amateur cup or something.'[171] One reason that some did not connect what they knew about the First World War to how they thought about the Second was that they expected it to be so different. Peter Taylor, a member of a motorised Territorial Army unit, felt the greater mobility provided by vehicles would ensure the Second World War was completely different to the First.[172] Likewise, Derrick Thurgood, who had enlisted in the elite Reconnaissance Corps in search of wartime adventure, 'expected it to be entirely different ... I thought it would be a mobile war, I thought it would be tanks and armoured cars, er parrying and thrusting, I didn't for a moment think that there would be dug in trenches, as there were in the eastern front ... but we weren't getting any images from there'.[173]

Others highlighted the importance of air power as a revolutionary technology. Brian Spragg had heard about the Great War from his father, and grandmother, had read about it, and felt that *All Quiet* had left an impression. Yet, he felt he had not made any connection between the First and Second World Wars at the time, 'knowing the First World War was a trench warfare basically, and you know thousands going over the top regardless of what was coming at them, a different war altogether, and more mobile war was coming up ...'.[174] Not only had the pilot become a prominent hero in interwar juvenile fiction and film, but aerial warfare dominated interwar imaginings of future war. The Great War had marked the Home Front as a target by demonstrating that aerial attack was possible and that the maintenance of civilian commitment to the war effort was crucial. Over the 1930s, the British government became preoccupied with how to best defend against the swift and devastating air attack that was anticipated at the outbreak of a future war.[175] Between 1927 and 1934 the RAF held annual 'well-publicised exercises designed to test the ability of bombers to penetrate London's air defences'; the bomber almost always got through.[176] The potential for airborne oblivion was made visible to the British public in a number of ways: newsreels of the Spanish Civil War,[177] discussion in the press,[178] and representations in popular fiction. One of the better remembered examples is H. G. Wells's *The Shape of Things to Come* (1933) and its film adaptation, *Things to Come* (1936), but this might have shared bookshelves with titles like *The Gas War of 1940* (1931),[179] *Cry Havoc!* (1933), *The Poison War* (1933), *The Air War of 1936* or *Air Reprisal* (1938), for example. This body of representations informed public expectations that aerial warfare would be central to future conflicts, and thus that the Second World War might be very different from the First.[180]

The majority of young men, however, seem to have expected the Second World War to be like the First, at least when it came to infantry service. Arthur Flint chose to join an armoured unit because he 'felt no wish to sort of get slaughtered like the infantry were in the 14–18 war'.[181] A 30-year-old clerk, reserved at the time of writing to MO, wrote:

> If I am called up for service, I'll do all I can to get a job in the Army at which I will be MOST useful, and I don't mean BEHIND a bayonet. I have no desire to impale anyone on the business end of a rifle. If the worst happens and I'm put in the P.B.I. then God help any bugger that gets in the way, of either the point or the bullet.[182]

It is noteworthy that the Great War acronym Poor Bloody Infantry was sufficiently common parlance in January 1940 that the respondent saw no need to spell it out. The perceived probability of infantry service, and a sense of the infantry's Great War experience as negative, was a significant reason that Army life in particular was not anticipated with excitement and enthusiasm. A 23-year-old told MO in January 1940, 'I'm going to try and keep out of the infantry if I am called up, I don't want to go into muddy trenches, going to try for despatch rider.'[183]

As we have seen, the Great War was understood as the Army's war, and particularly the infantryman's war. This understanding was numerically accurate, but had also been reinforced in post-war

Attitudes to service

representations, as discussed in Chapter 1. One way that young men responded to this understanding was to seek to serve in a different role. Yet, especially if a man planned to serve in something other than the Army, the Great War might still appear disconnected from his own service. For instance, Spragg, who had consumed lots of representations of the Great War, said that his understanding of the Great War had not impacted upon his thoughts because 'it was always at the back of my mind that aviation was what I wanted and the RAF preferably'.[184] Tom Knowlton, whose father was a Great War veteran, who had occasionally heard Great War stories from veteran colleagues, who saw *All Quiet,* and who read avidly about Great War air aces and thought *Ships With Wings* was a 'wonderful' film, did not feel his attitude was shaped by his understanding of the Great War. The Second World War was an opportunity to fly, a job he had aspired to but would otherwise have been unable to afford to access.[185] A similar line of thought was visible in Don Browne's narrative. He had imagined the Second World War as an opportunity for adventure, and he recalled the sincere hope amongst his friends that the war would last long enough for them to serve, but only in the Navy: 'I didn't want to go into the Army, because I'd been brought up about the First World War and going over the top with bayonets and I thought I could and never ever do that ....'[186] Impressions of the Great War commonly shaped young men's understandings of Army service, and deterred many from it, but any such lessons or influences could be dismissed as irrelevant by those anticipating enlisting for war in the skies or on the seas.

Conclusion

Varied motivations affected whether men waited to be conscripted or volunteered. Men typically waited because they prioritised their duty to their families, because conscription removed the need to consider volunteering or because they were in no rush to enter the forces before they had to. While Britain's men were overwhelmingly compliant with conscription, most were not enthusiastic about the prospect. Some volunteers were keen, expressing a desire for adventure and a sense of patriotism, but volunteering also gave men greater opportunity to exercise agency over their service. Arguably, in

210   *Joining up in the Second World War*

relation to wartime control of manpower both the State and citizens learned from the First World War: the State learned that conscription and reservation was necessary to control who enlisted; Britons learned legitimate ways to negotiate with the State and balance the desires and responsibilities of the individual with their responsibility as citizens. A significant proportion of servicemen volunteered, in part or often solely, to have control over where they served. A desire to avoid the Army, particularly the infantry, was a significant reason for the popularity of the RAF and the Royal Navy, and in many cases that desire was directly informed by men's understandings of the Great War. That Britain operated a manpower system that allowed men to exercise agency about how and where they served, or at the very least created the illusion of agency by asking them express a service preference, had an unintended consequence: an individual was more likely to consent to service of some kind, even if they were strongly averse to the prospect of infantry service because of their understanding of the Great War, because they could (or thought they could) affect how they would serve.

Many young men drew upon their understandings of the Great War when thinking about their service. Those who expected the Army's war to be similar often drew on their understandings of the last war to try to identify safe service roles. That normally led them away from the infantry towards tanks or the artillery, or into the Royal Navy or the RAF. In reality, provided he had not volunteered to go into a front-line infantry or tank unit, a man who went into the Army actually had a better chance of returning home alive. The particular nature of the RAF and Royal Navy's war contributed to their higher death rates: 5.5 per cent in the Navy, 5.87 per cent in the RAF and only 3.8 per cent in the Army.[187]

Not everyone, however, looked back to the Great War. This was sometimes because they expected the Second World War would be a different kind of war altogether, and sometimes because they expected *their* role would be different. Young men's understandings of the Great War were strongly connected to the Army, and the infantry in particular. As we saw in Chapters 1 and 2, in popular culture, and in veterans' narratives too, representations of the Great War privileged trenches and men 'going over the top'. Those who anticipated serving other roles did not necessarily connect the two conflicts.

Attitudes to service

Both veterans' narratives and cultural texts shaped young men's attitudes towards the Second World War, but this relationship was more complicated than the assumption that consumption shaped attitudes. Within oral enlistment narratives, and in MO responses about influences upon attitudes to the Second World War, references to accounts of the Great War from veterans, particularly family members, were more common than those to representations in popular culture. The relative paucity of references to popular culture suggests that individuals privileged first- or second-hand representations of the conflict in their narratives and their conscious understandings. When men did refer to cultural representations of the Great War they tended not to point to the now canonical war books and instead drew on a much wider body of representations. These findings complicate the assumption that cultural representations of the Great War determined Britons' responses to the outbreak of the Second World War.

Knowledge of a veteran's service did not need to be detailed to be influential. One veteran's narrative alone could be more influential than any number of books or films, but the meanings that individuals took from their encounters with the legacy of the Great War were not necessarily what one might assume. Even those who encountered the horrific consequences of modern warfare when brought close up to wounds did not necessarily believe that they would suffer the same fate, and young men who had lost their fathers to the last great conflict were not inevitably put off participation in the next.[188]

While MO was concerned that men lacked fire and fury, the prevalence of reluctant, if determined, resignation in fact fitted well with the temperate masculinity that would become hegemonic in public discourse during the Second World War. The temperate model required bravery and willingness to fight, but was set against the jingoistic militarism associated with Nazi Germany. In practice, and as will be discussed in Chapter 5, men's subjective masculinities diverged from the temperate construction – the First World War had not removed the possibility of imagining war as hyper-masculine adventure, and the desire to avoid combat was not strictly playing the game and was positioned as hypo-masculine – but in practice temperate masculinity was broad enough that it could envelop masculinities along this spectrum within respectable male citizenship.

212   *Joining up in the Second World War*

The uniformed combatant remained the most vaunted masculine identity, though, and broad public opinion about wartime service was still reflected by the First World War recruiting song that opined, 'We don't want to lose you but we think you ought to go.' These personal testimonies suggest that most men would have responded, 'I'd prefer I wasn't needed, but if I am then I suppose I will.'

Notes

1 MOA, TC, Worktown, 52/A: GT, Militiamen, 11 November 1939.
2 Morley, 'The Memory of the Great War and Morale During Britain's Phoney War', especially p. 16. For quote, pp. 1–2.
3 Parker, *Manpower*; Fennell, *Fighting the People's War*, pp. 64–6.
4 For instance, Broad's *Conscription in Britain* places much greater emphasis on politics and processes than on men's attitudes. Jonathan Fennell reflects on attempts to evade or defer service in *Fighting the People's War*, pp. 63–6, and Todman reflects on this and rates of conscientious objection in *Britain's War, A New World*, pp. 411–13.
5 Hayes, *Challenge of Conscience*; Barker, *Conscience, Government, and War*; Robb, 'The "Conchie Corps"'; Tobias Kelly, 'Citizenship, Cowardice and Freedom of Conscience: British Pacifists in the Second World War', *Comparative Studies in Society and History*, 57 (2015) pp. 694–722.
6 Allport, *Browned Off and Bloody-Minded*, pp. 60–75.
7 Houghton, *The Veterans' Tale*, pp. 208–9, 211–13.
8 *Ibid.*, pp. 208–13.
9 Sheffield, 'Shadow of the Somme', pp. 30–1. See also Strachan, 'The Soldier's Experience in Two World Wars'.
10 Trott, *Publishers, Readers and the Great War*, pp. 75–80.
11 Houghton, *Veterans' Tale*, pp. 210, 214–15.
12 Houghton's memoirists were predominantly middle and lower-middle class; *Veterans' Tale*, p. 25.
13 MO January 1940 Directive, Question 7 [Attitudes to conscription].
14 Within the following discussion, all references to Directive Replies [DR] are to Question 7 of the January 1940 Directive, unless otherwise stated. 164 men answered Question 7.
15 Some respondents did not express their attitude towards conscription, particularly those who simply stated that they did not expect to be conscripted, yet it was possible to access the attitudes of respondents from all stages of the process.

Attitudes to service

16 MO DR1279.

17 MO DR1338, RAF designer.

18 The regional distribution of the respondents to this directive matches that of England, and to a lesser extent Scotland, relatively well, but there are very few Welsh respondents, and, like most Directives, a disproportionately high number from South-East England.

19 MO, *US*, 3, pp. 5–8. Other aspects of MO's analysis are deserving of critical scrutiny. MO, probably due to their belief in the benefits of providing the masses with information, implied that uncertainty about when individuals would be conscripted was damaging to morale, and asserted that 'Directly, the first dates were given, a million men felt calmer.' It is a sensible suggestion, but not one that can be derived from the Directive Replies.

20 *Ibid.*, p. 5.

21 Adrian Gregory, 'British "War Enthusiasm" in 1914: A Reassessment', in *Evidence, History and the Great War: Historians and the Impact of 1914–18*, ed. by Gail Braybon (New York: Berghahn Books, 2008) pp. 67–85; Catriona Pennell, *A Kingdom United: Popular Responses to the Outbreak of the First World War in Britain and Ireland* (Oxford: Oxford University Press, 2012).

22 David Silbey, *The British Working Class and Enthusiasm for War, 1914–1916* (London: Frank Cass, 2005). See also Pennell, *A Kingdom United*, pp. 227–8.

23 Jay Winter, 'Army and Society: the Demographic Context', in *Nation in Arms: A Social Study of the British Army in the First World War*, ed. by Ian F. Beckett and Keith Simpson (Manchester: Manchester University Press, 1985) pp. 193–209 quoted in Silbey, *The British Working Class and Enthusiasm for War*, p. 127.

24 MO DR2380.

25 MO DR1330. See also DR2349.

26 MO DR2199.

27 MO DR1341.

28 MO DR2402.

29 MO DR2273.

30 MO DR2074.

31 See also MO DR1309 who worried about paying a mortgage on Army wages; DR1237; DR1174.

32 MO DR2375. See also DR2360.

33 MO DR2090. See also DR2085.

34 MO DR2377. See also DR1612, DR2362, DR2358.

35 MO DR1182. See also DR2418.

36 MO DR1264.

214 *Joining up in the Second World War*

37 MO DR2378.
38 MO DR2370.
39 MO DR2222.
40 MO DR2303. See also DR2372, DR2357.
41 MO DR2346. See also DR1962, DR1381, DR1518.
42 MO DR1532.
43 MO DR2353.
44 MO DR2349.
45 See MO DR1093, DR2085, DR1532.
46 MO DR2386.
47 J. M. Winter, 'The Demographic Consequences of the War', in *War and Social Change: British Society in the Second World War*, ed. by Harold Smith (Manchester: Manchester University Press, 1986) pp. 151–78 (p. 152).
48 See, for example, MO DR1264.
49 MO DR2102. See also DR1118, DR2237.
50 MO, *US, Mass-Observation's Weekly Intelligence Service*, 5, 2 March 1940, p. 3.
51 David Englander and Tony Mason examined politics in the January 1940 Directive Reponses, and concluded that 'an active interest in politics does not appear to have been shared by many [soldiers]'. 'The British Soldier in World War II', Warwick Working Papers in Social History, 1984, p. 16.
52 MO DR2419 and DR1416.
53 MO DR2363.
54 MO DR1291, DR1345, DR1465, DR2368.
55 MO DR1457.
56 MO DR2102.
57 MO DR1241.
58 MO, *Us*, 5, p. 8.
59 *Ibid.*, p. 3.
60 MO DR2355.
61 MO DR1213. See also DR1478.
62 MO DR2364. See also DR1526. Some in reserved occupations were willing to serve: DR2132 considered himself 'fortunate' to be reserved but was 'quite ready to take a more directly active part' if the exemption was removed. See also DR2276.
63 MO DR2237, DR1412.
64 MO DR2354. See also DR2131.
65 Both references, already cited, to 'King and Country' in the January DRs responses were negative.
66 Pennell, *A Kingdom United*, pp. 227–8.

Attitudes to service 215

67 Morley, 'The Memory of the Great War and Morale During Britain's Phoney War'.
68 MO FR 274– [Attitude of Civilians to Military/Talk about conscription on the streets].
69 Parker, *Manpower*, table IV, p. 485.
70 Stephens (Morley, 2010).
71 This was also a potential issue for potential conscientious objectors with dependants: MO DR1122, January 1940 Directive. (For more on this, see Robb, 'The "Conchie Corps" '). Conversely, Sydney Leech (IWM-SA-22623, 2002) attempted to accelerate enlistment so that his wife could move in with her parents, thus avoiding having three Austrian refugees billeted in the "empty" rooms of their rented marital home.
72 Knowlton (Morley, 2010). Similarly, Thomas Leask (IWM-SA-21602) waited to be conscripted so that he would be entitled to an allowance from his firm.
73 Stagg (Morley, 2010).
74 Adrian Gregory, *The Last Great War. British Society and the First World War* (Cambridge: Cambridge University Press, 2008) pp. 92–4.
75 *Ibid.*, p. 75.
76 *Ibid.*, p. 95.
77 William Reid, IWM-SA-27208, 2004. He later volunteered when the Fleet Air Arm were looking for pilots.
78 Thomas Illman, IWM-SA-18438, 1998. See also Drake, IWM-SA-20791; Cox, IWM-SA-22167; Sweetland, IWM-SA-10452.
79 Abbott (Morley, 2010).
80 Lowe (Morley, 2010). See also Abbott (Morley, 2010).
81 Lowe (Morley, 2010).
82 Stephen Smith (pseudonym), interviewed by Linsey Robb, 16 May 2013 (Scottish Oral History Centre, 050/043) quoted in Pattinson, McIvor, and Robb, *Men in Reserve*, p. 113.
83 Ministry of Labour and National Service. Report for the years 1939–46. [CMD 7225] House of Commons Parliamentary Papers Online, p. 13.
84 Malling (Morley (& Cash & Dann), 2010).
85 Wyke (Morley, 2010). See also Douglas Baines, IWM-SA-13147, 1993.
86 Todd, IWM-SA-29069.
87 John Winstanley, IWM-SA-17955, 1998. Percival Tyson, also in the TA, expressed a similar attitude and framed it as a result of being young: 'with being only a young lad I thought it was gonna be great'. Percival Tyson, IWM-SA-10309, 1988.

88 Houghton, *Veterans' Tale*, chapter 7.

89 Browne (Morley, 2010).

90 Adverts were issued encouraging ROs to volunteer for the RAF as pilots or observers, which implied aircrew were performing a more important function. Alison Chand, 'Second World War in Glasgow and Clydeside: Men in Reserved Occupations 1939–1945' (Unpublished PhD Thesis, University of Strathclyde, 2012) p. 80.

91 Sell, IWM-SA-10403.

92 Patterson, IWM-SA-8901.

93 Stagg (Morley, 2010).

94 Hayes (Morley, 2010).

95 Cash (Morley (& Dann & Malling), 2010).

96 Pragnell (Morley (& Marriot), 2010).

97 French, *Raising Churchill's Army*, p. 64. 29 per cent of conscripts expressed a preference for the RAF and 18 per cent for Navy; Parker, *Manpower*, table VI, pp. 488–90.

98 Except those rejected because they were unfit, or conducting Essential Work.

99 Florence (Morley, 2010).

100 The Ministry of Labour and National Service tried to end the service option; see Broad, *Conscription in Britain*, p.144.

101 Carmichael, IWM-SA-10297.

102 Bowdler, IWM-SA-22342.

103 Interviewees felt this, and it was also suggested by MO research – see Francis, *The Flyer*, p. 20 drawing on MO FR 895 Public Attitudes to RAF News, October 1941.

104 Ratio of conscripts to volunteers – 0.9:1, based on Parker, *Manpower*, table IV, p. 485.

105 Ratio of conscripts to volunteers – 1.2:1, based on *ibid*.

106 Ratio of conscripts to volunteers – 3.2:1, based on *ibid*.

107 Army accepted 650,400 volunteers and 61,300 Direct Officer Intake. Royal Navy accepted 296,200 volunteers and 31,000 DOI. RAF accepted 511,800 volunteers and 27,600 DOI. Parker, *Manpower*, table IV, p. 485; French, *Raising Churchill's Army*, p. 64.

108 Broad, *Conscription in Britain*, p. 144.

109 Webster (Morley, 2010); Reid, IWM-SA-27208.

110 Thurgood (Morley, 2010); Webster (Morley, 2010).

111 Howard (Morley, 2011). See also Alf Wkye (Morley, 2010) discussed earlier in this chapter.

112 Gordon Gent, IWM-SA-18255, 1999.

113 Frank Clements, National Museum of the Royal Navy, 278/1994–3*2, 1994.

Attitudes to service

114 *National Service: A Guide to the Ways in Which the People of This Country May Give Service; with a Message from the Prime Minister* (London: HMSO, 1939).
115 MO, *Home Propaganda* (1941) pp. 37–9.
116 *Joining Up*, p. 30.
117 *Ibid.*, pp. 39–46.
118 *Ibid.*, pp. 57–62. The guide suggests that these are the rates payable to men of 26 or above, but is somewhat ambiguous in its totality.
119 *Ibid.*, pp. 56–9.
120 Cox, IWM-SA-22167.
121 Wyke (Morley, 2010); Baines, IWM-SA-13147.
122 Cash (Morley (& Dann & Malling), 2010).
123 Dann (Morley (& Cash & Malling, 2010).
124 Knowlton (Morley, 2010).
125 MO January 1940, DR 1424.
126 Hayes (Morley, 2010).
127 Illman, IWM-SA-18438.
128 Frank Webster, 'This Question of Conscription', 28 March 1939. Interviewee's personal papers.
129 Webster (Morley, 2010).
130 Morley, 'The Memory of the Great War and Morale During Britain's Phoney War', pp. 6, 14.
131 For a fuller exploration of this material, see *ibid.*
132 MO February 1940, DR 1046.
133 Morley, 'The Memory of the Great War and Morale During Britain's Phoney War', p. 3.
134 MOA, TC Worktown, 9 May 1940. Similar sentiment was expressed in MOA 42/G: short report on territorial army, 15 February 1938.
135 MO DR1220, February 1940 Directive.
136 Sheffield, 'Shadow of the Somme'.
137 MO FR 274.
138 Thurgood (Morley, 2010).
139 Atkinson, IWM-SA-18738.
140 Hayes (Morley, 2010).
141 Donovan, IWM-SA-20316.
142 MO DR2348, January 1940 Directive. He ultimately joined the RAF.
143 MO DR2349, January and February 1940 Directives.
144 Ronald Mallabar, IWM-SA-11211, 1989. See also Harold Vanderwolfe, IWM-SA-13426, 1993. Carmichael, IWM-SA-10297; Riggs (IWM-SA-22346) opted to go in his uncle's service arm.
145 Wilson, IWM-SA-17985.
146 Parkhouse, IWM-SA-15476.

218   *Joining up in the Second World War*

147 Kirby, IWM-SA-16084.
148 Another factor was his fear that he would not be able to accept the ethos of the Army and would ultimately get into a fight with a superior. Hayes (Morley, 2010).
149 Wyke (Morley, 2010).
150 Atkinson, IWM-SA-18738. Those who expressed a conscientious objection could also be influenced by those with experience from the Great War. Quaker, F. R. Davies, considered refusing when conscripted to the Non-Combatant Corp rather than his preferred RAMC. His uncle said, 'his own time in Prison as a conscientious objector in the first war had ruined his digestion for life, and he advised against refusal. So I went.' F. R. Davies, *Some Blessed Hope: Memories of a Next to Nobody* (Lewes, 1996) p. 37 quoted in Robb, 'The "Conchie Corps"', p. 417.
151 Eric Johnson (Morley, 2016).
152 Eric Wakeling, *The Lonely War: A Story of Bomb Disposal in World War Two by One Who Was There* (Worcester: Square One, 1994) p. 7.
153 Cash (Morley (& Dann & Malling), 2010).
154 Henry Brewis, IWM-SA-12707, 1992.
155 Abbott (Morley, 2010).
156 Thurgood (Morley, 2010); Brand, IWM-SA-27347.
157 Spragg (Morley, 2010).
158 Pragnell (Morley (& Marriot), 2010).
159 Derrick Thurgood was particularly aware that talk of the First World War upset his mother, though this made him more interested in it as a child. Thurgood (Morley, 2010).
160 Wilfred White, IWM-SA-16718, 1996. Mothers also attempted to prevent enlistment in the Great War; see Pennell, *A Kingdom United*, pp. 53–4.
161 White, IWM-SA-16718.
162 Stephens (Morley, 2010).
163 Woodhams (Morley, 2010).
164 Pragnell (Morley (& Marriot), 2010). Houghton observes pilots explaining their service choice in the same way – an attempt to avoid the Army – in their memoirs. Houghton, *Veterans' Tale*, p. 210.
165 Pearson (Morley, 2011).
166 See Peter Berresford Ellis and Jennifer Schofield, *By Jove., Biggles! The Life Story of Captain W E Johns* (Watford: Norman Wright, 2003).
167 Houghton makes the same observation, *Veterans' Tale*, pp. 214–17.
168 Patterson, IWM-8901.

Attitudes to service

169 Johns, *Biggles of the Camel Squadron*, p. 55, quoted in Budgen, *British Children's Literature*, p. 86.

170 Carmichael, IWM-SA-10297.

171 Hay (Morley, 2010).

172 Taylor, IWM-SA-10484. For men who expected it to be different, see also Sidney Parsons, IWM-SA-14052, 1994 and Harper, IWM-SA-10923.

173 Thurgood (Morley, 2010). Les Temple (Morley, 2010) also expected very different methods.

174 Spragg (Morley, 2010).

175 Mackay, *Half the Battle*, pp. 17–22, 31–9.

176 Brett Holman, 'The Air Panic of 1935: British Press Opinion between Disarmament and Rearmament', *Journal of Contemporary History*, 46.2 (2011) pp. 288–307 (pp. 293–4).

177 See Helen Jones, *British Civilians in the Front Line. Air Raids, Productivity and Wartime Culture, 1939–1945* (Manchester: Manchester University Press, 2006) p. 58.

178 See Holman, 'Air Panic'.

179 This sold 100,000 copies. Martin Ceadel, 'Popular Fiction and the Next War, 1918–1939', in *Class, Culture and Social Change: A New View of the 1930s*, ed. by Frank Gloversmith (Sussex: Harvester Press, 1980) p. 171.

180 Mackay, *Half the Battle*, pp. 40–1. For discussion of the plot and critical reception of *The Shape of things to Come* and *Things to Come*, see Susan Grayzel, *Britain at Home and Under Fire. Air Raids and Culture in Britain from the Great War to the Blitz* (New York: Cambridge University Press, 2012) pp. 117–19.

181 Flint, IWM-SA-899. First World War weaponry and techniques were expected by Riggs, IWM-SA-22346. It was expected to be a 'continuation of what happened at the end of the First World War' by Sweetland, IWM-SA-10452. Unpleasant images of Great War infantry service were drawn upon by Carmichael, IWM-SA-10297 and Patterson, IWM-SA-8901, suggesting their expectation it would be similar.

182 MO DR1178. See also DR2244.

183 MO DR 2364, January 1940 Directive.

184 Spragg (Morley, 2010).

185 Knowlton (Morley, 2010).

186 Browne (Morley, 2010).

187 Winter, 'The Demographic Consequences of the War', pp. 163–4.

188 Winstanley, IWM-SA-17955; Leech, IWM-SA-22623; George Dann (Morley (& Cash & Malling), 2010).

5

Masculinity in the Second World War

Introduction

Young men's understandings of the Great War may not have dissuaded them from participating in the Second World War. Nor did they necessarily weaken the relationship between military participation and masculinity in young men's subjective constructions of what it was to be a man. This chapter develops the interpretation laid out so far by concentrating on how understandings of masculinity affected attitudes to and experiences of service. It examines the importance men placed on military service, and its visual embodiment through uniforms, and whether social constructions of masculinity exerted pressure upon young men to serve. The first section explains how masculinity is conceptualised. The second highlights the disconnect between scholarly suggestions about the Great War's legacy in relation to masculinity and research about gender in public discourse during the Second World War, and explains the wartime masculinity that occupied a hegemonic position in public discourse. In the third and fourth sections, oral history interviews and MO material are used to examine the centrality of military participation to men's subjective conceptions of wartime masculinity, and how these related to the hegemonic wartime masculinity constructed in public discourse. Men's attitudes to those outside the full-time Forces – conscientious objectors, those in reserved occupations (ROs) and the Home Guard – are explored, before turning to the ways that masculinity was evident in men's discussion of their own enlistment and service. Consideration of how constructions of masculinity shaped men's attitudes towards enlistment runs throughout the chapter.

Masculinity in the Second World War   221

The chapter demonstrates that men's understandings of wartime masculinity did shape their attitudes to service, but it also demonstrates that men's subjective conceptions of masculinity were often divergent from the 'temperate' masculinity that was hegemonic in Second World War Britain. Some men desired military involvement or combat, perceived elements of service as glamorous, and anticipated an exciting adventure. This conception was more closely aligned to a much older perception of service as a masculine rite of passage. However, the majority of men probably did perceive the connections between masculinity and military participation in terms of duty, defence of home and family, and reluctant acceptance of the need to serve. It should be recognised that the key shift between the First and Second World Wars was not the wholesale rejection of military participation but rather the increased acceptability of publicly expressing a willingness to fight mixed with a preference for not having to do so. Significantly, this chapter also shows that men generally understood hegemonic wartime masculinity as bound up with the status of combatant, particularly in the air, and perceived similar hierarchies of wartime masculinity. Even though not all aspired to the hegemonic version of masculinity, and some served begrudgingly rather than sincerely willingly, this understanding nevertheless shaped their attitudes towards military service. The considerable variation in men's subjective conceptions of masculinity that is shown highlights that national discourse did not necessarily dictate individuals' ideas, but the temperate framework was flexible enough to contain and permit such diversity.

Conceptualising masculinity

Any given society, at any given time, through public discourse and social expectations and practices, encourages and validates sets of behaviours and attributes as gendered ideals. The 'hegemonic masculinity', in Connell's useful conceptual framework, is it not necessarily the most common masculinity in a given society at a given time, but it is the masculinity most 'respected for men of a particular age group'.[1] It is a dominant ideal type established through public discourse, which 'convinc[es] the generality of men that there is no other way of "being a man"'.[2] It sits at the top of a

222 *Joining up in the Second World War*

hierarchical framework into which other subordinate masculinities can be positioned in relation to both the hegemonic masculinity and femininities.[3] Constructions of national identity and citizenship can also shape acceptable gendered behaviour, particularly during wartime,[4] and the hegemonic masculinity is not universally or wholly applicable but is contingent upon other elements of an individual's identity, such as class and age.[5] Nevertheless, masculinity is not only a social construct but is also a subjective identity.[6] John Tosh writes men 'must live by a code which affirms their masculinity', and such 'lived masculine identities' draw upon available cultural forms.[7] Similarly, the hegemonic masculinity and men's subjective masculinities are connected in Judith Butler's notion that individuals strive to 'perform' socially constructed gender identities.[8] Men who accept the hegemonic masculinity will attempt to enact it, and failure to do so will result in a sense of personal deficiency or emasculation.[9] In practice, a gender identity, like other aspects of social conformity, is something that individuals go to differing lengths to achieve. Men might only wish to be *perceived* as conforming to the hegemonic masculinity, to avoid being seen as possessing a subordinate masculinity. As Peniston-Bird stated about men's bodies, 'Men did not have a choice whether to conform or reject hegemonic masculinity: they positioned themselves in relation to it.'[10]

Drawing on Connell's formulation, we might envisage a hierarchical framework of multiple masculinities, with the hegemonic masculinity surrounded by concentric rings of subordinate masculinities of decreasing status. During wartime, roles involving combat, risk, and high levels of fitness or/and skill tend to be closer to the centre. Defining the hierarchy is, however, made very difficult by the number of potential variants. The fighter pilot appears to have been *the* hegemonic masculinity of Second World War Britain, encapsulating ideas of chivalry and fair play, but he required less physical and more mental capacity than the front-line infantryman, who could also ultimately be in much closer proximity to killing. As we will see, when soldiers referred to airmen as 'Brylcreem Boys', they were posing an implicit query about their masculinity – when airmen used the term about themselves, they were claiming access to an idealised masculinity. Attitude or spirit was also central to understandings of wartime masculinity, though its rehabilitative power was limited.[11] The willing voluntarism of an unfit

Masculinity in the Second World War 223

RAF armourer might place him closer to the hegemonic masculinity than the conscript reluctantly serving in an infantry regiment. To further complicate matters, non-military roles can be as masculine as some military roles.[12] Increasingly technological warfare made this particularly apparent; radar operators might be physically detached from battle but integral to it, and did not require all the traditional soldierly attributes. The existence and performance of an *alternative* masculinity might provide personal and/or social acceptance. For example, Alison Chand suggests that men in ROs could retain a sense of masculinity through a focus on pre-war masculine attributes, within a community where many others were doing the same.[13] Similarly, one my interviewees felt that the public thought more of men in the forces than of civilians, but that firemen were 'on a par with the forces'.[14] Nevertheless, public perceptions were much less nuanced than the potential variables; the inability to create a rigid hierarchy did not prevent people from drawing a boundary between sufficient and deficient masculinities in wartime Britain. The masculinity of those within military uniform was largely accepted, though the Home Guard came close to straddling the boundary, whilst that of those outside uniform was open to challenge and scrutiny.

Scholars have used the term 'military masculinity' to describe either the set of characteristics required of servicemen by the military, or the socially expected behaviour of men during wartime. To avoid confusion, here, where the military's requirements are of interest only in so far as they shape the public understanding of the relationship between warfare and masculinity, societal expectations of men during the Second World War are referred to with the term 'wartime masculinity'.

Connecting wartime masculinities

The historiographical literature relating to the First and Second World Wars does not always intersect. In 1914 the hegemonic masculinity was that of the soldier hero.[15] Some scholars have contended, however, that the Great War challenged the place of military participation in conceptions of masculinity, and that masculinity was reshaped during the inter-war years.[16] Certainly, combat in the

224   *Joining up in the Second World War*

Great War challenged the connection between agency and heroism and survival and victory, and potentially undermined the relevance of the previously held characteristics of the ideal soldier, and therefore man. The prevalence of shell shock, which demonstrated men of all classes could not endure the mental strains of modern warfare indefinitely, challenged understandings of 'character' and stoicism. Michael Roper suggests that one lesson of the Great War, which 'struck at the heart of manliness', was that character could not prevent fear; instead, the ability to endure despite fear became the hallmark of courage.[17] Men might plausibly have rejected military participation as national duty and an essential characteristic of masculinity in the wake of such an illustrative display of the costs of this principle, as some scholars who focus upon the 'disillusioned war writers' suggest.[18]

George Mosse and Alison Light suggest that in inter-war Britain masculinity was constructed as softer, more domestic, pacifistic, and anti-heroic.[19] Sonya Levsen argues that by the late 1920s Cambridge students were less inclined to consider themselves 'soldiers ready for their summons'.[20] Alternatives to military masculinity were available, and while they wished to honour the worthwhile sacrifice of Great War dead, celebrating peace was an increasingly popular way to do this. Debating societies increasingly supported pacifist motions, similar to the widely noted 1933 Oxford Union debate which passed the motion 'This house will in no circumstances fight for its King and Country'.[21] Whether such results reveal people's viewpoints rather than which side made the strongest argument is questionable, though; none of those who voted for the Oxford Union motion subsequently conscientiously objected.[22] Gregory has suggested a literal interpretation: students would no longer fight for *King* and *Country*, for the patriotism associated with 1914 – although they might well fight (and did) for other things.[23]

Oxford and Cambridge represented a narrow social milieu, but Bond, Sheffield and Watson cite a similar trend towards peace in wider society, driven by the realisation of the human cost of the war.[24] This is normally illustrated with the Fulham East by-election,[25] the success of the 1935 'peace ballot' and the subsequent popularity of the Peace Pledge Union.[26] Whether or not these events can or should be interpreted as evidence of a single set of attitudes to peace, war and the international use of force is highly debatable:

Masculinity in the Second World War   225

it might be better to see them as highlighting the views of particular sections of society at particular political moments. Nonetheless, they do suggest that different versions of masculinity, in which the martial was less important or differently constructed, did open up for some people in some places between the wars.

In contrast to the emphasis on the popularity of the peace movement, and despite a scholarly concentration on canonical literature and disillusionment as a legacy of the Great War, the first and second chapters of this book demonstrated that inter-war popular culture and veterans continued to offer traditional and positive representations of the Great War, as an adventure and an arena for heroic or stoic manliness. In these representations military participation in wartime remained an integral part of what it was to be a man, and as these chapters showed, these were the representations that young men most often encountered. Scholars have suggested that the continuation of such depictions, and particularly the pleasure culture of war, may have ensured the survival of Edwardian masculine ideals.[27]

There is consensus amongst historians of gender in Second World War Britain, based on research about constructions of gender in public discourse during the Second World War, that military service remained an essential component of hegemonic masculinity from 1939 to 1945. Men and women were expected to contribute to the war effort, with the 'Good Citizen' constructed, Sonya Rose has argued, as a self-sacrificing, active contributor to the welfare of the nation, who subjugated self-interest for the benefit of the community.[28] This construction of active citizenship, Lucy Noakes states, worked to persuade people to perform wartime roles that 'were not necessarily roles that everyone was happy to undertake'.[29] Significantly, though, these wartime roles were gendered: 'man as soldier and woman as wife, mother and war worker'.[30] While the formulation of active citizenship encouraged, and to some extent legitimised, women undertaking work that challenged traditional gender roles, the contests that occurred about women's involvement in particular roles served to articulate the essential boundaries of wartime masculinity and femininity, and the significance contemporaries placed significance on segregating combat as a masculine arena.[31] Women who joined military arms were designated auxiliaries, and were denied the use of weapons even in the most logical

226 *Joining up in the Second World War*

circumstances.[32] Just as ATS recruitment literature stated: 'The men will do the fighting, You must do the rest.' Indeed, Summerfield has described a 'wartime gender contract': 'Men, not women, were presumed ... to be "natural" warriors' and 'were pledged to fight for women, who undertook to maintain home and family'.[33] The contestation surrounding women's military participation, and the limitations imposed upon their roles, demonstrates the extent to which men, not women, were expected to fight the nation's wars, and combat roles remained the pinnacle of wartime masculinity.

Nevertheless, Rose suggests that the hegemonic masculinity during the Second World War was softer than during the First; the soldier hero was blended with 'the homely, more feminine ideals of masculinity inherited from' the 'interwar anti-hero' to form a 'temperate masculinity': good humoured, rational, stoic, chivalrous and fair spirited, physically strong, brave and modestly heroic if necessary, but lacking in bravado and aggression.[34] This ' "kinder, gentler" manliness, which was equated with Britishness', was 'an unstable mix';[35] performing it successfully required a man to be in 'military dress'. The man outside uniform risked being 'seen as a "bad citizen", even though there were millions of men on the home front "doing their bit" for the country'.[36] If public discourse had not made societal expectations clear enough, the announcement of conscription legally marked military service as the civic obligation of the young man, and ensured that the masculinity of those outside uniform was open to scrutiny. Conscientious objectors were widely criticised and represented as cowardly and effeminate, with questions posed about their sexuality.[37] Similarly, men at work outside military uniform were often represented in public discourse as possessing subordinate masculinities – they were assistants, not equals.[38]

Existing research about wartime roles in cultural discourse during the Second World War and the resolute defence of combat as a masculine sphere suggest its continued centrality to hegemonic wartime masculinity. This does not fit neatly with the idea that masculinity had been significantly reconstructed in response to the experiences of 1914–18. Historians have, however, paid less attention to whether individuals' subjective understandings of masculinity mirrored these ideal constructions and how this affected their attitudes to wartime service. Recent studies have shed much

Masculinity in the Second World War   227

needed light on the subjective masculinities of men outside uniform – in the Home Guard and in reserved occupations – and these works inform this one in useful ways.[39] How the man *in* uniform experienced being at war and how this affected masculine subjectivities has also received some attention.[40] Martin Francis focused on masculinity amongst combatant aircrew in the wartime RAF, and posits a change towards a more reflective martial masculinity, readier to acknowledge the challenges to traditionally male traits implicit in the experience of combat.[41] Frances Houghton makes a similar argument about memoirists who served in explicitly 'sharp-end' roles across all forces: their narratives chart a coming of age, from naive, enthusiastic (even gung-ho) warriors who, upon combat experience, recognised a more temperate and less heroic masculine reality.[42] That Houghton's memoirists presented themselves as enthusiastic about the prospect of military participation and expected action to be both adventure and rite of passage mirrors some of my findings.[43] Nevertheless, it remains necessary to explore attitudes to military service and masculinity in greater breadth because, as Houghton points out, her memoirists were an atypical sample of servicemen.[44] As well as having a war story that both that veteran and publisher deemed worth telling, Houghton's (typically middle-class) memoirists had often been involved military forces prior to the outbreak of the war, often had rank and had mostly chosen to enter explicitly combatant roles.[45] Given their decisions, and that public schools encouraged a masculinity that emphasised stoicism, civic duty and heroic chivalry, it would be surprising if these men had not begun their wars as keen fighters. Their path made a story-worthy war more likely and was different to that taken by the majority of British men, particularly those who *tried* to limit their war to the mundane. Houghton is careful to avoid generalising from their experience, but the composition of the sample limits the relevance of the findings to the different questions this chapter addresses. Still absent from the historiography is a significant body of research that unpicks the subjective conceptions of masculinity held by men *in* uniform during the Second World and who were brought up after the Great War, and that focuses on pulling these two threads together. This chapter starts to address this deficit, and to improve our understanding of masculinity in Britain after the Great War.

228 *Joining up in the Second World War*

Conchies, shirkers and Dad's Army: non-military masculinity in Second World War Britain

Men's subjective understandings of wartime masculinity were seldom directly addressed in narratives of enlistment and service. Nonetheless, they were evident as men discussed their attitudes to military service, particularly why it was desirable, and as they discussed the consequences of wearing or not wearing a uniform. Indeed, their descriptions of and attitudes towards men (including themselves prior to enlistment) who were *outside* the full-time forces highlight their understandings of the importance of military service to wartime masculinity. Therefore, this analysis begins with an examination of what men thought about conscientious objectors, and those in reserved occupations or the Home Guard.

'Evading their responsibilities': conscientious objectors

In April 1940, MO surveyed 250 people in Fulham about COs. Around a third were sympathetic, particularly the young, while around two-fifths were antagonistic, some violently so, and antagonism was more entrenched than tolerance.[46] MO, counterintuitively, suggested that 'the less likely people are to be conscripted themselves the more antagonistic they seem to become to the idea that other people can evade conscription'.[47] In August and September of 1940, when Britain appeared under significantly greater threat, MO repeated their questions in Fulham. Similar proportions expressed either pro-pacifist (12 per cent) or strong anti-pacifist sentiment (25 per cent), but far fewer people reported tolerance and a full third were 'moderately anti'.[48] Attitudes had hardened.

Those who supported COs tended to comment on their bravery, with comments like 'Needs a lot of pluck, don't it, facing everybody.' Tolerance was more common than sympathy, and still tended to include qualifications about COs sincerity. One said, 'They've got as much right to their views as anyone, if they're really COs.' Another said, 'If a man's honestly a CO I think he had a perfect right to be one.' Tolerance was often begrudging; as one woman said, 'Well I understand their point of view and I even sympathise, but if the other boys have got to fight, they should really, too.'

Masculinity in the Second World War   229

What MO termed 'mild criticism' centred upon the idea that everyone should participate in the war effort. Doubts about COs' sincerity combined with fears they might benefit from others' sacrifice, perhaps gaining lucrative war work, caused antagonism. Accusations of cowardice were common within the stronger criticism. One said, 'I think they are cowards, looking after themselves', while another said, 'Cowards ... they didn't ought to have ration cards.'[49] Suspicions of cowardice undermined their masculinity; as one woman tellingly commented, 'I don't think they're men.' In Liverpool, a fifth of those asked their opinion of COs said they were 'afraid to fight and should be made to'. One replied, 'Some are yellow, some are truly of that conviction. I should put them on work of national importance. They must pull their weight.' The State was, of course, directing them to such work, but even COs serving with the Non-Combatant Corps sometimes encountered open antagonism; soldiers would start fights in pubs and members of the NCC were denied service by some businesses;[50] a café owner told one 'We don't serve the NCCs here. It's the missus, not me. She lost a brother in the last war and would rather put the shutters up than take money from anyone who wears your badge.'[51]

John Hall Williams, who was a CO, recalled being sent an anonymous postcard labelling him a traitor.[52] White Feather campaigns, which sought to shame men not in uniform, were not as widespread as during the last war.[53] Still, there were calls in parliament for men who were exempt from service on medical grounds to be issued with a badge to deter undeserved criticism from passersby, and men who had been discharged wounded were given the King's Badge to indicate their service.[54] My interviewees also remembered antagonistic feelings, and that most people 'had no time for COs' during the Second World War.[55] Only one had considered objection themselves, and few had known COs. Their attitudes mirror those found by MO. A small number sincerely felt that COs were entitled to their opinion, but only a minority admired them. George Stagg felt the decision was for each individual's conscience, and that COs 'must have had some convictions' to go before the tribunal. Moreover, he recognised 'a lot of 'em done jobs that I would never have done', such as stretcher-bearing in the Royal Army Medical Corps.[56] Some were indifferent, particularly if Objectors were forced to join the war effort, but their position remained questionable.[57]

230 *Joining up in the Second World War*

George Dann thought COs were undermined by 'the minority of people who were, shall we say, were cowards, who didn't want to go in and get killed and they ... dodged in other words'.[58] Similarly, Frank Webster's attitude highlighted the importance of that ambiguity: he 'never felt antagonistic' towards a CO colleague, 'probably because I knew that he wasn't a shyster', but 'generally I don't suppose I was very pleased with the fact that they were, course then you come to the word conscientious, I mean that's the main thing, some were, some weren't ...'.[59]

As many interviewees had negative attitudes as had held sympathetic or tolerant ones. Some felt that the benefits of citizenship were contingent upon fulfilling one's obligation to defend the nation, and Reg Elson felt 'bitter' that the protection and food which some fought and died for might be received by a 'conscientious objector [who] in my book has no rights to any of that whatsoever'.[60] Others believed that an individual should not be able to shirk the burden of wartime service. Brian Spragg said, 'Well I for one, did object to [COs] really, and most of my friends did as well because you know, somebody has got to do it', and he and his peers 'were quite prepared to do military service of some sort or other'.[61] Peter Woodard said, 'We tended to look down on [COs]'. 'As a lad I suppose you got a feeling that the war is on and pull their finger out and join up and beat these damn Germans.' He would not have objected himself: 'you've got to do your duty after all is said and done'.[62] Maurice Marriot agreed: 'I didn't think much to them ... because I mean none of us wanted war or anything but we felt it was our duty', and while COs were brave 'the general thought was that they were getting out of you know going into the Army, the forces'.[63] This observation mirrored that of MO diarist Len England, who reported that 'the men in the Army feel that [COs] are getting away with it'.[64]

Two testimonies provided particularly clear illustrations that a man's lack of willingness to serve in the military could be perceived as emasculating them. Percy Walder thought very little of COs, and said 'nothing would turn me into that'. He questioned the sexuality, and thus masculinity, of men entering ROs, and characterised COs with the same terms. He suggested that it was effeminate men who objected: 'barbers and these blokes who worked in like tailors and those sort of things, what I call a soft-hand man who would never

Masculinity in the Second World War   231

done anything sort of thing'.[65] Reg Day felt that most men were reluctant combatants, but felt 'like everybody else' that COs were

> cowards, cowards, I mean I'm no hero but I'm not a coward either … they were cowards, I mean they backed right out of the whole thing, I was only going to go and do half way as I thought, I mean you know, meaning I wouldn't be doing the full bit which would to be going right up the very front end, I'd be going as near as I could get to actually doing it … I've still got the eye half blind.

Here Day demonstrates a clear hierarchy of service based upon proximity to combat. His poor eyesight, rather than his courage or will, prevented him from progressing past 'half way' and 'doing the full bit which would be going right up the very front end'. This still, however, put him above COs, who were 'cowards' because they lacked will even if they had the physical capacity. Overall, these findings support Linsey Robb's conclusion that '[f]or many [COs] were still shirkers and cowards who had fundamentally rejected a key part of their male duty. For others the objector's seeming desire to choose only the palatable parts of wartime service seemed palpably unfair.'[66] COs themselves were evidently not attempting to embody the hegemonic wartime masculinity,[67] but others' attitudes towards them illustrate that uniformed military service and willingness to fight if needed continued to be significant components of most Britons' conceptions of wartime masculinity.

'Jammy bastards': men in reserved occupations

The civilian man had been represented as a shirker in the Great War and civilian workers' efforts were absent from post-war memorialisation; when the Second World War Schedule of Reserved Occupations was devised there was concern about 'scrimjacks'.[68] Robb stresses that 'Reserved Occupation' was not a singular wartime identity in a dichotomous relationship with the serviceman during the Second World War; different civilian occupations were depicted differently in public discourse and occupied different positions in the hierarchy of wartime masculinity.[69] For instance, firemen and merchant seamen – the 'most exalted civilian wartime occupation'[70] – whose roles were easily connected to the war effort,

232   *Joining up in the Second World War*

required bravery because of inherent danger, and in the case of merchant seamen could also involve fighting with the enemy, featured in public discourse in ways that paralleled the heroism of servicemen and that positioned men in these roles as close to the wartime hegemonic ideal. Meanwhile men working in agriculture were rendered invisible by the focus on the work of the Women's Land Army and campaigns to encourage amateurs to dig for victory, and the man in industry, pushed aside by a focus on women entering new roles, was 'most definitely the man behind the man behind the gun'.[71]

Men's subjective attitudes to ROs make visible the importance of occupying a *military* role to enact masculinity as distinct from the importance of fulfilling civic and patriotic duty through participation in the war effort. Some of my interviewees expressed disappointment in friends attempting to avoid military service by entering ROs, and attempted to avoid non-uniformed roles themselves, which suggests that membership of the fighting forces was an important component of their subjective conceptions of wartime masculinity.

Men in ROs received significantly greater acceptance, and less hostility, than COs. Many interviewees had simply accepted that ROs were making their contribution. As Bob Woodhams said, 'if they're exempt and they don't want to go and they're doing a worthwhile job then that's fair enough, if they're working on munitions and anything to help the war effort ... 'cos they're doing the same job but in a civilian way like, it's all helping, ...'.[72] Some did not see such work as an equal contribution to being in the services, though. Arthur Howard said, 'we always referred to [ROs] as jammy bastards, we thought "Well it's alright for you, you've got a cushy number"'.[73] Derrick Thurgood would not stand a drink for a reserved man and said that 'they were seen as certainly dodging the column'.[74]

The moral legitimacy of reservation appears to have been heavily dependent upon *when* an individual had entered the role. Peniston-Bird has suggested that 'Working in a reserved occupation was only acceptable if the individual longed to join the Armed Forces, but nobly sacrificed his desire for the good of the country.'[75] Don Browne was clearly thinking of those who were kept in ROs, perhaps unwillingly, when he accepted that 'you didn't really have a

Masculinity in the Second World War 233

choice did you, I mean if you was the age [then] you went or if you were a reserved occupation you stayed at your job because it was obviously an important job, a war job'.[76] Interviewees depicted men who had deliberately entered ROs after the outbreak, however, in terms that challenged their masculinity and perceived their behaviour as unacceptable. John Malling, who volunteered for the RAF from his position at A. V. Roe's, manufacturer of the Lancaster bomber, observed:

> a lot of young fellows ... who wanted to get themselves reserved would come to A.V. Roe's ... their mums and dads didn't want them to fight the wars, wanted them to be safe [....] We didn't think much of it but it was legitimate for them to do it, they came into a reserved occupation, we needed people to fill the vacancies and you are getting the right types who didn't want to fight.

While Malling recognised that it 'pleased everybody' as those who wanted to fight were replaced by those who did not, it was seen as 'a way out, escaping call-up' and 'they were frowned upon' by the existing employees.[77] Malling's framing subtly but clearly emasculates such men; that their motivation was safety implies cowardice, and that it was their parent's decision both denies agency and denotes immaturity. Percy Walder left an RO at Hawker, manufacturer of the Hurricane fighter-plane, for the RAF. Like Malling, he described men entering ROs at Hawker in critical terms that certainly implied effeminacy and appear, given his initial coyness, to have implied homosexuality. Both characterisations suggested he perceived them to possess subordinate masculinities. Initially, Walder said, '[T]hey were bringing in what we call, I shouldn't use the right word because it's the wrong word probably, but still, what I meant, people who had never got their hands dirty if you like, one way or another, hairdressers if you like, put it a bit vaguely.' He later referred to them as 'people who had been ... in a shop selling clothes and whatnot, not what I call a manual man ...'. At the end of the interview, he described them again, perhaps revealing the word he had earlier avoided:

> [T]here were all sorts coming in there [Hawker], I've got a funny word which I use, posers I call 'em, whatever, pansy boys, they got rings on their fingers and long fingernails and whatever but they're

234 *Joining up in the Second World War*

not, they are either tailors or whatever, but that's me I'm rough and ready [....] right smart git I remember coming in now, the old fingernails were lovely and he had posh shirts ha-ha-ha-ha oh dear but there you are.[78]

Walder's description of clean, well-presented, effeminate appearance suggested these were men unfamiliar with, and potentially unsuited to, this kind of workplace and who were not acculturated to the 'rough and ready' hard masculinity traditionally associated with heavy industrial manufacturing.

Even if they thought ROs were legitimate, some individuals clearly conceived ROs as subordinate roles to those in the military. Peter Woodard said that 'if you couldn't be in the forces then you just had to do what you could do otherwise, whether it be in munitions or [whatever]'. The implication that ROs were inferior to military roles was repeated when he said that he was glad not to be reserved because 'there was a war on and you'd got to be your best, that was it'.[79] The notion of a hierarchy was also apparent in Les Temple's reflections. He remembered those who opted to enter mining were 'looked down on a bit' because they had 'tried to get out of the services sort of thing you see'. Asked about the comparative masculinity of men inside and outside uniform, Temple said that being in the services 'was the ultimate' but that Bevin Boys and ROs were 'a grade below servicemen'. They were 'looked upon as being unable to get in the service and they may not have been fit enough to get in the service, just about fit enough to go down the mine, you see, which wasn't a glamour situation' and some felt they were more feminine.[80]

Men's reluctance to be in ROs further suggests that this position did not satisfy wartime masculinity. Although it was noted in Chapter 3 that a minority of men would have gladly accepted reservation to avoid military service, most interviewees said that they would have been unhappy to be reserved, and a significant number knowingly left positions where they were, or would have become, reserved. This was certainly not always related to masculinity; Ted Roberts left skilled war work for the Army simply because he had always wanted to join when he came of age and was not about to let the opportunity presented by the war pass.[81] The following examples show, however, that a desire to meet either personal or

Masculinity in the Second World War 235

public conceptions of wartime masculinity did in some cases motivate the move from ROs into uniform.

Bill Lloyd burnt his reservation paperwork and deceived his boss to be conscripted. He thought he 'must have been the only skilled moulder in the British Army', but explained that 'all my mates had gone [to war], I'd lost a brother, my brothers had gone, and I thought well I'll take it'.[82] Similarly, a friends' enlistment was key in Walder's decision to volunteer for the RAF from a RO. Walder had not questioned his civilian role 'because we were there to build things for the war' but once his friends had joined he felt left out 'in a sense' and 'they went in and it looked like the natural thing, they were in it and I had to get in it, that's really what it was I suppose'.[83] Ronald Oates's boss arranged for his reservation and provided paperwork to present at his medical examination. Ronald, however, felt he had to be in uniform to do his bit:

> I felt no, I'm going into the services, I'm going to play my part, my brother's in the services I've got to be part of the services so I, I never told my director these feelings [and] I never surrendered that letter, because I didn't want to be a key worker ....

Ronald recognised ROs were necessary, but his insistence upon joining the forces to play his part implied that 'key workers' did not meet his conception of wartime masculinity.[84] George Forster's narrative suggested that he felt others did not perceive ROs as meeting wartime masculinity. When reserved despite volunteering, Forster was disappointed because 'what does it look like, all your friends going and you're still stuck at home'. That his disappointment was expressed in relation to how others would perceive him, rather than his own desire to fight, suggests that it was meeting societal expectations that drove his attempt to enlist. Deferred students could experience the same discomfort – a 19-year-old wrote to MO: 'a large number of my friends who were in the Territorials were of course called up, and I do feel as though people are comparing me unfavourably with them'.[85] These examples make clear that masculinity was comparative, and notably the comparisons were made with men in close proximity – brothers, friends and peers; when they made these comparisons these men evidently did not feel that they would be making an equivalent contribution to the war effort without donning uniform.

236   *Joining up in the Second World War*

Not all men dreaded the prospect of being denied wartime masculinity by reservation. Joseph Drake, born in 1913, was willing to join the forces if he had to, and had joined Civil Defence, but his enlistment narrative conveys disappointment that a hoped-for RO did not materialise. He said, 'I had a heavy Goods Vehicle License so in some ways I thought I wouldn't be called up, however, my calling up papers came and I had to go.'[86] Some men would even bribe foremen to ensure they were reserved, which Chand argues demonstrates that they were uninterested in living up to a hegemonic masculinity.[87] Drake was notably older than many of my interviewees. Studies of men in ROs suggest that older men were more likely to prioritise staying at home, while younger men were more likely to be keener to enter the forces.[88] This suggestion is broadly supported here.[89] It might be that older men had more commitments which tied them to home or required them to avoid unnecessary risks, as outlined in Chapter 4, or that young men more readily perceived or were more interested in potential adventure in warfare, which had been depicted in popular inter-war representations of warfare. Temperate masculinity, which required men to be willing to serve but not necessarily eager, permitted older men to prioritise their other responsibilities for as long as they could. Alternatively, we might argue that the hegemonic masculinity of wartime Britain was more applicable to younger men since it privileged attributes they possessed in any case; moreover, reservation policies which reserved older men ahead of younger colleagues legitimised their desire to stay, and these policies meant older men in ROs were less likely to feel pressured because their immediate peers were in the forces.

The comparative pressure to serve in the forces could also be reduced by living in a region with a high concentration of essential industries. My interviewees often suggested that a sense that they were making an inferior contribution compared to friends or family members encouraged them to leave ROs or volunteer before their conscription date. Several of my interviewees remembered being challenged in the street about why they were not in uniform, and Pattinson notes that slurs aimed at young men who were not in the forces were reported as the cause of suicides.[90] Conversely, studies of men in ROs suggest that being within a community of reserved men lessened feelings of emasculation and pressure to enlist.[91]

Certainly, being in an area where most men were not in uniform and locals understood it was probably because they were reserved reduced the chances of being challenged in the street about why you were not uniform.[92]

Studies of men in ROs also find that many, particularly those who had offered to serve in the forces, were 'comfortable with their reserved status', able to build a masculine identity around their wartime contribution, or traits specific to the workplace rather than to wartime, such as skilled or dangerous labour, physical exertion and earning capacity.[93] Excepting earning, these were the attributes of men in ROs that Rose and Robb highlight were emphasised in public discourse.[94] In addition, both Chand and Peniston-Bird have argued that those who could connect their employment directly to the war effort were able to cast their manhood in military terms, reinforcing the idea that participation in the war effort was key to wartime masculinity.[95]

The attitudes expressed by men who went on to become servicemen have commonalities with the findings of Chand and Pattinson, McIvor and Robb about the attitudes expressed by men who were reserved. Much as some of my interviewees would not have welcomed reservation, Pattinson *et al.* say that some of their interviewees felt 'stuck', denied an experience their peers were having,[96] and half of their interviewees attempted to leave ROs, because 'military service was evidently a powerful lure to young men' and membership of the Armed Forces was an important component of their subjective conceptions of wartime masculinity.[97] Pattinson, McIvor and Robb are certainly correct to argue for recognition of the complexity of lived experiences of wartime civilian masculinities – a thread that also runs throughout this chapter – and to stress that many reserved men did not experience their status as emasculating.[98] It is not contradictory, however, to argue, as I have shown here, that the attitudes which men *in uniform* demonstrated towards both COs and those in ROs suggest that many of them subjectively conceived those in these roles as possessing subordinate masculinities to men in the forces. COs were not being patriotic because they refused to be involved in the war, and accusations that their objections were a pretence to disguise their cowardice attacked their masculinity. A reserved man's willingness to fight was also ambiguous. As Frank Webster said:

238 *Joining up in the Second World War*

> I think there were some who couldn't go and would of and others who were glad they didn't, I know one in particular, I don't mean he was, what can I say, don't know how to put it, I don't say he was a coward but he just didn't want it ... I think he was in a what do they call it [JM: a reserved occupation?] Yeah that's it a reserved occupation and i think there was some in reserved occupations who you thought hhhhmmm [little chuckle].

Central to this tension was the ambiguity about willingness to participate in the war effort, defined above all by the act of combat. COs were determinedly stating their lack of willingness, while ROs might have found a way to shirk military service. This is why a military uniform was so crucial to hegemonic masculinity in wartime: it was a very clear signal of intent – indeed, one that could be clearer than the ambiguous feelings many men *in uniform* actually had about their military service.

'What a privilege to have a real rifle to walk around with ...': the Home Guard

Chris Rose joined the Home Guard before reaching conscription age, and remembered he got a 'khaki uniform like the soldiers were wearing, and er feeling so proud in it, used to walk down the road in it sometimes ...'. When asked why he had joined he remembered his motivation was 'being a soldier I suppose, trying to be a man [little laugh]'.[99] Joining the Home Guard was one way to access military uniform, and thus signal one's willingness to serve, yet the masculinity Home Guard service provided could be fragile. Reg Day felt his ill-fitting uniform undermined his credibility and therefore his masculinity. Similarly, James Donovan's uniform was

> about two sizes too big for me, the collar [laughter] was about 6 inches bigger than what my neck was but er, you didn't have enough guns to go round, so you used to have to share them, we used to go out on patrol and you would have one rifle and five rounds

and his training exercises were farces that concluded prematurely at the pub.[100] Summerfield and Peniston-Bird have demonstrated that the appearance, equipment and training of the Home Guard, as well as its recruits' age and fitness, posed questions about the

Masculinity in the Second World War 239

organisation's military efficacy, which rendered the masculinity of the force unstable.[101] Nevertheless, they suggested that Home Guard membership could be a route to being a 'man' in wartime. Although Donovan highlighted the force's weaknesses, he appeared proud of his service. The enlistment narratives examined here support Summerfield and Peniston-Bird's argument that men joined the force both because of a desire to 'do their bit' and a desire to be demonstrably involved with the military.[102]

James Oates expected to be conscripted into the Army, and even married in preparation. When he was reserved because his work 'bricking up windows in hospitals and schools, putting up air raid shelters' was ARP work he 'felt guilty like any young man, so I joined the Home Guard'.[103] Oates's guilt demonstrates he conceived military service to be a crucial element of wartime masculinity, and his response demonstrates that he saw Home Guard membership as providing some compensation for his otherwise threatened masculinity. Similarly, Les Shepherd recalled that his father, reserved as a shipyard boilermaker, got into trouble for volunteering for the full-time Forces so persistently, even trying his luck in different towns; ultimately he joined the Home Guard instead.[104] By changing from 'civvies' into uniform the Home Guard member moved closer to the wartime masculine ideal of the combatant. Members commonly reported having taken pride in their uniforms,[105] which was so similar to that of the Army that members were sometimes mistaken for soldiers.[106] Thomas Leesk joined the Home Guard rather than the ARP because he wanted a uniform and a rifle.[107] Cyril Price was in the ARP and said he 'envied one's friends in the Home Guard because they actually had a Lee Enfield rifle, we didn't have rifles, what a privilege to have a real rifle to walk around with ...'.[108] That envy is significant; like the uniform, a rifle was desirable as a signifier of proximity to combat and it ensured people knew the bearer held a certain position and masculine status.

The absence of these signifiers could also be important. When recalling his service in the Local Defence Volunteers, the precursor to the Home Guard, Frank Webster pointed to his lack of uniform and having to equip himself with a broomstick for rifle drill, as evidence that the 'Look Duck and Vanish brigade' was farcical, and referred to *Dad's Army* to illustrate this:

240 *Joining up in the Second World War*

> I mean when old *Dad's Army* comes on now and he says 'Going home, catching the train, nine to five or something' and he comes home ready with his gun, well it's similar to that but we didn't have a gun ... I watch *Dad's Army* and I know it sounds preposterous, which parts of it are, but oh dear, until the Home Guard then became more established and I think it was really a force to be reckoned with later on, but not during the LDV days [laughter].[109]

Webster compared the LDV with the RAF, which he subsequently joined, saying that he 'went on to higher things'.[110] The importance which young men might place upon being 'visibly in the fighting forces' is suggested by the elaborate ruse orchestrated by 18-year-old Christopher Redmond, detailed by Summerfield and Peniston-Bird. Redmond, unable to enlist due to reservation, feared being perceived as a CO. He thus joined the Home Guard, and 'then I looked like a soldier'. The townsfolk, however, understood he was not a 'proper soldier'. He successfully enrolled on a distant training course and would return periodically on 'leave' wearing his Home Guard uniform minus the Home Guard shoulder patches.[111] This instance also illustrates his conception of the Home Guard as a subordinate masculinity to that of the full-time forces, a conception which was suggested in a number of different ways in young men's testimonies. For instance, when Victor Waterhouse said, 'I felt I was doing "my bit" in the Home Guard as I was unfit for National Service', he demonstrated that his service gave him a sense of worth, but implicit in his statement is the notion that had he been fully fit his service in the Home Guard would have been an insufficient contribution.[112]

Those who were too young to enter the full-time forces could also use the Home Guard to access wartime masculinity, though they emphasised that it was temporary and that the full-time forces were more desirable. Woodhams, for example, joined the LDV (underage) and proudly sat for photographs in his ill-fitting uniform; nevertheless his motivation for joining was 'to pass the time away' until he could join the Navy, having aged out of Sea Cadets.[113] Similarly, Reg Day 'thought that if I could get in the Home Guard I will have covered that bit between getting old enough to join up and I will have been doing something in uniform'. His desire to be part of the war effort was enhanced by the fact that his older peers 'were all going in the forces and you felt out of it, you felt as though, you

Masculinity in the Second World War 241

... weren't doing anything to help when you felt, you wanted to be helping your country'. Having joined, Day was proud to be '*in* something, you know, I was in a uniform and in something and I was helping'. Despite being employed in a role that could have seen him reserved, Day only perceived himself to be involved in the war effort once he was in uniform. Getting into uniform was a positive step which he was proud of, but the Home Guard was imagined as a temporary solution until he too could join the full-time forces, alongside those whose enlistment had left him feeling 'out of it'.[114] Ken Hay joined the Home Guard aged 15, and acknowledged that although the 'overriding thing' was that 'you felt that erm you are doing your bit' 'some people who took the Mickey out of you [because...] when you went on parade there were blokes who were limping by from [Great] war wounds ... or alternatively through age ...'. Therefore 'there was a certain attraction about being in [Army] uniform, I think that applied to most people, which the Home Guard bits didn't satisfy, and it looked good being on leave.'[115]

These narratives suggest that it was important to some men to occupy a military role, and that military uniform provided a masculine identity. They also suggest, however, that the masculinity of the Home Guard was subordinate: those unable to join the full-time forces looked to it as a substitute, and those able to join the full-time services saw the Home Guard as a temporary position from which they 'progressed'; young men often positioned the Home Guard as something from which they matured into full-time service when they came of age. In combination, this suggests that in many men's subjectivities the hegemonic masculinity was connected to the combatant Armed Forces, and they sought to occupy that role. Pattinson, McIvor and Robb note the poignant characterisation of selfhood offered by one of their interviewees: Craig Inglis, a reserved cobbler and later Bevin Boy, who recalled his feelings about his brothers in uniform: 'oh a wis proud of them. We thought they were the bee's knees.' Inglis, however, 'wis naebody'.[116] One of my interviewees, Fred Pond, recalled he had initially hoped to become an RAF air gunner: 'I was boasting, you know, I was a boy and I wanted to become somebody.'[117]

242 *Joining up in the Second World War*

Military service and wartime masculinity

As was shown in the previous two chapters, men's motivations and attitudes to military service were many and varied; they might relate to any of (or any combination of) duty (to the State or to one's family), masculinity, adventure, ambition, reluctant acceptance or the war as an opportunity to alter their circumstances. The desire to perform hegemonic wartime masculinity was not important in every man's enlistment. Some considered service solely or primarily within public and private conceptions of duty and patriotism, probably best combined under the umbrella of active citizenship – albeit a citizenship constructed in highly gendered ways. For instance, Reg Elson thought all men should be willing to take arms in defence of the nation when called, but framed his dislike of COs as related to refusal to participate in a communal endeavour rather than effeminacy. Nonetheless, it is clear that, for many men, military service mattered as an articulation of masculinity, and it is significant that one of the most important sites for discussion of this topic was the importance of being in uniform.

'I think it was the attraction of the uniform that made up my mind'

Rose argued that performing wartime masculinity required men to be 'visibly members of the fighting forces'.[118] As we have seen, the citizenship and the masculinity of the man outside uniform was decidedly ambiguous. He might be reserved, unfit, an objector or simply a shirker. Military uniform was thus the most important signifier of wartime masculinity. On the streets of wartime Britain uniform demarcated those performing roles that fulfilled wartime masculinities from those whose positions were indeterminate. Men connected military uniform to masculinity in a number of ways that suggest they perceived military roles to be closer to the hegemonic wartime masculinity. Their testimonies suggest that they subjectively valued uniform, and that they understood its cultural capital and the threats posed by its absence.[119]

Many interviewees found being in uniform an attractive prospect. Jack Abbott was unenthusiastic about military service – 'you

Masculinity in the Second World War 243

wouldn't wish it on yourself' – but nevertheless excited about being in uniform.[120] He admitted he had not thought about what service entailed beyond 'marching about' and asked to join the Royal Marines because 'it's got a smarter uniform, I like the blue sash and the red stripe and the pink hat [laughter] you know, jolly smart the Royal Marines ...'.[121] Others based their preference on the appearance of the uniform, like Jack Pragnell, who had intended to join the Fleet Air Arm rather than the RAF because the uniform was nicer and either service would satisfy his aim of flying. Bob Woodhams and his friends discussed what they wanted to join, and he recalled 'there weren't many said Army'. He thought this was because:

> the uniform was only a blouse, buttoned up at the neck, weren't nothing to look at it really to encourage anyone to go in the Army really, and I think this is the big thing, the uniform attracted a lot of people, cos the RAF was a smart uniform, and the Army was a terrible uniform ... baggy old jacket and that blouse.[122]

That some young men framed their desire to serve in terms of getting into uniform, rather than a desire to defeat the enemy or perform a particular wartime activity, suggests the importance of signifying masculinity to others. Woodhams could have been reserved, but a desire 'just to get into uniform' punctuated his narrative.[123] Before the war Woodhams wanted to join the Merchant Navy, 'but course when it all started I thought uniform, I'll go for the Royal Navy'. He had seen his brother in his Navy uniform with 'the big bell bottoms and the Chinley collars and what have you, yeah so I liked that, and I thought yeah I'll have some of that, you know, but that was what really attracted me, but I did want to go to sea'. He noted the 'merchant navy never got a uniform you see, so I think it was the attraction of the uniform that made up my mind'.[124] Later in his interview, Woodhams said, 'I think most of us at that time wanted to get into the forces, regardless ... [we] didn't have a clue what it was about, but it was the fact they wanted to get into uniform.' He lied about his age and joined the Navy aged 16. He said, 'at the time I was keen to serve in the war, bearing in mind I had four brothers above me in the forces ...'. Again, Woodhams's motivations illustrate the need to position oneself relative to your peers.

In some instances, the value placed upon the possession of military uniform clearly related to the social enactment of

244   *Joining up in the Second World War*

masculinity – Redmond, the Home Guardsman already discussed, is an extreme example. This is also evident, however, in the fact that men took pride in their uniforms, and compared them with those of other forces and other ranks within their own force. Other items that signified military participation were also prized. Men on deferred service in the RAF Volunteer Reserve wore silver badges, which Air Training Cadets jealously remembered; Bob Lowe recalled those with these badges 'were the cat's pyjamas because they were already in the RAF then of course'.[125] Maurice Marriot and Jack Pragnell remembered their pride in the badges:

> MAURICE We were on deferred service for a while.
> JACK   [Interrupting] We were in civvy clothes but we were in.
> MAURICE We all had little silver badges, do you remember those silver badges, RAFVR which were very proud of, all the aircrew got these badges which went in the lapel and we were very proud of these badges.
> JACK   To show you were a volunteer.[126]

These badges marked an individual out as a member of the RAF, a sought-after service, but they also removed the ambiguity created by being 'in civvy clothes' in a similar fashion to a Home Guard uniform. Similarly, the desirability of being a pilot was suggested by George Cash's memory of being 'so proud of [wearing] the white flash to indicate that we were under training for flying ...'.[127]

Men's common perception that women found men in uniform more attractive than civilians also suggests the masculinity of service roles.[128] Don Browne explained his desire to join the Navy in terms of liking the uniform and the idea that 'you pulled the birds'.[129] Derrick Thurgood felt his girlfriend could not wait 'to be seen on my arm in my reconnaissance outfit'.[130] Pond always wore his RAF uniform on dates, and Marriot commented that one attraction was 'thinking of all the girlfriends we'd get when we were fighter pilots and all that [laughter]'.[131] Rupert Parkhouse, who had connected pilots with sexual success since a pre-war air show, said, 'One of the great things about [service] was of course, donning one's uniform. I remember being extremely proud of the hat, looking at myself in the mirror in my room, thinking you know, what a handsome chap I looked ....'[132] Francis writes that the RAF uniform was

Masculinity in the Second World War 245

'associated with both heroism and sexual magnetism', particularly if it included a set of wings.[133] As Peter Woodard recalled, at dances women 'were attracted by your pilot's wings or your half brevee'.[134] Lowe said, 'I was quite keen, you know, I was going in the RAF, getting a uniform, prance around like I was the cat's pyjamas.'[135] Lowe felt that the RAF uniform was not only the best quality of the three services, but that it was the most alluring to women:

> our ordinary uniform had brass buttons ... it was only [Army] dress uniforms that had brass buttons, they just had a short tunic, khaki grey, we were quite, oh yeah they always used to say that the RAF got the girls more, 'til the Yanks come along and knocked ours off.

The hierarchy of the services that was often expressed in people's preferences was mirrored in Lowe's analysis of which was the most attractive to women: 'oh the RAF definitely first, I think the Navy came next, I think the Army were the bottom line sort of thing'.[136] The hierarchical conception of the forces' standing in Britain is also fundamental to the idea that the 'Yanks come along and knocked ours off'; many interviewees remembered American servicemen with the phrase 'Overpaid, oversexed and over here', although in this context these markers of masculinity were an expression of jealous complaint rather than admiration.

More generally, men remembered uniform increased their self-confidence. Charles Sinclair, for whom the uniform was 'a big attraction' to joining the forces, said wearing it 'makes you feel confident, you walk down the street in an Army uniform, you feel pretty good'.[137] Charles Jeffries associated masculinity with military uniform when he recalled his pride when he 'put that uniform on and strutting around, oh yes, and I felt more so when I joined the Highland Regiment' because it was 'an elite unit'.[138] During our interview George Cash stood up to demonstrate swaggering when he explained his RAF uniform made him feel he 'was IT'. He remembered many of the young men in his area were 'going off into the Army and they were coming home with their nice private's uniforms and all the rest of it, one or two managed to get into the Navy and they looked even smarter but I thought myself it's not for me ...'. With the Battle of Britain the RAF were in the public eye, and he recalled 'the RAF uniform in certain areas where I lived, you know people looked at you with respect so to speak, and eventually

246 *Joining up in the Second World War*

when you passed out you got your wings and you got your stripe, by gum, you're king of the castle'.[139] Reg Day similarly said that pilots could 'come home and swank', and Pond said uniform gave you confidence and 'if you was RAF you were top-notch you know, you were right at the top'.[140]

Some said simply that having a uniform prevented them appearing inferior.[141] Browne said that 'everybody was in the same boat, I mean you would have stood out if you had been in civvies'. George Stagg did not feel superior once in the Army 'because if you walked down the street and there was 200 people there 150 would be in uniform ... so you were one of the crowd. If I hadn't been in uniform I'd have felt really out of place, really and truly. I'd have hid behind a tree.'[142] The sense that most people were in uniform was inaccurate in relation to the proportion in the full-time forces but many more people had Home Guard uniforms and symbols of participation such as ARP armbands and helmets. The sense that everyone was in uniform may well have increased as the war continued and uniformed men became more ubiquitous. Day, who did not enlist until the latter half of 1941, said that uniforms would have been glamorous but they were 'ten a penny, you see every shape and size just down the street'.[143] Webster, tellingly, said that once he was in uniform he 'didn't necessarily feel superior, I just felt that erm, as I said just before, at least I was doing what is required of everybody'.[144]

'I just thought well you're expected': negotiating societal expectations

Men's testimonies show that many perceived, and often accepted, that men were expected to serve in the forces in wartime. Ted Roberts felt servicewomen did 'a hell of a job, it saved a lot of men and they put a lot of good food on the table, and they done a bloody good job in the offices *to relieve men to go to do what they should be there for* ... [my emphasis]'.[145] Women, too, expressed their belief that men should be fighting. Hay recalled women asking accusingly: ' "My son's in the Army, why aren't you?" ... because I was tall they thought I was old enough to be in the Army, I got a lot of that'.[146] Lowe got the same.[147] Neither perceived this to have

Masculinity in the Second World War 247

pressured them to enlist, but it could. Summerfield and Peniston-Bird cite the example of Tex Laws who recalled being 'taunted in the street: "Bloody great boys. Ought to be in the Guards" ... so eventually I became a Home Guard", before call up'.[148]

In the winter of 1939, Arthur Howard went to see *The Four Feathers*. Leaving the pictures, Howard's friend Frank, prompted by a recruiting sergeant's pre-show appeal, said, 'What are we going to do? We will have to join something or they will be sticking a white feather on us.' Frank wanted to join the RAF, and Howard agreed to do the same. Having travelled from Buxton to Manchester to volunteer, Howard, 19, was told he would have to join the RAF Volunteer Reserve. He thought, 'I've come all this way and I'm bloody joining something' and tried the Army, but could only sign for twelve years' regular service, and thinking his mother would 'play hell' if he joined the Navy, given sinking of the *Royal Oak* the previous week, he accepted the RAFVR. Howard 'was quite happy to go when I made my mind up' but considered it 'something I had to do' rather than an adventure. Asked if he 'felt it your duty to serve in the forces, or was it something that you just wanted to do?', he related his decision to patriotism and to social expectation: 'We're British aren't we, well English not bloody British, but oh no, we were, you think to yourself, well we've got to pull together and you know that's all, I didn't go because I thought it would be a holiday or nothing you know, I just thought well you're expected.'[149]

Social expectation was also apparent in Tom Neary's narrative of his enlistment following call-up in October 1939: 'you knew it was your duty, erm, and of course other lads were joining up so you know, it had to be done'.[150] He explained that there was not the enthusiasm associated with the outbreak of the Great War, but 'you knew it had to be done so, and the cause was right as we assumed, so we joined you know, that was it'. Hay spoke of military service as an obligation rather than a desire; he framed his Home Guard enlistment as 'doing his bit', and said he thought 'well I think I *ought* to go in the Army and I *ought* to go in the service [my emphasis]'. Still, this feeling appears to have been influenced by comparisons to the men around him, particularly his brother who was already serving in the Commandos and would 'come home with his fighting knife down here ... his badge with the dagger ... you know, the bees' knees'. Hay came to feel that he was not

248   *Joining up in the Second World War*

doing my bit, my brother was doing his bit, he had served in Norway and now he had served and was wounded at St Nazaire, and other people who had gone in the Army [or] ... Navy and what not used to come on leave ... these are the chaps who are doing their bit and they've all got something, and I'm outside this, I mean being in the Home Guard didn't get me into that club as such ....[151]

This can be interpreted as a recognition of the social expectation of active citizenship and sacrifice, but the framing reveals the importance of masculinity: when he compared himself to other men who were doing their bit they had 'all got something' and were included in 'club', while Hay's service was insufficient and left him in deficit.

Traditional understandings of military service as duty were certainly not dead, as others' testimonies show. As Gordon Mellor expressed, 'there was still what you might call Victorian sense of duty in youngsters ... King and Country, all these things were in the background and you absorbed them without really thinking about it very much'.[152] Patriotic duty was central to Samuel Pearson's narrative; it was 'always drilled into us that it was your duty if ever you were called to fight for your King and country and I always believed in that'. He lived in a strongly patriotic area and felt conscious others were in the forces, including his older brother who had been conscripted as war broke out.[153] Shortly after turning 20 in 1941, Pearson volunteered for the Navy from his RO making rubberised military clothing: 'I thought to myself that I had to go, I needed to go, it wasn't right for me doing that war work.' Instead, he felt he 'had to go and fight for the King and country, not being a hero type'.[154] While he stressed that it was not about bravado, combat was central to Pearson's conception of duty; had he had a non-combatant or administrative role in the forces he 'wouldn't have thought I was really doing my duty' because he would not have felt involved.

Just because men accepted service did not mean that they aspired to the most hyper-masculine roles. For instance, Jim Stephens was 'very happy' when he was initially conscripted to a searchlight regiment, because:

you are basically at home ... and you weren't in the frontline, the frontline troops are the infantry, they are the frontline troops, they are the boys that took all the hammering, ... [searchlights] were

Masculinity in the Second World War　　　249

> non-combatants units, the combat units were the infantry and the
> artillery ... so I was quite happy [JM: okay] I make no bones about it
> but [little laugh] as I said before that was wishful thinking.[155]

That he made 'no bones about it' indicates that his attitude diverged
from the ideal. Duty was not only used to explain a belief in service
as a patriotic obligation, but sometimes to explain reluctant acceptance of inevitable military service. Alan Watcham, for example,
appears to have been a reluctant soldier, and expressed his bitterness that his call-up had not come six months later when he would
have been compensated for his drop in pay. Nonetheless, when the
war came he 'never thought about anything else but well I was 21
and the country needed me and that sort of thing ...'.[156]
The number of men who undertook military service against
their private wishes but without negotiating some kind of civilian
position through reservation or objection suggests that some men
accepted military service to conform to constructions of masculinity. They accessed a military identity that protected their masculinity from scrutiny, while attempting to negotiate participation in
the forces in the manner that they found least objectionable. Mr
Sweetland, for example, distanced himself from a military masculine identity, saying he had been brought up to shun uniform, and
plainly did not want to enter the forces. Yet, rather than find a way
out of service, he waited until he was called up, and promptly set
about moving from his assigned role of signaller to a clerking post,
his pre-war job.[157] Sweetland exercised his own agency so that he
could remain in uniform whilst experiencing as little discomfort as
possible. Similarly, Thomas Illman, born 1923, also 'wasn't a keen
soldier to be honest', and took opportunities to move away from
combat roles.[158]
Others appear to have opted for uniformed roles because it
masked attitudes that would otherwise have challenged their masculinity. Hugh Jenkins detailed his psychic battles over military
service, but his choices illustrate the draw of military identity in
wartime, and perhaps that uniform could suggest public conformity. Jenkins sincerely contemplated conscientious objection and was
considering joining the Friends Ambulance Unit when he learned
the Observer Corps was recruiting and seized the opportunity to
join. He was able to reconcile the Observer's non-combatant and

250   *Joining up in the Second World War*

defensive activities with his pacifism, but the only reason this role was preferable to the Friends Ambulance unit seems to have been that it was military and therefore more masculine. He subsequently joined RAF Fighter Command, which he conceptualised as defensive, gallant, and noble because they never bombed civilians. This allowed him to access a still more masculine role without compromising his principles.[159]

'Brylcreem Boys': the ambiguities of a high technology war and the hierarchy of military masculinity

Although being in or out of uniform was a significant demarcation in wartime Britain, men also understood that a more complex hierarchy of wartime roles existed. Performing a particular wartime masculinity was not the key driver in Les Temple's enlistment, but his testimony nevertheless demonstrates his conception of a clear hierarchy. Asked whether servicemen were 'seen as sort of any more or less manly than those who weren't in the services', Temple said, 'Well, yes, I mean that was the ultimate, getting into the services to fight a war.' In comparison, for him, those in ROs and Bevin Boys were 'a grade below servicemen'. The RAF uniform was something to be proud of once 'you got your stripes and … your wings', and as aircrew 'the girls used to look to go out with you' and there was 'a bit of glamour to it' because 'you were on operations, you were in a dangerous situation'. This highlights that proximity to combat and to danger were related to wartime masculinity. Temple would not, however, have 'felt very good' to have a ground crew position in the RAF because he 'wasn't looking to be a mechanic or … radio operator on the ground but they used a lot of ladies, er WAAFs on the ground for th[at] you see, and I wouldn't have been happy about it'. Doing the same job as a WAAF, he 'wouldn't have felt that I was contributing enough' to ending the war.[160]

Interviewees regularly recalled the glamour of the RAF, and associated with it was the moniker 'the Brylcreem Boys'. Whilst the RAF pilot may have been widely regarded as the hegemonic wartime masculinity, investigation of the term 'Brylcreem Boys' demonstrates the existence of different military masculinities, and competition between those in different roles.[161] Most aircrew members felt the

Masculinity in the Second World War 251

term had only applied to aircrew, though some ground crew members applied the term to themselves.[162] Most recalled this as a derogatory, teasing term used by the Army, though some members of aircrew reported ground crew using it too.[163] The Army's resentment of the RAF, occasionally seen as resulting from the RAF's sexual allure,[164] was most commonly perceived to be a result of the more comfortable and luxurious life of the RAF, particularly aircrew.[165] Lowe recalled 'they used to call us the Brylcreem Boys, we had sheets on the beds, [the Army] just had a blanket'. The RAF uniform was softer, smarter and more elaborate than the Army's coarse khaki battledress, and 'we had shirts and ties, they didn't, theirs used to button up to the neck', and aircrew were well paid, promoted quickly, and 'they used to have egg and bacon in the morning when they got back you see'.[166] The term Brylcreem Boys, then, was an ambiguous one. It simultaneously denoted glamour and style and was used by those in other services to imply a dandified femininity which had need of such comforts and which even lacked substance.

This could be, but was not necessarily, connected to attempts to undermine the heterosexual allure of RAF aircrew. Jack Pragnell, when asked whether any roles were more 'manly' than others, said that as aircrew they 'were treated as poofs sort of thing by some of the public, oh fancy boys sort of thing, fancy boys of the air force' because they were 'spoilt'.[167] 'Pansy' was the definition Howard gave for Brylcreem Boys.[168] Pond said Byrlcreem Boys meant the RAF were 'sissy boys' relative to the Army, and when asked for clarification, he offered 'nancy boys' as an alternative, adding, 'they were the sort that would get a whistle if the Army was in a gang and the RAF went by'.[169] Although implications of homosexuality were used to deride the RAF, its members doubted this stemmed from any belief this was true. Pond thought the criticism was because 'we were dressed better than they were, we had a uniform where we had a collar and tie, they didn't, [laughs] I'm sure that's what it was, we could have shoes, they had to have army boots ...'.[170] Woodard also connected the criticism to the level of attention RAF members paid to their appearance, 'especially as I say this collar and tie' but he also had not perceived it to be 'because they thought we were you know AC/DC or something like that [laughter]'.[171]

Frank Webster associated the Brylcreem Boys teasing not only with the RAF's 'smarter uniform ... collar and tie and belt and

252 *Joining up in the Second World War*

buttons and all that', but also with the RAF's perceived absence at Dunkirk,[172] and a class difference between the RAF and the Army:

> the majority of the RAF ground crew were tradesmen ... but you might have had somebody who was below par or something like that in the Army but there is just that step up, well however you look at it, all our blokes were educated, I don't know if that's a reasonable explanation, but there was a difference yeah.[173]

Therefore, 'Brylcreem Boys' might also be seen as a delineator rooted in classed divisions between manual and non-manual work. This tessellates with the interviewees' emphases of luxury and their 'smarter' uniform, particularly wearing a collar and tie, a traditional demarcation between white- and blue-collar work. It also connects to the reality that aircrew were better paid, and more quickly promoted than the majority of Army recruits.

Another way to locate the use of 'Brycreem Boys' is within a discourse about the nature of military capability and the use of physical power. While it was well known that flyers had to pass their medical A-1, and especially that eyesight was important, size and strength became less relevant – indeed, Francis notes the slight, feminine appearances of well-known pilots. The fact that flyers were well educated and commanding sophisticated technology also stood out in public perceptions. This required not only intellectual ability but a different kind of courage to, say, infantry service. Francis observes that this 'created a space in the wartime RAF for men who possessed potentially "feminine" attributes or sensibilities'. The use of the term 'Brylcreem Boys' suggests that flyers' masculinity was challenged by some Britons, supporting Francis's suggestion that 'British masculinity in the 1940s was still in transition.'[174]

It was not only those in or looking at the RAF who perceived a hierarchy – the importance of proximity to combat in wartime masculinity is highlighted in others' testimony about potential wartime roles, too. Hay, whose enlistment was influenced by his comparisons with his brother's service in the commandos, similarly seems subconsciously to have conceived of a hierarchy of wartime roles, in which those also performed by women were less masculine than others. When asked if he would have felt 'less like you are doing your duty or possibly less manly ... if you had been placed in a quartermaster role or moving supplies around rather than being in a fighting role ...', he pondered the correct wording before saying:

Masculinity in the Second World War   253

> I felt being in the infantry that I was doing all I could do that was
> expected of me, if I'd been doing a more sedentary thing like you're
> suggesting at the quartermaster's stores I think I would have been a
> bit fed up with myself, I think I would have [pause] felt that this could
> have been left of the girls and that we ought to be doing something a bit
> more manly than this, I don't think I'd have much to boast about ....

Reg Day could have been reserved as a driver for a company salvaging aviation parts, but he had wanted to be more involved in the war. He explained that he had not seen assisting aviation production as a sufficient contribution because this was something his wife was doing. If a woman could do his job, he could be freed to perform a role more directly connected to combat: an RO 'wasn't near enough to the war for me, see when I was here [RAF Dunsfold] I was putting bombs on aeroplanes that were going to kill Germans, that was what I wanted, they wanted our country and bugger them'.[175] It is noteworthy that for Day, just as for some in ROs, the ability to draw a direct connection between his action and the war effort elevated the masculine status of his role and had some recuperative power. Similarly, while some in ROs found masculinity in the association of their role with a 'hard man' physicality, the usage of Brylcreem Boys shows that the masculinity of those in military roles that did not require this physicality could draw challenge. A number of these testimonies also confirm scholars' findings that the masculinity conferred by a uniformed role could be undermined if women were also fulfilling the role, such as in Air Raid Precautions or RAF trades.[176] There was, then, not a simple binary opposition between those in and out of the services, but a complex, and in some ways contested, hierarchy of wartime masculinities. Being in the services and in uniform was significant, but men understood the masculinity associated with a role to be affected by its relationship to physical work, endurance and proximity to combat.

Wartime masculinities

As was shown in Chapter 4, volunteering was commonly a way men negotiated joining their preferred service or perhaps limiting danger or discomfort, rather than necessarily expressing patriotism and desire to serve. Such self-interest ran counter to Rose's formulation of temperate masculinity. In some ways narratives such as

254   *Joining up in the Second World War*

Temple's, that show a desire to occupy positions most associated with hegemonic masculinity combined with a desire for strident, aggressive, heroic, glamorous participation, are also divergent from temperate masculinity. For instance, rather than accepting military service as an unfortunate but necessary interlude, Pragnell's attraction to the RAF was more enthusiastic than temperate: '… the flying was all the glory … the prestige, the newspapers were full of our boys in the air … there was a bit of sort of bravado about it I suppose, a bit of semi-heroics …'.[177] Marriot similarly desired the 'excitement and the glamour of it, it wasn't much you know sort of fighting for King and country and all that sort of thing, the things you hear about you know get at the enemy and all that'.[178]

Thurgood had also 'wanted to get into the war as people did' and sought an active role: 'I wouldn't have minded being an infantryman, but I didn't want to get put into something like the Pay Corps or the Catering Corps.' He had wanted to be a pilot but, knowing his eyesight was too poor, was attracted by a different elite, active, combatant role. Already a Home Guard, he opted (underage) to volunteer for the Reconnaissance Corps, which he found appealing because it was an elite unit and had an 'extraordinarily attractive hat badge with a spear with lightning coming out of it and yellow and green Reconnaissance on the shoulder and all those sorts of things which impress young men, very young men, or did then during the war'. The opportunity to learn to drive armoured cars and use every weapon 'was marvellous' and he said this appeared 'fairly glamorous' when they saw newsreels from El Alamein. Thurgood himself points to youth as one of the factors in this interest – the military badge impressing young men during the war – supporting the observation that the aspiration to perform a hegemonic masculinity had a greater pull upon young men. Similarly, in the preceding chapters we have heard the narratives of men, like Thurgood, who were keen to embark upon a military adventure, which was also divergent from temperate masculinity.[179] We have also heard the expectation that military uniform increased sexual allure; the apparent pursuit of promiscuity intersects with youthful masculinity but was not a component of the temperate masculine template, and is at odds with ideas of chivalry.

This is not to say that temperate masculinity was not exhibited during the Second World War. It is well reflected in the reluctant but

Masculinity in the Second World War 255

genuine acceptance of military service as an obligation that characterised a number of men's memories. Gordon Gent knew that joining the forces would negatively impact his business, and therefore his family, but prioritised a sense of fair play and moral character when he dismissed his family's suggestion that he play the system to obtain reservation: he 'wouldn't hear tell of it, "No" I said "No, I don't want anything like that," I said "I won't volunteer, I'll not leave you till I have to, but ... I don't want to have it handled like that".'[180] Enactments of temperate masculinity were not limited to the narratives of older men. Spragg had wanted to fly since childhood, and when the war presented the opportunity to become a fighter pilot he gladly accepted, but he was not interested in the glamour and esteem attached to the role. Instead, he emphasised the subtle distinction that he and his friends were 'prepared to do' military service, but 'I wouldn't like to be as strong as wanted.'[181]

Others' motivations could fit within a temperate masculinity, but only uncomfortably. Pond, for instance, said he wanted to serve 'because of the country, I had to do my part. Somebody had to do it. It sounded thrilling to me.'[182] Woodard successfully volunteered to serve in RAF aircrew and, like most RAF recruits, his enlistment narrative centred upon his desire to fly. Yet deeper questioning revealed that he was engaged in a pragmatic attempt to balance personal preferences rather than fulfil a desire to participate in the war effort. He said of his volunteering: 'I can't say there was anything really heroic about it or anything like that, it was just the fact that the war was on and we knew we'd be in the forces eventually if the war carried on, which was the likelihood it was going to anyway, and we wanted to get into something we wanted to do.' He later reiterated that he had not considered the idea of doing his bit for the country, rather he was aware that the 'potluck' of conscription was looming.[183] The public construction of British masculinity as temperate, lacking in heroism or jingoism, surely made the position of men like Woodard easier, as they needed only to publicly accept service and do what was asked of them to comply with it. Temperate masculinity might therefore be better conceived not as an all-encompassing hegemony that determined behaviour, but as a public construction that enabled sufficient space for individuals to negotiate between the public and the very different and disparate private masculinities that existed in wartime Britain. This is

256 *Joining up in the Second World War*

not to refute Rose's suggestion that a temperate masculinity dominated constructions of masculinity in the public sphere during the Second World War. Indeed, men's testimonies make clear that they well understood what the hegemonic wartime masculinity was and where its boundaries were, and some had internalised these expectations. Instead, it is to suggest that looking beneath the level of public constructions at men's subjective masculinities during the same period reveals diversity, negotiation and private contestation of temperate masculinity. Men's subjective conceptions of masculinity did not always align with the national discourse. Crucially, the hegemonic framework was flexible enough to contain Britons' diverse understandings. This flexibility was created by the fact that, in relation to enlistment at least, public assessments of a man's compliance, based on willingness and motivation, were imprecise (hence the precarious position of men in reserved occupations). In practice, military uniform symbolised compliance; so long as it was worn it could camouflage the wearer's over-enthusiasm, private objection or ambivalence.

Conclusion

Asked how important 'it was to be seen doing your bit' during the Second World War, Reg Day said:

> Well I think you would have been ashamed if you didn't, I think you would have, well you'd have felt like jumping in the river, if you you know, if you couldn't have done it, I'm sure the shame would have been shame, and everybody would have looked at you with shame if you hadn't been in it ....[184]

We have seen that, for Day, doing your bit as a man required military service. Indeed, this examination of enlistment narratives demonstrates that military service in wartime was integral to many men's subjective conceptions of masculinity. Men's attitudes to COs and those in ROs suggest that they felt men should be at least willing to participate in military service. COs were actively rejecting this, while the willingness of those in ROs was ambiguous. Those who sought reservation to avoid military service were criticised as shirkers and depicted as emasculated. Joining the Home Guard could

Masculinity in the Second World War 257

demonstrate willingness and enact a more acceptable wartime masculinity. Both those who could not join, and those waiting to join, the full-time forces used the Home Guard in this way, although it also functioned, sometimes simultaneously, as a sincere expression of their desire to participate in the war effort. Still, descriptions of the Home Guard as a temporary solution, and the force's dubious masculinity in public discourse, emphasise it was subordinate to the full-time forces.

Examination of the hierarchies men conceived, and the fact that some went to great lengths to avoid reservation, suggests the importance of specifically military participation in subjective conceptions of masculinity. This is reinforced by how military uniform was connected to masculinity: men spoke of it as a desirable possession, took pride in it and felt more confident and attractive in it. The overt comparisons and judgements some made about the roles being performed by women and by other men further emphasise that military participation was important to performing wartime masculinity specifically, as well as to performing the more flexible gendered obligations of the active wartime citizen.

There was, however, considerable variation in men's subjective masculinities in wartime Britain, and men attempted to position themselves at varying distances from the hegemonic wartime masculinity. There are distinct parallels here with Summerfield's identification of heroic and stoic narratives amongst women war workers, although some certainly sat in between these two poles.[185] Heroic women were keen to be involved in the war effort and determined to obtain roles connected to it, while stoic women had thought about service in relation to 'personal rather than national goals'.[186] Some 'heroic' men clearly strove to perform hegemonic wartime masculinity, but this was less important to others who sought to balance societal expectations with their personal desires, and 'stoically' endured service. The societal expectation was clear, and they anticipated that shame and emasculation might result from a failure to at least approximate wartime masculinity. Thus, while many aspired to get into uniform to access that masculine image, those less keen on participation often found ways to negotiate their service whilst remaining publicly compliant with wartime masculinity.

Throughout this chapter, men's testimonies have shown the influence of small social groups upon their feelings and actions. It

258   *Joining up in the Second World War*

was the enlistment of siblings, friends or colleagues that spurred men to enlist or caused feelings of personal inadequacy, rather than national discourses. This, combined with the findings of Chand and Pattinson, McIvor and Robb about communities where a significant proportion of the population were reserved, suggest the need for regional studies of *military* enlistment narratives to establish how attitudes towards military service might vary depending on the extent of regional military participation.

It has also been suggested that the masculinities British men in combatant roles expressed often varied from a construction of British masculinities as temperate. While most were reluctantly accepting of military service, some, particularly amongst the young, saw military service as an opportunity for adventure and glamour, an idea that was closely related to a masculinity more associated with the First than the Second World War, and that was informed by the inter-war pleasure culture of war. In addition, some young men wanted to experience war, an interest that appears to have been related to their exclusion from the Great War. More common than jingoistic enthusiasm, though, was acknowledgement that military service was a man's duty. The meanings attached to this varied significantly. At its most patriotic level, it referred to a sincere belief that an individual should willingly undertake military service for the benefit of the nation, and at the other end of the spectrum it was used to describe the unwilling acceptance of inescapably imposed service. In contrast to seeking adventure, some men's enlistment narratives reveal that they resented being forced to enlist and were unwilling to serve, so wished to limit their wartime involvement. Seeing little way out, they sought the least objectionable ways to comply. This might involve securing a reserved occupation or, more commonly, trying to secure a non-combatant role in the forces, often by volunteering. Although very different to the more hyper-masculine attitudes just discussed, this too demonstrates a divergence from temperate masculinity, potentially disguised within legitimate wartime roles.

Patriotism was a motivation for some, but was far from a universal drive to accept military service, and in some testimonies masculinity can be seen as a stronger influence. As Riggs put it, his enlistment was 'following the herd in some ways rather than seething patriotism'.[187] Peniston-Bird discussed how oral histories of the Second

Masculinity in the Second World War
259

World War might be shaped by the dominance of the 'People's War' narrative in relation to the modern-day currency of patriotism. She suggests that while 'all in it together' and 'doing your bit' were sentiments that both an interviewee and interviewer could be expected to understand, and which are uncontested in the dominant narrative, patriotism was more difficult to express. Like Peniston-Bird, I found my interviewees would reach for Empire Day and lessons about the scale of the British Empire in their youth, to explain or justify the patriotism that they remembered.[188] It is also possible, however, that the weakness of the association between patriotism and the Second World War in popular narratives enabled my interviewees to move away from and ultimately reject or place minimal emphasis upon King and country as explanations of enlistment. Over the course of an interview, they could transition to the nuanced explanations we have seen here which allow space for self-interested motivations and acknowledge that duty was accepted in part because it was so difficult to reject. That it proved so difficult to reject may be partly explained by the fact that commonly encountered representations of war in general, and the Great War in particular, in inter-war Britain continued to link military service with masculinity.

Notes

1 Pattinson, *Behind Enemy Lines*, p. 114, drawing on Connell, *Masculinities*, p. 76.

2 John Tosh, 'Hegemonic Masculinity and the History of Gender', in *Masculinities in Politics and War: Gendering Modern History*, ed. by Stefan Dudink, Karen Hagemann and John Tosh (Manchester: Manchester University Press, 2004) pp. 41–60 (p. 44).

3 Tosh, 'Hegemonic Masculinity', p. 42.

4 Rose, *Which People's War?*; Noakes, *War and the British*.

5 Tosh, 'What Should Historians do with Masculinity? Reflections on Nineteenth-century Britain', *History Workshop Journal*, 38.1 (1994) pp. 179–202 (p. 182); Raewyn Connell, *Masculinities* (Cambridge: Polity, 2005) p. 76.

6 Tosh, 'What Should Historians do with Masculinity?, p. 198.

7 *Ibid.*, p. 181.

8 Judith Butler, *Gender Trouble* (Abingdon: Routledge, 2007) pp. 185–93.

260   *Joining up in the Second World War*

9 Tosh, 'Hegemonic Masculinity', p. 47.
10 Peniston-Bird, 'Classifying the Body', p. 45.
11 *Ibid.*, pp. 31–48.
12 Paul Highgate, ' "Soft Clerks" and "Hard Civvies": Pluralizing Military Masculinities', in *Military Masculinities: Identity and the State*, ed. by Paul Highgate (London: Praeger, 2003) pp. 27–42.
13 Chand, *Masculinities on Clydeside*.
14 Samuel Pearson (Morley, 2011). This mirrored public discourse about wartime firemen: see Robb, *Men at Work*, chapter 4.
15 Dawson, *Soldier Heroes*; Paris, *Over the Top* and *Warrior Nation*.
16 Showalter, 'Rivers and Sassoon'; Bogacz, 'War Neurosis and Cultural Change'; Bourke, *Dismembering the Male*; Benyon, *Masculinities and Culture*; Boyd, 'Knowing Your Place'; Glover and Caplan, *Genders*.
17 Roper, 'Between Manliness and Masculinity', p. 353.
18 Fussel, *Great War and Modern Memory*; Hynes, *A War Imagined*.
19 Pattinson, *Behind Enemy Lines*, p. 13.
20 *Cambridge Review*, 24 October 1924, p. 33 in Levsen, 'Constructing Elite Identities', p. 167.
21 Levsen, 'Constructing', pp. 143–83.
22 Martin Ceadel, 'The 'King and Country' Debate, 1933: Student Politics, Pacifism and the Dictators', *The Historical Journal*, 22 (1979) pp. 397–422 (p. 422); Trott, *Publishers, Readers and the Great War*, p. 77.
23 Gregory, *Silence*, p. 151.
24 Bond, *Unquiet Western Front*; Sheffield, *Forgotten Victory*; Watson, *Fighting Different Wars*.
25 Sheffield, 'Shadow of the Somme', p. 30.
26 Sheffield, *Forgotten Victory*, p. 9; Calder, *People's War*, p. 494.
27 Paris, *Over the Top*, p. 161. See also Bond, *Unquiet Western Front*; Paris, *Warrior Nation*; Sheffield, *Forgotten Victory*; Strachan, 'The Soldier's Experience in Two World Wars'; Watson, *Fighting Different Wars*.
28 Rose, *Which People's War?*, Introduction, specifically pp. 18 and 27.
29 Noakes, *War and the British*, p. 48.
30 *Ibid.*, p. 52; Rose, *Which People's War?*, p. 6.
31 Lucy Noakes, ' "Serve to Save": Gender, Citizenship and Civil Defence in Britain 1937–41', *Journal of Contemporary History*, 47.4 (2012) pp. 734–53; Summerfield, ' "Gun not a Dishcloth!" '.
32 See, for example, Gerard De Groot, 'Whose Finger on the Trigger?', pp. 444–6; De Groot, ' "I Love the Scent of Cordite in Your Hair": Gender Dynamics in Mixed Anti-Aircraft Batteries during the Second World War', *History*, 82.265 (1997) pp. 73–92 (pp. 83–4); Penny

Masculinity in the Second World War   261

Summerfield and Corinna Peniston-Bird, 'Women in the Firing Line: The Home Guard and the Defence of Gender Boundaries in Britain in the Second World War', *Women's History Review*, 9.2 (2000) pp. 231–55. Pattinson suggests that representations of women in SOE, the only (potentially) combatant role they were permitted, stressed their femininity to redress the imbalance resulting from their proximity to combat. *Behind Enemy Lines*, pp. 4–5.

33 Penny Summerfield, ' "My Dress for an Army Uniform": Gender Instabilities in the Two World Wars', Inaugural Lecture delivered at the University of Lancaster, 30 April 1997, p. 6.

34 Quote, Rose, *Which People's War*, p. 287, see also pp. 152–3, or chapter 5. Rose is drawing upon Alison Light's *Forever England: Femininity, Literature and Conservatism between the Wars* (London: Routledge, 1991) in which it is suggested that the inter-war years saw an anti-heroic masculinity with a distaste for romantic language of national pride. See pp. 8–10 of Light, *Forever England*.

35 Rose, *Which People's War?*, p. 287.

36 *Ibid.*, p. 287.

37 *Ibid.*, pp. 170–8.

38 Robb, *Men at Work*; Rose, *Which People's War?*; Summerfield, *Reconstructing Women's Wartime Lives*, pp. 120–1.

39 Summerfield and Peniston-Bird, *Contesting Home Defence*, chapter 7; Pattinson, McIvor and Robb, *Men in Reserve*; Chand, *Masculinities on Clydeside*.

40 Joanna Bourke has examined one aspect of the male experience in *An Intimate History of Killing: Face-to-Face Killing in Twentieth Century Warfare* (London: Granta Books, 2000).

41 Francis, *The Flyer*.

42 Houghton, *Veterans' Tale*, chapter 7; Houghton, 'Becoming "a Man" During the Battle of Britain'.

43 *Ibid.*, pp. 208–13.

44 *Ibid.*, p. 243.

45 *Ibid.*, p. 25 and chapter 7.

46 Unless otherwise stated, discussion of MO and COs is informed by MO File Report 312 'Conscientious Objectors', 30 July 1940, particularly Section D [Social Pressure on COs].

47 MO File Report 610 [Attitudes to Conscientious Objectors, March 1941]. This report drew upon the research within FR 312 and 405.

48 MO File Report 405 [16.9.40 Supplementary Report on COs].

49 More violent suggestions were made: they should be 'burned' or 'put up against a wall and shot'.

262 *Joining up in the Second World War*

50 Robb, 'The "Conchie Corps"', pp. 411–34 (pp. 425–6).
51 Ernest Spring, *'Conchie': The Wartime Experiences of a Conscientious Objector* (London, 1975) p. 51, cited in Robb, 'The "Conchie Corps"', p. 426.
52 John Hall Williams, IWM-SA-15323, 1995.
53 Rose, 'Temperate Heroes', p. 191.
54 Peniston-Bird, 'Classifying the Body', pp. 40–1.
55 Howard (Morley, 2011); Lesley Temple (Morley, 2010); Knowlton (Morley, 2010); Wally Harris (Morley, 2010); Woodhams (Morley, 2010); Cash (Morley (& Dann & Malling), 2010); Day (Morley, 2011); Derrick Thurgood (Morley, 2010).
56 Stagg (Morley, 2010). Cash and Pond respected their bravery. Cash (Morley (& Dann & Malling), 2010); Pond (Morley, 2011).
57 Stephens (Morley, 2010); Browne (Morley, 2010); Pragnell (Morley (& Marriot), 2010).
58 Dann (Morley (& Cash & Malling), 2010).
59 Frank Webster (Morley 2011).
60 Edward (Ted) Roberts (Morley, 2010); Elson (Morley, 2010).
61 Spragg (Morley, 2010).
62 Woodard (Morley, 2011).
63 Marriot (Morley (& Pragnell), 2010). See also Malling (Morley (& Cash & Dann), 2010).
64 MO, TC 6/2//E, Miscellaneous, Attitudes in the Forces (Army) to Conscientious Objectors 26.11.44 (Len England).
65 Walder (Morley, 2010).
66 Robb, 'The "Conchie Corps"', p. 433.
67 *Ibid.*, pp. 411, 433–4.
68 Pattinson, '"Shirkers", "Scrimjacks" and "Scrimshanks"?', pp. 710–14, 716.
69 Robb, *Men at Work*, pp. 134–5.
70 *Ibid.*, p. 129.
71 *Ibid.*, quote p. 75. On men in agriculture, see chapter 2. See chapter 4 for firemen and chapter 5 for merchant seamen.
72 Woodhams (Morley, 2010); Elson (Morley, 2010); Lowe (Morley, 2011); Spragg (Morley, 2010); Roberts (Morley, 2010); Woodard (Morley, 2011); Browne (Morley, 2010).
73 Howard (Morley, 2011).
74 Thurgood (Morley, 2010). See also Woodard (Morley, 2011).
75 Peniston-Bird, 'Classifying the Body', p. 40.
76 Browne (Morley, 2010).
77 Malling (Morley (& Cash & Dann), 2010).
78 Walder (Morley, 2010).

Masculinity in the Second World War 263

79 Woodard (Morley, 2011). The relationship between this inferiority and masculinity was apparent in Reg Day's testimony, already cited. Day (Morley, 2011).

80 Temple (Morley, 2010). This mirrored the views of reserved men's female colleagues: Summerfield, *Reconstructing Women's Wartime Lives*, pp. 121–32; Alison Chand, 'Glasgow's War and Masculine Identities in the Reserved Occupations 1939–1945: Wartime Women's Perspectives on Glasgow's Working Men', in *War, Memory and Biography. United Academics Journal of Social Sciences* (April 2011) pp. 12–16; Chand, *Masculinities on Clydeside*, pp. 28–9.

81 Roberts (Morley, 2010).

82 William Lloyd, IWM-SA-13283,1993. Spragg would have felt 'not very happy, in my frame of mind then' to be an RO. Spragg (Morley, 2010).

83 Walder's repeated emphasis on the service of his friends is not inconsistent with a less heroic motive, which in one narration triggered his volunteering. He had been caught leaving work early and threatened with removal from his RO and service in the Army, and if he were going in the forces preferred the RAF. Walder (Morley, 2010).

84 Ronald William Oates, IWM-SA-17931,1998. See also, his brother, James Lawrence Burgess Oates, cited in relation to the Home Guard, James Oates, IWM-SA-17984, 1998.

85 MO DR1483, January 1940 Directive.

86 Drake, IWM-SA-20791.

87 Barry Keenan, interview with Alison Chand, 25 January 2011, cited in Chand, *Masculinities on Clydeside*, p. 43.

88 Chand, *Second World War in Glasgow*, pp. 132–8. Pattinson, McIvor and Robb, *Men in Reserve*, pp. 100, 113. Pattinson, '"Shirkers", "Scrimjacks" and "Scrimshanks"?', p. 718.

89 See Gent, IWM-SA-18255, Cox, IWM-SA-22167 and Drake, IWM-SA-20791. All were notably less keen to serve before they had to, and were all amongst the older (archival) interviewees.

90 Pattinson, '"Shirkers", "Scrimjacks" and "Scrimshanks"?', p. 720.

91 Pattinson, McIvor and Robb, *Men in Reserve*, p. 126; Pattinson, '"Shirkers", "Scrimjacks" and "Scrimshanks"?', p. 711; Chand, *Second World War in Glasgow*, pp. 116–22.

92 Chris Rose (Morley, 2016).

93 For quote, Pattinson, McIvor and Robb, *Men in Reserve*, p. 127, see also conclusion; Chand, *Second World War in Glasgow*, see pp. 109–14, and pp. 117–18 for physical strength; Pattinson, '"Shirkers", "Scrimjacks" and "Scrimshanks"?', p. 724.

94 Rose, *Which People's War?*, pp. 186–92; Robb, *Men at Work*.

264 *Joining up in the Second World War*

95 Chand, *Second World War in Glasgow and Clydeside*, pp. 100–101. Little distinction is drawn in this argument between masculinity and active citizenship, however. Peniston-Bird, 'Classifying the Body', p. 37.

96 Pattinson, McIvor and Robb, *Men in Reserve*, pp. 104–5.

97 For quote, *ibid.*, pp. 95–6; see also p. 117 for importance to sense of self. Pattinson, '"Shirkers", "Scrimjacks" and "Scrimshanks"?', p. 718.

98 Pattinson, McIvor and Robb, *Men in Reserve*, pp. 330–1.

99 Rose (Morley, 2016).

100 Donovan, IWM-SA-20316; Day (Morley, 2011).

101 Summerfield and Peniston-Bird, *Contesting Home Defence*, p. 16.

102 *Ibid.*, chapter 7.

103 James Oates, IWM-SA-17984.

104 Les Shepherd (Morley, 2022).

105 Woodhams (Morley, 2010); Day (Morley, 2011).

106 Summerfield and Peniston-Bird, *Contesting Home Defence*, p. 222.

107 Leask, IWM-SA-21602.

108 Price, IWM-SA-28775.

109 Webster (Morley, 2011). Webster's negotiation of *Dad's Army* here well supports arguments made by Peniston-Bird, '"I Wondered Who'd Be The First To Spot That."'.

110 Webster (Morley, 2011).

111 Summerfield and Peniston-Bird, *Contesting Home Defence*, pp. 225–6.

112 Victor Waterhouse, cited in Summerfield and Peniston-Bird, *Contesting Home Defence*, p. 209.

113 Woodhams (Morley, 2010).

114 Day (Morley, 2011).

115 Hay (Morley, 2010).

116 Craig Inglis, interviewed by Linsey Robb, 10 May 2013 (Scottish Oral History Centre, 050/48), quoted in Pattinson, McIvor and Robb, *Men in Reserve*, p. 104.

117 Pond (Morley, 2011).

118 Rose, *Which People's War?*, p. 153.

119 Pattinson, McIvor and Robb found the same was true of men in reserved occupations. See *Men in Reserve*, pp. 98–9.

120 Pragnell (Morley (& Marriot), 2010).

121 Abbott (Morley, 2010).

122 Noakes shows that the ATS uniform was also seen by some as inferior to that of the WAAF and the WRNS. *Women in the British Army*, pp. 108–9. Tessa Stone has shown that some women also opted for the

Masculinity in the Second World War

WAAF based on the appearance of the uniform, Stone, 'Creating a (Gendered?) Military Identity', p. 618.

123 Woodhams (Morley, 2010).

124 Marriot said that the Merchant Navy were 'worst off' because 'there was nothing glamorous about the job' and the casualties were heavy. The lack of uniform may have been one reason that it was not glamorous. Marriot (Morley (& Pragnell), 2010).

125 Lowe (Morley, 2011).

126 Pragnell and Marriot (Morley, 2010).

127 Cash (Morley (& Dann & Malling), 2010).

128 See also Woodhams (Morley, 2010).

129 Browne (Morley, 2010).

130 Thurgood (Morley, 2010). See also Mallabar, IWM-SA-11211.

131 Marriot (Morley (& Pragnell), 2010).

132 Parkhouse, IWM-SA-15476.

133 Francis, *The Flyer*, p. 23. For women talking about attraction of pilots, see pp. 23–5.

134 Woodard (Morley, 2011).

135 Lowe (Morley, 2010).

136 Lowe (Morley, 2011).

137 Charles Sinclair, IWM-SA-10230 (1988).

138 Charles Jeffries (Morley 2010).

139 Cash (Morley (& Dann & Malling), 2010).

140 *Ibid.* Day (Morley, 2011); Pond (Morley, 2011). This was also expressed within flyers' memoirs. Francis, *The Flyer*, p. 24.

141 See also Mellor (Morley, 2010).

142 Browne (Morley, 2010). Stagg (Morley, 2010).

143 Day (Morley, 2011).

144 Webster (Morley 2011).

145 Roberts (Morley, 2010).

146 Hay (Morley, 2010).

147 Lowe (Morley, 2010).

148 Tex Laws, Correspondence, 3 May 2000, cited in Summerfield and Peniston-Bird, *Contesting Home Defence*, p. 219.

149 Howard (Morley, 2011).

150 Tom Neary, IWM-SA-18736, 1999.

151 Hay (Morley, 2010).

152 Mellor (Morley, 2010).

153 Pearson (Morley, 2011) and Pearson (Morley (& Platts & Hayes), 2011).

154 Pearson (Morley (& Platts & Hayes), 2011).

155 Stephens (Morley, 2010).

266 *Joining up in the Second World War*

156 Alan Watcham, IWM-SA-11210, 1989.
157 Sweetland, IWM-SA-10452.
158 Illman, IWM-SA-18438.
159 Lord Hugh Gater Jenkins, IWM-SA-12507, 1992.
160 Temple (Morley, 2010).
161 This might exist between or even *within* services. Francis discusses the demarcations and competition between those in different roles within the RAF – Ground Crew/Air Crew, Bomber Command/Fighter Command/ Officer/NCO. See Francis, *The Flyer*, pp. 44–62. Stone has also highlighted the hierarchies perceived between WAAFs in the wartime RAF. Stone, 'Creating a (Gendered?) Military Identity'.
162 Day (Morley, 2011) and Pond (Morley, 2011).
163 Temple (Morley, 2010); and Pragnell (Morley (& Marriot), 2010).
164 Day (Morley, 2011); Knowlton (Morley, 2010).
165 Woodard (Morley, 2011); Meades (Morley, 2010); Pragnell (Morley (& Marriot), 2010).
166 Lowe (Morley, 2010 and 2011).
167 Both Pragnell and Marriot said that submariners were manlier and they would not have done that. Pragnell and Marriot (Morley, 2010) 1/1.
168 Howard (Morley, 2011).
169 Pond (Morley, 2011).
170 *Ibid.*
171 Woodard (Morley, 2011).
172 For discussion, see Francis, *The Flyer*, pp. 18–19.
173 Webster (Morley, 2011). Howard also made the distinction between the Army as 'Rough' and the RAF, Howard (Morley, 2011).
174 Francis, *The Flyer*, pp. 129–30.
175 Day (Morley, 2011).
176 Noakes, 'Serve to Save', p. 737; Jutta Schwarzkopf, 'Combatant or Non-Combatant? The Ambiguous Status of Women in British Anti-Aircraft Batteries during the Second World War', *War & Society*, 28.2 (2009) pp. 105–31 (p. 119); Stone, 'Creating a (Gendered?) Military Identity', pp. 610–12. See also Penny Summerfield and Corinna Peniston-Bird, 'The Home Guard in Britain in the Second World War: Uncertain Masculinities?', in *Military Masculinities: Identity and the State*, ed. by Paul Highgate (London: Praeger, 2003) pp. 57–69.
177 Pragnell (Morley (& Marriot), 2010).
178 Marriot (Morley (& Pragnell), 2010). As has already been noted, there were numerous popular representations of aerial warfare in juvenile literature, like Biggles, and cinema that gave an impression of glamour and encouraged young men in their desire to join the RAF.

Masculinity in the Second World War

179 Seibert, IWM-SA-18485; Donovan, IWM-SA-20316; Wilson, IWM-SA-17985; Winstanley, IWM-SA-17955; Tyson, IWM-SA-10309; Todd, IWM-SA-29069.
180 Gent, IWM-SA-18225. Jim Hayes also repeatedly ignored opportunities to evade military service because he felt it was morally objectionable. Hayes (Morley, 2010).
181 Spragg (Morley, 2010).
182 Pond (Morley, 2011).
183 Woodard (Morley, 2011).
184 Day (Morley, 2011).
185 Summerfield, *Reconstructing Women's Wartime Lives*, pp. 78–99.
186 *Ibid.*, p. 99.
187 Riggs, IWM-SA-22346.
188 Peniston-Bird, ' "All in it together" ', p. 75.

Conclusion

By examining how understandings of the Great War shaped men's attitudes and decisions about military enlistment during the Second World War this book adds to our understandings of Second World War enlistment, masculinity and the legacy of the Great War. Original oral history interviews conducted specifically for this purpose have been used alongside archival oral histories and material from the Mass Observation Archive to understand how these men encountered and responded to representations of the Great War in popular culture and from Great War veterans themselves, and whether and how they drew on their understandings of the Great War when faced with the prospect of participation in their own war.

Chapter 1 investigated young men's encounters with, and subjective responses to, representations of the Great War in popular culture in inter-war Britain. It showed that young men encountered a huge variety of representations of the Great War, but, particularly for those from working-class homes, this typically did not include the poetry, plays and memoirs normally presumed to make up the canon of war literature. Boys' story papers, illustrated histories and films were far more frequently encountered texts. These materials tended to depict the war in traditional, positive terms. The paucity of references to 'disillusioned' high literature, even amongst those participating in Mass Observation, should inform our assessments of its relative impact on attitudes. Conversely, young people were almost universally involved in commemorating the Great War, but even those who were directly involved in commemorative acts typically did not feel that they had taken much from Armistice events other than the knowledge that many had died in the Great War. Importantly, Chapter 1 also showed that young men's subjective

Conclusion 269

responses to the representations they encountered were even more wide-ranging than the representations themselves. The consumption of a cultural text did not equate to being imbued with, or even necessarily fully understanding, its intended message. Audiences' interpretations were varied, sometimes in unpredictable ways, as were the ways in which they might later deploy these understandings. This examination of subjective responses has shown the difficulty of assessing the impact of representations in popular culture without looking at how individuals reacted, and has highlighted the complexity and nuance within reactions. Historians and literary scholars should be far more hesitant than they typically have been in stating that any given text shaped the thoughts and attitudes of an entire cohort of people.

Chapter 1 illustrates the need to expand the historiography of the legacy of the Great War to consider how the conflict was represented in an even broader range of media. Not only were young men's understandings more often informed by representations of the Great War in popular culture, rather than elite literature, but the oral histories also pointed to engagement with periodicals, encyclopaediae and children's histories of the Great War and to the ubiquity of photographic images of the Great War in different media. These artefacts were remembered as sources of understanding about the Great War, but remain under-studied sources. The argument for a broader field of enquiry is made even more forcefully in Chapter 2. Cultural representations of the Great War were ever-present in inter-war Britain, but so were millions of its veterans.

Chapter 2 explored what young men in inter-war Britain had heard about the Great War from its veterans, and significantly expands our knowledge about a previously understudied area. It shows that we should adapt our conception of the Great War veteran. It has previously been suggested that events where veterans gathered might enable them to reminisce, and that they preferred to discuss their happier memories.[1] This chapter shows that many veterans also provided information about their war experiences to young men, albeit occasionally, within the domestic sphere and outside the home, far more commonly than has previously been acknowledged. While most veteran fathers were reticent about the Great War, the majority still narrated at least basic details about their service to their sons. Those with veteran fathers commonly learned about their wounds and how they had been sustained, and a significant minority heard occasional detailed narratives about aspects of their fathers' war experiences. These more extensive narratives were varied, just like veterans' narratives within cultural texts, but young men heard more about positive elements of war experience than about horrific ones. Indeed, Chapter 2 demonstrates that some veterans were selective in what they discussed, and this appears generally to have denied young men access to more unpleasant elements of the war. Young men might hear about the war in similar ways from veterans they knew outside the family, including colleagues and neighbours, and some young men also learned about veterans' war experiences indirectly, through photographs, medals, mementoes and second-hand stories. Notably, the personal nature of the impressions gained from such narratives seems to have made them significant in young men's understandings of the Great War. This chapter makes an important contribution then, because it demonstrates that veterans' narratives, however fleeting and ephemeral, were an important facet of the body of representations of the Great War from which Britain's inter-war youth learned about and understood the Great War.

Chapters 3 and 4 address men's attitudes to enlistment in the Second World War. These attitudes have seldom been considered, but they help us to understand the reasons behind some of the ways that men sought to serve during wartime, and shed light on consent and coercion during the Second World War. They show that British men held a wide variety of attitudes towards peacetime and wartime conscription. Some men, particularly young men, were distinctly enthusiastic about military service. Explicit, jingoistic patriotism was rarely expressed, but expectations of adventure and excitement were far from absent. Most men, however, accepted military service reluctantly; their reluctance stemmed from the disruption it would cause to their professional and domestic lives, or the simple fact that they would not have chosen to go to war, rather than ideological objections towards the war. That Hitler in particular appeared unambiguously evil to most Britons – an antipathy probably based more on his apparent determination to have a war than on any detailed knowledge of Nazism's ideological programme – probably limited opposition in any case. Ideas about duty and patriotism were not straightforward, but men used these terms to

Conclusion 271

describe various levels of willingness. Nevertheless, the conception that wartime military service was a man's duty, however reluctantly accepted, was critical to the lack of social conflict around the introduction and implementation of conscription.

The early implementation of manpower controls was itself a legacy of the Great War. While this removed the requirement for men to actively consider how they would enter the military services (or how they would stay out) this research has highlighted the need for historians to pay attention to the extent to which Britain's men could take an active role in shaping their war experience before it began. Conscription generated little outward dissent, and a negligible proportion of men removed themselves from the war effort. Rather than simply indicating a sense of inviolable duty to the State or enthusiastic willingness to fight, however, the lack of opposition to conscription was due in part to the level of agency men retained, so long as they could establish how to exercise it. Chapter 3 showed that men who understood the changing manpower controls in wartime Britain retained a number of choices and could potentially exercise a surprising degree of agency, which many of them used to negotiate the terms of their service in self-interested ways while remaining within the bounds of the system.

Chapter 4 showed that both a sense of patriotism and wish for adventure motivated men to volunteer, but also highlighted that volunteering was also an important method of exercising agency over which service one would join or which role one would have, and such self-interested voluntarism was common. Certainly, the majority of men who enlisted would have preferred to serve in the RAF or the Royal Navy. Importantly, here we can see a key legacy of the Great War: many men, drawing on their understandings of the Great War, sought to avoid service in the Army, and particularly the infantry. They used their understanding to identify safe(r) services, and images of infantry slaughter and bayonet fighting did not inspire them to join the Poor Bloody Infantry. Yet, it must be noted that a minority of those who drew on their understandings of the Great War were not only keen to serve but *wanted* to serve in infantry units, particularly to follow in their fathers' footsteps. While individuals' subjective experiences defy easy categorisation, Chapter 4 nonetheless shows that representations of the Great War in both veterans' narratives and cultural texts shaped young men's

272 *Joining up in the Second World War*

attitudes towards service, and in particular how they wanted to serve. Crucially, however, the influence of these representations was as complex and varied as the narratives themselves. Knowledge of a veteran's service often seems to have had greater impact than representations in popular culture. This reinforces the argument that veterans' narratives at an extremely individual level were an important part of how young men encountered the last conflict in interwar Britain.

Chapter 4 also shows that assessing the reactions of audiences, rather than critics, to all of these representations can provide a more nuanced understanding of what these representations meant to those who consumed them. Positive and traditional representations of the Great War within popular culture (including, we might now add, within veterans' narratives) were not, however, the only reason that young men were able to see the Second World War in terms of an adventure, or an arena for heroic actions. This chapter also showed that young men did not universally look to the First World War when thinking about their own service in the Second. Some simply did not connect the two; it was 'just history'.[2] Others expected the war would be very different, particularly if they anticipated service in the RAF or the Royal Navy, and so concluded the Great War was not relevant. For most, to a greater degree than the Army, imaginings of war with these services retained the possibility of exciting, adventurous service, untainted by the Great War.

Chapter 5 makes a significant contribution to the history of men and masculinity in the Second World War. Its examination of the importance of military service to the performance of masculinity in wartime Britain in the subjective conceptions of men who entered the three Armed Forces answers the calls of historians, including Michael Roper and John Tosh, to examine masculinity as a subjective identity as well as a cultural construction.[3] While the Great War may have influenced the form of the softer and less jingoistic temperate masculinity that was the hegemonic ideal in public discourse in Britain from 1939–45, that construction still privileged the man in uniform and retained military participation as the key signifier of masculinity. When we look instead at men's subjective conceptions we find that military service also remained key to most men's understandings of their role in wartime. The ways that men thought and spoke about men who were outside the forces, about

Conclusion

273

military uniform and its effects on their sense of self, and how they coveted certain roles over others, show that they understood the importance of *military* participation, rather than wider active citizenship, to the hierarchy of wartime masculinities.

Nevertheless, Chapter 5 shows that although men typically understood what the hegemonic masculinity was, the extent to which men sought to perform it varied significantly and their own conceptions of masculinity were diverse. In many ways traditional conceptions of the link between masculinity and war survived the Great War. Many men sincerely felt that service was their duty and they were willing to do it to maintain their own identity. Others were more enthusiastic participants who strove to achieve heroic and hyper-masculine roles and some perceived war as holding potential excitement, glamour and adventure. The Great War had not removed the possibility of imagining warfare in these traditional ways; indeed, such imaginings could be informed by the inter-war pleasure culture of war, which included depictions of the Great War. Imaginings of war as adventure, as test of masculine character and rite of passage, and as duty, could all be informed by representations of the Great War and could encourage men's curiosity about whether or not they could do it. Other men, despite their reluctance and private desire to prioritise their own wishes over the national war effort, recognised that to be publicly compliant with wartime masculinity they must stoically accept that they must agree to military participation if it was asked of them. Even if they sought to delay or avert this request, or just took no action to hasten it, their recognition of, and compliance with, societal expectation indicates the resilience of Edwardian understandings of war and masculinity.

Chapter 5 showed, then, that the public construction of temperate masculinity did not dictate and was not a perfect mirror of all British men's subjective conceptions of wartime masculinity. Instead, looking at men's attitudes to enlistment highlights diversity, negotiation and private contestation. Many sought to shape their service so that it was more suited to their own private attitudes and aspirations. The reluctant but acceptant resignation that many – probably a majority – of men felt about their Second World War enlistment meshed quite well with temperate masculinity; they could not be accused of bravado or aggression, but they were willing. Yet others, particularly young men, were too enthusiastic

274 *Joining up in the Second World War*

about service and too keen to be heroes, and at the other end of the spectrum were those who were not sufficiently willing to take part. Yet temperate masculinity was resilient to these divergent attitudes because public assessments of a man's compliance were, in practice, based on the presence or absence of a military uniform. So long as most men complied with conscription and the manpower system temperate masculinity was secure, and this was never in doubt. Understandings of the Great War did shape men's attitudes to service in the Second World War in multiple ways: it informed men's reluctance to serve and tempered the enthusiasm of some; it deterred many from serving in the Army and particularly the infantry; but men typically considered *how* they might participate, not whether they would. The Great War did not pose such a challenge to the connection between masculinity and military service that large numbers of men questioned whether they would don military uniform between 1939 and 1945.

Notes

1 See Todman, ' "Sans Peur et Sans Reproche" ', p. 1105; and Gregory, *Silence*, pp. 51–93.
2 MO DR 1310, male, unemployed, born 1921, February 1940 Directive.
3 Michael Roper, 'Slipping Oout of View: Subjectivity and Emotion in Gender History', *History Workshop Journal*, 59.1 (2005) pp. 57–72 (p. 57); Tosh, 'What Should Historians Do with Masculinity?'.

Bibliography

Primary sources

Oral history interviews conducted by Joel Morley

Abbott, Jack. 30 July 2010, 24 August 2010 and 9 December 2010.
Browne, Don. 28 September 2010.
Burney, David. 30 March 2016.
Cash, George. 22 September 2010, 6 October 2010 and 27 October 2010. With Dann and Malling.
Curtis, Wilfred. 10 February 2011 and 24 March 2011. With Gwendoline Saunders.
Dann, George. 22 September 2010, 6 October 2010 and 27 October 2010. With Cash and Malling.
Day, Reg. 16 March 2011 and 18 May 2011.
Elson, Reg. 25 August 2010.
Etty, John. 30 March 2016.
Florence, Allan. 17 September 2010.
Folkes, Brian. 29 March 2016.
Foster, Philip. 19 April 2016.
Gould, Harold. 14 March 2016.
Hagger, Dennis. 24 September 2015.
Harris, Ralph. 21 July 2010.
Harris, Wally. 20 July 2010.
Hay, Ken. 19 August 2010.
Hayes, Jim. 1 September 2010.
Holloway, Ron. 18 April 2016.
Howard, Arthur. 28 February 2011.
Johnson, Eric. 23 May 2016.
Jeffries, Charles (Wag). 9 September 2010.
Kinnear, Bob. 22 September 2015.
Knowlton, Thomas. 13 September 2010.
Lowe, Bob. 17 November 2010 and 15 March 2011.
Malling, John. 22 September 2010, 6 October 2010 and 27 October 2010. With Dann and Cash.

276 Bibliography

Marriot, Maurice. 10 September 2010. With Pragnell.
McKenzie, Robert. 17 September 2015.
Meades, Ron. 1 September 2010.
Mellor, Gordon. 17 August 2010, 7 November 2010 and 7 December 2010.
Owen, Denys. 1 April 2016.
Parkes, Harry (Bevin Boy). 20 March 2016.
Pearson, Samuel. 1 March 2011.
Pearson, Samuel. 2 September 2010. With Hayes and Platts.
Pettet, Leonard. 23 June 2016.
Platts, Ben. 2 September 2010. With Hayes and Pearson.
Pond, Fred. 9 April 2011, 21 April 2011 and 5 May 2011.
Pragnell, Jack. 10 September 2010. With Marriot.
Reed, Frank. 1 June 2016.
Roberts, Edward (Ted). 26 July 2010.
Robinson, Phillip. 31 March 2016.
Rose, Chris. 1 June 2016.
Sewell, Ernest. 15 April 2016.
Smith, Bernard (pseudonym). 4 November 2016.
Spragg, Brian. 27 September 2010.
Stagg, George. 15 September 2010.
Stephens, Jim. 11 September 2010.
Stoddart, Jack. 21 September 2015.
Temple, Lesley. 21 August 2010.
Thurgood, Derrick. 29 July 2010.
Walder, Percy. 5 October 2010.
Waterhouse, Gordon. 31 March 2016.
Walker, Henry (pseudonym). 28 September 2015.
Webster, Frank. 19 November 2010, 19 January 2011.
Woodard, Peter. 14 and 15 April and 13 May 2011.
Woodhams, Robert (Bob). 20 September 2010.
Womack, Ronald. 15 April 2016.
Wyke, Alf. 14 September 2010.

Personal papers and correspondence from interviewees

Browne, Don. Personal papers.
Pond, Fred. *Keen to Do Our Bit.* Self-published memoir, 2010.
Webster, Frank. Personal papers.

Oral histories from the Imperial War Museum Sound Archive

Atkinson, Bob. (18738). With Bob Watkins, 1999.
Ayers, Ron. (21093). With Peter Hart, February 2001.
Baines, Douglas. (13147). With Conrad Wood, 1993.
Beddows, Herbert. (20373). With Conrad Wood, 2000.

Bibliography

Bell, William Henry. (22585). With Conrad Wood, 2002.
Boardman, Arthur Douglas. (10047). With Conrad Wood, 2000.
Bowdler, Norman. (22342). With Nigel de Lee, 2001.
Brand, Stanley. (27347). With Richard McDonough, 2005.
Brewis, Henry Charles Francis. (12707). With Harry Moses, 1992.
Burnett, Arthur. (24905). With Jo White, 2003.
Carmichael, Ian. (10297). With Conrad Wood, 1988.
Cheetam, Arthur. (14779). With Conrad Wood, 1994.
Chilton, Thomas. (27345). With Richard McDonough, 2005.
Cosgrove, Henry Frank. (10177). With Conrad Wood, 1988.
Coster, William. (28723). With Richard McDonough, 2006.
Cox, Alfred. (22167). With Debbie Frith, 2001.
Davis, Albert. (12709). With Harry Moses, 1990.
Donovan, James. (20316). With Peter Hart, March 2000.
Drake, Joseph. (20791). With Tom Tunney, 2000.
Elliott, George. (10602). With Harry Moses and Chris Thistletwaite, 1993.
Flint, Arthur. (899). With Colin Lovelace, 1977.
Forster, George. (12824). With Peter Hart, date unknown.
Gent, Gordon. (18255). With Harry Moses, 1999.
Griffiths, Richard. (29574). With Richard McDonough, 2007.
Grogan, Gwyn St George Elger. (22368). With Conrad Wood, 2002.
Gross, Anthony. (4621). With Julian Andrews, 1980.
Guest, Marge and Stan. (7261). With Peter Grafton, 1981.
Hall, Charles. (9230). With Conrad Wood, 1986.
Hall-Williams, John Eryl. (15323). With Lyn E. Smith, 1995.
Hammerton, Ian Charles. (8939). With Nigel de Lee, 1985.
Hann, Fredrick William. (3962). With Katherine P. Barratt, 1978.
Harper, Harold. (10923). With Peter Hart, 1990.
Hillman, Jesse James. (4612). With Margaret A. Brooks, 1980.
Hutchinson Brookes, Robert. (10148). With Conrad Wood, 1988.
Iceton, George Edward. (11938). With Harry Moses, 1989.
Illman, Thomas Edgar. (18438). With Conrad Wood, 1998.
Jalland, William Herbert Wainwright. (11944). With Nigel de Lee, 1991.
Jenkins, Lord Hugh Gater. (12507). With Lyn E. Smith, 1992.
Kidston, Montgomerie. (892). With Colin Lovelace, 1977.
Kilby, Edward. (16084). With Peter Hart, 1995.
King, Russel. (18512). With Harry Moses, 1998.
King, Tom. (9571). With Jon Newman, 1986.
Knight, William Phillip. (6627). With Conrad Wood, 1983.
Le Cheminant, William John. (12546). With Conrad Wood, 1992.
Leask, Thomas. (21602). With Harry Moses, 2001.
Leech, Sydney. (22623). With Conrad Wood, 2002.
Lloyd, William Edward. (13283). With Conrad Wood, 1993.
Mallabar, Ronald. (11211). With Harry Moses, 1989.
Mann, James Arthur. (18513). With Harry Moses, 1998.
Neary, Tom. (18736). With Bob Watkins, 1999.
Nimmins, Thomas. (11941). With Harry Moses, 1991.

278 *Bibliography*

Oates, James Lawrence Burgess. (17984). With Conrad Wood, 1998.
Oates, Ronald William. (17931). With Conrad Wood, 1998.
Parkhouse, Rupert. (15476). With Conrad Wood, 1995.
Parsons, Sidney. (14052). With Conrad Wood, 1994.
Patterson, Charles. (8901). With Peter Simkins, 1985.
Pearson, Alastair Stevenson. (12151). With Conrad Wood, 1991.
Price, Cyril. (28775). With Richard McDonough, 2006.
Pugh, Alec. (10880). With Conrad Wood, 1989.
Radwell, Des. (28531). With Nick Haslam, 2005.
Reid, William St Clair. (27208). With Richard McDonough, 2004.
Riggs, John. (22346). With Nigel de Lee, 2001.
Rodgers, John Crawford. (11202). With Harry Moses, date unknown.
Saward, Leslie. (12834). With Conrad Wood, 1991.
Seibert, Charles. (18485). With Peter Hart, 1998.
Sell, Harold. (10403). With Peter Hart, date unknown.
Sinclair, Charles. (10230). With Conrad Wood, 1988.
Smith, Arthur. (27348). With Richard McDonough, 2005.
Spearman, William James. (9796). With Conrad Wood, 1987.
Sweeney, H. Y. (11556). With Stephen Ambrose, 1983.
Sweetland, Mr (10452 – catalogued as Sidney Parsons). With Conrad Wood, 1988.
Taylor, Peter Douglas. (10484). With Conrad Wood, 1988.
Thomas, Jack. (27342). With Richard McDonough, 2005.
Tobin, Cornelius Joseph. (17566). With Conrad Wood, 1997.
Todd, Richard. (29069). With Nigel de Lee, 2006.
Tyson, Percival Goodman. (10309). With Conrad Wood, 1988.
Underdown, Stuart Vernon. (31699). With Toby Brooks, 2008.
Vanderwolfe, Harold George. (13426). With Peter Hart, 1993.
Walker, Robert Henry. (13137). With Conrad Wood, 1993.
Waller, George Edward Anthony. (15239). With Conrad Wood, 1995.
Watcham, Alan Hughes. (11210). With Harry Moses, 1989.
White, Wilfred Scott. (16718). With Harry Moses, 1996.
Wilson, John Leo. (17985). With Conrad Wood, 1998.
Wilson, Thomas. (11106). With Harry Moses, date unknown.
Winstanley, John. (17955). With Conrad Wood, 1998.
Wright, Edward George. (12786). With Conrad Wood, 12 October 1992.

Oral histories from the National Museum of the Royal Navy, Portsmouth

Cambrook, Commander Clement. (2004/51 (2*1)). With Bill Alexander, 2004.
Clements, Frank. (278/1994 (3*2)). With Chris Howard Bailey, 1994.
Cobb, David. (299/1991 (1*1)). With Chris Howard Bailey, 1991.
Drummond, Geoffrey. (1993/1 (2*1)). With Chris Howard Bailey, 1993.

Bibliography 279

Dunne, Lt Commander Gordon Dunne. (445/1991). With Chris Howard Bailey, 1991.

Frost, Frank. (441/1994). With Chris Howard Bailey, date unknown.

Hill, Frances Frederick. (92/7). With Chris Howard Bailey, date unknown.

Pack, Captain Arthur James. (1993/445(4)). With Chris Howard Bailey, 1994.

Tindall, Kevin. (2004/88 (2*1)). With Capt. William Alexander, 2004.

Mass Observation Archive

Mass Observation January 1940 Directive Replies, Question 7 [Attitudes to conscription].

Mass Observation February 1940 Directive Replies, Question 8 [Influence of childhood impressions].

Mass Observation Topic Collections:

6–2–E, Miscellaneous, Attitudes in the Forces (Army) to Conscientious Objectors 26.11.44 (Len England).

Worktown, 9 May 1940.

27/A Armistice Day 1937.

Worktown, 52/A: GT, Militiamen, 11 November 1939.

29, Microfiche Reel 142. Section 1/b [Observations in Stepney, 29.7.40].

29, Microfiche Reel 142. Section 1/c. [Verbatim responses to Military Training Bill Street Surveys, 26 and 27 April 1939].

29, Microfiche Reel 142. Section 1/c. [Harrisson, letter to Darlow, 28 April 1939].

Mass Observation File Reports:

FR42/G – [short report on Territorial Army, 15 February 1938].

FR 33 – [February 1940].

FR 62 – [Literary Questionnaire, March 1940].

FR 274 – [Attitude of Civilians to Military/Talk about conscription on the streets].

FR 312 – [Conscientious Objectors, July 1940].

FR 361 – [Attitudes to Military Training Bill, 1939].

FR 405 – [16.9.40 Supplementary Report on COs].

FR 553 – [Activities of Youths].

FR 610 – [Attitudes to Conscientious Objectors, March 1941].

FR 827 – [Public Opinion on Service and Civilian Pay].

FR 1009 – [Manpower and Conscription, December 1941].

FR 1080 – [Adolescents in Wartime].

FR 1402 – [Attitudes to Civilian War Work, 1942].

MOA1.2.27.1.E – [Attitudes to conscription, 1939].

MOA1.2.64.2.J.3 – [Attitudes to wartime work in coal mines].

MOA1.2.75.5.c.4 – [Manpower conscription questionnaire results, 1941].

MOA1.5.17.52.a.49 – ['Overheards' in Bolton about Conscription and Evacuation].

280 *Bibliography*

Mass Observation publications

Clothes Rationing Survey. An Interim Report prepared by Mass Observation for the Advertising Service Guild. Change, No. 1. Bulletin of the Advertising Service Guild, August 1941.

Home Propaganda, A report prepared by Mass Observation for the Advertising Services Guild. Change, No. 2. Bulletin of the Advertising Service Guild, September 1941.

Madge, Charles and Harrisson, Tom (eds), *First Year's Work 1937–38 by Mass Observation* (London: Drummond, 1938).

Mass Observation, *Britain* (London: Penguin, 1939).

Mass Observation, *War Begins at Home* (London: Chatto & Windus, 1940).

Mass Observation, *The Pub and the People: A Worktown Study* (London: Gollancz, 1987).

US, *Mass-Observation's Weekly Intelligence Service*, 17 February 1940 and 2 March 1940.

Government papers

Ministry of Labour and National Service. Report for the years 1939–46. [CMD 7225] House of Commons Parliamentary Papers Online.

National Archives, CAB 24/285. Cabinet. Military Training Bill. 30 April 1939.

———— CAB 65/2/53. War Cabinet. Conclusions of a Meeting of the War Cabinet. 19 December 1939.

———— CAB 67/1/22. The Calling Up of Men for the Armed Forces. Memorandum by the Minister of Labour and National Service. 28 September 1939.

———— CAB 67/3/40. War Cabinet. The Calling Up of Men for the Armed Forces. Memorandum by the Minister of Labour and National Service. 15 December 1939.

———— CAB 67/6/16. War Cabinet. Manpower available for the Armed Forces. 30 April 1940.

———— CAB.67/9/12. War Cabinet. The National Service (No. 2) Bill.

———— CAB 68/4/12. War Cabinet. Eighth report submitted by the Minister of Labour and National Service covering the period 16 December–31 December 1939.

Parliamentary debates

Hore Belisha, Volume 346, House of Commons Debates, 5th Series, 5 May 1939, col. 2230.

Sir V. Warrender, Volume 347, House of Commons Debates, 5th Series, 10 May 1939, col. 493.

Bibliography

Published primary sources

Gallup, George, *The Gallup International Public Opinion Polls, Great Britain, 1937–1975* (1976).

Hammerton, J. A. (ed.), *The War Illustrated: A Pictorial Record of the Conflict of the Nations*, vol. 5 (London: Amalgamated Press Ltd, 1916).

Johannsen, Ernst, *Brigade Exchange, A telephone story of the Great War* (New York; Los Angeles: Samuel French, 1932).

Joining Up. A Complete Guide to Those Joining the Army, Navy or Air Force, Etc (London: War Facts Press, 1940).

The National Register: United Kingdom and Isle of Man. Statistics of Population on 29 September 1939. Report and Tables (London: HMSO, 1944).

National Service: A Guide to the Ways in Which the People of This Country May Give Service; with a Message from the Prime Minister, Ministry of Labour (London: HMSO, 1939).

Pollard, Robert, *You and the Call-Up. A Guide for Men and Women* (London: Blandford Press, 1942).

Radio Times

Wakeling, Eric, *The Lonely War: A Story of Bomb Disposal in World War Two by One Who Was There* (Worcester: Square One, 1994).

Websites

BBC Genome database, extracted from *Radio Times*: https://genome.ch.bbc.co.uk/genome (accessed 12 February 2024).

BBC People's War website, Arthur Finn, Article ID A4119851 written 1994, contributed 2005 by his daughter, www.bbc.co.uk/history/ww2peopleswar/stories/51/a4119851.shtml (accessed 8 January 2024).

Carlson, Jessamy, 'Battle Babies', 18 February 2016, https://blog.nationalarchives.gov.uk/battle-babies/ (accessed 8 January 2024).

Foster, Ann-Marie, 'The Next of Kin Memorial Plaque and the Family Connection', https://blogs.kent.ac.uk/munitions-of-the-mind/2019/07/08/the-next-of-kin-memorial-plaque-and-the-family-connection/ (accessed 8 January 2024).

Imperial War Museum, 'Next of Kin Memorial Plaque, Scroll and King's Message', www.iwm.org.uk/history/first-world-war-next-of-kin-plaque (accessed 8 January 2024).

Selected secondary literature

Books

Abrams, Lynn, *Oral History Theory* (London: Routledge, 2010).

Abrams, Mark, *Social Surveys and Social Action* (London: William Heinemann; printed in France, 1951).

282 Bibliography

Addison, Paul and Crang, Jeremy (eds), *Listening to Britain: Home Intelligence Reports on Britain's Finest Hour, May–September 1940* (London: Vintage Digital, 2011).

Allport, Alan, *Browned Off and Bloody-Minded. The British Soldier Goes to War, 1939–1945* (Yale: Yale University Press, 2015).

Anderson, Julie, *War, Disability and Rehabilitation in Britain. Soul of a Nation* (Manchester: Manchester University Press, 2011).

Barker, Rachel, *Conscience, Government and War: Conscientious Objection in Great Britain 1939–45* (London: Routledge & Kegan Paul, 1982).

Barr, Niall, *The Lion and the Poppy: British Veterans, Politics, and Society, 1921–1939* (Westport, Conn.: Praeger, 2005).

Becket, Ian F. W., *The Great War 1914–1918* (Harlow: Routledge, 2007).

Benyon, John, *Masculinities and Culture* (London: Open University Press, 2002).

Berresford Ellis, Peter, and Schofield, Jennifer, *By Jove., Biggles! The Life Story of Captain W E Johns* (Watford: Norman Wright, 2003).

Bond, Brian, 'British Anti-War Writers and Their Critics', in *Facing Armageddon. The First World War Experienced*, ed. by H. Cecil and P. Liddle (London: Leo Cooper, 1996) pp. 810–30.

—— *The Unquiet Western Front: Britain's Role in Literature and History* (Cambridge: Cambridge University Press, 2002).

Borland, Katherine, 'That's not what I said" Interpretive Conflict in Oral Narrative Research', in *The Oral History Reader*, ed. by Robert Perks and Alistair Thomson (London: Routledge, 2006) pp. 310–21.

Bourke, Joanna, *Dismembering the Male: Men's Bodies, Britain and the Great War* (London: Reaktion, 1996).

—— *An Intimate History of Killing: Face –to-Face Killing in Twentieth Century Warfare* (London: Granta Books, 2000).

Boyd, Kelly, 'Knowing Your Place; The Tensions of Masculinity in Boys' Story Papers 1918–1939', in *Manful Assertions: Masculinities in Britain since 1800*, ed. by Michael Roper and John Tosh (London: Routledge, 1991) pp. 145–67.

—— *Manliness and the Boys' Story Paper in Britain: A Cultural History, 1855–1940* (Basingstoke: Palgrave Macmillan, 2003).

Bracco, Rosa Maria, *Merchants of Hope: British Middlebrow Writers and the First World War, 1919–1939* (Oxford: Berg, 1992).

Broad, Roger, *Conscription in Britain, 1939–1963: The Militarization of a Generation. British Politics and Society* (London: Routledge, 2006).

Brown, R. Douglas, *East Anglia 1939* (Lavenham: Terence Dalton, 1980).

Budgen, David, *British Children's Literature and the First World War. Representations since 1914* (London: Bloomsbury, 2020).

Butler, Judith, *Gender Trouble* (Abingdon: Routledge, 2007).

Calder, Angus, 'Mass Observation 1937–1949', in *Essays on the History of British Sociological Research*, ed. by Martin Bulmer (Cambridge: Cambridge University Press, 1985) pp. 121–36.

Bibliography 283

—— *People's War: Britain, 1939–45* (London: Pimlico, 1992).

Ceadel, Martin, *Pacifism in Britain 1914–1945: the defining of a faith* (Oxford: Clarendon Press, 1980).

—— 'Popular Fiction and the Next War, 1918–1939', in *Class, Culture and Social Change: A New View of the 1930s*, ed. Frank Gloversmith (Sussex: Harvester Press, 1980) pp. 161–84.

—— *Semi-Detached Idealists: The British Peace Movement and International Relations, 1854–1945* (Oxford: Oxford University Press, 2000).

Cecil, Hugh, 'British War Novelists', in *Facing Armageddon. The First World War Experienced*, ed. by H. Cecil and P. Liddle (London: Leo Cooper, 1996) pp. 801–16.

Chand, Alison, *Masculinities on Clydeside: Men in Reserved Occupations 1939–1945* (Edinburgh: Edinburgh University Press, 2016).

Chibnall, Steve, 'Pulp Versus Penguins: Paperbacks Go to War', in *War Culture: Social Change and Changing Experience in World War Two Britain*, ed. by Pat Kirkham and David Toms (London: Lawrence & Wishart, 1995) pp. 131–49.

Cohen, Deborah, *The War Come Home: Disabled Veterans in Britain and Germany, 1914–1939* (Berkeley: University of California Press, 2001).

Connell, Raewyn, *Masculinities* (Cambridge: Polity, 2005).

Connelly, Mark, *The Great War, Memory and Ritual: Commemoration in the City and East London, 1916–1939* (London: Royal Historical Society, 2002).

Cornish, Paul, ' "Just a boyish habit" British and Commonwealth War Trophies in the First World War', in Nicholas J. Saunders and Paul Cornish (eds), *Contested Objects. Material Memories of the Great War* (Abingdon: Routledge, 2009) pp. 16–25.

Crang, Jeremy, *The British Army and the People's War* (Manchester: Manchester University Press, 2000).

Cunningham, Hugh, *The Invention of Childhood* (London: BBC Books, 2006).

Damousi, Joy, *The Labour of Loss. Mourning Memory and Wartime Bereavement in Australia* (Cambridge: Cambridge University Press, 2010).

Dawson, Graham, *Soldier Heroes: British Adventure, Empire, and the Imagining of Masculinities* (London: Routledge, 1994).

Dennis, Peter, *Decision by Default: Peacetime Conscription and British Defence, 1919–1939* (London: Routledge and Kegan Paul, 1972).

—— *The Territorial Army, 1906–1940* (Woodbridge: Boydell, 1987).

Draaisma, Douwe, *Why Life Speeds Up as You Get Older: How Memory Shapes Our Past* (Cambridge: Cambridge University Press, 2001).

Fennell, Jonathan, *Fighting the People's War. The British and Commonwealth Armies and the Second World War* (Cambridge: Cambridge University Press, 2019).

284 *Bibliography*

Field, Geoffrey G., *Blood, Sweat and Toil. Remaking the British Working Class, 1939–1945* (Oxford: Oxford University Press, 2011).

Francis, Martin, *The Flyer: British Culture and the Royal Air Force, 1939–1945* (Oxford: Oxford University Press, 2008).

French, David, *Raising Churchill's Army: The British Army and the War Against Germany, 1919–1945* (Oxford: Oxford University Press, 2000).

Fussell, Paul, *The Great War and Modern Memory* (Oxford: Oxford University Press, 2000).

Glover, David and Caplan, Cara, *Genders* (London: Routledge, 2000).

Goot, Murray, 'Mass Observation and Modern Public Opinion Research', in *The SAGE Handbook of Public Opinion Research*, ed. by Wolfgang Donsbach and Michael W. Traugott (London: SAGE, 2008) pp. 93–103.

Grayzel, Susan, *Women's Identities at War. Gender, Motherhood and Politics in Britain and France during the First World War* (Chapel Hill, North Carolina: The University of North Carolina Press, 1999).

—— *Britain at Home and Under Fire. Air Raids and Culture in Britain from the Great War to the Blitz* (New York: Cambridge University Press, 2012).

Gregory, Adrian, *The Silence of Memory: Armistice Day 1919–1946* (Oxford: Berg, 1994).

—— 'British "War Enthusiasm" in 1914: A Reassessment', in *Evidence, History and the Great War: Historians and the Impact of 1914–18*, ed. by Gail Braybon (New York: Berghahn Books, 2008) pp. 67–85.

—— *The Last Great War. British Society and the First World War* (Cambridge: Cambridge University Press, 2008).

Hanna, Emma, *Sounds of War: Music in the British Armed Forces during the Great War* (Cambridge: Cambridge University Press, 2020).

Hayes, Denis, *Challenge of Conscience: The Story of the Conscientious Objectors of 1939–1945* (London: Allen and Unwin, 1949).

Heathorn, Stephen, *Haig and Kitchener in Twentieth-Century Britain* (Farnham: Ashgate, 2013).

Hetherington, Andrea, *British Widows the First World War: The Forgotten Legion* (Barnsley: Pen and Sword, 2018).

Hickman, Tom, *Called Up, Sent Down* (Stroud: Sutton, 2008).

Highgate, Paul, ' "Soft Clerks" and "Hard Civvies": Pluralizing Military Masculinities', in *Military Masculinities: Identity and the State*, ed. by Paul Highgate (London: Praeger, 2003) pp. 27–42.

Higonnet, Margaret, Jenson, Jane, Michel, Sonya and Collins Weitz, Margaret (eds), *Behind the Lines: Gender and the Two World Wars* (New Haven: Yale University Press, 1987).

Hinton, James, *Nine Wartime Lives: Mass Observation and the Making of the Modern Self* (Oxford: Oxford University Press, 2010).

—— *The Mass Observers. A History, 1937–1949* (Oxford: Oxford University Press, 2013).

Holman, Brett, *The Next War in the Air: Britain's Fear of the Bomber, 1909–1941* (Ashgate: Surrey, 2014).

Bibliography

Houghton, Frances, 'Becoming "a Man" During the Battle of Britain: Combat, Masculinity and Rites of Passage in the Memoirs of "the Few"', in Lindsey Robb and Juliette Pattinson (eds), *Men, Masculinities and Male Culture in the Second World War* (Basingstoke: Palgrave, 2018) pp. 97–120.

—— *The Veterans' Tale. British Military Memoirs of the Second World War* (Cambridge: Cambridge University Press, 2019).

Howlett, Peter, *Fighting with Figures: A Statistical Digest of the Second World War*, Central Statistical Office (London: HMSO, 1995).

Hubble, Nick, *Mass-Observation and Everyday Life: Culture, History, Theory* (Basingstoke: Palgrave Macmillan, 2006).

Hucker, Daniel, *Public Opinion and the End of Appeasement in Britain and France* (Farnham: Ashgate, 2011).

Hynes, Samuel, *A War Imagined: The First World War and English Culture* (London: Bodley Head, 1990).

Isherwood, Ian Andrew, *Remembering the Great War. Writing and Publishing the Experiences of World War I* (London: Bloomsbury, 2020).

Jones, Helen, *British Civilians in the Front Line. Air Raids, Productivity and Wartime Culture, 1939–1945* (Manchester: Manchester University Press, 2006).

King, Laura, *Family Men: Fatherhood and Masculinity in Britain 1914–1960* (Oxford: Oxford University Press, 2015).

Kushner, Tony, *We Europeans: Mass-observation, 'Race' and British Identity in the Twentieth Century* (Aldershot: Ashgate, 2004).

Leed, Eric J., *No Man's Land: Combat & Identity in World War I* (Cambridge: Cambridge University Press, 1979).

Lomas, Janis, 'Soldiering On: War Widows in First World War Britain', in *The Home Front Iin Britain*, ed. by Maggie Andrews and Janis Lomas (Basingstoke: Palgrave Macmillan, 2014) pp. 39–56.

Mackay, Robert, *Half the Battle: Civilian Morale in Britain during the Second World War* (Manchester: Manchester University Press, 2003).

McAleer, Joseph, *Popular Reading and Publishing in Britain, 1914–1950* (Oxford: Clarendon, 1992).

McCarthy, Helen, *The British People and the League of Nations. Democracy, Citizenship and Internationalism, c1918–45* (Manchester: Manchester University Press, 2011).

McCartney, Helen, *Citizen Soldiers: The Liverpool Territorials in the First World War* (Cambridge: Cambridge University Press, 2005).

McKibbin, Ross, *Classes and Cultures. England 1918–1951* (Oxford: Oxford University Press, 1998).

Meyer, Jessica, *Men of War: Masculinity and the First World War in Britain* (Basingstoke: Palgrave Macmillan, 2009).

—— 'Wounded in a Mentionable Place: The (In)visibility of the Disabled Ex-Serviceman in Inter-War Britain', in *Veterans of the First World War: Ex-Servicemen and Ex-Servicewomen in Post-War Britain and Ireland*, ed. by Oliver Wilkinson and David Swift (Abingdon: Routledge, 2019).

Bibliography

Moorhouse, Geoffrey, *Hell's Foundations: A Town, Its Myths and Gallipoli* (London: Hodder & Stoughton, 1992).

Newlands, Emma, *Civilians into Soldiers. War, the Body and British Army Recruits 1939–1945* (Manchester: Manchester University Press, 2014).

Nicholls, Robert, *The Belle Vue Story* (Manchester: Neil Richardson, 1992).

Noakes, Lucy, *War and the British: Gender, Memory and National Identity, 1939–1991* (London: I. B. Tauris, 1998).

—— *Women in the British Army: War and the Gentle Sex, 1907–1948* (London: Routledge, 2006).

—— '"War on the Web": The BBC's "People's War" Website and Memories of Fear in Wartime in 21st Century Britain', in *British Cultural Memory and the Second World War*, ed. by Lucy Noakes and Juliette Pattinson (London: Bloomsbury Academic, 2013) pp. 47–66.

Noakes, Lucy and Pattinson, Juliette, eds. *British Cultural Memory and the Second World War* (London: Bloomsbury Academic, 2013).

Paris, Michael, 'Enduring Heroes: British Feature Films and the First World War, 1919–1997', in *The First World War and Popular Cinema. 1914 to the Present*, ed. by Michael Paris (Edinburgh: Edinburgh University Press, 1999) pp. 51–73.

—— *Warrior Nation: Images of War in British Popular Culture, 1850–2000* (London: Reaktion, 2000).

—— *Over the Top: The Great War and Juvenile Literature in Britain* (Westport, Conn.: Praeger, 2004).

Parker, Henry Michael Denne, *Manpower. A Study of War-Time Policy and Administration* (London: United Kingdom Civil Series, 1957).

Pattinson, Juliette, *Behind Enemy Lines: Gender, Passing and the Special Operations Executive in the Second World War* (Manchester: Manchester University Press, 2007).

Pattinson, Juliette, McIvor, Arthur, and Robb, Linsey, *Men in Reserve: British Civilian Masculinities in the Second World War* (Manchester: Manchester University Press, 2017).

Pennell, Catriona, *A Kingdom United: Popular Responses to the Outbreak of the First World War in Britain and Ireland* (Oxford: Oxford University Press, 2012).

Peniston-Bird, Corinna, 'Oral History. The Sound of Memory', in *History Beyond the Text: A Student's Guide to Approaching Alternative Sources*, ed. by Sarah Barber and Corinna Peniston-Bird (London: Routledge, 2009) pp. 105–21.

Popular Memory Group, 'Popular Memory: Theory, Politics, Method', in *Making Histories: Studies in History*, ed. by R. Johnson, G. McLennan, B. Schwartz and D. Sutton (London, 1982) pp. 205–52.

Pugh, Martin, *We Danced All night. A Social History of Britain between the Wars* (London: Vintage, 2009).

Reeves, N., 'Through the Eye of the Camera', in *Facing Armageddon. The First World War Experienced*, ed. by H. Cecil and P. Liddle (London: Leo Cooper, 1996) pp. 780–800.

Bibliography

Ritchie, Donald, *Doing Oral Histroy: A Practical Guide* (Oxford: Oxford University Press, 2003).

Robb, Linsey, *Men at Work: The Working Man in British Culture, 1939–1945* (Basingstoke: Palgrave Macmillan, 2015).

Roper, Michael, 'Maternal Relations: Moral Manliness and Emotional Survival in Letters Home During the First World War', in *Masculinities in Politics and War: Gendering Modern History*, ed. by Stefan Dudink, Karen Hagemann and John Tosh (Manchester: Manchester University Press, 2004) pp. 295–316.

—— *The Secret Battle: Emotional Survival in the Great War* (Manchester: Manchester University Press, 2009).

—— 'Subjectivities in the Aftermath: Children of Disabled Soldiers in Britain after the Great War', in Jason Crouthamel and Peter Leese (eds), *Psychological Trauma and the Legacies of the First World War* (Basingstoke: Palgrave, 2016) pp. 165–92.

—— *Afterlives of war. A Descendant's History* (Manchester: Manchester University Press, 2023).

Rose, Jonathan, *The Intellectual Life of the British Working Classes* (New Haven: Yale University Press, 2002).

Rose, Sonya O., *Which People's War?: National Identity and Citizenship in Britain 1939–1945* (Oxford: Oxford University Press, 2003).

—— 'Temperate Heroes: Concepts of Masculinity in the Second World War Britain', in *Masculinities in Politics and War: Gendering Modern History*, ed. by Dudink, Hagemann and Tosh, pp. 177–98.

Saunders, Nicholas J., 'Apprehending Memory: Material Culture and War, 1919–1939', in *The Great World War, 1914–1945*, vol. 2, ed. by John Bourne, Peter Liddle and Ian Whitehead (London: Harper Collins, 2001) pp. 476–88.

—— *Trench Art. Materialities and Memories of War* (Oxford: Berg, 2003).

—— *Killing Time. Archaeology and the First World War* (Stroud: The History Press, 2010).

Sheffield, Gary, 'The Shadow of the Somme: The Influence of the First World War on British Soldiers' Perceptions and Behaviour in the Second World War', in *A Time to Kill: The Soldier's Experience of the War in the West, 1939–1945*, ed. by Paul Addison and Angus Calder (London: Pimlico, 1997) pp. 29–39.

—— *Forgotten Victory: The First World War: Myths and Realities* (London: Review, 2002).

Showalter, Elaine, 'Rivers and Sassoon: The Inscriptions of Male Gender Anxieties', in *Behind the Lines: Gender and the Two World Wars*, ed. by Margaret Higonnet, Sonya Michel, Jane Jenson and Margaret Collins Weitz (London: Yale University Press, 1987) pp. 61–9.

Silbey, David, *The British Working Class and Enthusiasm for War, 1914–1916* (London: Frank Cass, 2005).

Silkin, Jon (ed.), *The Penguin Book of First World War Poetry* (Harmondsworth: Penguin, 1979).

288 Bibliography

Strachan, Hew, 'The Soldier's Experience in Two World Wars: Some Historiographical Comparisons', in *A Time to Kill: The Soldier's Experience of the War in the West, 1939–1945*, ed. by Paul Addison and Angus Calder (London: Pimlico, 1997) pp. 369–78.

Summerfield, Penny, *Reconstructing Women's Wartime Lives: Discourse and Subjectivity in Oral Histories of the Second World War* (Manchester: Manchester University Press, 1998).

—— '"She Wants a Gun not a Dishcloth!" Gender, Service and Citizenship in Britain in the Second World War', in *A Soldier and a Woman*, ed. by G. J. DeGroot and C. M. Peniston-Bird (Harlow: Pearson, 2000) pp. 119–34.

—— 'The Generation of Memory. Gender and the Popular Memory of the Second World War in Britain', in *British Cultural Memory and the Second World War*, ed. by Lucy Noakes and Juliette Pattinson (London: Bloomsbury, 2014) pp. 25–45.

Summerfield, Penny, and Peniston-Bird, Corinna, 'The Home Guard in Britain in the Second World War: Uncertain Masculinities?', in *Military Masculinities: Identity and the State*, ed. by Paul Highgate (London: Praeger, 2003) pp. 57–69.

—— *Contesting Home Defence: Men, Women and the Home Guard in the Second World War* (Manchester: Manchester University Press, 2007).

Tebbutt, Melanie, *Being Boys. Youth, Leisure and Identity in the Inter-War Years* (Manchester: Manchester University Press, 2012).

Thompson, Paul, *The Voice of the Past* (Oxford: Oxford University Press, 2000) pp. 129–30.

—— 'The Voice of the Past: Oral History', in *Oral History Reader*, ed. by Robert Perks and Alistair Thomson (London: Routledge, 2006) pp. 25–31.

Thomson, Alistair, *Anzac Memories: Living with the Legend* (Oxford: Oxford University Press, 1994).

—— 'Unreliable Memories? The Use and Abuse of Oral History', in *Historical Controversies and Historians,* ed. by William Lamont (London: UCL Press, 1998) pp. 23–34.

—— 'Memory and Remembering in Oral History', in *The Oxford Handbook of Oral History*, ed. by Donald Ritchie (Oxford: Oxford University Press, 2007).

Todman, Dan, *The Great War: Myth and Memory* (London: Hambledon and London, 2005).

—— *Britain's War, Into Battle, 1937–1941* (London: Allen Lane, 2016).

—— *Britain's War: A New World, 1942–1947* (London: Allen Lane, 2020).

Tomczyszyn, P., 'A Material Link between War and Peace: First World War Silk Postcards', in *Matters of Conflict: Material Culture, Memory and the First World War*, ed. by N. J. Saunders (Abingdon: Routledge, 2004).

Tonkin, Elizabeth, *Narrating Our Pasts: The Social Construction of Oral History* (Cambridge: Cambridge University Press, 1995).

Bibliography 289

Tosh, John, 'Hegemonic Masculinity and the History of Gender', in *Masculinities in Politics and War: Gendering Modern History*, ed. by Stefan Dudink, Karen Hagemann and John Tosh (Manchester: Manchester University Press, 2004) pp. 41–60.

Trott, Vincent, *Publishers, Readers and the Great War. Literature and Memory since 1918* (London: Bloomsbury, 2017).

Van Emden, Richard, *The Quick and the Dead: Fallen Soldiers and their Families in the Great War* (London: Bloomsbury, 2011).

Van Emden, Richard and Humphreys, Stephen, *All Quiet on the Home Front: An Oral History of Life in Britain during the First World War* (Chatham: Headline Book Publishing, 2004).

Vickers, Emma, *Queen and Country: Same-Sex Desire in the British Armed Forces, 1939–45* (Manchester: Manchester University Press, 2013).

Watson, Janet, *Fighting Different Wars: Experience, Memory, and the First World War in Britain* (Cambridge: Cambridge University Press, 2004).

Wilkinson, Oliver, 'Ex-Prisoners of War, 1914–1918. Veteran Association, Assimilation and Disassociation after the First World War', in *Veterans of the First World War: Ex-Servicemen and Ex-Servicewomen in Post-War Britain and Ireland*, ed. by Oliver Wilkinson and David Swift (Abingdon: Routledge, 2019) Ebook.

Winter, J. M., 'The Demographic Consequences of the War', in *War and Social Change: British Society in the Second World War*, ed. by Harold Smith (Manchester: Manchester University Press, 1986) pp. 151–78.

—— *Sites of Memory, Sites of Mourning: The Great War in European Cultural History* (Cambridge: Cambridge University Press, 1995).

—— *The Great War and the British People* (Hampshire: Palgrave Macmillan, 2003).

—— 'Shell Shock, Gallipoli and the Generation of Silence', in *Beyond Memory: Silence and the Aesthetics of Remembrance*, ed. by Alexandre Dessingue and Jay Winter (Abingdon: Routledge, 2016) pp. 195–208.

Winter, J. M. and Antoine Prost, *The Great War in History. Debates and Controversies, 1914 to the Present* (Cambridge: Cambridge University Press, 2005).

Yow, Valerie, 'Do I Like Them Too Much? Effects of the Oral History Interview on the Interviewer and Vice Versa', in *Oral History Reader*, ed. by Robert Perks and Alistair Thomson (London: Routledge, 2006) pp. 54–72.

Articles

Badsey, S., 'Battle of the Somme: British War Propaganda', *Historical Journal of Film, Radio and Television*, 3.2 (1983) pp. 99–115.

Bingham, Adrian, 'Writing the First World War after 1918. Journalism, History and Commemoration', *Journalism Studies*, 17.4 (2016) pp. 392–7.

Bishop, Libby, 'A Reflexive Account of Reusing Qualitative Data: Beyond Primary/Secondary Dualism', *Sociological Research Online*, 12.3 (2007) pp. 43–56.

Bibliography

Bogacz, Ted, 'War Neurosis and Cultural Change in England, 1914–22: The Work of the War Office Committee of Enquiry into "Shell-Shock"', *Journal of Contemporary History*, 24.2 (1989) pp. 227–56.

Bornat, Joanna, 'A Second Take: Revisiting Interviews with a Different Purpose', *Oral History*, 31.1 (2003) pp. 47–53.

Brookshire, Jerry H., '"Speak for England", Act for England: Labour's Leadership and British National Security Under the Threat of War in the Late 1930s', *European History Quarterly*, 29.2 (1999) pp. 251–87.

Ceadel, Martin, 'The "King and Country" Debate, 1933: Student Politics, Pacifism and the Dictators', *The Historical Journal*, 22 (1979) pp. 397–422.

———— 'The First British Referendum: The Peace Ballot, 1934–5', *The English Historical Review*, 95 (1980) pp. 810–39.

Chambers II, John Whiteclay, '"All Quiet on the Western Front" (1930): The Antiwar Film and the Image of the First World War', *Historical Journal of Film, Radio and Television*, 14.4 (1994) pp. 377–411.

Chand, Alison, 'Glasgow's War and Masculine Identities in the Reserved Occupations 1939–1945: Wartime Women's Perspectives on Glasgow's Working Men', *War, Memory and Biography. United Academics Journal of Social Sciences*, (2011) pp. 12–16.

Crowson, N. J., 'The Conservative Party and the Call for National Service, 1937–39: Compulsion Versus Voluntarism', *Contemporary Record*, 9 (1995) pp. 507–28.

Curtis Walters, Emily, 'Between Entertainment and Elegy: The Unexpected Success of R. C. Sherriff's *Journey's End* (1928)', *Journal of British Studies*, 55 (2016) pp. 344–73.

De Groot, Gerard, 'Whose Finger on the Trigger? Mixed Anti-Aircraft Batteries and the Female Combat Taboo', *War in History*, 4.4 (1997) pp. 434–53.

———— ' "I Love the Scent of Cordite in Your Hair": Gender Dynamics in Mixed Anti-Aircraft Batteries during the Second World War', *History*, 82.265 (1997) pp. 73–92.

Ekstiens, Modris, 'All Quiet on the Western Front and the Fate of a War', *Journal of Contemporary History*, 15.2 (1980) pp. 345–66.

Foster, Ann-Marie, '"We Decided the Museum Would Be the Best Place for Them": Veterans, Families and Mementos of the First World War', *History and Memory*, 31.1 (2019) pp. 87–117.

Francis, Martin, 'Attending to Ghosts: Some Reflections on the Disavowals of British Great War Historiography', *Twentieth Century British History*, 25 (2014) pp. 347–67.

Gallwey, April, 'The Rewards of Using Archived Oral Histories in Research: The Case of the Millennium Memory Bank', *Oral History*, 41.1 (2013) pp. 37–50.

Hammett, Jessica, '"It's in the Blood, isn't it?" The Contested Status of First World War Veterans in Second World War Civil Defence', *Cultural and Social History*, 14.3 (2017) pp. 343–61.

Bibliography

Harper, Sue, 'A Lower Middle-class Taste-Community in the 1930s: Admissions Figures at the Regent Cinema, Portsmouth, UK', *Historical Journal of Film, Radio and Television*, 24.4 (2004) pp. 565–87.

Heathorn, Stephen, 'The Mnemonic Turn in the Cultural Historiography of Britain's Great War', *The Historical Journal*, 48 (2005) pp. 1103–24.

Hinton, James, 'The "Class" Complex': Mass-Observation and Cultural Distinction in Pre-War Britain', *Past & Present*, 199.1 (2008) pp. 207–36.

Holman, Brett, 'The Air Panic of 1935: British Press Opinion between Disarmament and Rearmament', *Journal of Contemporary History*, 46.2 (2011) pp. 288–307.

Hucker, Daniel, 'Franco-British Relations and the Question of Conscription in Britain, 1938–1939', *Contemporary European History*, 17.4 (2008) pp. 437–56.

Huxford, Grace, 'The Korean War Never Happened: Forgetting a Conflict in British Culture and Society', *Twentieth Century British History*, 27.2 (2016) pp. 195–219.

K'Meyer, Tracy E. and Glenn Crothers, A., '"If I See Some of This in Writing, I'm Going to Shoot You": Reluctant Narrators, Taboo Topics, and the Ethical Dilemmas of the Oral Historian', *The Oral History Review*, 34.1 (2007) pp. 71–93.

Kelly, Andrew, 'All Quiet on the Western Front: "brutal cutting, stupid censors and bigoted politicos" (1930–1984)', *Historical Journal of Film, Radio and Television*, 9.2 (1989) pp. 135–50.

Kelly, Tobias, 'Citizenship, Cowardice and Freedom of Conscience: British Pacifists in the Second World War', *Comparative Studies in Society and History*, 57 (2015) pp. 694–722.

Kuhn, Annette, 'Cinema-going in Britain in the 1930s: Report of a Questionnaire Survey', *Historical Journal of Film Radio and Television*, 19.4 (1999) pp. 531–43.

Langhamer, Claire, '"The Live Dynamic Whole of Feeling and Behaviour": Capital Punishment and the Politics of Emotion, 1945–1957', *Journal of British Studies*, 51.2 (2012) pp. 416–41.

Levsen, Sonya, 'Constructing Elite Identities: University Students, Military Masculinity and the Consequences of the Great War in Britain and Germany', *Past and Present*, 198 (2008) pp. 143–83.

Liddle, Peter H. and Richardson, Matthew J., 'Voices from the Past: An Evaluation of Oral History as a Source for Research into the Western Front Experience of the British Soldier, 1914–18', *Journal of Contemporary History*, 31.4 (1996) pp. 651–74.

Luckins, Tanja, 'Collecting Women's Memories: The Australian War Memorial, the Next of Kin and Great War Soldiers Diaries and Letters as Objects of Memory in the 1920s and 1930s', *Women's History Review*, 19.1 (2010) pp. 21–37.

Mansell, James G., 'Musical Modernity and Contested Commemoration at the Festival of Remembrance, 1923–1927', *The Historical Journal*, 52.2 (2009) pp. 433–54.

Mayhew, Alex, '"A War Imagined": Postcards and the Maintenance of Long-Distance Relationships during the Great War', *War in History*, 28.2 (2019) pp. 1–31.

McCarthy, Helen, 'Democratizing British Foreign Policy: Rethinking the Peace Ballot, 1934–1935', *Journal of British Studies*, 49 (2010) pp. 358–87.

Meyer, Jessica, 'Separating the Men from the Boys: Masculinity and Maturity in Understandings of Shell Shock in Britain.' *Twentieth Century British History*, 20.1 (2009) pp. 1–22.

Moran, Joe, 'Mass-Observation, Market Research, and the Birth of the Focus Group, 1937–1997', *Journal Of British Studies*, 47.4 (2008) pp. 827–51.

Morley, Joel, 'Dad "never said much" but ... Young Men and Great War Veterans in Day-to-Day-Life in Interwar Britain', *Twentieth Century British History*, 29.2 (2018) pp. 199–224.

———— 'The Memory of the Great War and Morale During Britain's Phoney War', *The Historical Journal*, 63.2 (2020) pp. 437–67.

Noakes, Lucy, 'Serve to Save': Gender, Citizenship and Civil Defence in Britain 1937–41', *Journal of Contemporary History*, 47.4 (2012) pp. 734–53.

———— 'A Broken Silence? Mass Observation, Armistice Day and "everyday life" in Britain 1937–1941', *Journal of European Studies*, 45 (2015) pp. 331–46.

O'Keefe, Eleanor K., 'The Great War and "Military Memory". War and Remembrance in the Civic Public Sphere, 1919–1939', *Journalism Studies*, 17.4 (2016) pp. 432–47.

Pattinson, Juliette, '"The thing that made me hesitate ...": Re-examining Gendered Intersubjectivities in Interviews with British Secret War Veterans', *Women's History Review*, 20.2 (2011) pp. 245–63.

———— '"Shirkers", "Scrimjacks" and "Scrimshanks"? British Civilian Masculinity and Reserved Occupations, 1914–1945', *Gender and History*, 28.3 (2016) pp. 709–27.

Peniston-Bird, Corinna, 'Classifying the Body in the Second World War: British Men in and Out of Uniform', *Body & Society*, 9.4 (2003) pp. 31–48.

———— ' "I Wondered Who'd Be the First to Spot That." Dad's Army at War, in the Media and in Memory', *Media History*, 13.2 (2007) pp. 183–202.

———— '"All in it together" and "Backs to the Wall": Relating Patriotism and the People's War in the 21st Century', *Oral History*, 40.3 (2012) pp. 69–80.

Portelli, Alessandro, 'The Peculiarities of Oral History', *History Workshop Journal*, 12.1 (1981) pp. 96–107.

Robb, Linsey, 'The "Conchie Corps": Conflict, Compromise and Conscientious Objection in the British Army, 1940–1945', *Twentieth Century British History*, 29.3 (2018) pp. 411–34.

Rodney, Earl Walton, 'Memories from the Edge of the Abyss: Evaluating the Oral Accounts of World War II Veterans', *The Oral History Review*, 37.1 (2010) pp. 18–34.

Bibliography

Roper, Michael, 'Re-remembering the Soldier Hero: The Psychic and Social Construction of Memory in Personal Narratives of the Great War', *History Workshop Journal*, 50 (2000) pp. 181–204.

—— 'Between Manliness and Masculinity: The "War Generation" and the Psychology of Fear in Britain, 1914–1950', *Journal of British Studies*, 44.2 (2005) pp. 343–62.

—— 'Slipping Out of View: Subjectivity and Emotion in Gender History', *History Workshop Journal*, 59.1 (2005) pp. 57–72.

Ryan, Kathleen, '"I Didn't Do Anything Important": A Pragmatist Analysis of the Oral History Interview', *The Oral History Review*, 36.1 (2009) pp. 25–44.

Schwarzkopf, Jutta, 'Combatant or Non-Combatant? The Ambiguous Status of Women in British Anti-Aircraft Batteries during the Second World War', *War & Society*, 28.2 (2009) pp. 105–31.

Sheridan, Dorothy, 'Ambivalent Memories: Women and the 1939–45 War in Britain', *Oral History*, 18.1 (1990) pp. 32–40.

Smith, Harold, 'The Womanpower Problem in Britain during the Second World War', *The Historical Journal*, 27.4 (1984) pp. 925–945.

Stone, Tessa, 'Creating a (Gendered?) Military Identity: The Women's Auxiliary Air Force in Great Britain in the Second World War', *Women's History Review*, 8 (1999) pp. 605–24.

Summerfield, Penny, 'Mass-Observation: Social Research or Social Movement?', *Journal of Contemporary History*, 20.3 (1985) pp. 439–52.

—— 'Gender and War in the Twentieth Century', *The International History Review*, 19.1 (1997) pp. 3–15.

—— 'Culture and Composure: Creating Narratives of the Gendered Self in Oral History Interviews', *Cultural and Social History*, 1 (2004) pp. 65–93.

Summerfield, Penny and Peniston-Bird, Corinna, 'Women in the Firing Line: The Home Guard and the Defence of Gender Boundaries in Britain in the Second World War', *Women's History Review*, 9.2 (2000) pp. 231–55.

Summerfield, Penny and Crockett, Nicole, '"You weren't taught that with the welding": Lessons in Sexuality in the Second World War', *Women's History Review*, 1.3 (1992) pp. 435–54.

Thomson, Alistair, 'ANZAC Memories. Putting Popular Memory Theory into Practice', *Oral History*, 18.1 (1990) pp. 25–31.

Thompson, Rowan G. E., '"Millions of eyes were turned skywards": The Air League of the British Empire, Empire Air Day, and the Promotion of Air-Mindedness, 1934–1939', *Twentieth Century British History*, 2 (2021) pp. 285–307.

Todman, Dan, '"Sans Peur et Sans Reproche": The Retirement, Death and Mourning of Sir Douglas Haig, 1918–1928', *The Journal of Military History*, 68.4 (2003) pp. 1083–1105.

Tosh, John, 'What Should Historians do with Masculinity? Reflections on Nineteenth-Century Britain', *History Workshop Journal*, 38.1 (1994) pp. 179–202.

294 *Bibliography*

Trott, Vincent, 'Remembering War, Resisting Myth: Veteran Autobiographies and the Great War in the Twenty-first Century', *Journal of War & Culture Studies*, 6.4 (2013) pp. 328–42.

Watson, Janet, 'Khaki Girls, VADs, and Tommy's Sisters: Gender and Class in First World War Britain', *The International History Review*, 19.1 (1997) pp. 32–51.

Willcock, H. D., 'Mass-Observation', *American Journal of Sociology*, 48.4 (1943) pp. 445–56.

Miscellaneous

Chand, Alison, 'Second World War in Glasgow and Clydeside: Men in Reserved Occupations 1939–1945' (Unpublished PhD Thesis, University of Strathclyde, 2012).

Courage, Fiona, 'The National Panel' Responds: Mass Observation Directives 1939–1945', Mass Observation Online, Essays.

'Daddy, What Did YOU Do in the Great War?', Saville Lumley for the Parliamentary Recruiting Committee, 1915. IWM PST0311.

'Desert Island Discs' with Percy Merriman, BBC Radio, 17 August 1964.

Englander, David and Mason, Tony, 'The British Soldier in World War II', Warwick Working Papers in Social History (1984).

Fisher, Tim, 'Fatherhood and the Experience of Working-Class Fathers in Britain, 1900–1939' (Unpublished PhD Thesis, Edinburgh University, 2004).

Jeffery, Tom, MOA Occasional Paper No. 10. 'Mass Observation: A Short History.' Mass Observation Online, Essays.

McKay, Thomas, 'A Multi-Generational Oral History Study Considering English Collective Memory of the Second World War and Holocaust' (Unpublished PhD Thesis, University of Leicester, 2012) pp. 75–6, 139–40.

Mercer, Neil, 'Mass Observation 1937–1940: The Range of Research Methods', Working Papers in Applied Social Research, no. 16 (University of Manchester, 1989).

'The Present Salutes the Past', *Cambridge Daily News*, 21 October 1939, p. 3.

Shepherd, Les, Conversation with author, 2022.

Stanley, Nick, 'The Extra Dimension: A Study and Assessment of the Methods Employed by Mass-Observation in its First Period, 1937–1940' (Unpublished PhD Thesis, Birmingham Polytechnic, 1981).

Summerfield, Penny, '"My Dress for an Army Uniform": Gender Instabilities in the Two World Wars', Inaugural Lecture delivered at Lancaster University, 30 April 1997.

Wainwright, P. J., 'The National Service Debate: Government Conscription and the Peace Movement in Britain, 1936–1942' (Unpublished PhD thesis, Stamford, 1993).

Index

All Quiet on the Western Front
50, 52–4, 57–61, 63, 204,
207, 209
Allport, Alan 9, 171–2
Armistice Day 45, 54, 63–7, 68,
70–5, 94, 101,
113–14, 268

BBC 62–7, 70
Bevin boys 16, 143, 201, 234,
241, 250
Biggles 44–6, 206
Brooke, Rupert 54–5

Chamberlain, Neville 129, 132,
134, 160
Chand, Alison 223, 236–7, 258
Churchill, Winston 46
conscientious objectors 150–2,
178–9, 228–31
conscription
approach of 129–34
introduction in peacetime 134
introduction and
implementation in
wartime 140–3
process of 148–53, 156
resisting 149–50, 152, 154–5
responses to peacetime
introduction 134–40, 160
success of conscripts preferring
Navy or RAF 189

Dawn Patrol 60, 206

Empire Day 71, 89, 259
enlistment
formal expression of preferences
148–9, 156–7, 189, 191
intake into armed forces 144
motivations for
volunteering 184–8
preferences 188–91, 245–6,
250–5
preferences and pay *see*
military pay
preference to avoid army service
188–9, 193–5, 204–5, 208–9
process of registration
148–50, 156
reasons to delay
volunteering 182–4
underage 240, 254
volunteering to avoid peacetime
conscription 138–9
volunteering to negotiate terms
of service 184, 188–9,
205, 254–6
Essential Works Order 147, 184

Festival of Remembrance 165–6

Goodbye To All That 50, 52
Graves, Robert *see Goodbye*
To All That

296 *Index*

Great War letters 100
Great War medals 73, 101, 108–9, 113–14
Great War memorabilia/artefacts 99–101
Great War photographs 99–100
Great War representations
  in encyclopedia 81, 204–5
  in film 56–61, 204–9
  in juvenile literature 42–6, 193, 206, 269
  in non-fiction 46–9, 269
  in poetry 54–5
  on radio 63–8
  in schools 68–70
  in stage and radio plays 61–3
  summary of effects 211
  from veterans *see* Great War veterans
Great War commemoration 70–5, 113–14, 268
Great War veterans
  effects of veterans' narratives 198–202, 206–7, 211
  extended narratives 102–12, 119–20
  number of veterans 1
  number of veterans in receipt of a war disability pension 2
  silences 94–7
  wounds 100–3

Hitler, Adolf 133, 134, 175, 181, 270
Home Guard
  Dad's Army 15, 239–40
  direction into 144
  Great War veterans in 114–17
  and masculinity 238–41, 247–8, 256–7
Home Intelligence reports 142–3
Houghton, Frances 9–10, 12–13, 172–3, 186, 227

Johns, W. E. *see* Biggles
Journey's End 50, 55, 57–9, 61–3

Kipling, Rudyard 55

League of Nations Union 74–5, 130

masculinity
  of conscientious objectors 230–1
  hegemonic Second World War construction in public discourse 225–7, 231–3
  of the Home Guard 238–41, 247–8, 256–7
  and manpower legislation 160–1
  and military medical examination 154–6
  and military uniform 238–46
  of reserved occupations 232–8, 248
  theoretical conceptualisation of 221–3
  wartime hierarchies of 245–6, 250–3
Mass Observation 22–5, 41–2
McCrae, John 55
medical examination
  attempts to cheat 154–5
  failure to attend 152
  perception of 152–3, 156, 229
  process 152–3
military pay 176, 182–3, 192–3
military training bill
  announcement of 134
  responses to 134–40

National Service Acts 140, 143–4, 161

oral history 3–4, 14–22, 40–1
Owen, Wilfred 54–5
Oxford Union debate (1933) 224

Pattinson, Juliette, McIvor, Arthur, and Robb, Linsey 237, 241, 258

Index

Peace Pledge Union 11, 74–5, 130, 151
Peniston-Bird, Corinna 15, 20–1, 232, 237, 239–40, 258–9
popular memory 4, 14–15

reserved occupations
  avoiding 184, 186, 202, 235, 239, 241, 253.
  perception of 231–8
  Schedule of Reserved Occupations 134, 142, 144–7, 149, 184
  seeking 180, 236
Remarque, Erich Maria *see All Quiet on the Western Front*
Roper, Michael 30, 121, 224
Rose, Sonya 11–12, 226, 237, 242, 255–6
  see also temperate masculinity

Sassoon, Siegfried 54–5
Schedule of Reserved Occupations *see* reserved occupations
Sheffield, Gary 10, 92, 109, 173, 197
Sherriff, R. C. *see Journey's End*
Summerfield, Penny 239–40, 257

temperate masculinity 5–6, 11–13, 26, 211, 221, 226–7, 236, 253–8, 272–4
Trott, Vincent 6–7, 28, 50, 173

Voluntary National Service Campaign (1939) 132–3
volunteering *see* enlistment

war books controversy 50–2
war widows 112–14, 197